DRAW
ANIMALS

OCEAN · RAINFOREST · DESERT · GRASSLAND

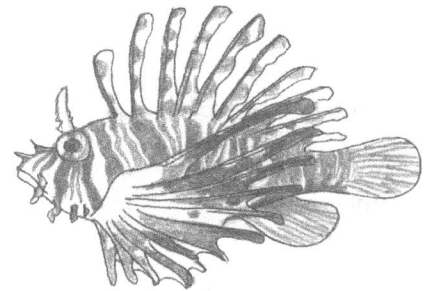

BY

DOUG DuBOSQUE

PEEL PRODUCTIONS, INC · VANCOUVER WA

What you will need

- A location with good light

- A pencil that's longer than your finger. Grades 2B or 3B work well.

- Use colored pencils if you have them!

- Sharpen your pencil when it gets dull!

- Find an eraser – the one on your pencil will disappear quickly. A knead-able one works best.

- For practice drawings, use recycled paper – for example, draw on the back of old photocopies or computer printouts.

- Plan to keep your drawings – put the date on each.

- Positive attitude. Forget "I can't." Say, "I'm learning. I'm figuring this out. I did this part well; now I'm going to work on the harder part. I'm not stopping until I get it RIGHT!"

Do-it-yourself portfolio

Save your work!

Whenever you do a drawing–or even a sketch–put your initials (or autograph!) and date on it. And save it. You don't have to save it until it turns yellow and crumbles to dust, but do keep your drawings, at least for several months. Sometimes, hiding in your portfolio, they will mysteriously improve! I've seen it happen often with my own drawings, especially the ones I knew were no good at all, but kept anyway.

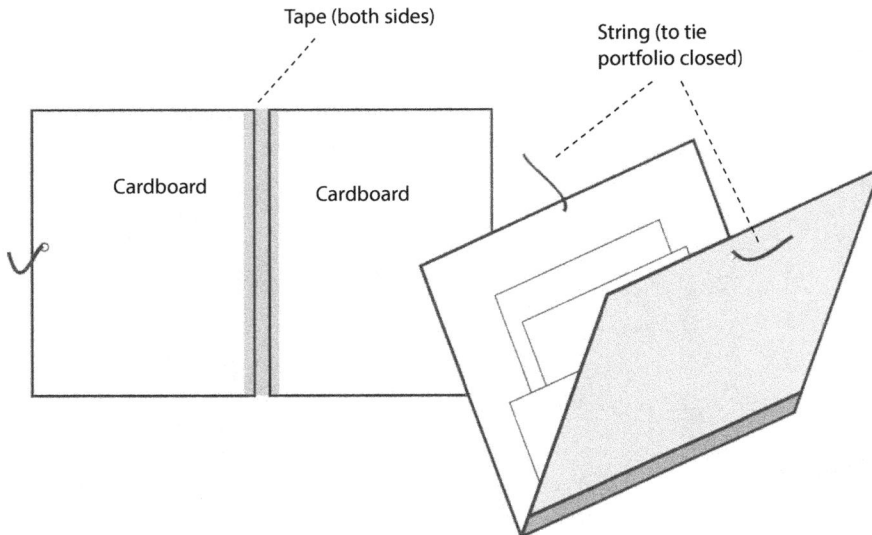

Tape (both sides)

String (to tie portfolio closed)

Cardboard

Cardboard

Published by Peel Productions, Inc., Vancouver, WA

Manufactured in the United States of America

Library of Congress Cataloging-in-Publication Data

Names: DuBosque, D. C., author, illustrator.
Title: Draw animals : ocean - rainforest - desert - grassland / By Doug DuBosque.
Description: Vancouver, WA : Peel Productions, Inc., 2015. | Previously published as four titles: Draw Ocean Animals, Draw Rainforest Animals, Draw Desert Animals, and Draw Grassland Animals.
Identifiers: LCCN 2015045273 | ISBN 9781943158003 (trade paper : alk. paper)
Subjects: LCSH: Marine animals in art--Juvenile literature. | Rain forest animals in art--Juvenile literature. | Desert animals in art--Juvenile literature. | Grassland animals in art--Juvenile literature. | Drawing--Technique--Juvenile literature.
Classification: LCC NC780 .D83 2015 | DDC 743/.6--dc23
LC record available at http://lccn.loc.gov/2015045273

Contents

DRAW
OCEAN ANIMALS

Three steps to a great drawing

1) Look carefully at your *reference material*. This could be an actual animal, or an image from a book or the internet. See the shapes and pieces and how they fit together. Next, lightly sketch the shapes in the right place.

   When you sketch lightly, you can easily correct any mistakes before they ruin your drawing.

2) Make sure you have all the shapes and pieces in the right place. Adjust lines, redraw pieces that don't look right, and erase sketch lines you no longer need.

3) Finally, spend as much time as you need to make your drawing jump off the page. Darken lines at emphasis points: joints, feet, points of claws, horns, spikes, and eyes, for example. Add fur, feathers, or scales, and shading. Clean up any smudges with your eraser, then date and save your drawing in a portfolio.

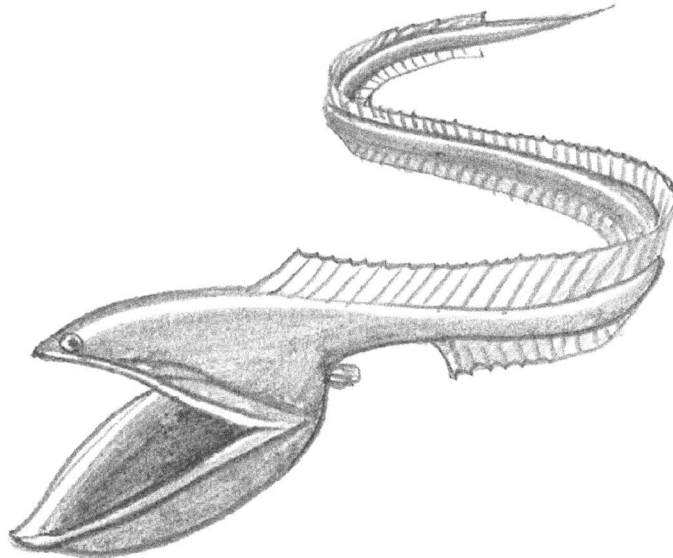

For colorful inspiration and ideas, follow our
Ocean Animals Pinterest feed:

drawbooks.com/ocean

Great White Shark

Carcharodon carcharias

Size: 6 m (19.5 ft). Diet: fish, seals, dolphins, unlucky humans. Large and aggressive! The great white shark has protective eyelids that cover the eyes during attacks.

1. Draw a long, flat oval. Add a box at one end for the head, and two lines tapering at the other end for the tail.

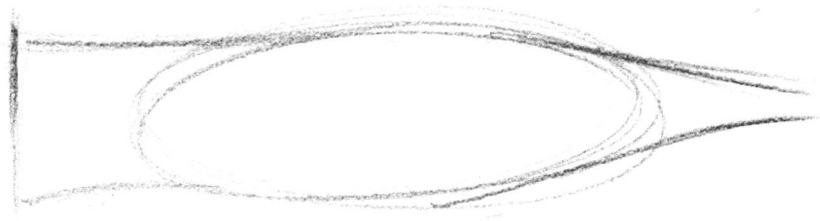

Nostril   Eye

2. Add mouth, teeth, eye, nostril, and gill openings.

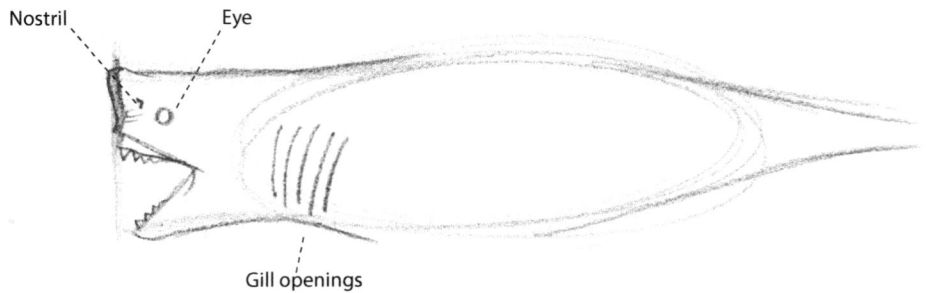

Gill openings

3. Next draw the triangle-shaped dorsal fin on top, behind the center of your oval. Draw the pectoral fin behind the gill openings.

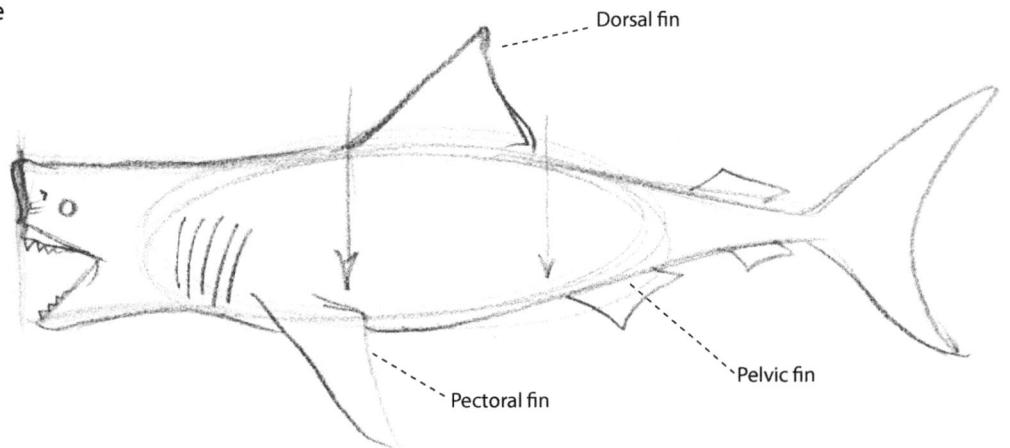

Dorsal fin

Pectoral fin

Pelvic fin

Draw the pelvic fin. It lies below the back of the dorsal fin. Add the two other small fins. Now draw the tail.

4. Add shading. Make the outlines and details bolder. Erase the lines you don't need.

Light snack

For help with details, see drawing tips on pages 54-57.

Always draw lightly at first!

Mako Shark

Isurus oxyrhincus

Size: 3-4 m (10-13 ft). Diet: tuna mackerel, herring, sardines, squid.

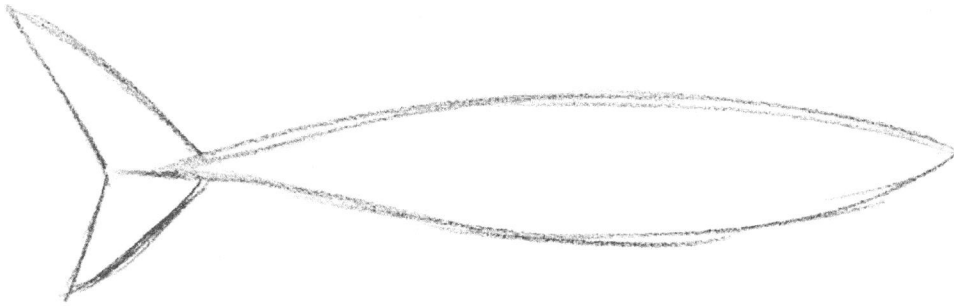

1. Start with a pointed oval. Notice the difference between the top and bottom.

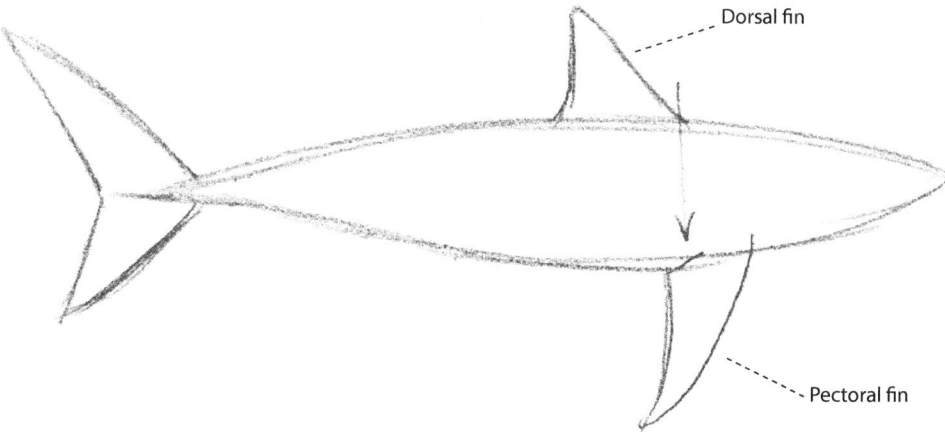

   Draw two triangles for the tail. Which is bigger?

Dorsal fin

Pectoral fin

2. Next, draw the dorsal fin, above the middle of the oval.

   The back of the pectoral fin lines up with the front of the dorsal fin. Draw it.

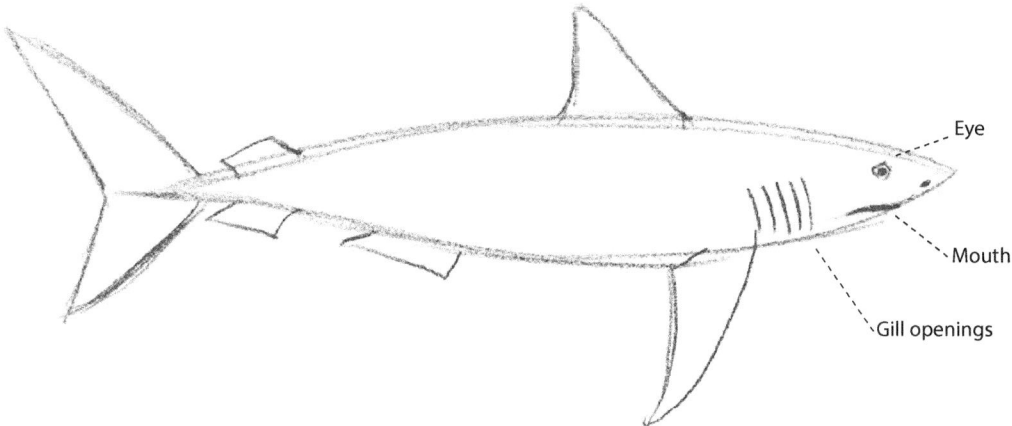

3 Add gill openings, eye, nostril, mouth, and other fins.

Eye

Mouth

Gill openings

4. Add shading. Sharpen details (did you catch the notch in the tail?). Clean up with your eraser.

Thresher Shark

Alopias vulpinus

Size: 6 m (19.5 ft). Diet: fish. Long tail is used to herd schooling fish, making them easier to catch.

Tail

1. Draw an oval with pointed ends. Add the tail. Make it as long as the body.

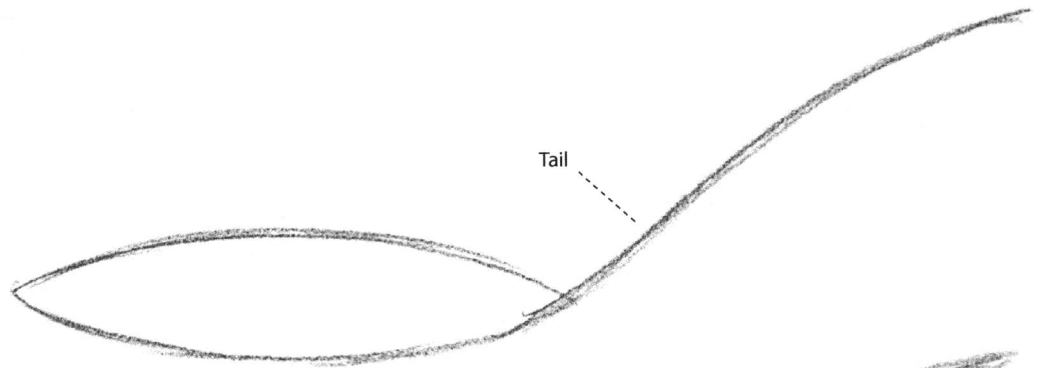

Dorsal fin

2. Add the dorsal fin above the middle of the body.

   Carefully look at the top and bottom part of the tail. Now draw them, lightly at first.

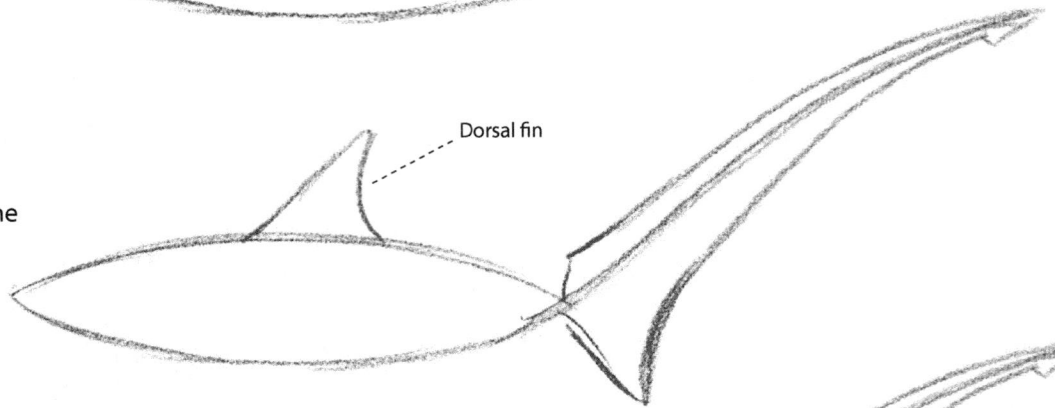

Gill openings

3. Add the other fins and details. Pay close attention to the spatial relationships (in other words, put things in the right places)!

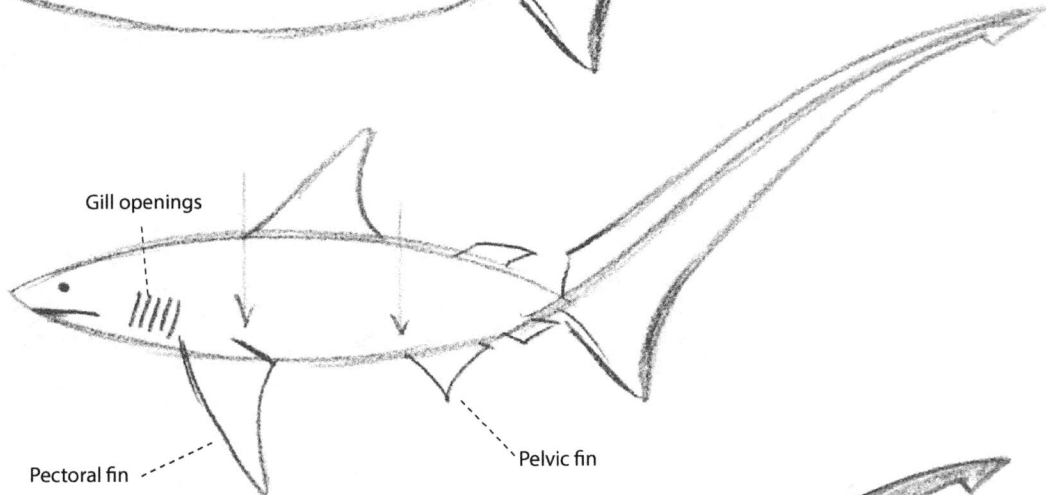

Pectoral fin

Pelvic fin

5. Add shading. Sharpen lines and details. Clean up any smudges with your eraser.

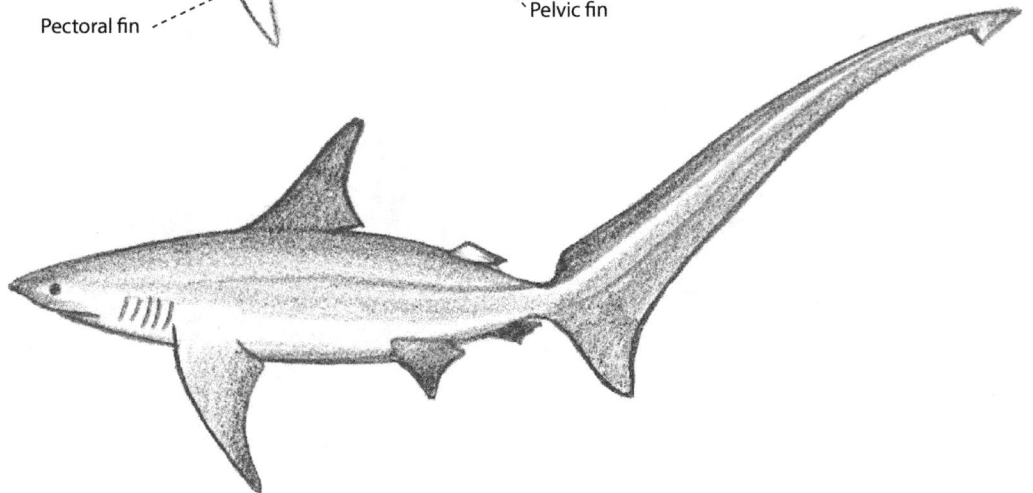

Cool looking shark!

For help with details, see drawing tips on pages 54-57.

Always draw lightly at first!

Odontaspis taurus

Size: 3.2 m (10.5 ft) Diet: fish. Lives at the bottom of shallow waters.

1. Draw a long, flat oval with a extending point at one end for the head, and a long, bending point at the other for the tail.

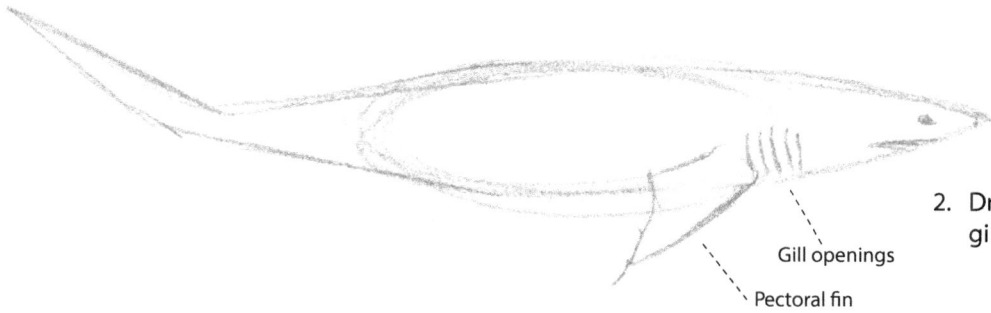

Gill openings

Pectoral fin

2. Draw the mouth and eye. Add gill openings and pectoral fin.

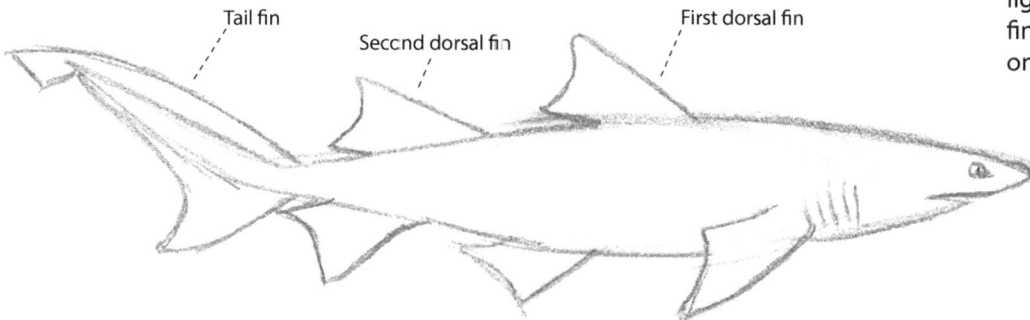

Tail fin   Second dorsal fin   First dorsal fin

3. Look at the tail fin. Draw it, lightly at first! Add the other fins, all about the same size as one another.

4. Add shading. Sharpen outlines and details Clean up any smudges with your eraser.

Hammerhead Shark

Sphyrna mokarran (Great hammerhead)

Size: 6m (19.5 ft) Diet: fish, especially rays. With eyes facing out to the side, hammerheads have to turn from side to side as they swim.

1. Start with a tilted oval. Add a curving triangle for the tail, and a pointed end for the head.

Tail

2. Look at the curved tail fin. Draw it. Now look at the angle of the head. Draw it carefully, paying attention to angles.

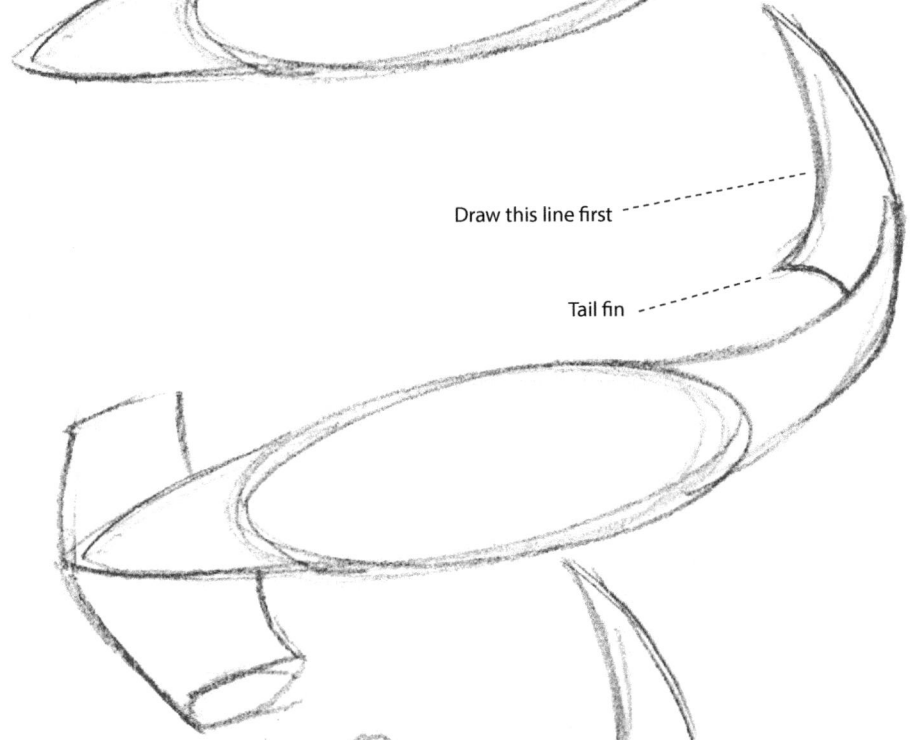

Draw this line first

Tail fin

3. Add the one eye you can see from this angle. Draw gill openings. Next add the pectoral and dorsal fins.

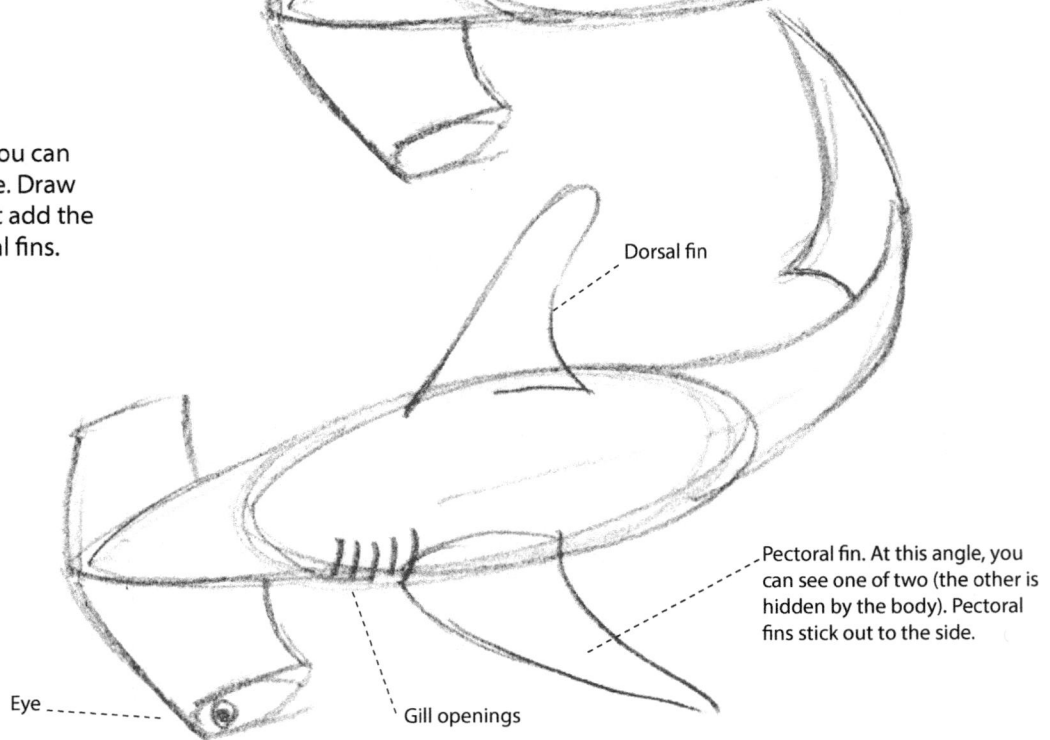

Dorsal fin

Pectoral fin. At this angle, you can see one of two (the other is hidden by the body). Pectoral fins stick out to the side.

Eye

Gill openings

10 *Draw Animals*

Always draw lightly at first!

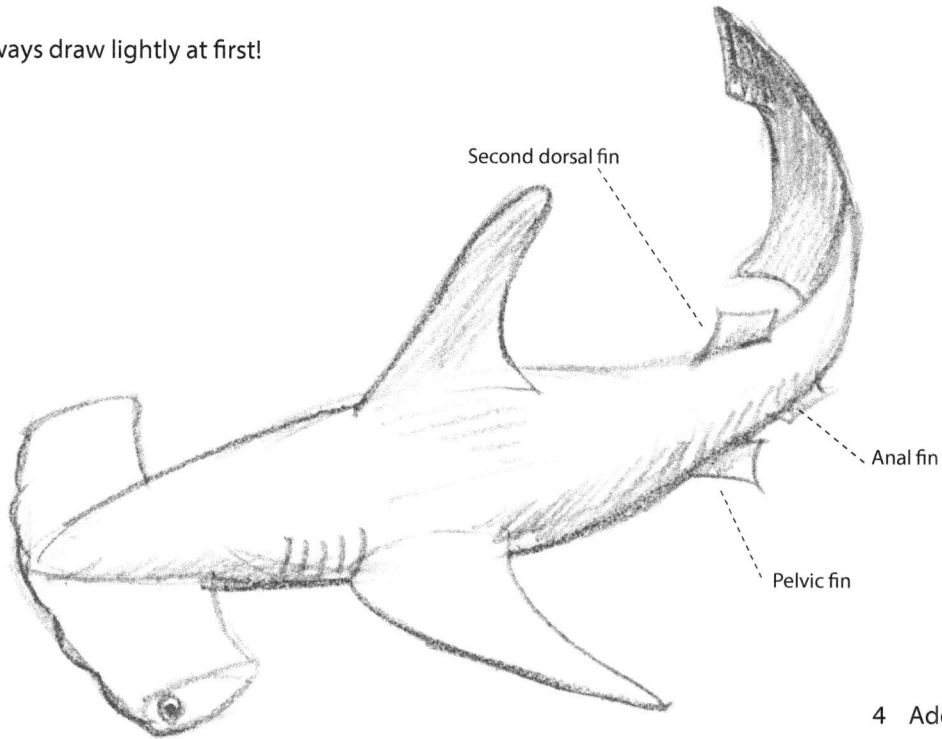

Second dorsal fin

Anal fin

Pelvic fin

4 Add the second dorsal, pelvic and anal fins.

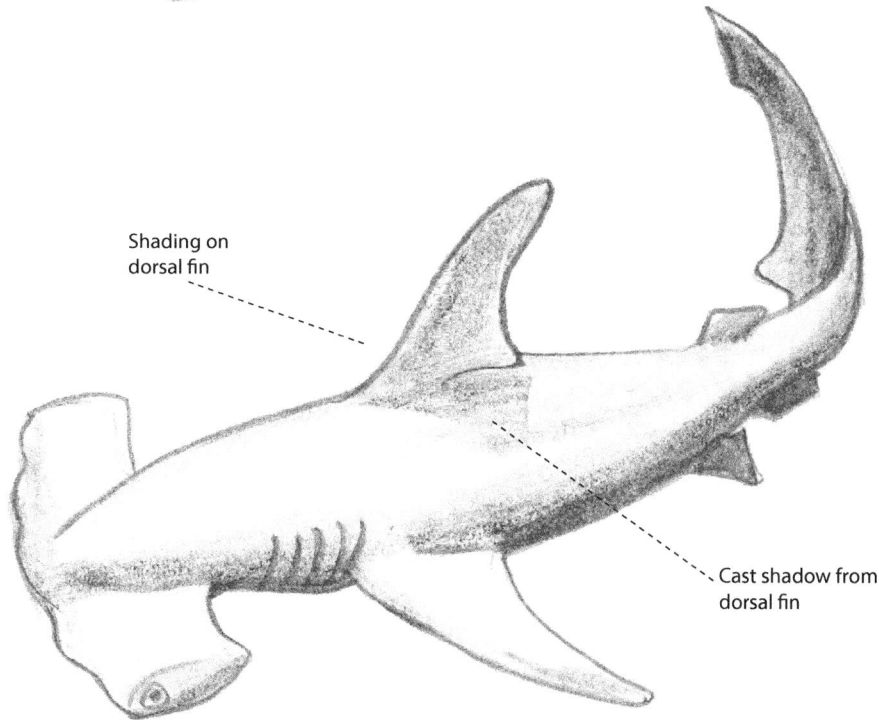

Shading on dorsal fin

5. Darken important lines and details. Add shading. Clean up by erasing any smudges or lines you no longer need.

Cast shadow from dorsal fin

Profile view of a Hammerhead shark, showing the shape of the tail more clearly. Scientists don't know why the head is that shape. Some think the winglike shape helps keep the shark swimming level.

Whale Shark

Rhincodon typus

Size: 15.2 m (50 ft). Diet: small fish, plankton. Filter feeder (notice the very large gill openings). The projections on the front of its mouth are not teeth. It's huge, but a very gentle shark.

Tail

Head

1. Draw a long, flat oval. Add a slanted box at one end for the head. Draw a long triangle at the other end for the tail.

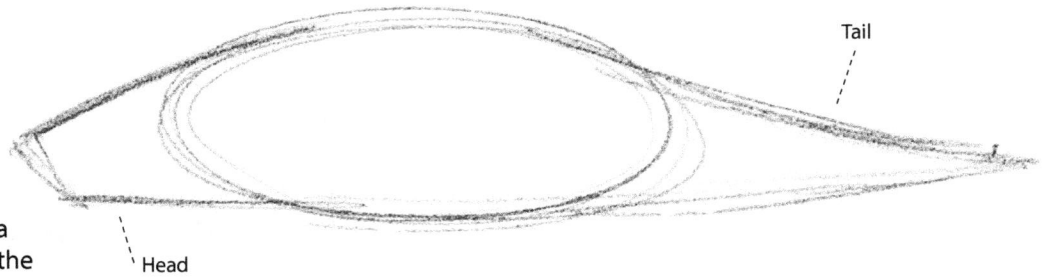

Eye–above back of mouth

First dorsal fin

Second dorsal fin

Large gill openings

Pelvic fins

Anal fin

Tail fins

2. Draw the dorsal fins at the back of the whale shark's body. Add large gill openings. Draw the pelvic, anal, and tail fins. Add the mouth and eye.

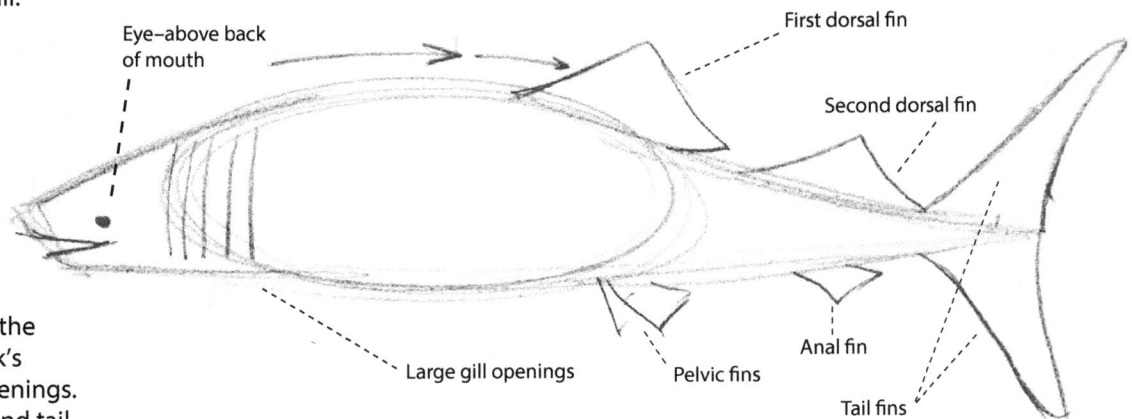

Pectoral fins

3. Next draw long ridges curving down the side and back of the shark's body. Add pectoral fins.

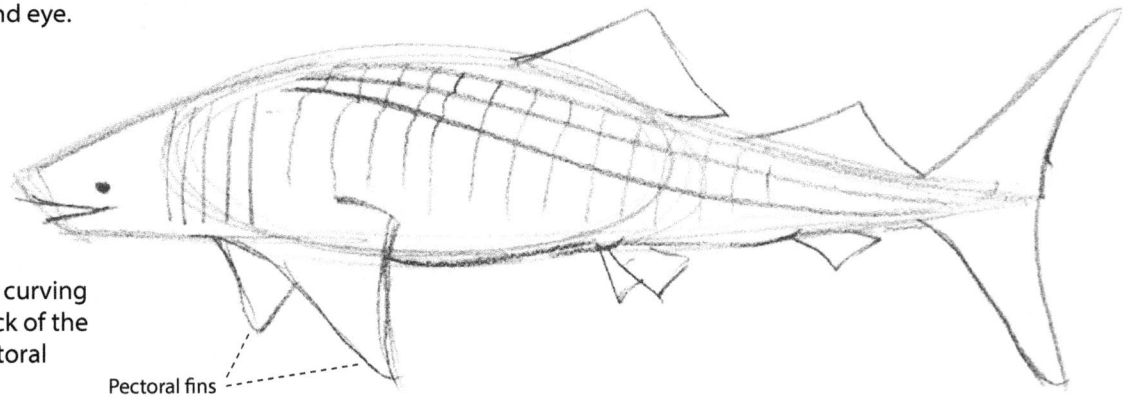

4. Add shading and patterns. Erase smudges and 'leftover' lines.

Always draw lightly at first!

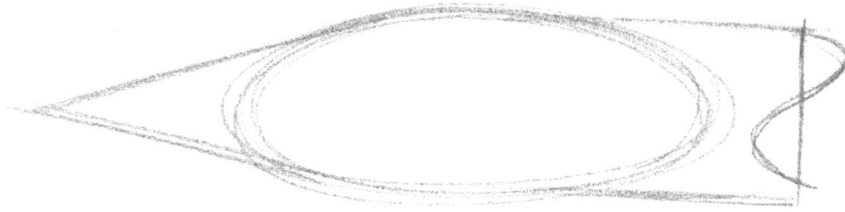

Basking Shark

Cetorhinus maximus

Size: 10.4 m (34 ft). Diet: plankton. Filter feeder. Swims along with its mouth wide open to catch plankton.

1. Draw a flat oval. Draw a box at one end, and a triangle at the other. A backward S curve forms the head.

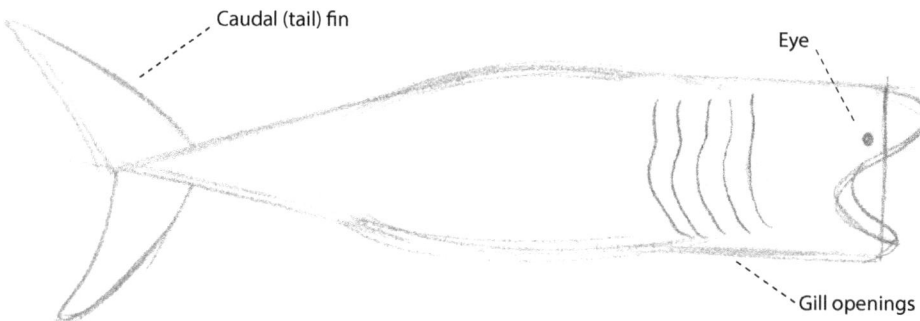

Caudal (tail) fin

Eye

Gill openings

2. Draw the eye and open mouth. Draw very large gill openings. Draw the caudal (tail) fin. Erase parts of the oval that you no longer need.

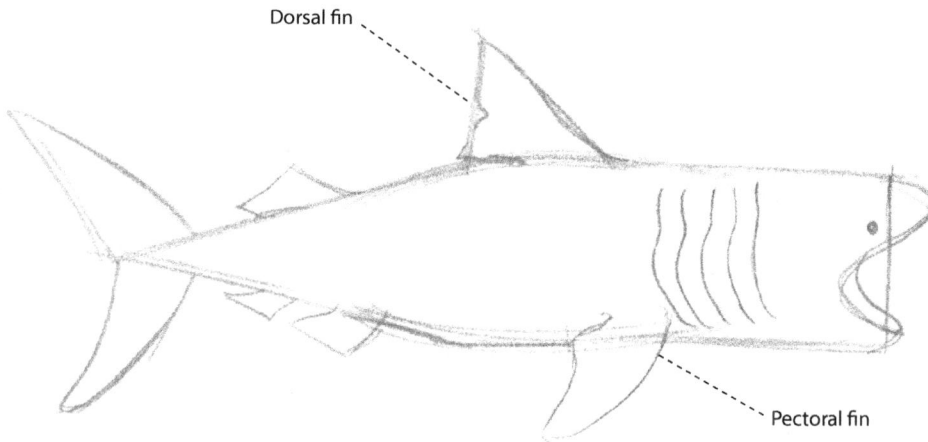

Dorsal fin

Pectoral fin

3. Put the dorsal fin above the middle of the oval. Draw the pectoral and remaining fins.

4. Finally, add shading and sharpen details. Clean up any smudges.

Port Jackson Shark

Heterodontus portusjacksoni

Size: up to 1.5 m (5 ft). Diet: probably mollusks, sea urchins and mollusks; feeds at night. Has stout spines in front of each dorsal fin.

Always draw lightly at first!

Head

Tail

1. Draw a long, flat oval with a rat-like tail. Add a slanting box shape for the head.

Spine

Dorsal fin

2. At the front of the oval, draw gill openings and the pectoral fin. Add the dorsal fin, with its pointed spine in the front.

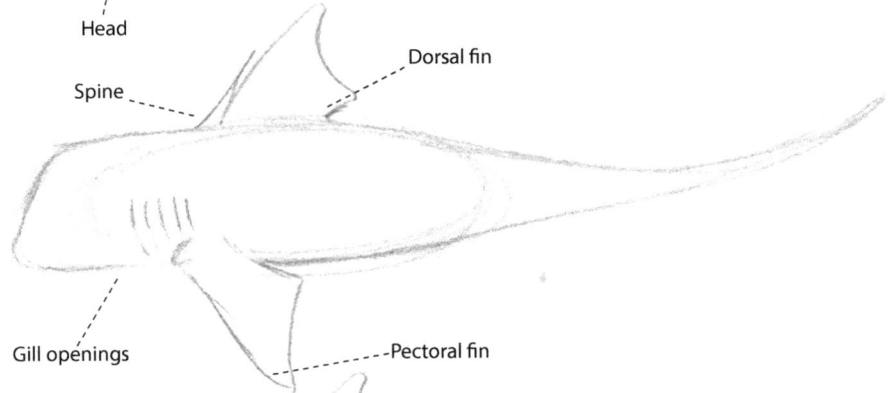

Gill openings

Pectoral fin

Lateral line

3. Draw the eye high in the head. Draw the mouth, quite unlike other sharks'. Carefully add the caudal (tail) fin, and the lateral line.

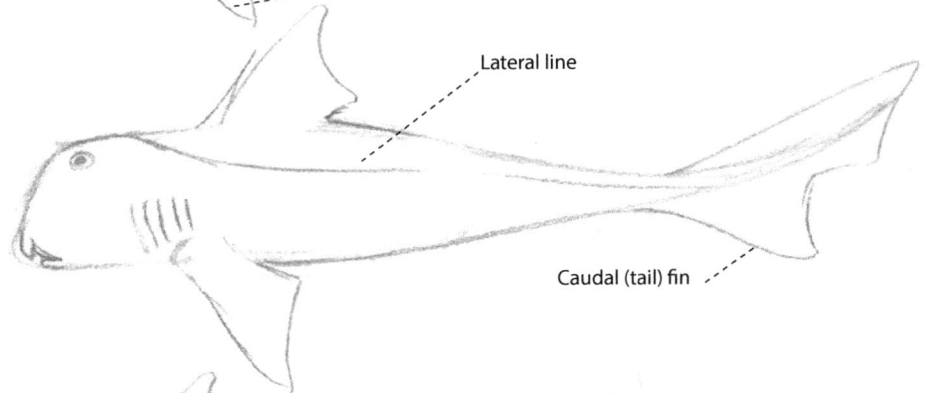

Caudal (tail) fin

Second dorsal fin

4. Draw the second dorsal fin, and the fins on the bottom.

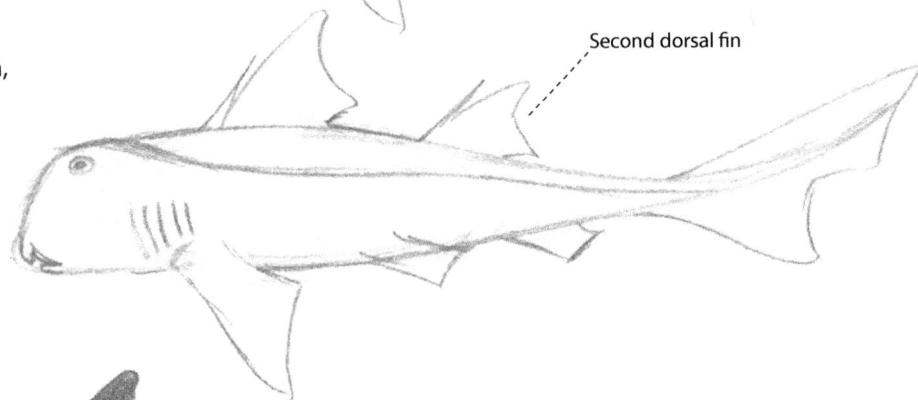

5. Add shading. Sharpen outlines and details. Clean up with your eraser.

For help with details, see drawing tips on pages 54-57.

Always draw lightly at first!

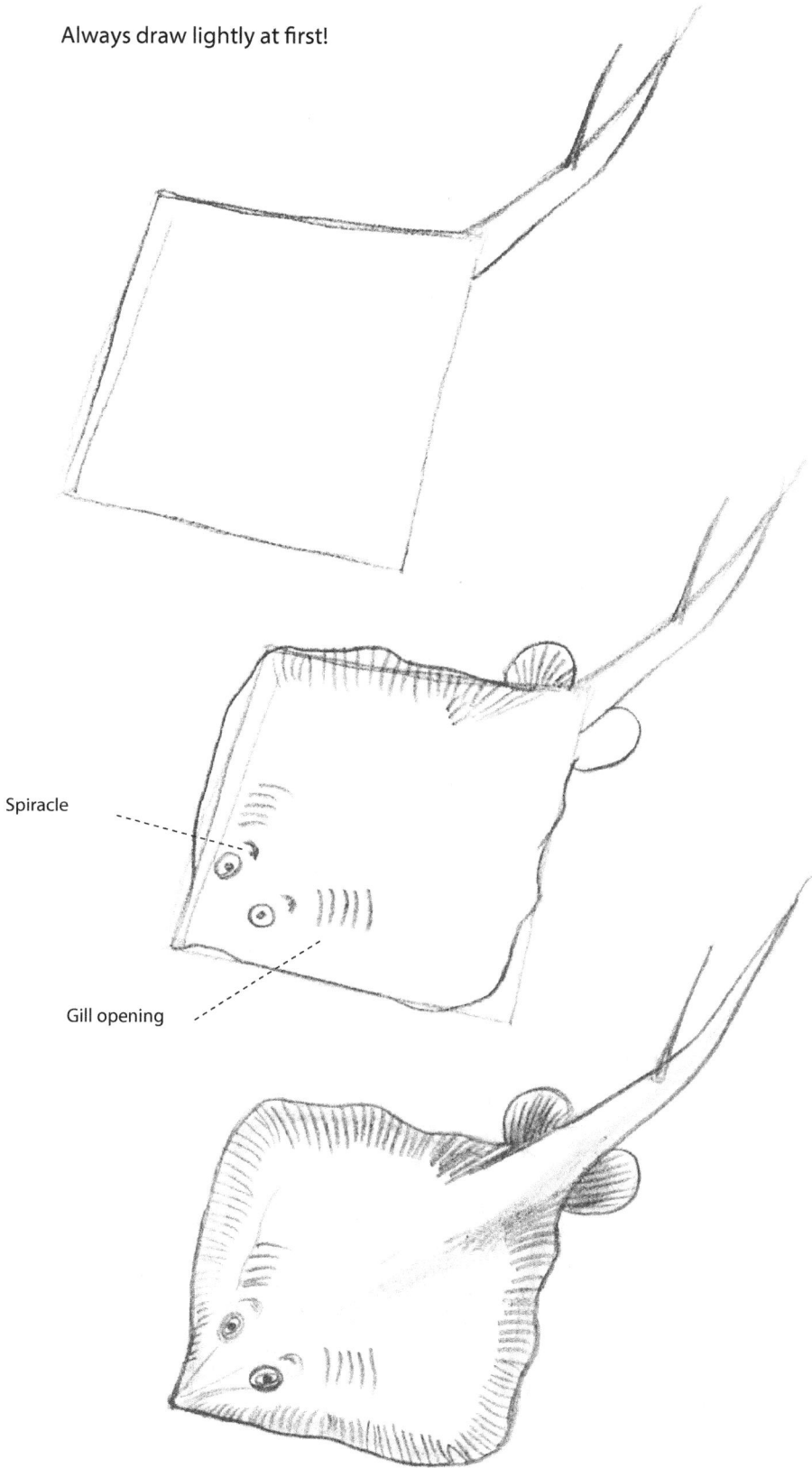

Sting Ray

Family dasayatidae

Size: 1.5 m (5 ft). Diet: Mollusks and crustaceans on the seabed. Graceful swimmers who live on sandy and muddy bottoms. The sharp spine can be used as a weapon. There are about a hundred species.

1. Start with a box shape. Add the pointed tail with its spine. This is where the 'sting' in stingray comes from.

Spiracle

Gill opening

2. Make the outline wiggly. Add eyes, gills, and spiracles, which are where the ray breathes in (its mouth is on the bottom; it breathes out through its gills). Carefully erase your straight lines.

3 Sharpen outlines and details. Add the little lines around the outside. Add shading. Clean up any smudges with your eraser.

Atlantic Manta

Manta birostris

Size: up to 6.7m (27ft) wide. Diet: plankton, fish and crustaceans. The 'hands' on either side of the mouth can be extended, or used as scoops to direct food into the mouth.

1. Draw a big, swooping curve.

2. Add a bump in the middle.

3. Next draw an arching curve to make one 'wing.'

4. Lightly draw in a C shape for the projections at either side of the mouth.

5. Add a line for the bottom of the closer wing. Draw the eye. Look carefully at my example to see how to finish the mouth.

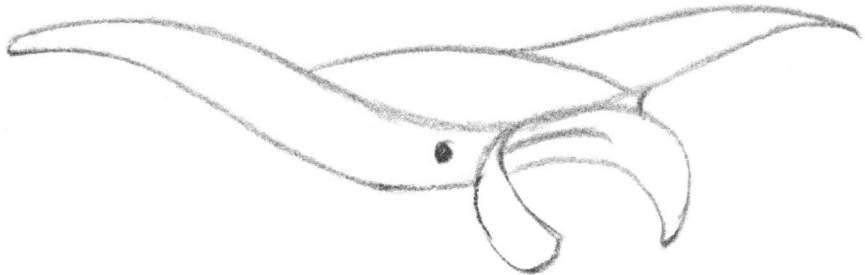

6. Add the tail. Sharpen outlines, add shading, and clean up any smudges with your eraser.

Always draw lightly at first!

Delphinapterus leucas

Size: 4-6 m (13-20 ft). Diet: fish and crustaceans from the sea bottom. White whales sing a variety of songs. Nineteenth century whalers called them sea canaries.

Tail

1. Draw a large, flat oval with another oval overlapping it. Add a triangular projection at the other end for the tail.

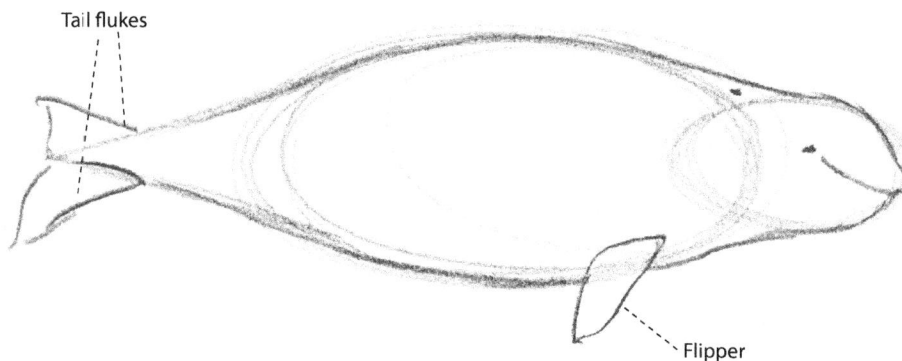

Tail flukes

Flipper

2. Add two small triangles for the tail flukes. Draw the flipper on the lower front of the big oval. Draw the mouth upward like a smile. Add the eye.

Blow hole

3. Erase what's left of the ovals. Go over outlines. This whale is very light in color, so there's not much shading to do. Clean up any smudges with your eraser.

Easy, eh?

For help with details, see drawing tips on pages 54-57.

Sperm Whale

Physeter catodon

Size: 11-20 m (36-66 ft). Diet: mainly large, deepwater squid.

1. Draw a long rectangle.

2. Add one big triangle and two small triangles for the tail flukes.

Tail fluke

Tail fluke

3. Draw a bump for the nose, and a long line for the mouth. Add the eye, and small flipper.

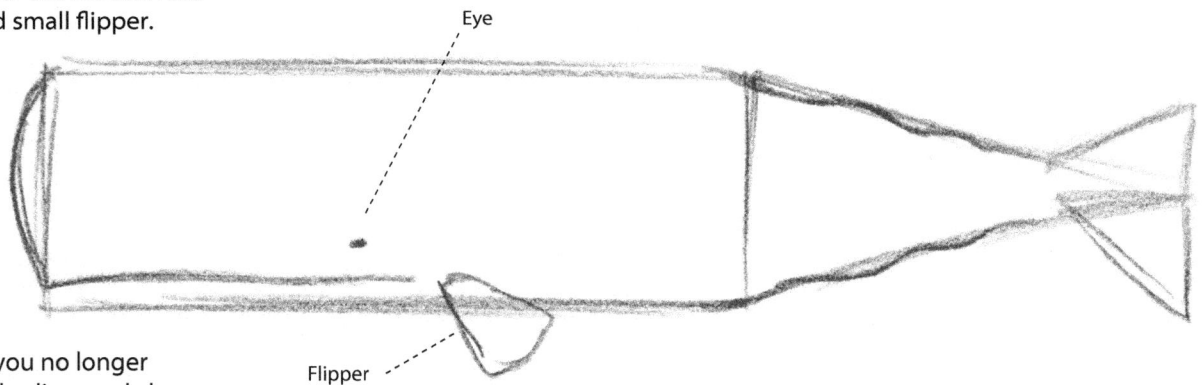

Eye

Flipper

4. Erase lines you no longer need, add shading, and clean up any smudges.

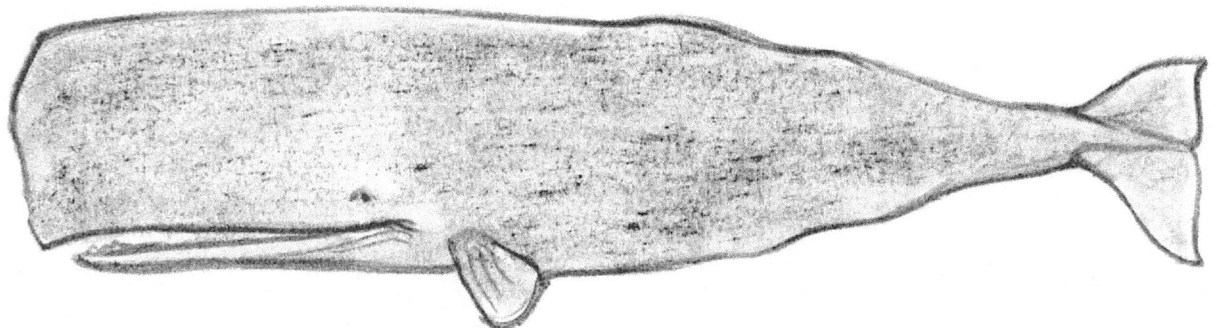

Always draw lightly at first!

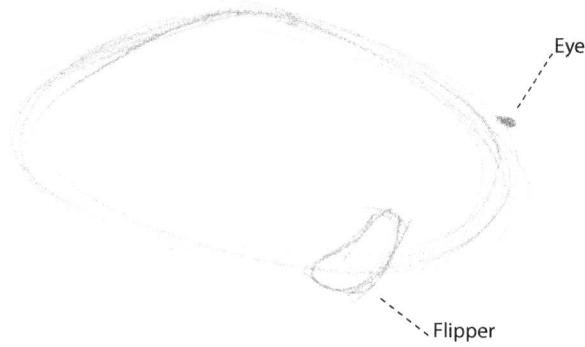

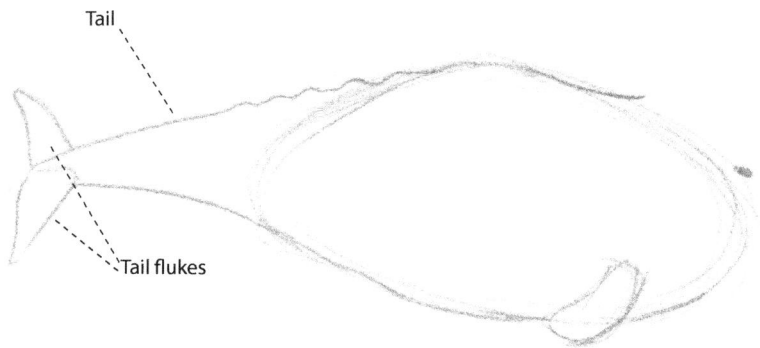

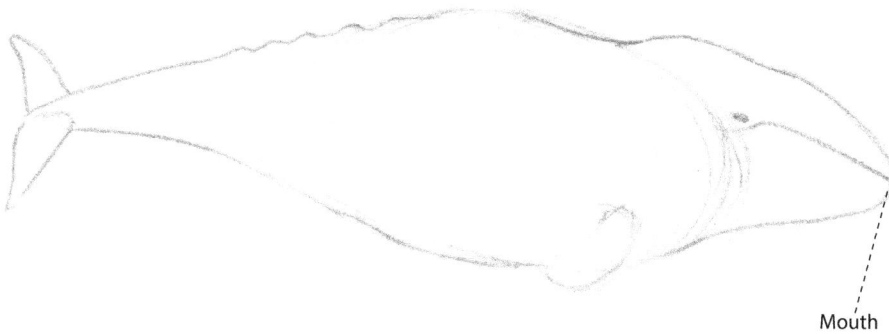

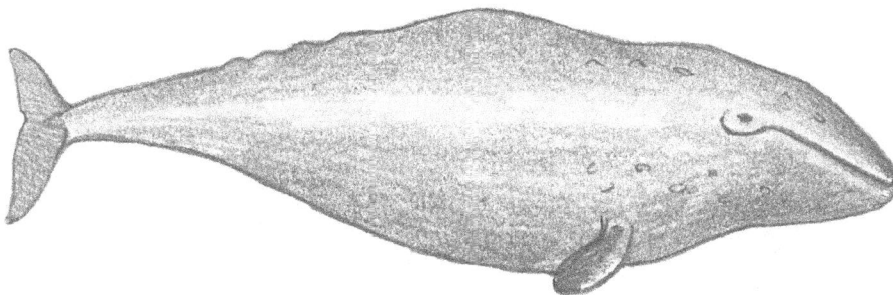

Gray Whale

Eschrichtius robustus

Size: 12-15 m (40-50 ft). Diet: planktonic shrimp, which it stirs up from the bottom, unlike other whales. Strains food through the baleen plates attached to upper jaw.

Eye

Flipper

1. Draw this oval carefully, with a slight point at the top and a sloping bottom. Add a dot where the eye will be. Draw the flipper.

Tail

Tail flukes

2. Draw the tail, with bumps. Add tail flukes.

3. Add the head, with a bump on the top. Draw a line for the mouth.

Mouth

4. Add shading. Sharpen outlines and details. Clean up any smudges with your eraser.

For help with details, see drawing tips on pages 54-57.

Blue Whale

Balaenoptera musculus

Size: 25-32 m (82-105 ft). Diet: plankton. Strains food through the baleen plates attached to upper jaw. The largest mammal that has ever existed. Feeds in polar waters during summer months, eating four tons of tiny shrimp each day. Migrates to warmer waters to breed. Endangered.

Always draw lightly at first!

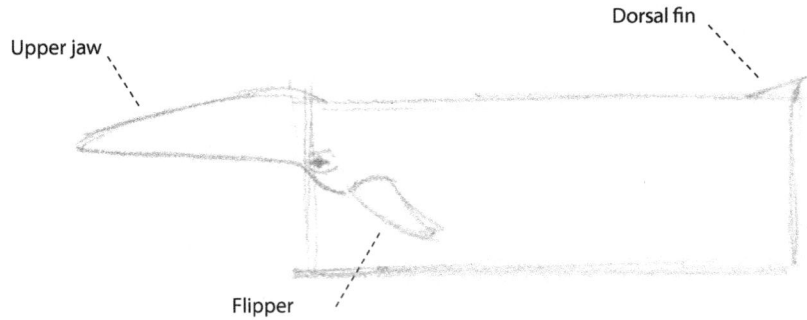

Dorsal fin

Upper jaw

Flipper

1. Draw a long rectangle. Add the little dorsal fin. Add the eye. Draw the flipper. Add the upper jaw.

Mouth

Tail flukes

Tail

Lower jaw

2. Taper the bottom of the whale's body upward, and extend it to form the tail. Extend the top line of the rectangle to meet it. Add the tail flukes. Draw the lower jaw, leaving space to show the baleen plates in the mouth.

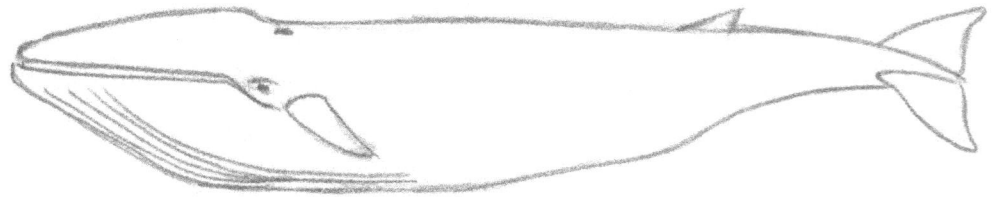

3. Erase parts of the rectangle you no longer need, and go over the outline. Add the grooves on the lower jaw.

Baleen

5. Add shading. Sharpen outlines and details (notice the baleen plates visible in the mouth). Clean up with your eraser.

Always draw lightly at first!

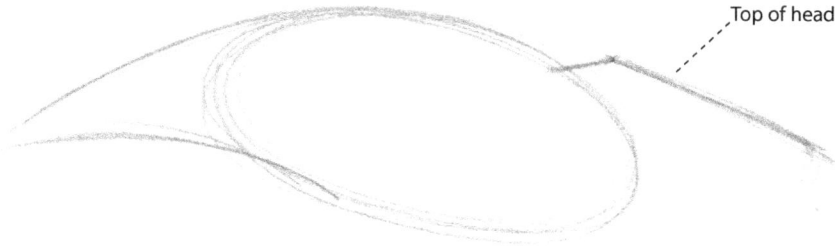

Tail

Top of head

Tail flukes

Flipper

Eye   Mouth

Lower jaw

Dorsal fin

Humpback Whale

Megaptera novaeangliae

Size: 14.6-19m (48-62 ft). Diet: plankton and fish. Strains food through the baleen plates attached to upper jaw. Many knobs and barnacles on body and very long flippers. Feeds in polar waters in the summer, and migrates to tropical waters for the winter. Endangered.

1. Draw a tilted oval. At the high end, make a curving-down triangle for the tail.

2 Draw the top of the head.

3. Add the bottom of the head. Add a long, slightly curving flipper with one bumpy side. Draw two triangle shapes for the tail flukes.

4. Add a line for the mouth. Draw the eye. Add curved lines on the lower jaw. Add bumps and barnacles on the head and flipper.

5. Draw the dorsal fin. Add shading. Sharpen outlines and details. Clean up any smudges with your eraser.

Great whale!

Listen to a recording of humpback whales singing!

Minke Whale

Balaenoptera acutorostrata

Size: 8-10 m (26-33 ft). Diet: plankton, fish, squid. Strains food through the baleen plates attached to upper jaw.

1. Draw a long, slightly curving line for the back. Add a curved line under it.

2. Draw the small dorsal fin. Add the small, rounded flipper. Add a slight bump at the head. Extend the bottom curved line upward to form the tail. Add tail flukes. Erase the part of the curve you no longer need.

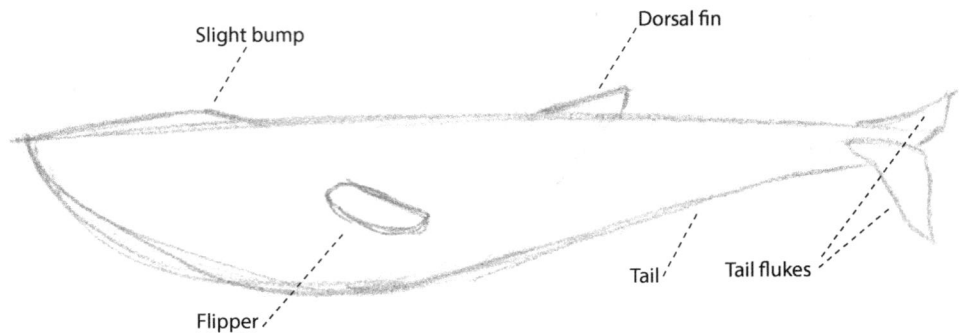

Slight bump

Dorsal fin

Flipper

Tail

Tail flukes

3. The mouth is at the top of the head, and turns down at the back. Draw the mouth, and the eye at the back of it. Draw the grooves on the lower jaw. You may find it easier to draw these with your paper upside down.

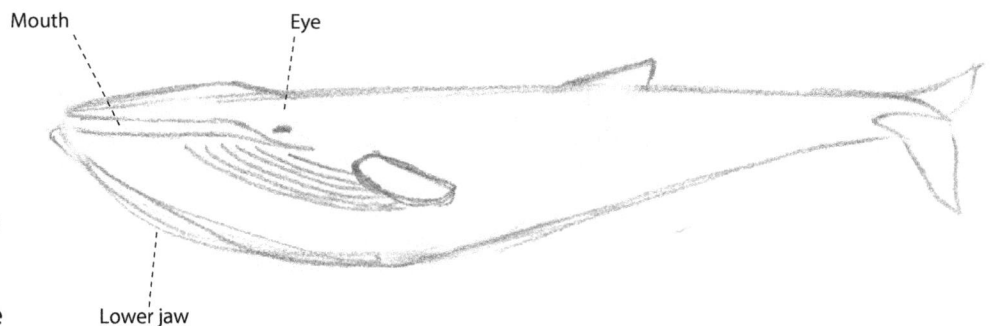

Mouth

Eye

Lower jaw

Baleen plates

4. Now, sharpen outlines and details. Add shading. Clean up any smudges with your eraser.

For help with details, see drawing tips on pages 54-57.

Always draw lightly at first!

Orcinus orca

Size: 7-9.7 m (23-32 ft). Diet: fish, squid, sea lions, birds. Males have the distinctive dorsal fin (smaller and curved on females and juveniles). Killer whales are black on top, and white on the bottom. Each has a unique pattern.

Head

Tail

1. Draw a long, flat oval. Add a triangle for the tail. Draw the head, with a bump on top.

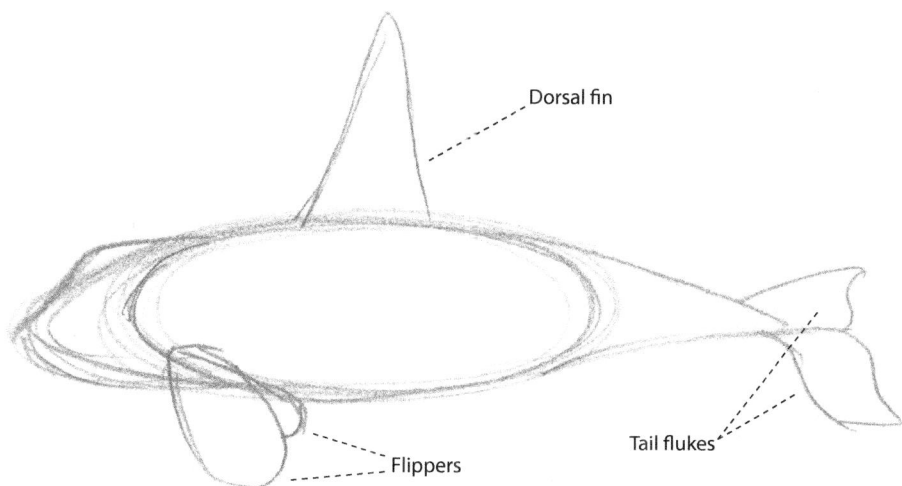

Dorsal fin

Tail flukes

Flippers

2. Draw a very tall dorsal fin on top. Add flippers and tail flukes.

3. Because of their strong black and white coloring, you may want to finish your drawing in ink or marker. Then you can carefully erase pencil lines.

Bowhead Whale

Balaena mysticetus

Size: 15-20 m (49-66 ft). Diet: plankton. The large vertical lines in the mouth are baleen, with which the whale strains plankton out of the water as it swims. Endangered.

Always draw lightly at first!

Tail

Tail fluke

1. Draw a box. Add three curving triangle shapes for the tail and tail flukes.

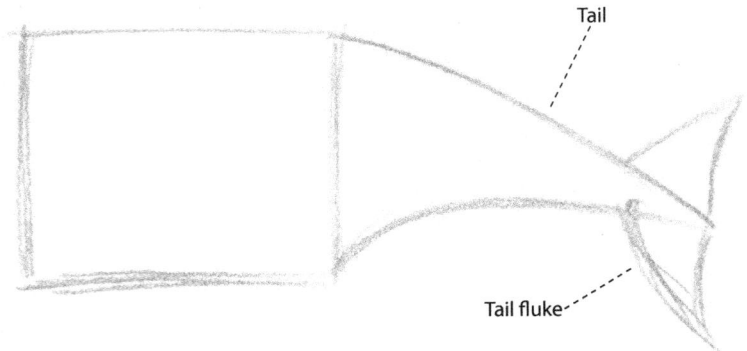

Upper jaw

Intersection of two lines at middle of box

Mouth

Eye

2. Draw the upper jaw. Notice where the mouth line and the box intersect. Add the eye.

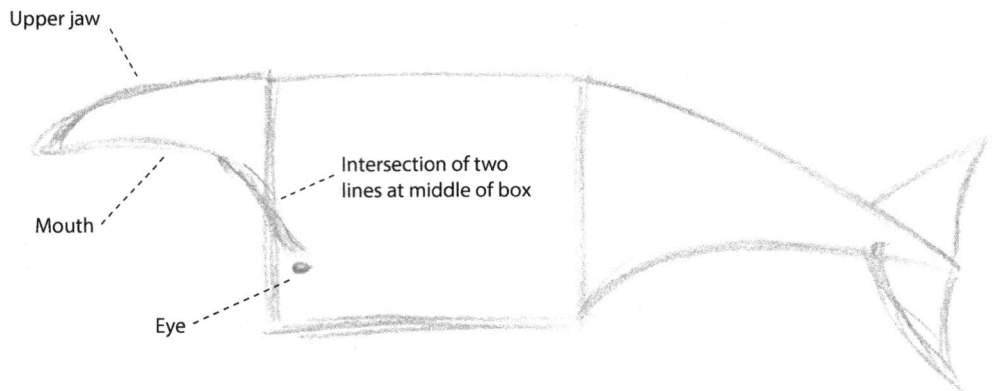

Baleen

3. Draw the flipper, then the bottom of the mouth, lower jaw, and baleen plates. Draw lightly and take your time! Add the flipper, and a bump on top.

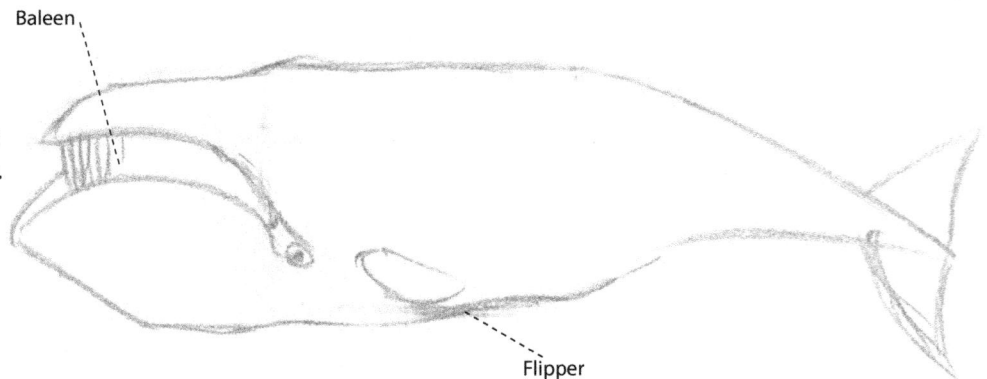

Flipper

4. Add shading. Sharpen outlines and details. Clean up any smudges with your eraser.

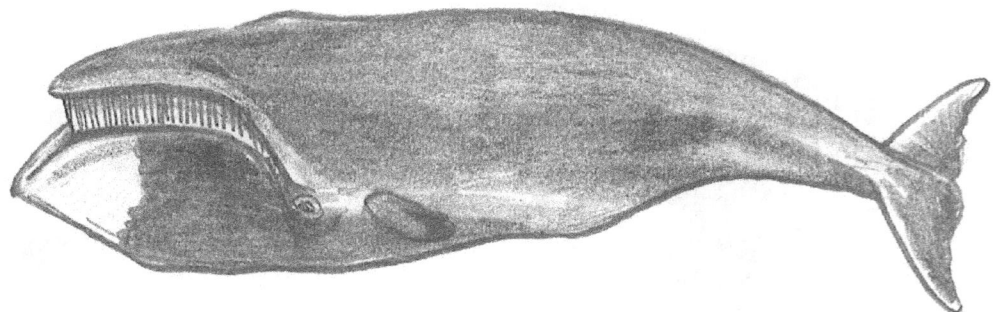

Always draw lightly at first!

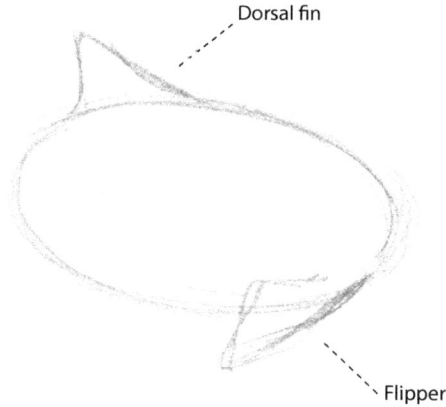

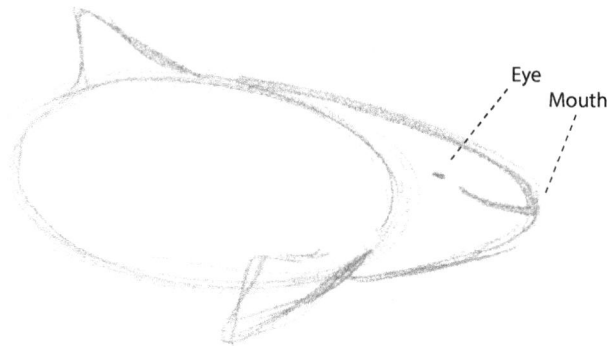

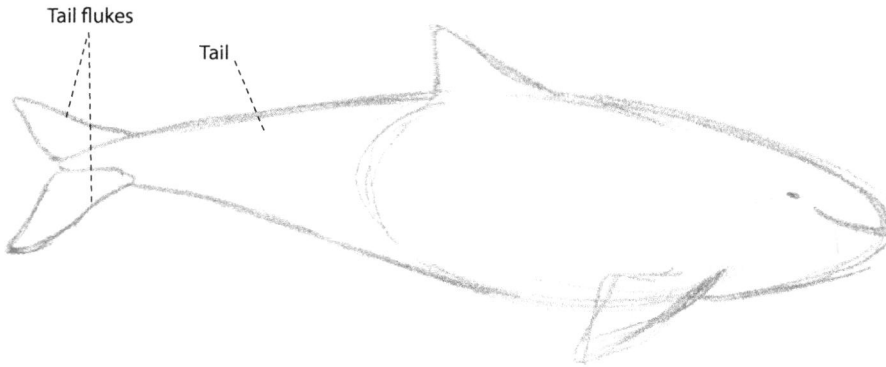

Harbor Porpoise

Phocoena phocoena

Size: 1.5-1.8 m (5-6 ft). Diet: fish. Harbor porpoises live in groups and 'talk' a lot. They can dive for up to six minutes, using clicking sounds and echolocation to find their prey.

Dorsal fin

Flipper

1. Start with an oval. Add the flipper at one end, and the dorsal fin at the other.

Eye
Mouth

2. Extend the oval to form the head. Draw the mouth and eye.

Tail flukes
Tail

3. Add the tail and tail flukes. Erase unneeded lines.

4. Add shading. Sharpen outlines and details. Clean up with your eraser.

For help with details, see drawing tips on pages 54-57.

Atlantic Bottlenose Dolphin

Tursiops truncatus

Size: 4 m (12 ft). Diet: fish. Highly intelligent animals who live in groups. These are the dolphins you usually see in movies or on television.

1. Draw a crescent shape.

2. Add a pointed nose, and two triangles for the tail flukes. Add the curved line on the side, and the eye.

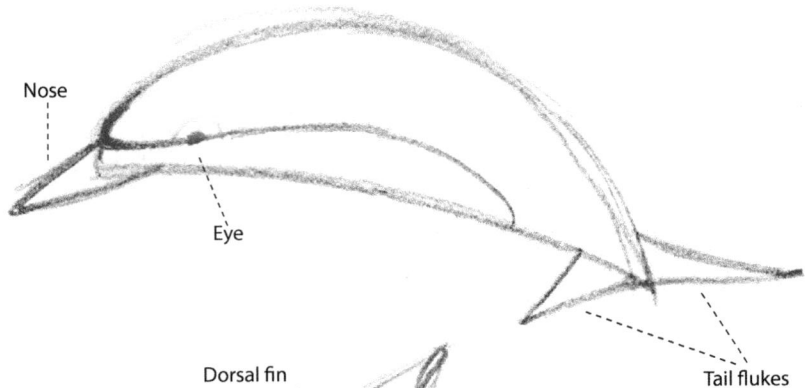

Nose

Eye

Tail flukes

3. Draw the flippers (you only see part of the far one, which I've shaded) and the dorsal fin.

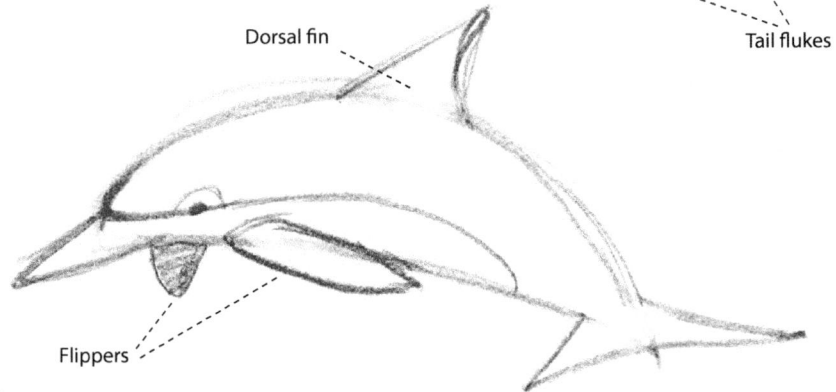

Dorsal fin

Flippers

4. Make your dolphin jumping out of the water if you like. Add shading. Sharpen outlines and details. Clean up any smudges with your eraser.

Harbor Seal

Phoca vitulina

Size: 5 ft (1.5 m). Diet: fish, squid, and crustaceans caught on 4-5 minute dives. Colors vary from light gray to dark brown or black. They come out of the water to spend much of their time on rocks. Unlike sea lions, seals' rear flippers do not turn forward. Seals have no ear flaps.

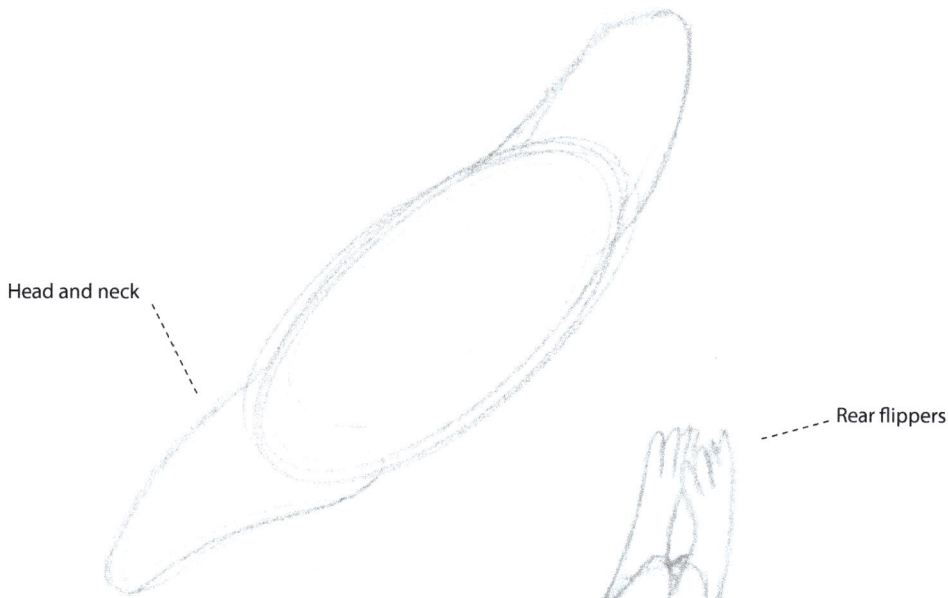

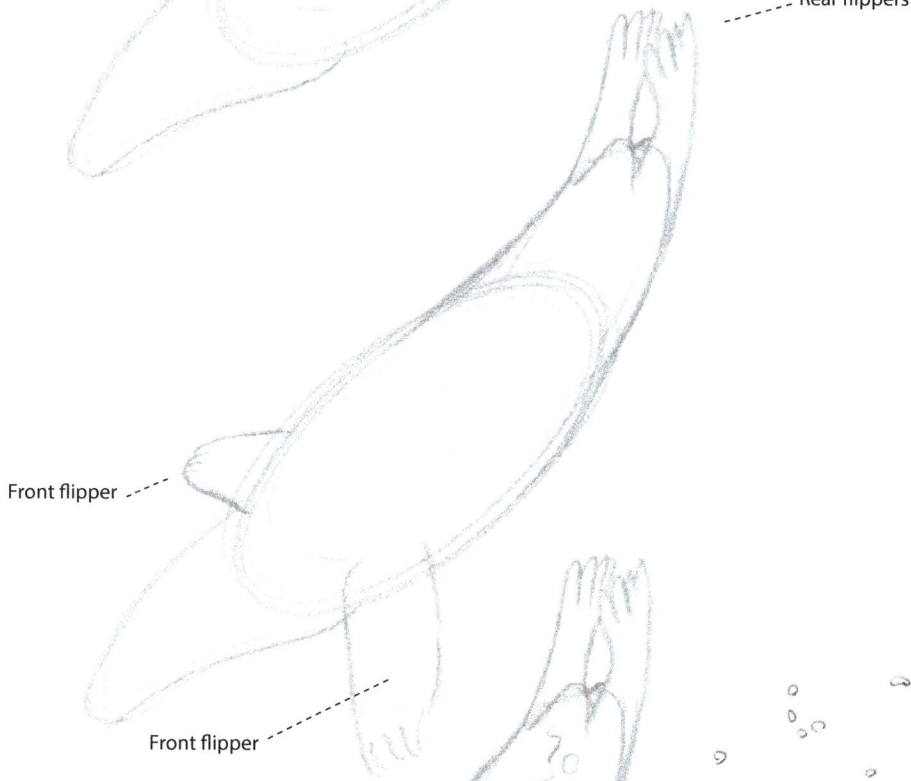

Head and neck

Rear flippers

Front flipper

Front flipper

1. Draw a long oval at an angle. Add curved shapes at both ends Pay special attention to the shape that will be the head and neck.

2. Add front and rear flippers.

3. Draw the eye and whiskers. Add a pattern if you want, or leave it a p ain color.

4. Sharpen outlines and details. Shade. Clean up any smudges.

California Sea Lion

Zalophus californianus

Size: 6 ft (1.8 m). Diet: fish, octopus, and squid. Unlike seals, sea lions can turn their rear flippers forward, which helps them move on land. Sea lions have ear flaps; seals don't.

Always draw lightly at first!

1. Draw three tilted ovals. Look carefully at how, and where they connect. Also look at how they tilt.

2. Draw the forward-facing rear flippers and the front flipper. Connect the two largest ovals.

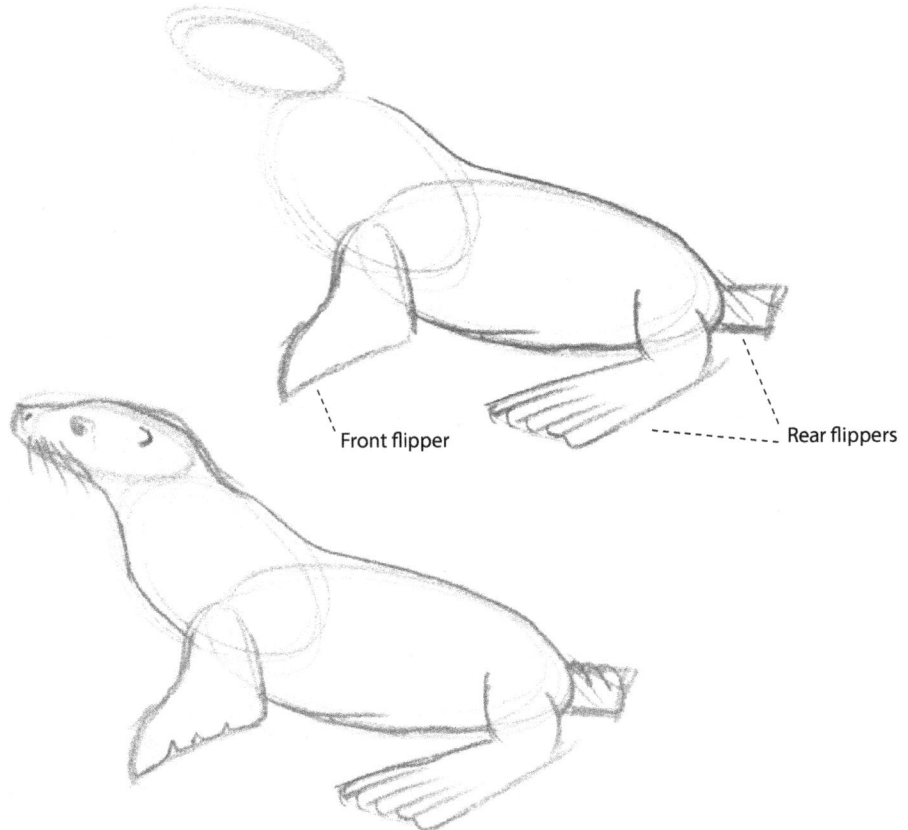

Front flipper

Rear flippers

3. Draw the head, and lines to connect it to the middle oval. Add the ear, nostril, eye, and whiskers.

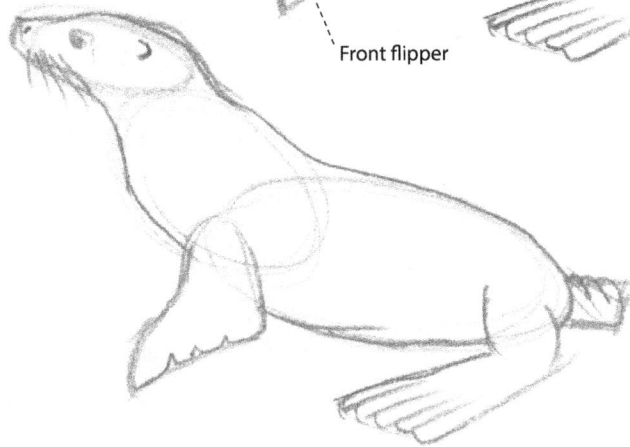

4. Now add shading. Notice how I use short strokes of the pencil to suggest fur. Sharpen outlines and details. Clean up any smudges with your eraser.

Always draw lightly at first!

Walrus

Odobenus rosmarus

Size: males 2.7-3.5 m (9-11.5 ft), females a bit smaller. Diet: mollusks, crustaceans, starfish, fish. They dive to feed, and use their tusks to help pick up food from the sea bottom.

1. Start with two simple shapes.

Eye

2. Add an oval for the head. Connect the back of the head in a smooth curve to the back. Draw the eye. Add the front flippers.

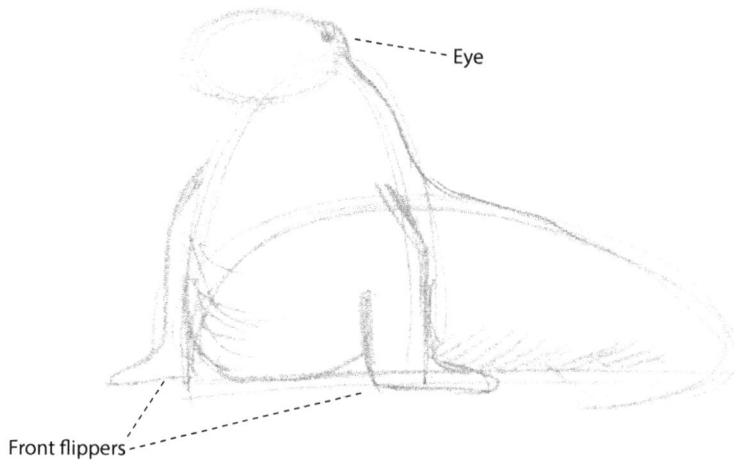

Front flippers

Mouth

Tusks

3. Draw mouth and tusks. Add wrinkles. Since the walrus has many wrinkles, you can use them to make the animal look more round (see Drawing Tips on page 55 for ideas about drawing with contour lines).

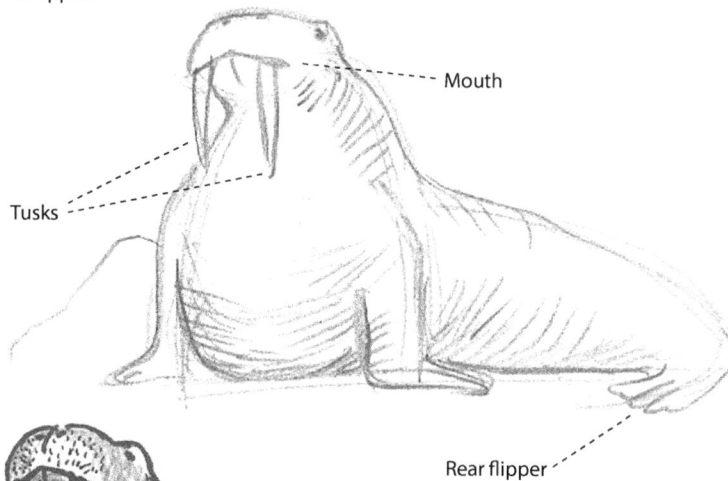

Rear flipper

4. Add shading. Sharpen outlines and details. Clean up any smudges with your eraser. I finished this drawing by going over key lines with a fine tip marker.

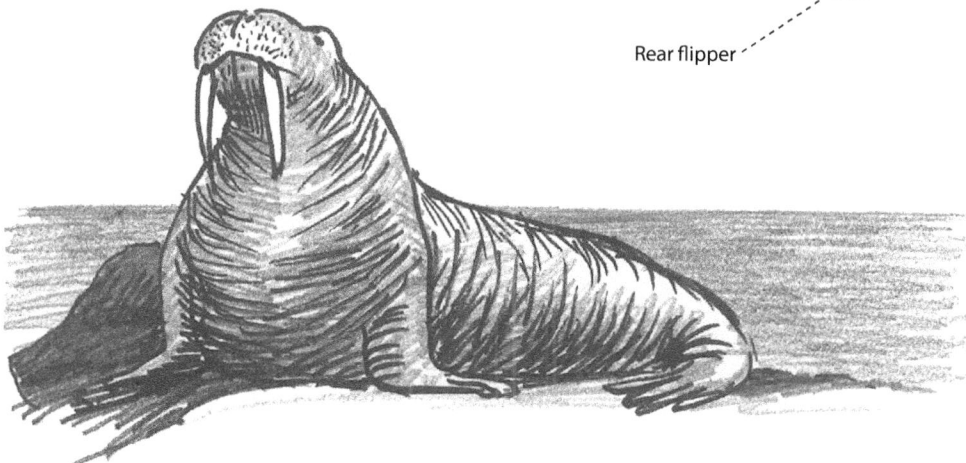

Northern Elephant Seal

Mirounga angustirostris

Size: males up to 6m (20 ft), females up to 3m (10 ft). Diet: fish and squid, caught on long, deep dives. Breed on offshore islands; were hunted almost to extinction but have recovered. Unlike sea lions, seals' rear flippers do not turn forward. Seals have no ear flaps.

1. Draw two ovals for the body. Extend both ends with partial ovals.

2. Connect the shapes to make the outline of the seal, with wrinkles. Draw flippers, front and back.

3. Carefully draw the head with its distinctive bulge, mouth and eye (sideways in this posture).

4. Add shading. Sharpen outlines and details. Clean up with your eraser.

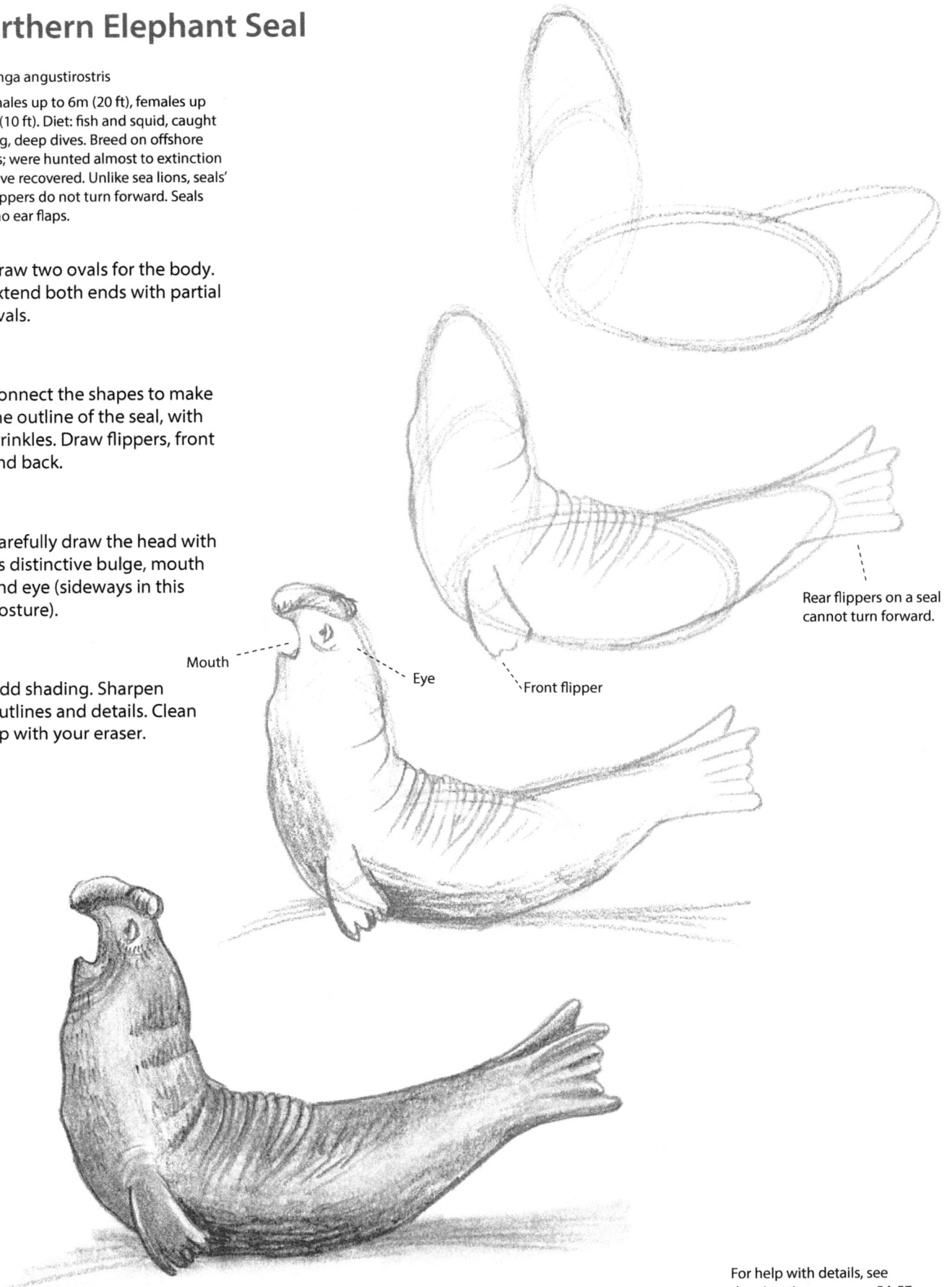

Mouth

Eye

Front flipper

Rear flippers on a seal cannot turn forward.

For help with details, see drawing tips on pages 54-57.

Manatee

Trichecus manatus (American manatee)

Size: up to 3m (10ft). Diet: mainly vegetation, found at night by touch and smell. Manatees sleep in shallow waters, coming to the surface every few minutes to breathe—without even waking up!

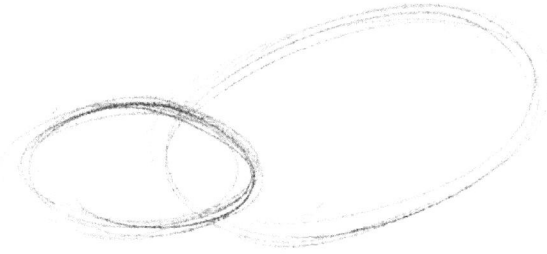

1. Draw two overlapping ovals.

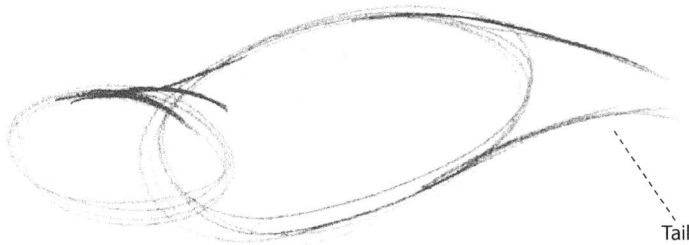

Tail

2. Add lines for wrinkles at the neck, and lines for the tail.

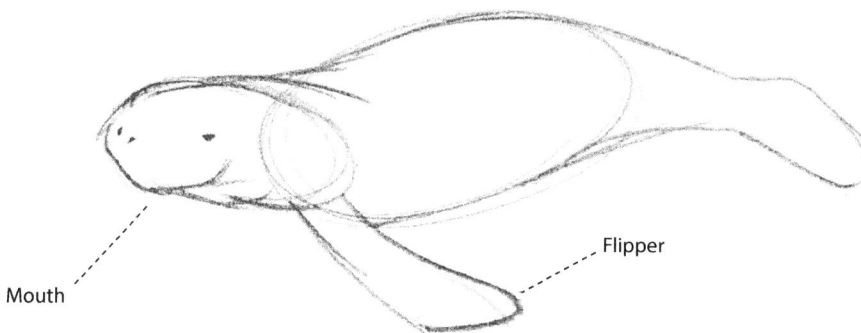

Mouth

Flipper

3. Draw the mouth and face. Add the rest of the tail and flipper.

ZZZ...

4. Add shading. Sharpen outlines and details. Clean up any smudges with your eraser.

Parrotfish

Scarus guacamaia (Rainbow Parrotfish)

Size: 1.2 m (4 ft). Diet: Algae and coral, which it scrapes off reefs with a parrot-like beak. Like some other parrotfish species, this one can create a mucus 'sleeping bag' around itself at night to protect it from predators.

Always draw lightly at first!

Tail

1. Start with a long oval. Add a point at one end and a rounded shape for a tail at the other end.

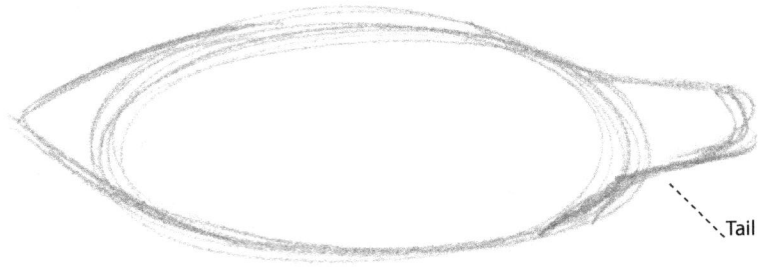

Dorsal fin

Pectoral fin

Tail fin

2. Add the dorsal fin. Next draw the pectoral fin. Add the pelvic, anal, and tail fins.

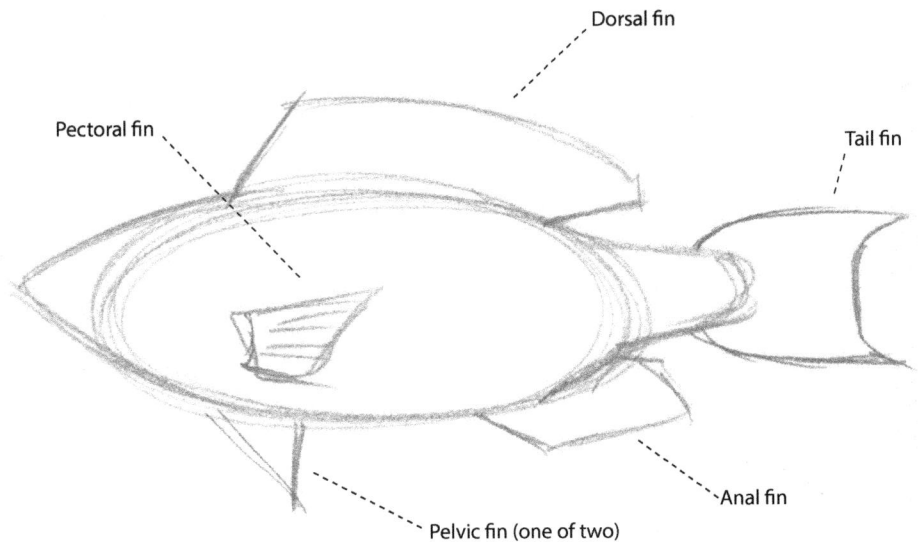

Pelvic fin (one of two)

Anal fin

3. Draw the mouth, eye, and gill openings. Add scales, spines in the fins, and shading. Sharpen outlines and details. Clean up any smudges with your eraser.

Gill openings

Always draw lightly at first!

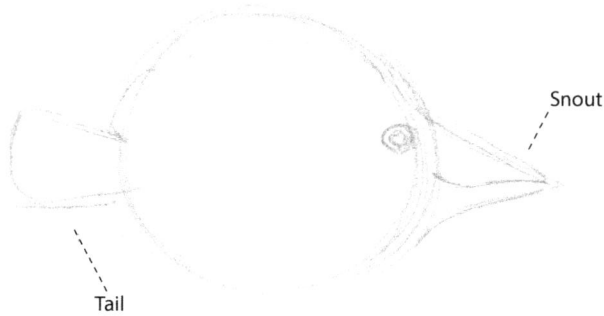

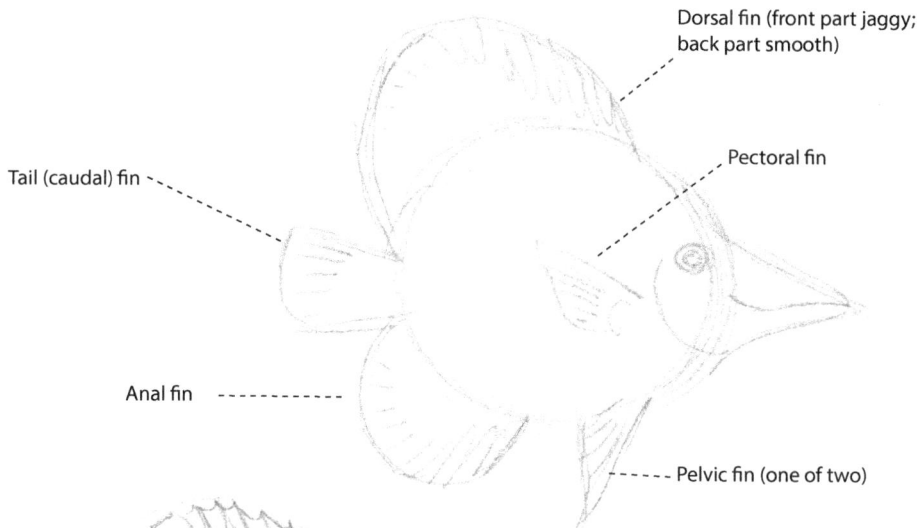

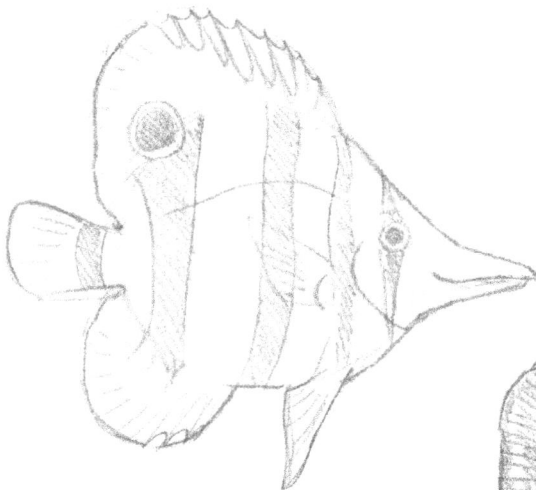

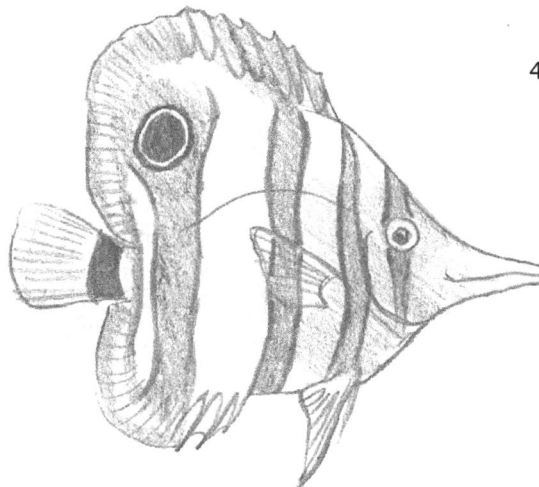

Snout

Tail

Butterflyfish

Chelmon rostratus (copperband or beaked butterflyfish)

Size: 20 cm (7.5 in). Diet: small plants and animals that it pulls out of crevices in coral. The big spot on the tail is probably to fool predators into thinking it's the eye. the eye itself is partially camouflaged by the stripe running through it.

Dorsal fin (front part jaggy; back part smooth)

Pectoral fin

Tail (caudal) fin

Anal fin

Pelvic fin (one of two)

1. Start with a light circle. At one end, in the middle, add the tail. At the other end, draw the long beaklike snout. Add a line for the mouth. Draw the eye.

2. Your next challenge is to draw all the fins with spines. Five fins are visible in this drawing. Draw them all!

3. Next, add the camouflage pattern, including the second 'eye' to fool attackers.

4. Darken the patterns. The eye and band on the tail are black. The stripes are copper-colored. Sharpen outlines and details. Clean up with your eraser.

For help with details, see drawing tips on pages 54-57.

Lionfish

Pterois volitans

Size: 38 cm (15 in). Lives in the Pacific and Indian Oceans. This is a "look but don't touch!" fish. Colorful fins conceal poisonous spines that will kill other fish and even people. Bright orange and reddish colors make this a very pretty fish. Just don't touch!

Always draw lightly at first!

Tail

'Eyebrow'

Barbels

Pectoral fin

Caudal fin

Anal fin

Dorsal fin

1. Start with a simple oval shape. Add a rounded part for the tail at one end, and a point at the other. Draw the eye. Notice where it lies on the oval.

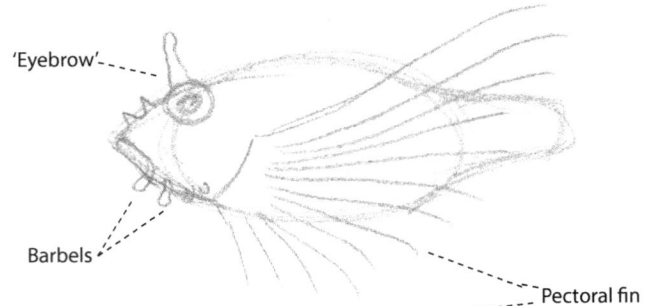

2. Add a line for the mouth, barbels on the chin, and the 'eyebrow' above the eye. Lightly draw radiating curved lines for the spines of the pectoral fin.

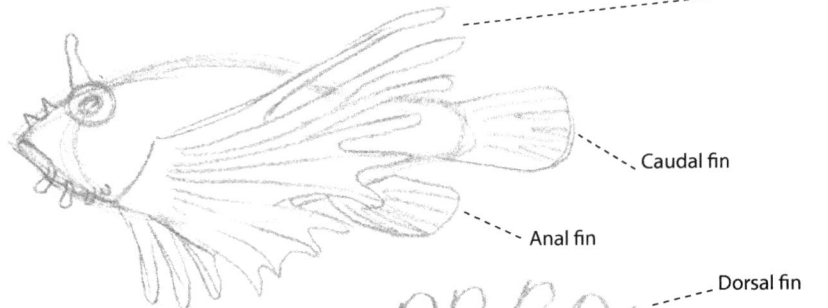

3. Complete the pectoral fin. Add the caudal (tail) fin and anal fin. Erase any body lines you no longer need.

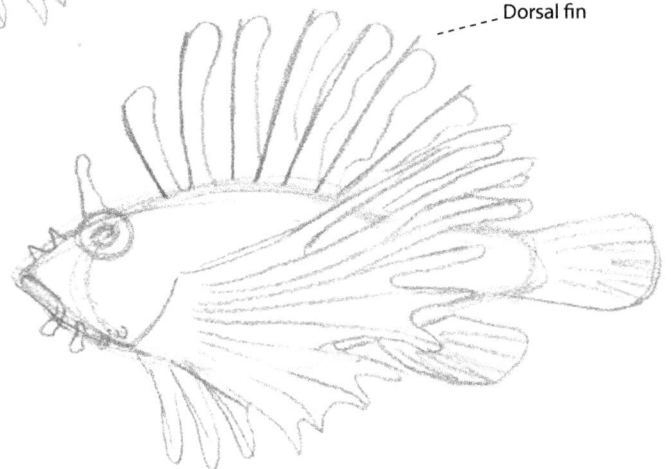

4. Add the large dorsal fin, which is in many parts. At the front of each is a spine.

5. To sharpen the lines, you can go over outlines and important details with a fine marker. Clean up with your eraser.

For help with details, see drawing tips on pages 54-57.

Always draw lightly at first!

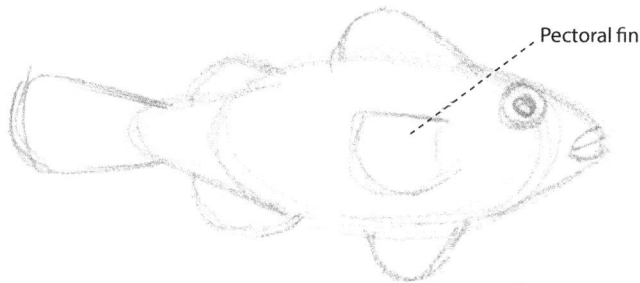

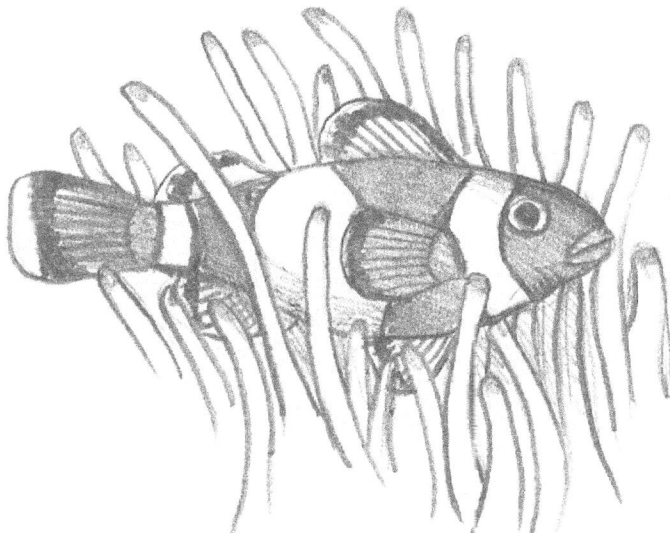

Tail

Pectoral fin

Amphiprion percula

Size: 6 cm (2.25 in). Diet: tiny crustaceans and other organisms. Lives in safety amidst the tentacles of sea anemones, which kill other fish.

1. Start with an oval. Add a rounded part at one end for the head. Draw a large eye and the mouth. Notice that the eye touches the outside of the oval. Add the tail.

2. Draw top and bottom fins in line with each other. Add the pectoral fin.

3. Add tentacles of the sea anemone, with some in front of the fish. Lightly erase lines they cross at the bottom of the fish.

4. Draw the bold pattern (orange, black and white if you're drawing in color). Add shading. Sharpen outlines and details. Clean up any smudges with your eraser.

Moray Eel

Mureana helena

Size:90 cm (35.5 in. Diet: fish, squid, cuttlefish. Hides in rock or coral crevices, waiting to lunge at prey swimming by.

This drawing involves depth, and it's a bit more complicated. For that reason, I've broken it down to one line at a time.

1. Start with a curvy line.

2. Add straight vertical lines at the ends and the curves. Hold your pencil flat on the paper if you have trouble seeing how to draw the vertical lines. Add more curved lines beneath the first ones, connecting to the vertical lines. See how you can turn it into a ribbon?

3. You may need a couple of tries to figure out the next few steps. Draw lightly at first! Pay special attention to the arrows.

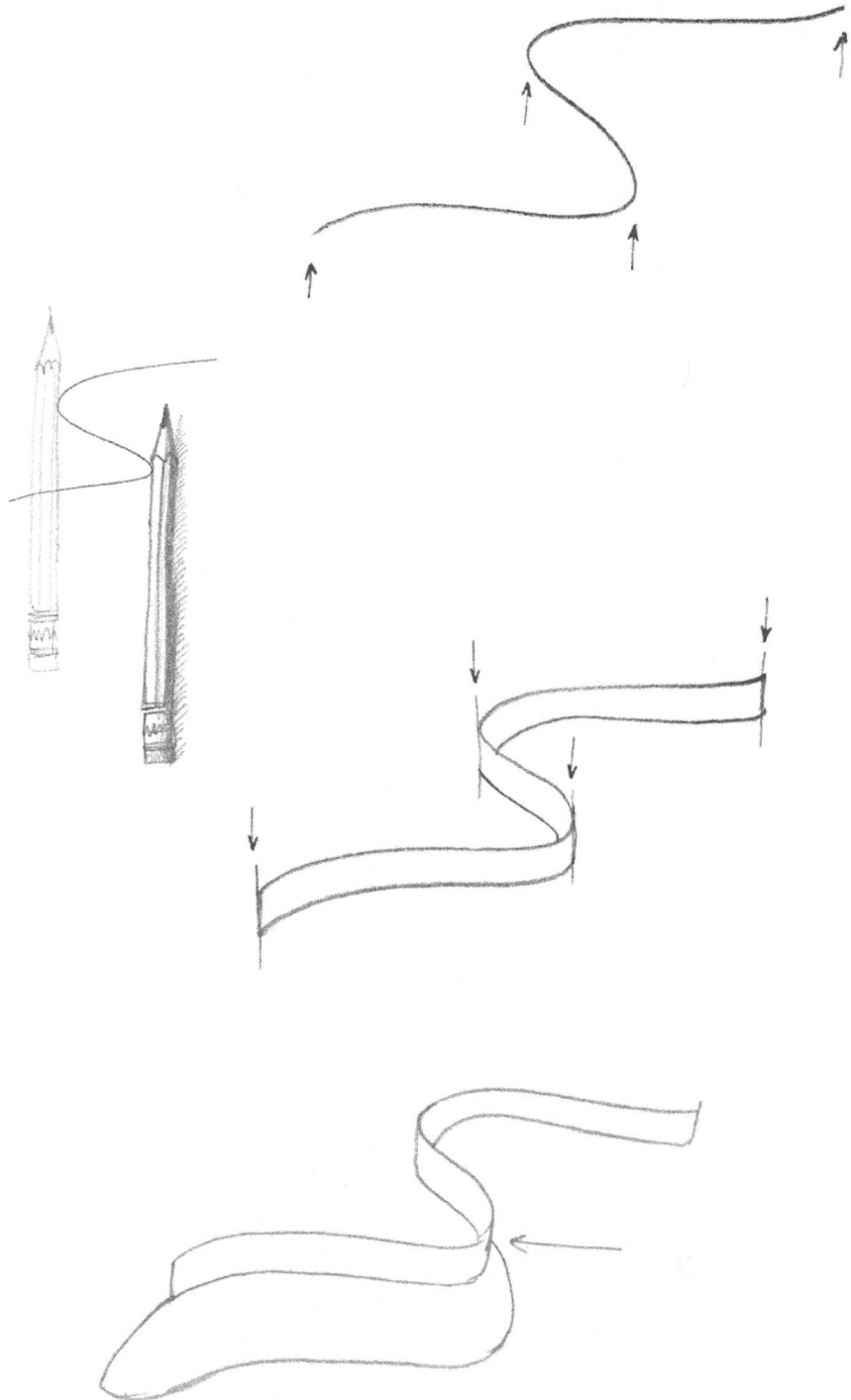

    From the left side of the ribbon, draw a sausage shape, your line ending at the arrow.

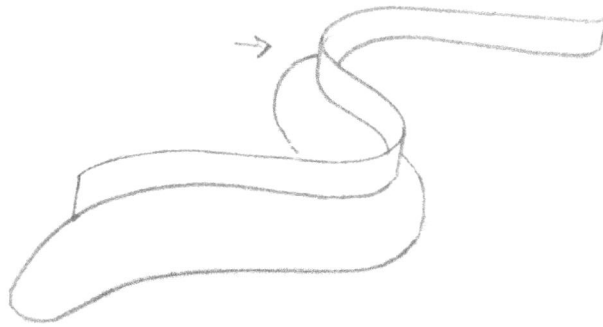

4. Draw a small line to make the second part of the body.

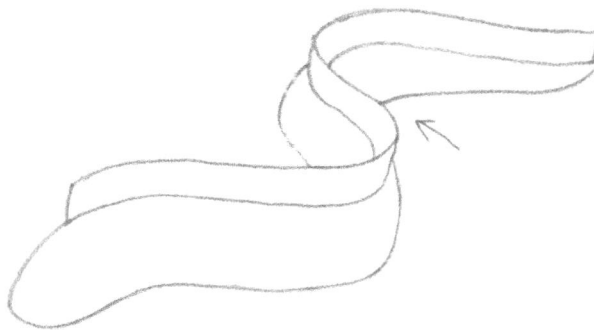

5. Add a third line. Now you've drawn the entire body of the eel. Take a moment to look at your drawing. Does it look like it's swimming toward you?

Cool!

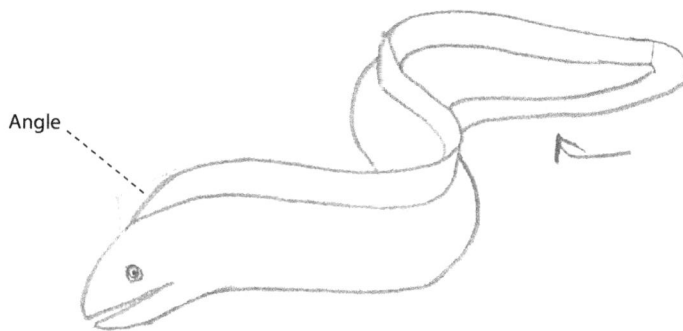

6. Next add the ribbon-like fin along the bottom of the eel. Draw the mouth and eye. Add an angle to the front of the dorsal fin.

Angle

7. Add shading and spots. See Drawing Tips at the end of the book for help with the pattern. Clean up any smudges with your eraser.

Marvelous moray!

Queen Triggerfish

Balistes vetula

Size: 33 cm (13 in). Diet: various invertebrates, primarily sea urchins. 'Trigger' in its name refers to the second dorsal spine, which can be locked against the first dorsal spine. The Triggerfish does this when alarmed, wedging itself in a crevice so that it's almost impossible to get out. When the 'trigger' spine is lowered, the fish swims out again.

Always draw lightly at first!

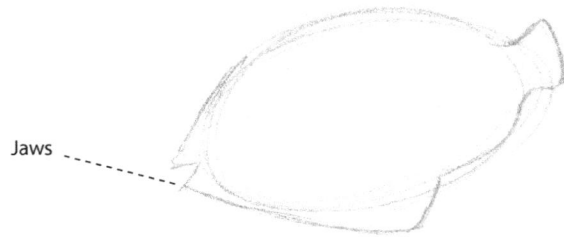

Jaws

1. Draw a tilted oval. Add the jaws and mouth. Extend the bottom jaw to make the body slightly pointed at the bottom. Draw a small shape for the base of the tail.

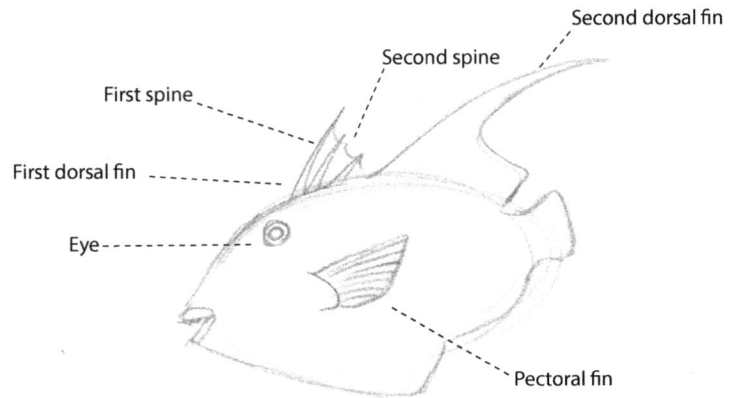

Second dorsal fin

Second spine

First spine

First dorsal fin

Eye

Pectoral fin

2. Draw the eye—notice how far back it is from the mouth. Add the pectoral fin. Draw the first dorsal fin with spines. Behind it, draw the long pointed second dorsal fin.

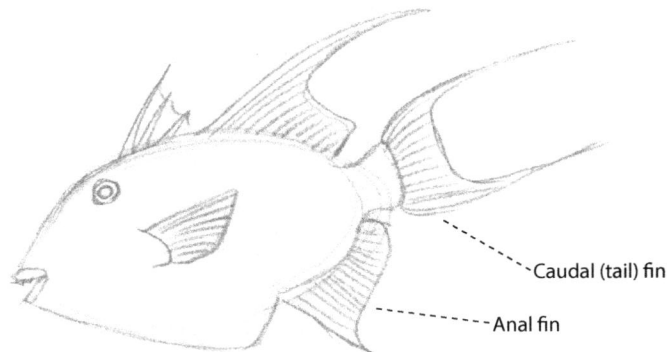

Caudal (tail) fin

Anal fin

3. Draw the tail (caudal) fin and the anal fin. Erase parts of the oval you no longer need.

4. Add stripes, fin patterns, scales and other details. Clean up any smudges with your eraser.

Snail

Oval

Arms

Soft body

Feelers

Acanthaster planci (Crown-of-thorns starfish)

Size: up to 40 cm (16 in) across. Diet: coral. In the mid-1960's, its population started growing, and large areas of coral reefs were destroyed. Did collectors kill too many Triton snails for their shells? Scientists don't know.

Charonia (Triton snail). This snail feeds on the starfish by spearing it with poison, then eating it. Unlike other animals, the snail isn't bothered by the sharp spines of the starfish.

This starfish is making its way slowly across a coral reef, killing coral. But a triton snail has found it, and is killing the starfish.

Snail eating starfish eating coral– chow time!

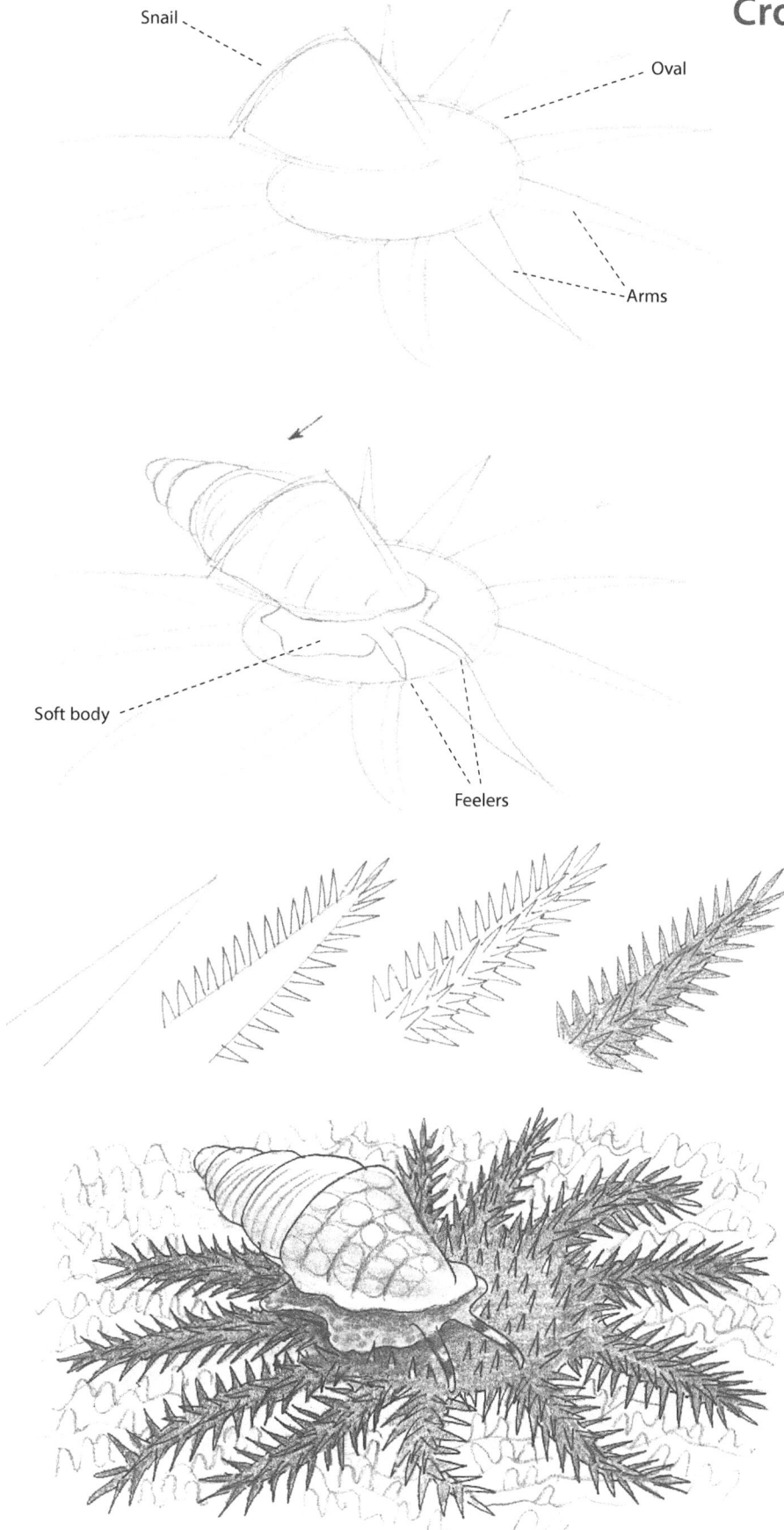

1. Draw the starfish as an oval, with pointed arms. Draw a triangular shape for the main part of the snail.

2. Add the back parts of the snail shell, and the soft body with feelers.

3. Complete the starfish arms by adding thorns on the outside and inside of each arm (I used a fine marker). Shade the arm gray, so the black thorns still show.

4. Draw light squiggly lines for the coral.

   Add shading and details to the snail. Clean up any smudges with your eraser.

Octopus

Class Cephalopoda, genus Octopus

Mollusk with eight tentacles, or arms, with suction cups. Related to squid, cuttlefish, and nautilus, an octopus has no bones. It moves by squirting water out of the siphon, an opening under its head. Has three hearts, can change colors, and shoots clouds of black 'ink' in self defense. Size: varies among 50 varieties, from 8 cm (3 in) to 8.5 m (28 ft). Diet: clams, crabs, lobsters, mussels and other shellfish. Octopuses live along coasts; not just in coral reefs.

Always draw lightly at first!

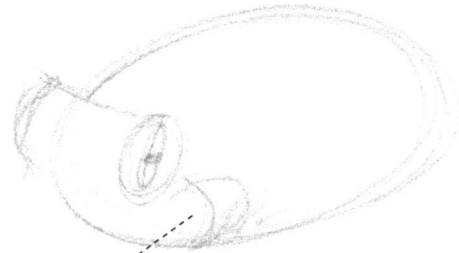

Siphon opening

1. Draw an oval for the body. Draw a cylinder shape for the head, with an eye at the end. Add the siphon opening.

Siphon

2. Draw the siphon. Because the octopus has no bones, the tentacles can go just about any direction. often they're curled. Draw its tentacles curling every which way. Make a fun design!

Tentacles

3. Draw suction cups on the bottom of each tentacle. When you like the design, you can go over your final lines with a fine-tip marker. Erase the pencil lines, add shading, and clean up with an eraser.

Always draw lightly at first!

Gills

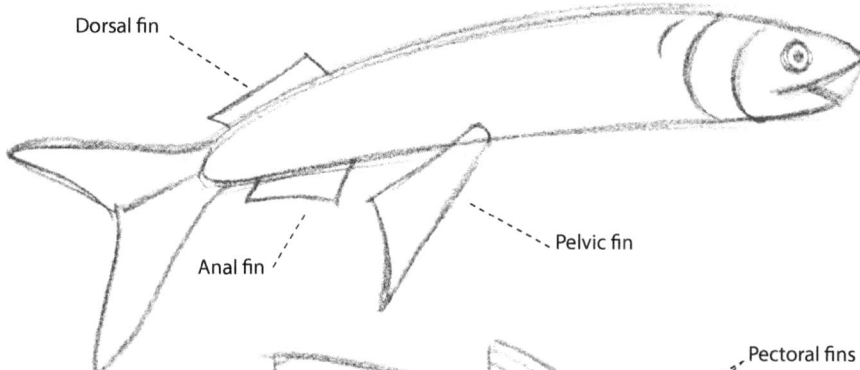

Dorsal fin

Anal fin

Pelvic fin

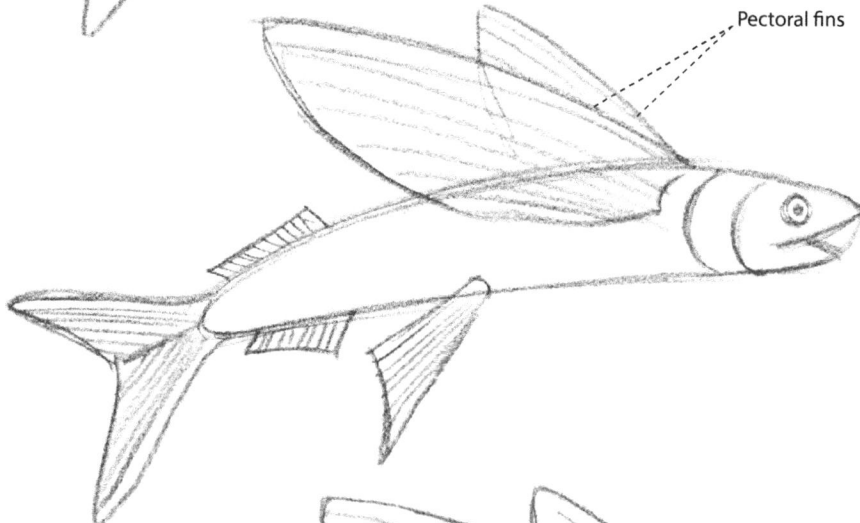

Pectoral fins

Flying Fish

Cypselurus heterurus (Atlantic flying fish)

Size: 30-43 cm (12-17 in). Diet: fish. Building up speed under water, flying fish jump clear of the surface and extend their pectoral fins, which lie against the body when swimming. With lift from these 'wings,' they can glide for 10 seconds or so, covering 90 m (300 ft) at 1.5 m (5 ft) above the surface. Why? Most likely to escape swimming predators.

1. Start with a long, curved, flat oval for the body. Add mouth, eye, and gills.

2. Add the tail fins, with the lower one longer than the upper. Draw the dorsal, pelvic, and anal fins.

3. Draw the pectoral 'wings.' Add lines to the fins.

4. Flying fish are fully scaled. Add shading, and scales (see Drawing Tips at the end of the book for ideas about drawing scales). Sharpen outlines and details. Clean up with your eraser.

Fantastic flying fish!

Tripod Fish

Bathypterois bigelowi

Lives at depths of 3000 m (9,800 ft). Stands on the bottom, on extended pelvic fins and its tail, waiting for prey.

Always draw lightly at first!

1. Start with a long, sausage-like body. Draw two 'legs' and the tail fin.

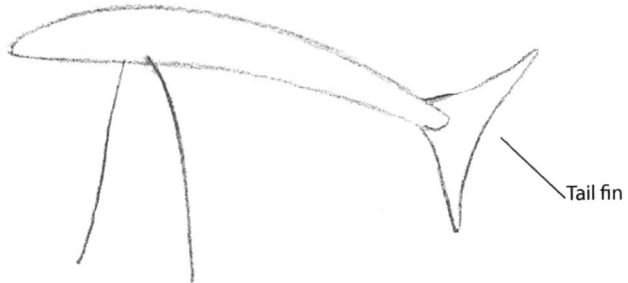

Tail fin

2. Turn the 'legs' into pelvic fins (no, fish don't have legs). Add the anal fin.

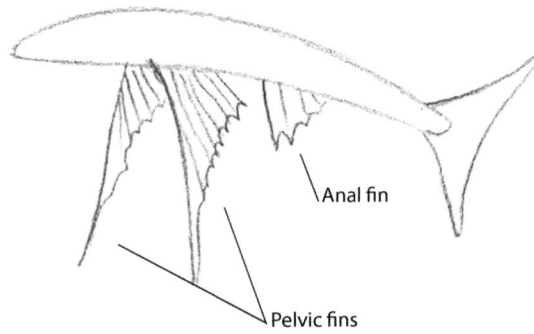

Anal fin

Pelvic fins

3. Draw long, curving pectoral fins above the body. Add mouth and eye.

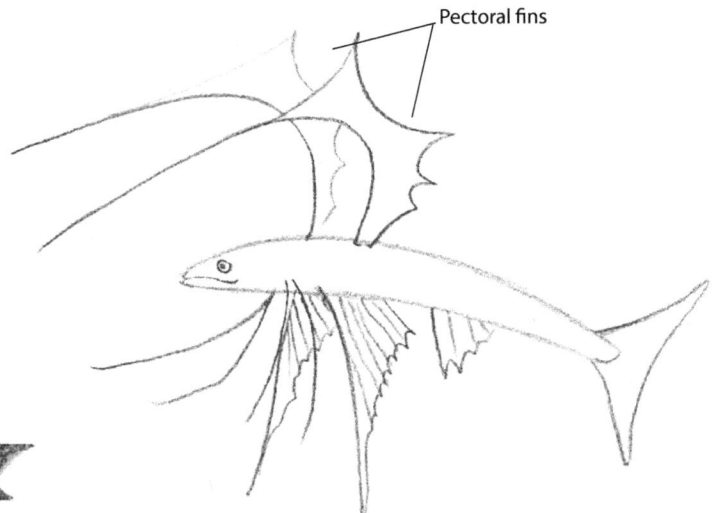

Pectoral fins

4. Add shading. Sharpen outlines and details. Clean up any smudges with your eraser.

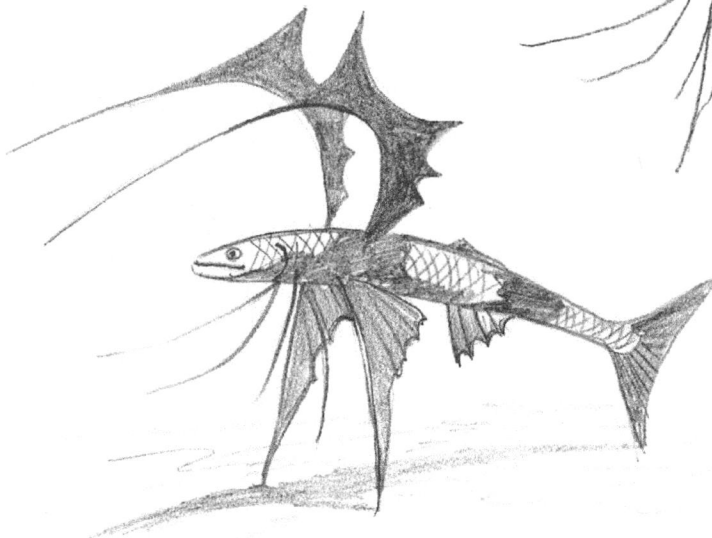

Angler 1

Linophryne arborifera

Size: 7 cm (3 in). This small (tiny compared to Angler 1) fish lives in the deep sea. The 'fishing rod' on its snout has a luminous lure. The chin barbel looks like a piece of seaweed. In the deep sea, where no sunlight penetrates, many animals have lights, to identify species and lure prey.

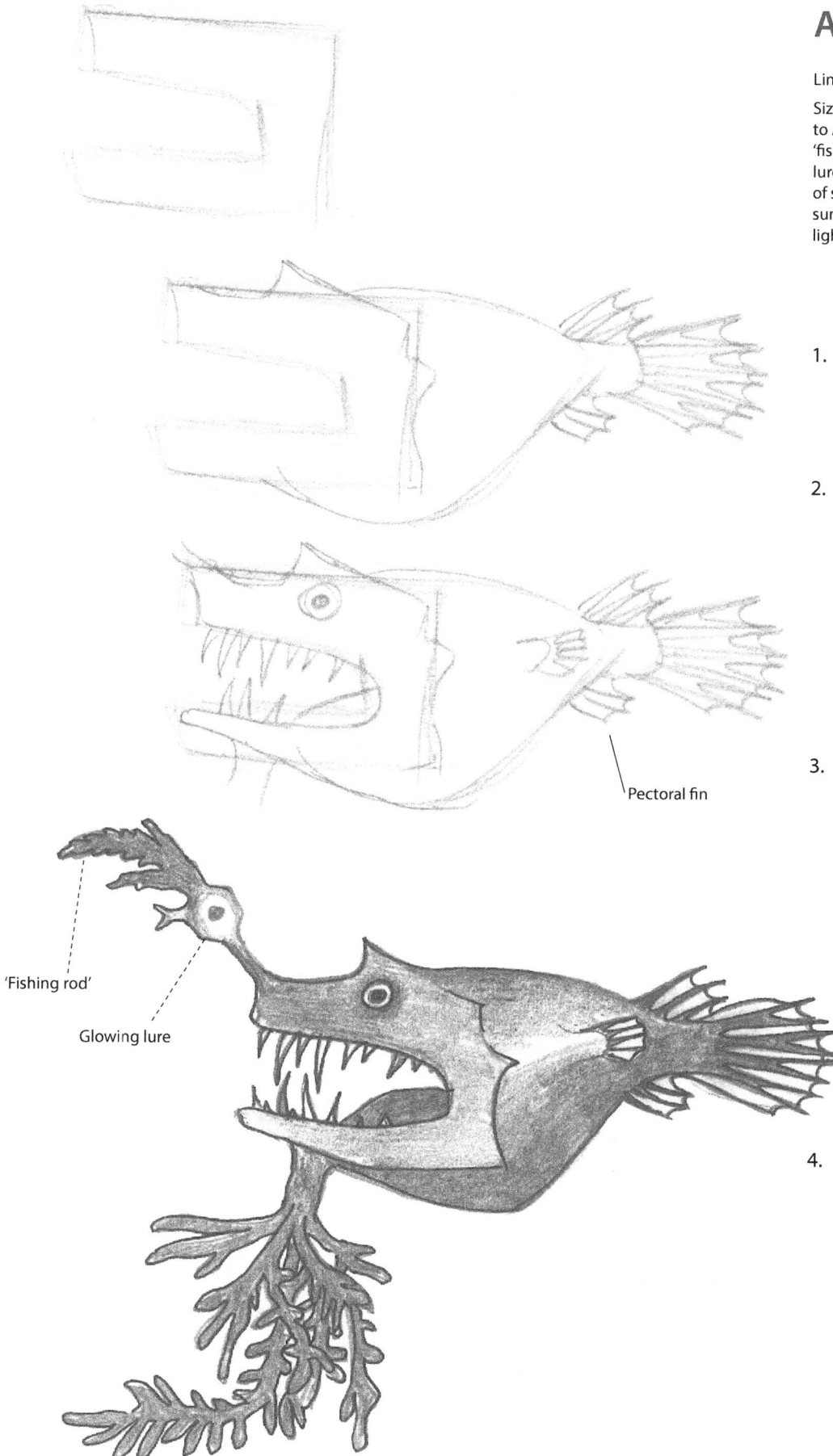

1. Start with a sideways U shape.

2. Extend the body back almost like a triangle. Add the tail, with its forked spines, plus the top and bottom fins. Draw the peak above the mouth.

Pectoral fin

3. Round out the mouth and add teeth (you may want to do some careful erasing first). Narrow the lower jaw as you make it rounder. Add the pectoral fin.

'Fishing rod'

Glowing lure

4. Add the distinctive chin barbel that looks like seaweed, and the 'fishing rod' on top with its glowing decoration. Add shading. Sharpen outlines and details. Clean up any smudges with your eraser.

Angler 2

Lophius piscatorius

Size: 1-2 m (3-6 ft). Diet: fish. Unusual flat coastal fish lies on the bottom, waiting for prey. The fringes at the edge of the body help conceal its outline. When it opens its huge mouth, its prey is sucked in with a large quantity of water. The water gets back out. The unfortunate prey stays in.

Always draw lightly at first!

Tail

1. Draw a flat oval, with an arc across the top of it for the center line of the fish's body. Draw the rough outline of the tail–lightly!

'Fishing rod'

Dorsal spines

Pectoral fin

2. Along the centerline (leave room for the mouth!) draw the 'fishing rod' and other dorsal spines. Add the pectoral fins and tail details.

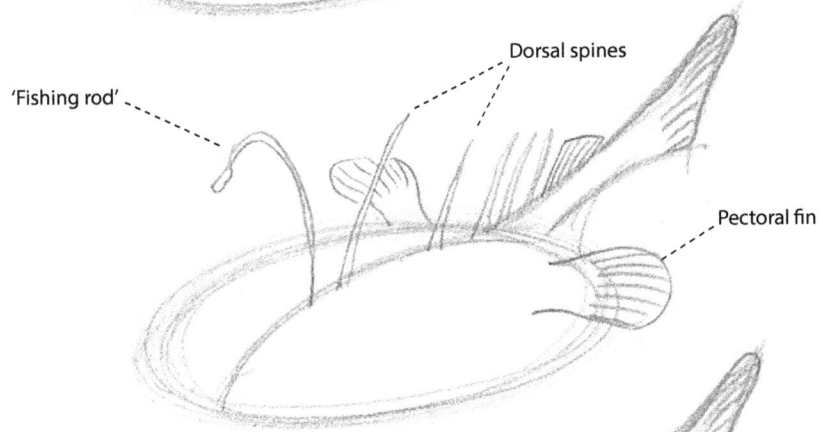

3. Draw the mouth with teeth. Add eyes. Draw lightly at first! Now comes the part requiring patience–slowly draw the frills around the outside edge. Do a little bit at a time, erasing part of the oval as you draw.

4. Add shading. Sharpen outlines and details. Clean up any smudges with your eraser.

Gulper Eel

Eurypharynx pelecanoides

Size: 61 cm (24 in). Diet: fish, crustaceans. Another deep sea fish. Lives at 1,400 m (4,500 ft) and below. Can feed on quite large fish even though it's not much of a swimmer. Thought to swim slowly with its mouth open catching whatever it can.

1. Start with a curvy ribbon (see moray eel on pages 38-39 if you're not sure how to do this). Extend the bottom line and add the eye.

2. Next draw the mouth, a sideways V. Curve the lower jaw up behind the mouth. Continue that line below the curve of the tail.

3. Add the inside section of the mouth. Drawing the remaining sections of the tail and fin can be confusing. I've tinted the part that is already drawn. The areas that aren't tinted are the parts you need to add now. Draw them.

4. Add lines on the fins, and shading. Sharpen outlines and details. Clean up any smudges with your eraser.

Atlantic Football Fish

Himantolophus groenlandicus

Size: 61 cm (24 in). Diet: fish attracted by the light in its forehead 'fishing rod.' This deep sea angler lives 100-300 m (330-980 ft) below the surface.

1. Start with an almost circular oval. Lightly divide it into four parts to help you place mouth and fins.

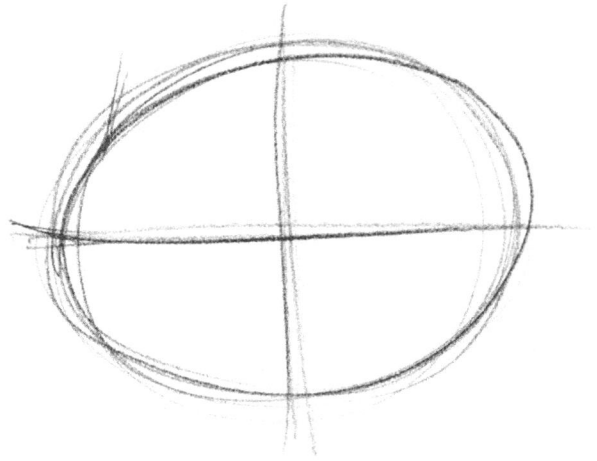

2. Draw the mouth. Notice that the front of the bottom jaw lines up with the centerline. Add teeth. Draw the eye and 'fishing rod.'

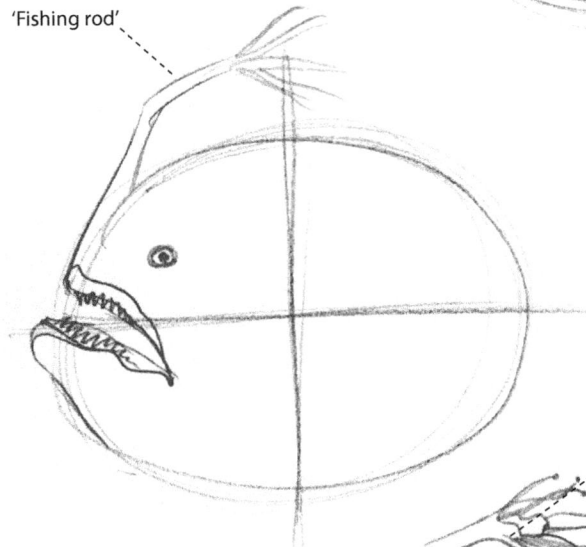

3. Draw the remaining fins.

4. Draw the forked spines in all the fins, and bony plates on the side of the fish. Add shading. Sharpen outlines and details. Clean up any smudges with your eraser.

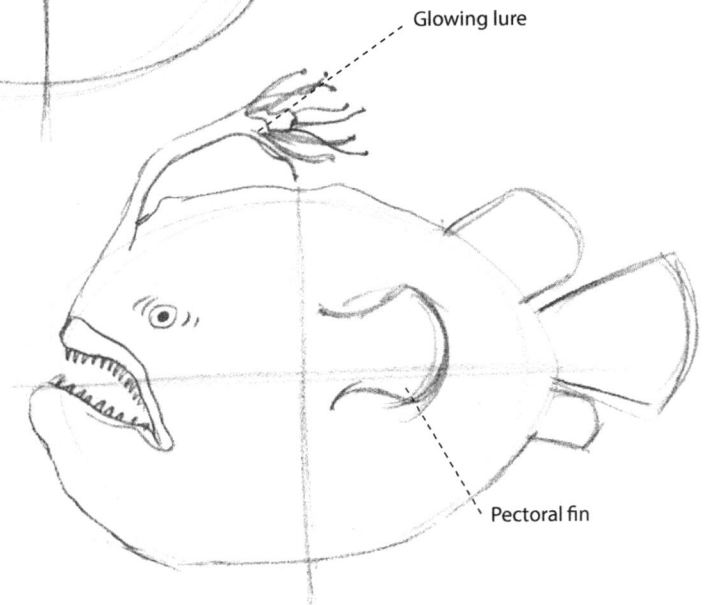

Congratulations! You have drawn one magnificently ugly fish.

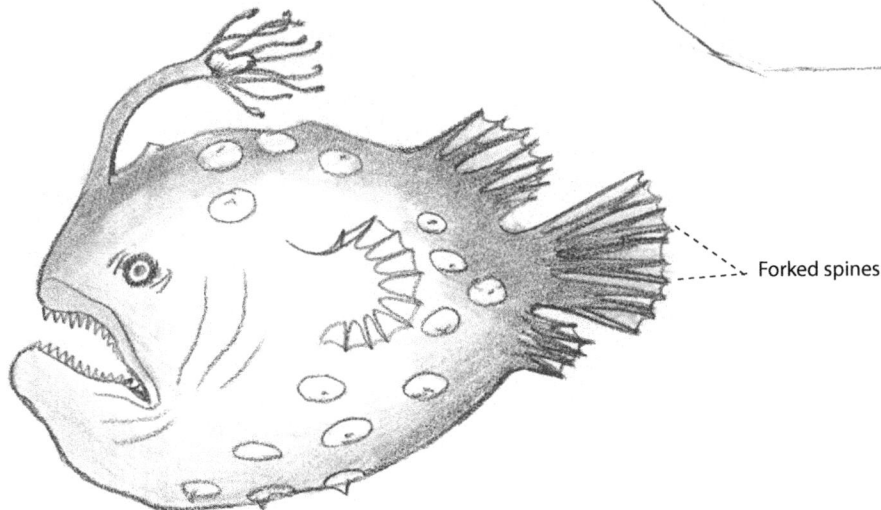

'Fishing rod'

Glowing lure

Pectoral fin

Forked spines

For help with details, see drawing tips on pages 54-57.

Cuttlefish

Sepia officinalis (common cuttlefish)

A mollusk related to octopus and squid. Can change color at will. Grab their prey with suction cups at the end of two long tentacles. They draw it into their beak, then inject it with poison.

Tentacles

1. Start with an oval, surrounded by the 'wings' the cuttlefish uses to swim.

2. Draw one eye looking straight toward you. Draw the other eye, noticing that you only see the side of it. To help you draw the shorter tentacles the same length, you can draw a light arc.

3. Add eight short tentacles and two longer ones.

4. Add patterns and shading. Sharpen outlines and details. Clean up any smudges with your eraser.

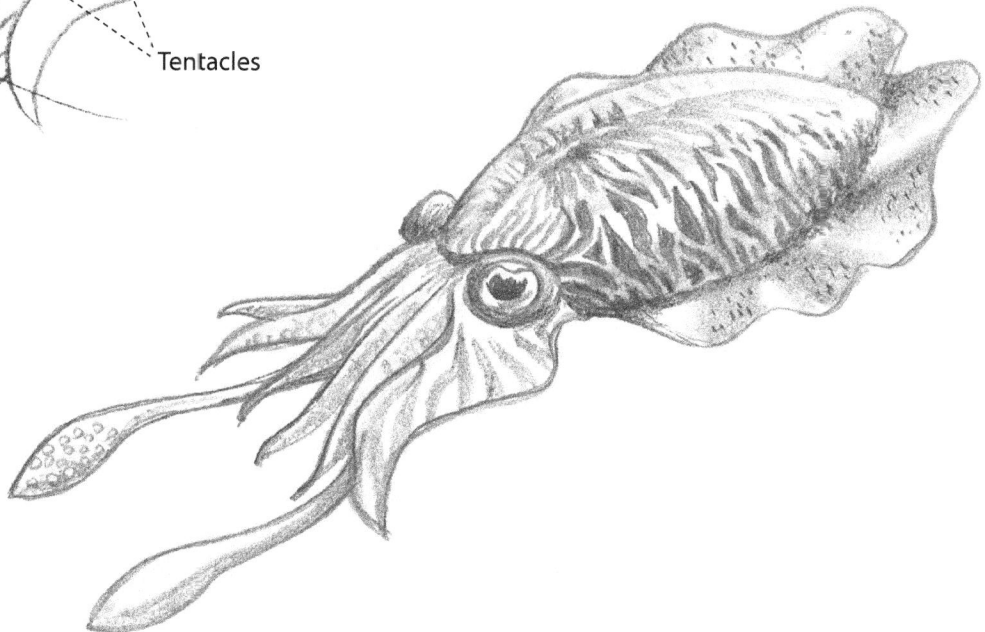

Squid

Loliginidae family

A mollusk related to octopus, cuttlefish, and nautilus. Size: Many varieties, ranging from less than 30 cm (1 ft) to 12 m (40 ft). Diet: fish, caught with suction cups on its ten arms. Two arms are longer, and used for drawing caught prey to the mouth. Squid move by jet propulsion, filling their body with water then shooting it out. They create clouds of 'ink' to confuse predators and escape.

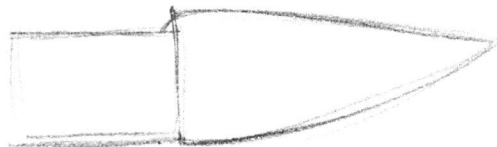

1. Start with a rectangle and a slightly larger triangle.

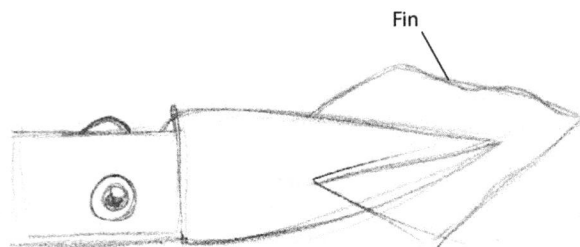

Fin

2. Draw the eye looking toward you, and the little bit you can see of the other eye. Add the fins.

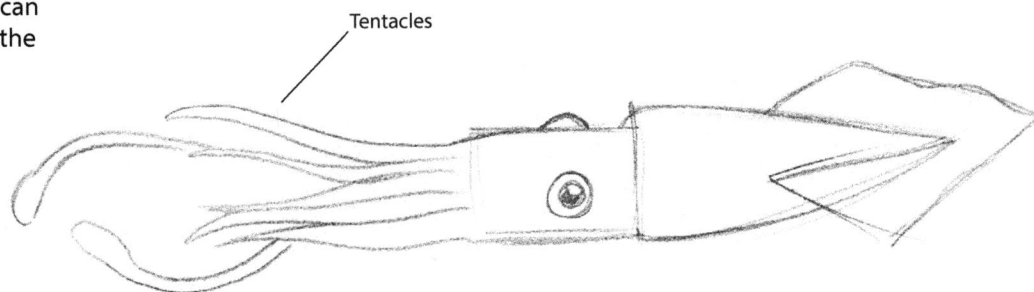

Tentacles

3. Add the tentacles. Two of them are longer, with little 'paddles' on the end.

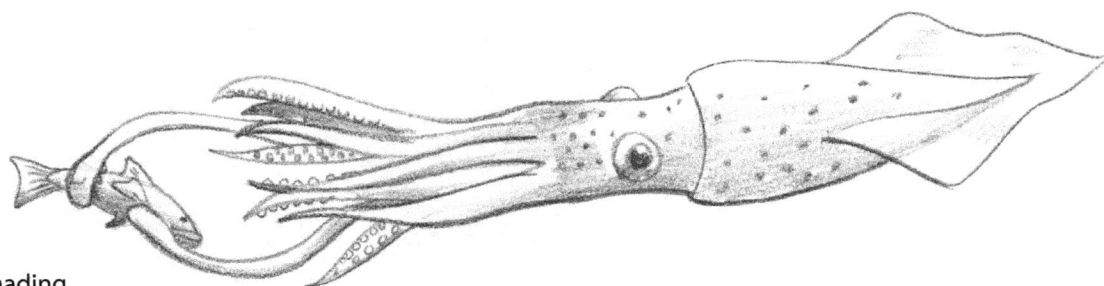

4. Add pattern and shading. Sharpen outlines and details. Clean up any smudges with your eraser.

A squid has ten tentacles, or arms (count them!)

Swordfish

Xiphias gladius

Size: 2-5 m (6.5-16 ft). Diet: small fish, squid. Function of the 'sword' isn't clear; it may be for striking at schooling fish or just to help the swordfish swim faster. This is a very fast fish!

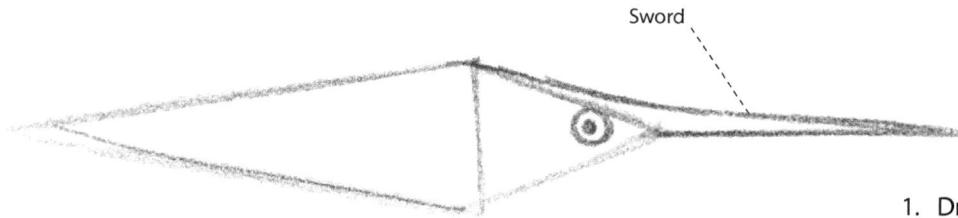

Sword

1. Draw two triangles for the body. The sword is part of the upper jaw, so draw it attached to the top of the small triangle. Add the eye.

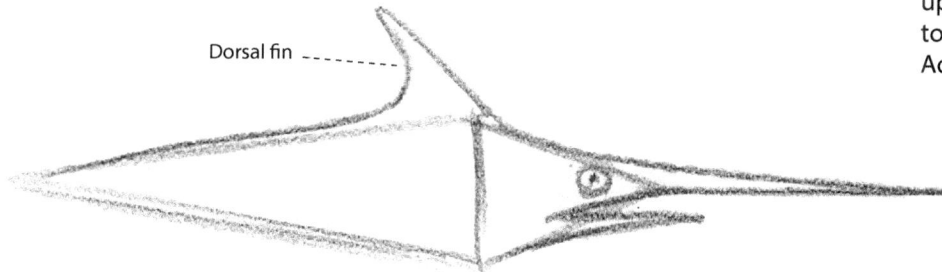

Dorsal fin

2. Next draw the dorsal fin and lower jaw.

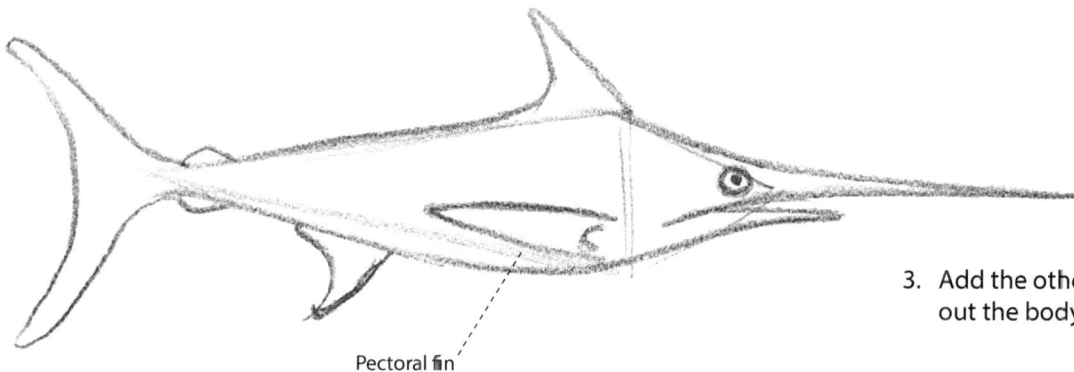

Pectoral fin

3. Add the other fins and round out the body shape.

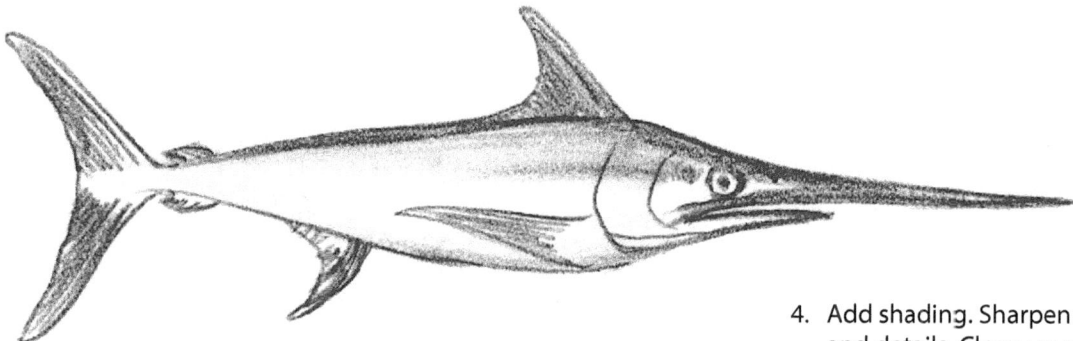

4. Add shading. Sharpen outlines and details. Clean up any smudges with your eraser.

For help with details, see drawing tips on pages 54-57.

Porcupinefish

Diodon hystrix

Size: 90 cm (35 in). Diet: crabs, mollusks, sea urchins. This fish has a most unusual defense—when threatened, it puffs itself up into an almost round ball, with spines sticking out all over!

1. Draw a flat oval. Add the mouth, which sticks out. Draw the eye. Add the two parts for the tail.

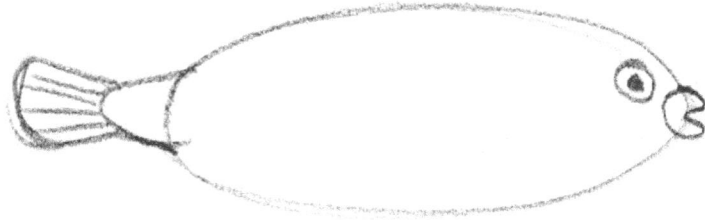

2. Add fins, with lines in them.

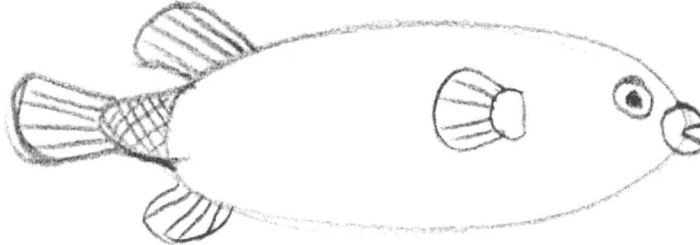

3. Draw spikes. They all point backwards when the porcupinefish is deflated.

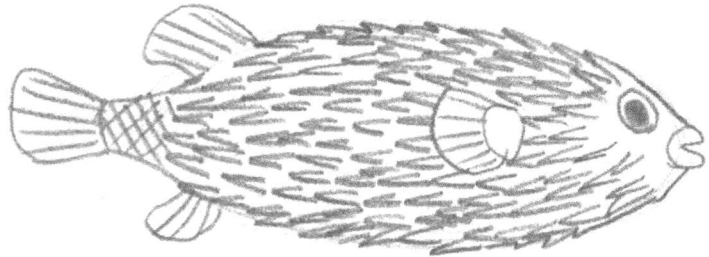

4. If you want to draw the fish expanded, do the same drawing, only this time starting with a circle.

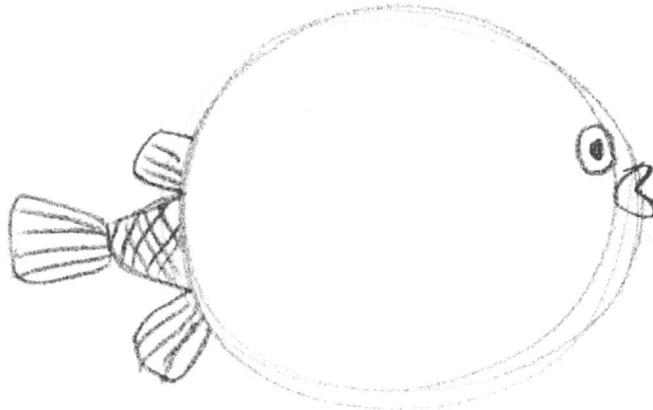

5. When expanded, the spines stick out from the center. I've drawn a few. You'll want to keep going until you've drawn them all.

California Halibut

Paralichthys californicus

Size: 1.5 m (5 ft). Diet: fish, particularly anchovies. Is in turn eaten by rays, sea lions, porpoises and people. Like the 500 or so other species of flatfishes, young halibut swim like normal fish, with an eye on either side of their head As they develop, one eye moves to the other side of the head. From then on, the fish swims on its side, with its eyes facing up. Flatfishes are bottom feeders.

Mouth

Tail

Dorsal fin

Lateral line

Pectoral fin

Gill openings

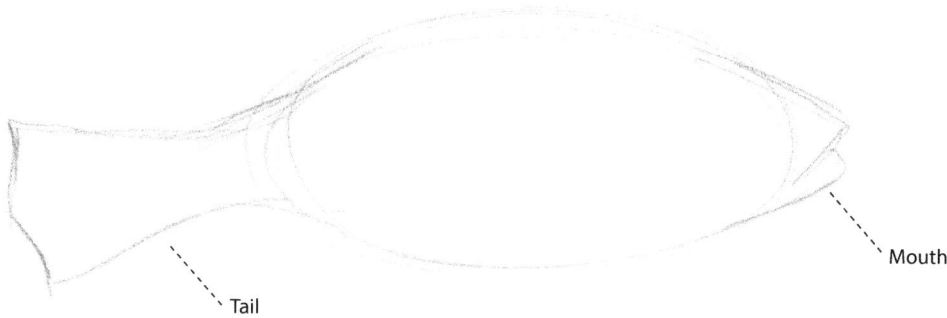

1. Draw an oval, with one end pointed. Draw the mouth. Add the tail.

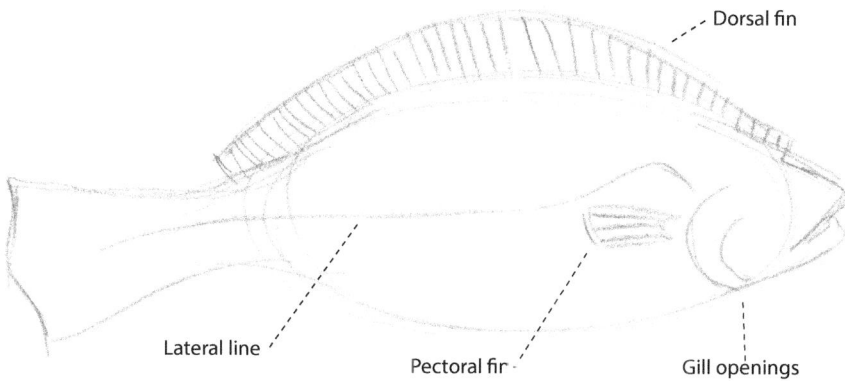

2. Draw the dorsal fin with spines. Draw the lateral line, pectoral fin, and gill openings.

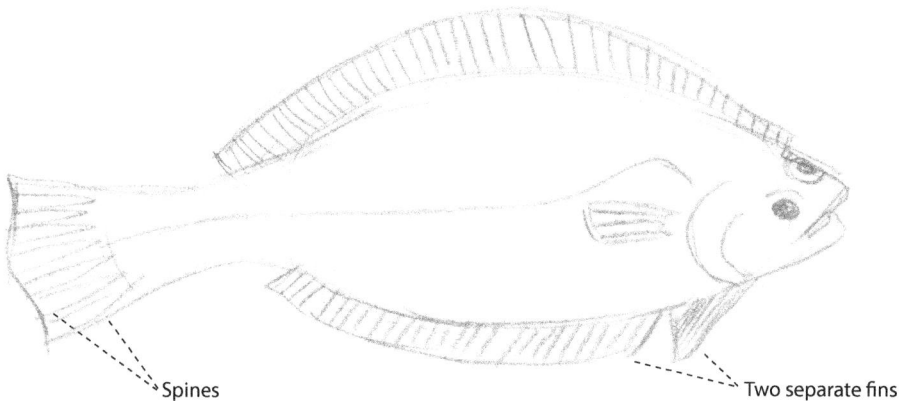

Spines

Two separate fins

3. Add the two separate fins on the bottom. Draw the eyes and spines in tail. Lightly erase lines you don't need.

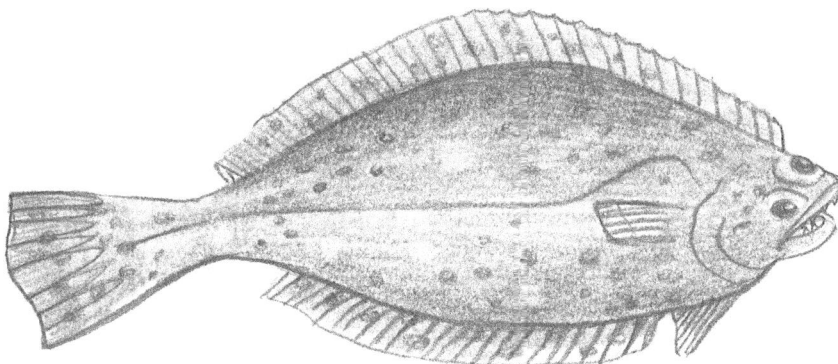

4. Add shading and spots. Sharpen outlines and details. Clean up any smudges with your eraser.

Green Turtle

Chelonia mydas

Size: 1-1.5 m (3-4 ft). Diet: sea grasses and seaweed, some jellyfish and crustaceans. *Endangered.*

Always draw lightly at first!

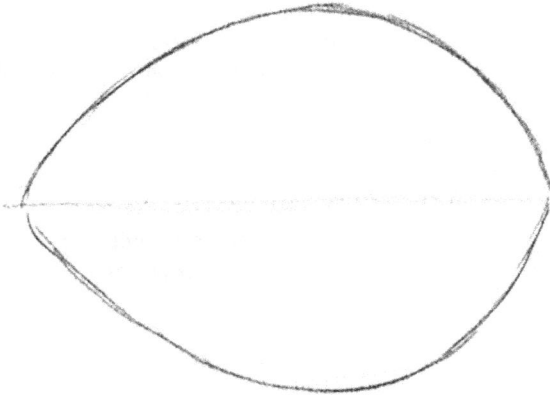

1. Draw the outside of the shell, with center line.

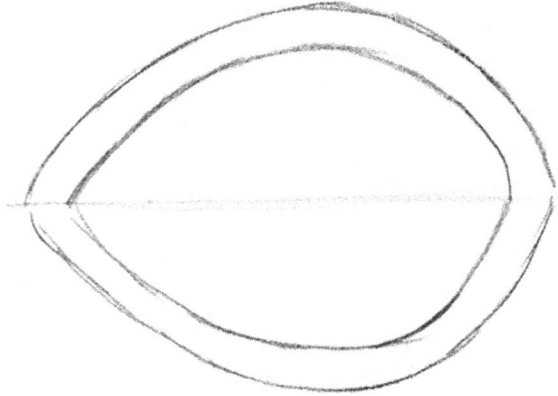

2. Draw the same shape inside the shell.

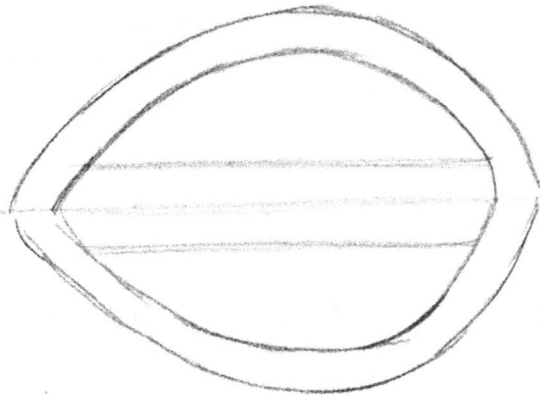

3. Draw a line either side of the center line.

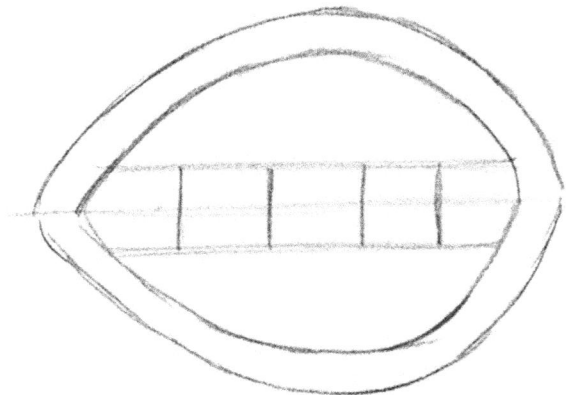

4. Divide the center into five spaces.

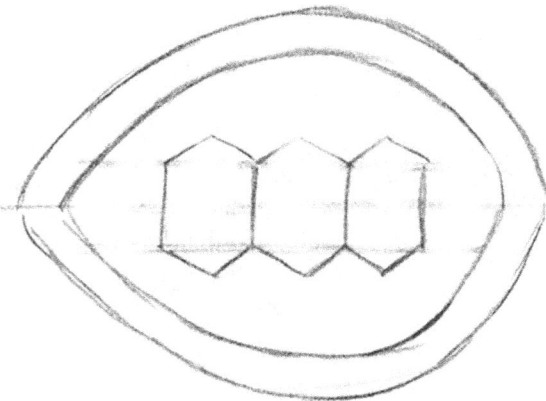

5. Turn the middle three spaces into hexagons.

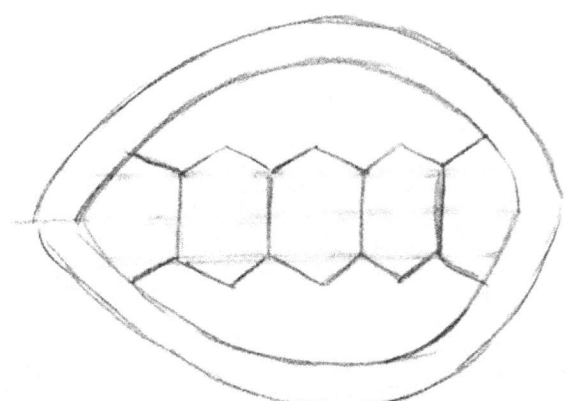

6. Draw lines for the front and back segments.

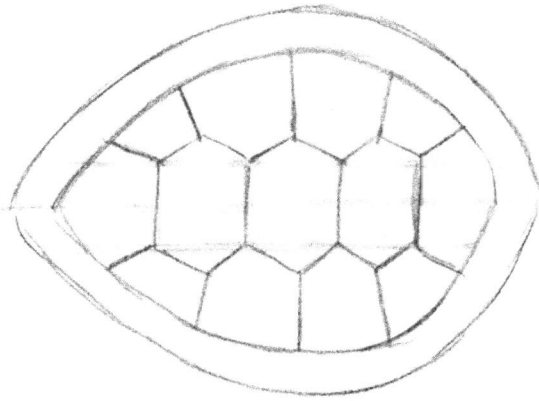

7. Draw radiating lines from the hexagon points.

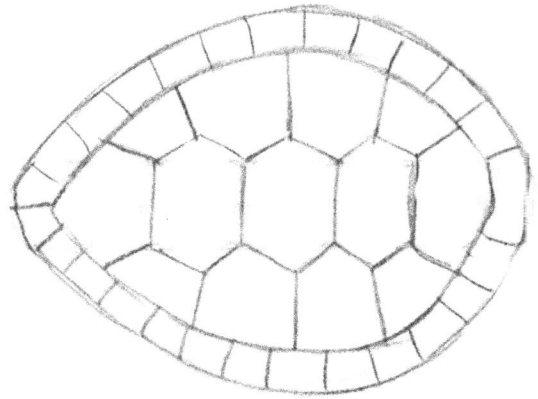

8. Make lots of little segments on the outside rim. Now the hard part is done!

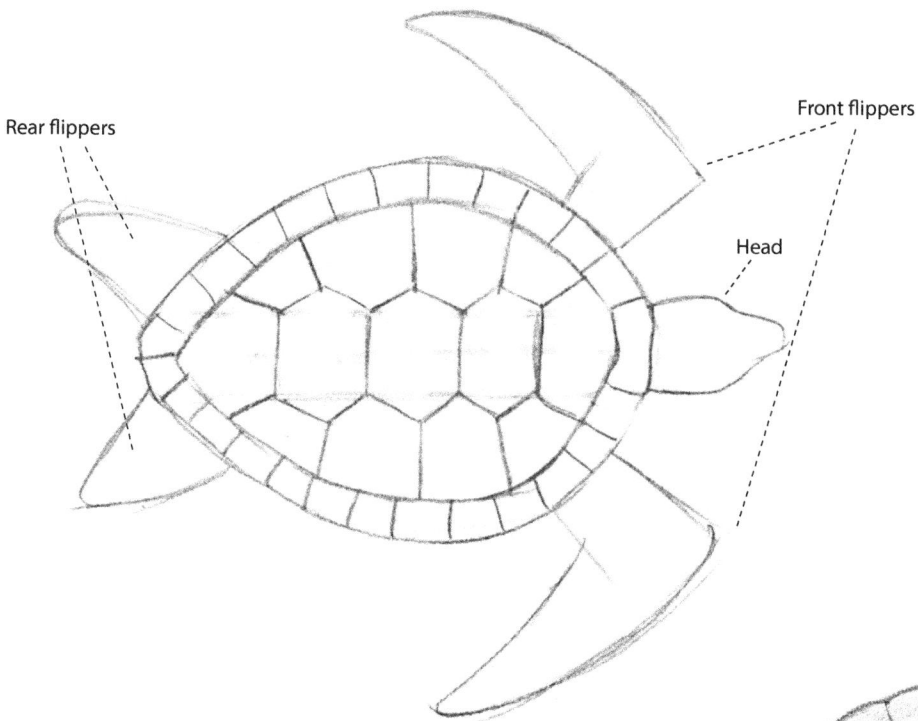

Rear flippers

Front flippers

Head

9. Add flippers and head. The front flippers have two parts. Notice which direction each part goes.

10. Draw the tail. Add shading and patterns of scales on the flippers and head. Sharpen outlines and details. Clean up any smudges with your eraser.

Tail

For help with details, see drawing tips on pages 54-57.

Drawing Tips

Scales and fins

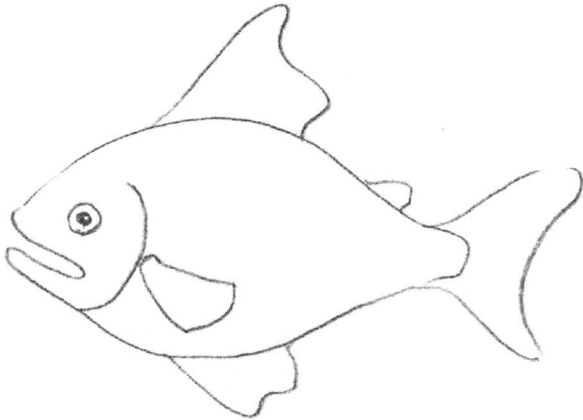

Start with your basic outline.

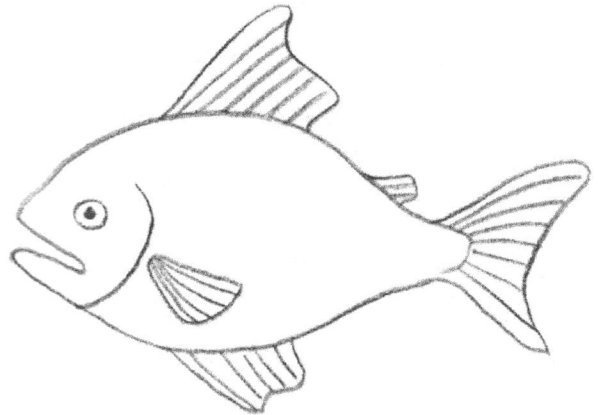

Add lines in the fins.

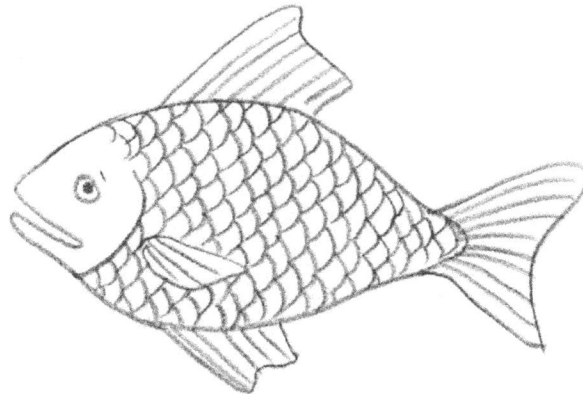

Make a very light 'checkerboard' with diagonal lines.
Then darken and round the edges of the diamond
shapes to make scales.

Always draw lightly at first!

Contour scales

It's not easy drawing scales evenly, but with a little practice, this technique might work well for you.

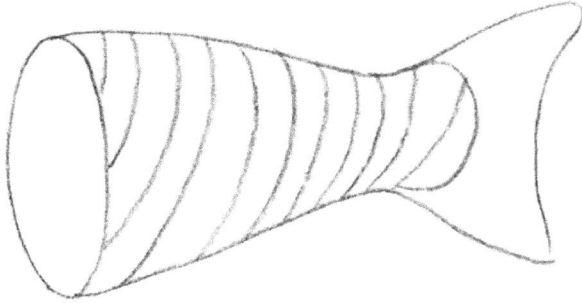

Angled contour lines

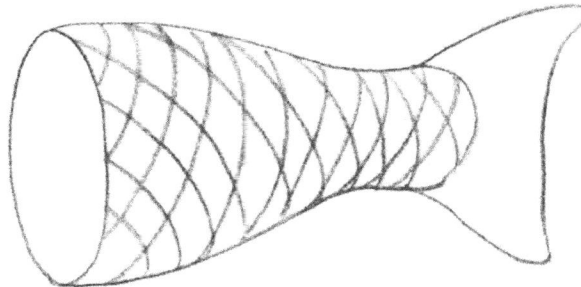

1. Draw angled contour lines around the fish (not vertical contour lines).

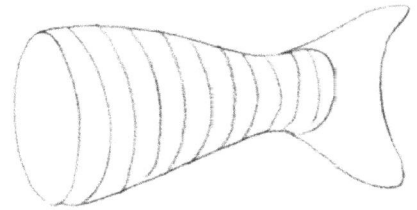

(Vertical contour lines–*not* what you want.)

2. Draw angled contour lines in the other direction, as evenly spaced as possible.

Angled contour lines going the other way

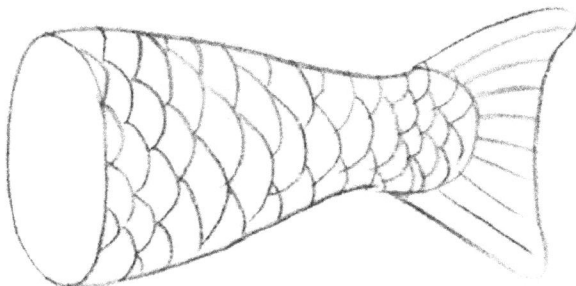

3. Carefully turn each small diamond shape into a scale shape. This will take some practice, but the results can be very impressive!

Scales!

Contours

1. Here's the outline of the moray eel from page 39. Because of the way it's drawn, the eel appears to be swimming toward you.

   Now let's shade it.

2. Just 'coloring' it with a pencil works, but you can do better. Here I've shaded the lazy way, using just back-and-forth lines.

3. A more effective approach: imagine the contours of the form–how the sides curve–and try to draw your shading lines so they follow the contours.

4. One step better is to think about light as you follow the contours. Make the top of the form a little lighter than the bottom. Can you see the difference, with the light and dark areas?

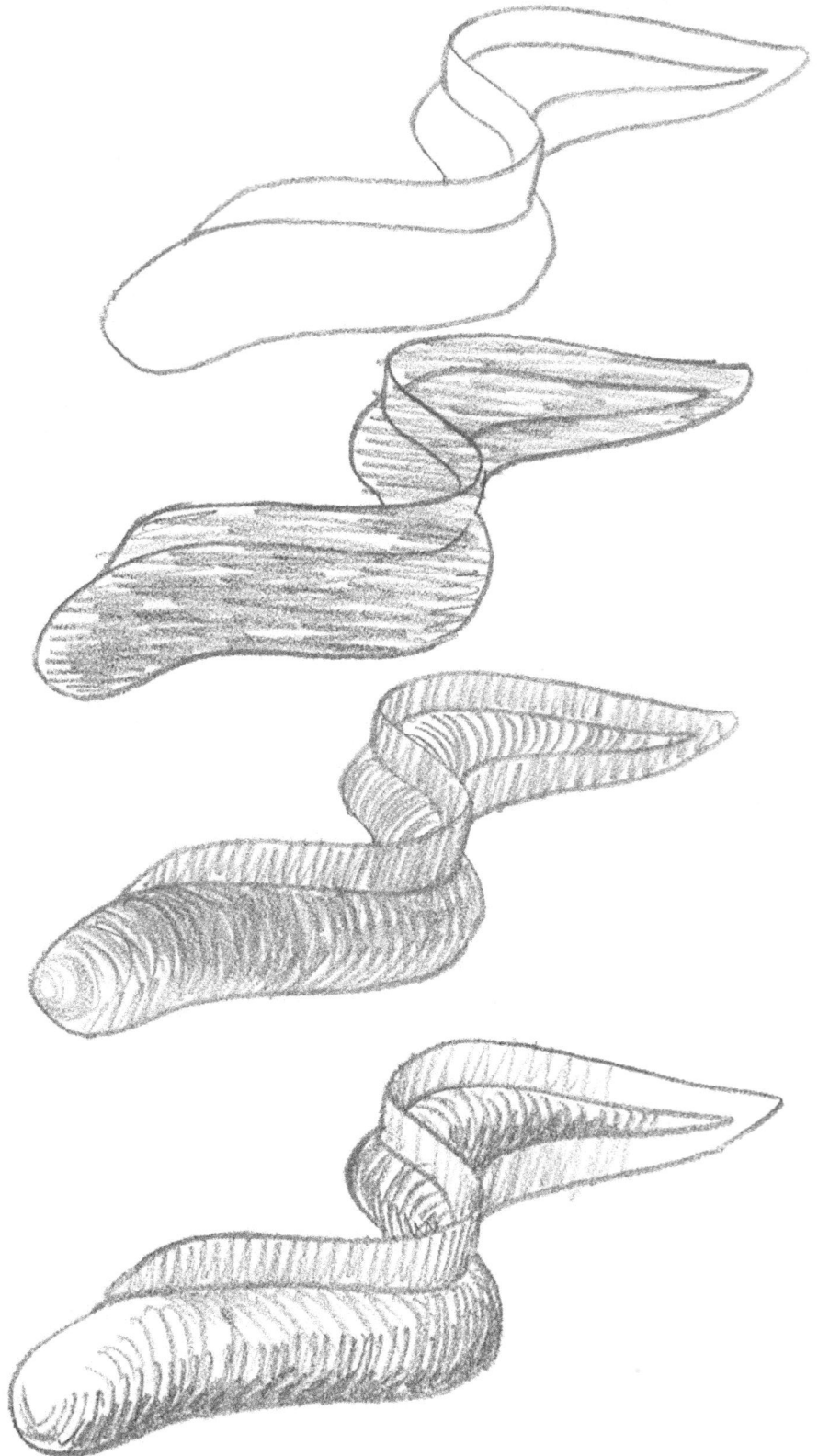

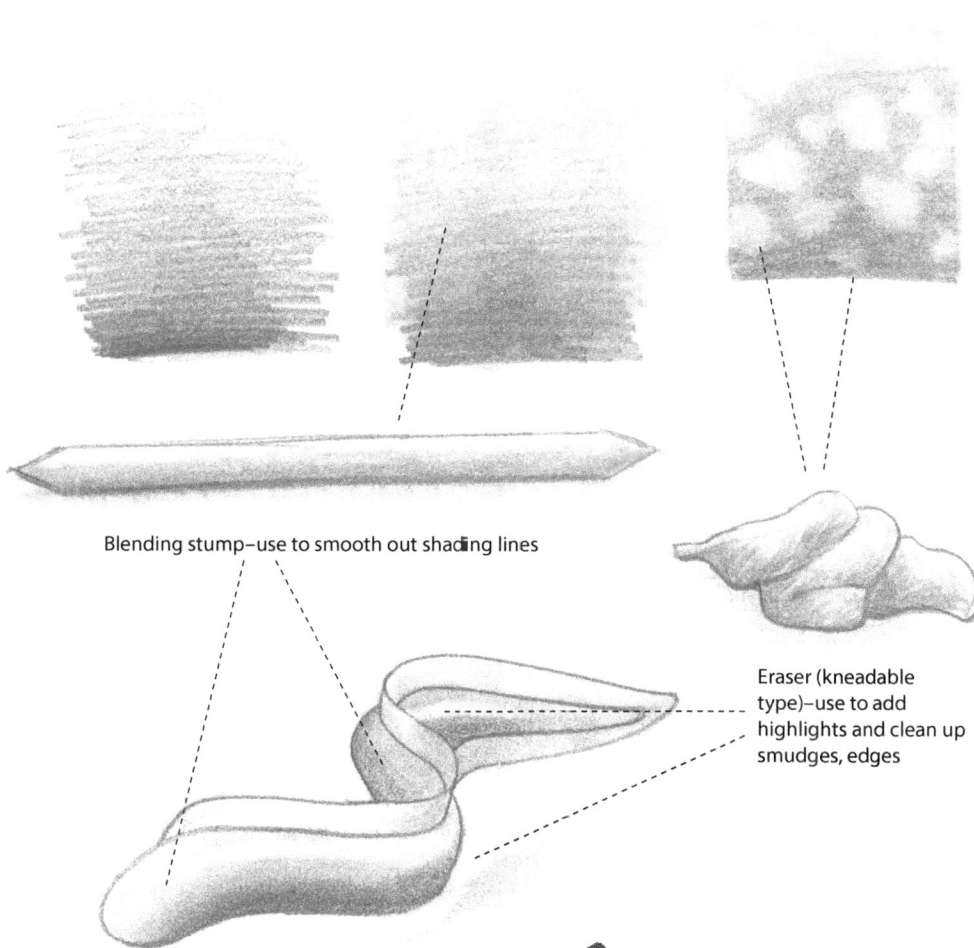

Shading

Sometimes the effect you want is a very smooth surface, with no contour lines showing on it. When that's the case, try using a blending stump.

First, carefully shade, trying not to make any obvious lines.

Next, blend the pencil marks with a blending stump (or a piece of paper or paper towel, or even your finger—that's kind of messy, though…).

Finally, use your eraser to add highlights and clean up any smudges. This technique may take some practice, but it's worth it!

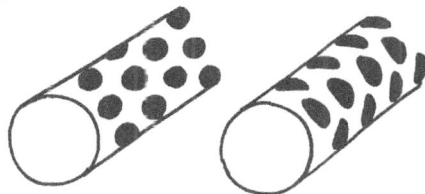

Blending stump—use to smooth out shading lines

Eraser (kneadable type)—use to add highlights and clean up smudges, edges

Contour patterns

Look at these two cylinders with spots on them. Which looks rounder? Why?

Notice that I've carefully drawn the pattern so that it appears to wrap around the right cylinder. When you add patterns to your drawings of ocean animals, look for ways to make the patterns 'bend' around the animal to show its form.

It takes practice, but it can make a big difference in your drawing!

DRAW
RAINFOREST
ANIMALS

Three steps to a great drawing

1) Look carefully at *reference material*. This could be an actual animal, or an image from a book or online. See the shapes and pieces and how they fit together. Next, lightly sketch the shapes in the right place.

   When you sketch lightly, you can easily correct any mistakes before they ruin your drawing.

2) Make sure you have all the shapes and pieces in the right place. Adjust lines, redraw pieces that don't look right, and erase sketch lines you no longer need.

3) Finally, spend as much time as you need to make your drawing jump off the page. Darken lines at emphasis points: joints, feet, points of claws, horns, spikes, and eyes, for example. Add fur, feathers, or scales, and shading. Clean up any smudges with your eraser, then date and save your drawing in a portfolio (see below).

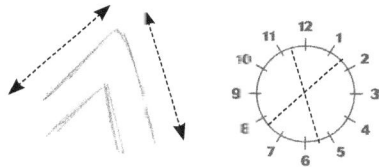

Clock faces appear from time to time. Use them as a reference to see the tilt of ovals, legs, and other angles in the drawing.

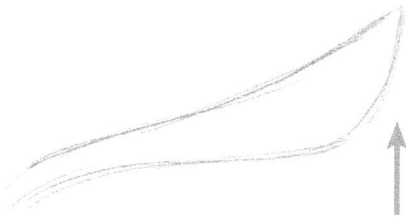

Arrows point out visual elements of the drawing—in this example, a curve that turns almost vertical.

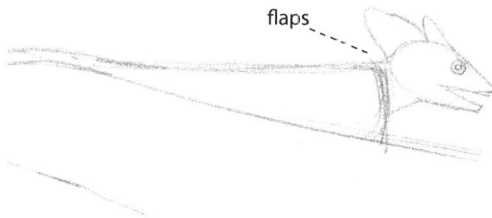

Labels will help you identify the parts of the animal mentioned in the instructions.

flaps

! Turn your paper as you draw to avoid smudging it with your hand.

For colorful inspiration and ideas, follow our Rainforest Animals Pinterest feed:

drawbooks.com/rainforest

Basilisk Lizard

Basiliscus plumifrons: South America.

Size: 80 cm (31 inches). Feeds on fruit and small animals during the day. Few four-legged animals can run on two legs the way this lizard does. It can even run a short distance across water!

1. Start with two slanting lines for the branch. Lightly draw a long triangle for the lizard's body. Add the long, curving tail.

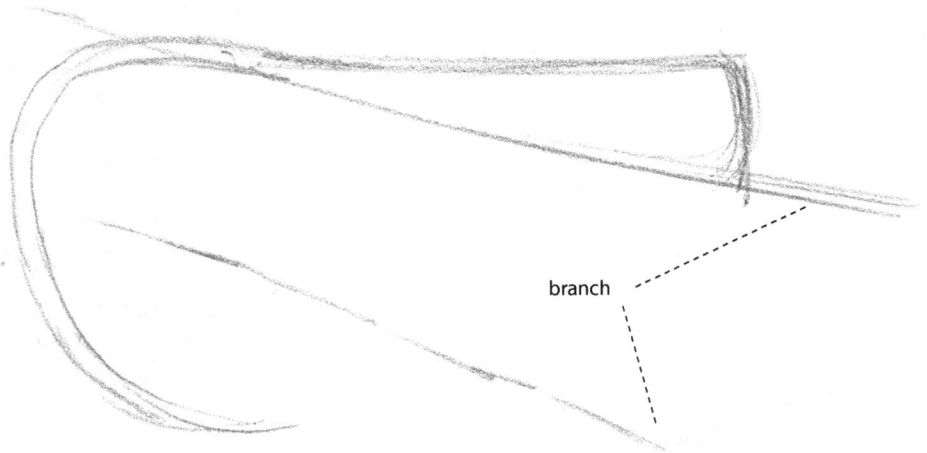

branch

upper jaw

flaps

2. Still drawing very lightly, make an oval for the head. Add the upper and lower jaws at one end. Draw the neck and flaps on top of the head. Carefully place the eye, above the back of the mouth.

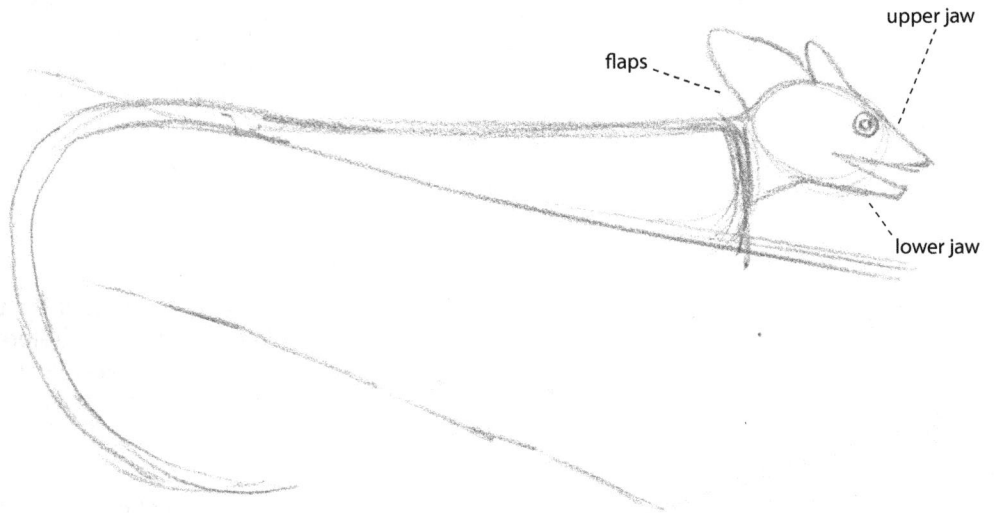

lower jaw

3. Look closely at the legs grabbing the branch. Draw the legs, one piece at a time.

   Draw lightly at first!

Sit back, take a deep breath, and really look at your drawing. Do all the proportions look correct? Is there anything you need to improve before continuing?

fins

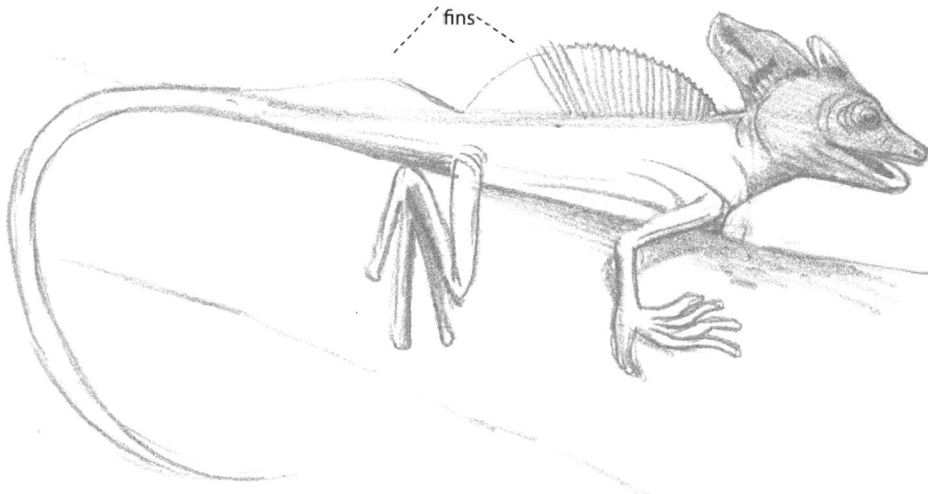

4. Lightly outline the fins on the back. Sharpen your pencil to put the fine lines inside them, and give them jagged edges. Add wrinkles on the face and body. As your pencil gets dull, start to add shading.

5. Shade slowly and carefully, using the side of your pencil if you find it helpful. Add stripes to the tail, and a cast shadow underneath. Use rough pencil marks to show texture.

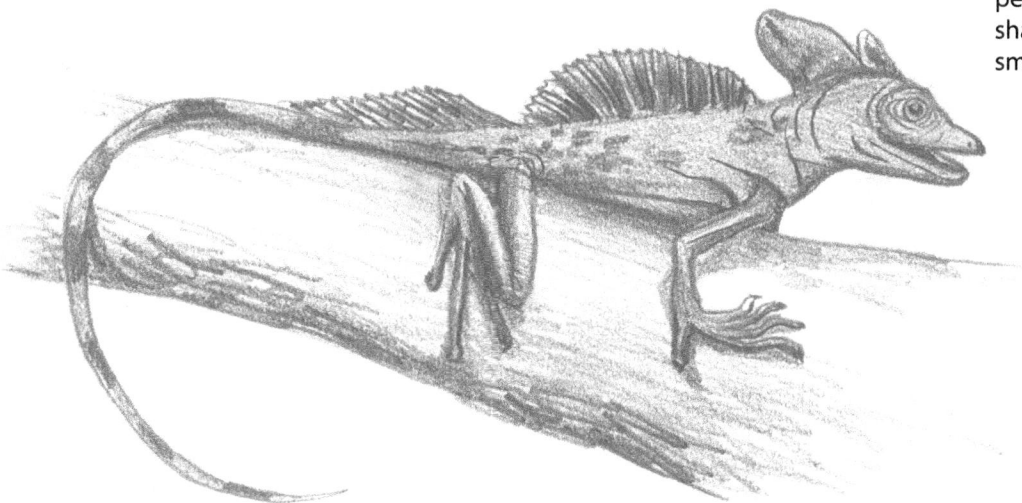

cast shadow

6. With a sharpened pencil, go over lines, darkening and adding emphasis. As your pencil gets dull, do more shading. Finally, clean up any smudges with your eraser.

Chimpanzee

Pan troglodytes: Africa. Intelligent and expressive animals, chimpanzees spend most of their time on the ground, walking on all fours and occasionally standing erect. They are good climbers. They eat plant materials, plus insects and eggs. They even use tools like twigs to extract ants or termites!

1

2

3

1. In this drawing, the face is important, so take time to get it right! Draw two light circles, with a tall oval touching the bottom of both.

radiating lines of fur go outward from the center of the head

2. Near the bottom of the lower oval, draw a line for the mouth. At the top of the oval, draw two nostrils with heart-shaped outline. Add curved lines for eyes.

4

3. Draw the lower lip. What other details do you see? Add them!

5

4. Add radiating lines to complete the head. Add ears.

5. Lightly draw two overlapping ovals for the body. Which is higher? Which is bigger? Which is flatter?

6. Look at the back legs. Which lines go straight up and down (vertical)? Where does each leg start? Which direction does it go? Now draw them – very lightly until you've got them just right.

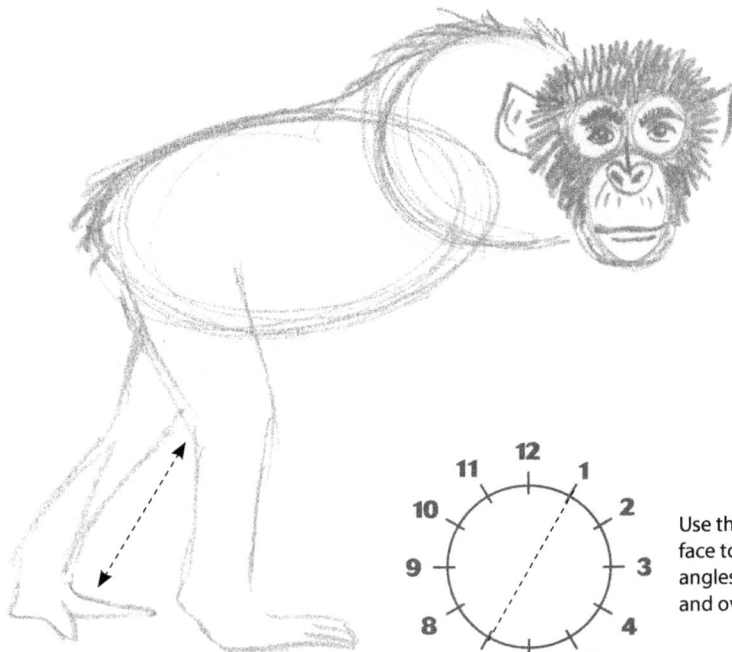

6

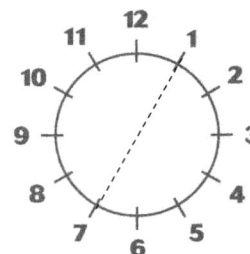

Use the clock face to compare angles of lines and ovals.

7. Lightly draw the arms. (If it helps you, add a line for the ground.) Look carefully at the shape of the arms and hands.

   Make short pencil guide lines showing the direction of the fur.

8. Following those guide lines, add fur to the body. Look how the ovals disappear—no need to erase! Add a slight cast shadow on the ground.

   Sit back, take a deep breath and really look at your drawing (perhaps in a mirror). Does it need darker fur? Sharper details on the face or hands? If so, do them now.

   Clean up any smudges with your eraser.

   Psssst ... if nobody's listening, make some chimp sounds.

cast shadow

Emerald Tree Boa

Boa caninus: South America

Size: 1.2 m (4 ft). Brilliant green snake with prehensile tail spends its life in trees, where it lies in wait for prey, often birds and bats. Fast, and a good swimmer.

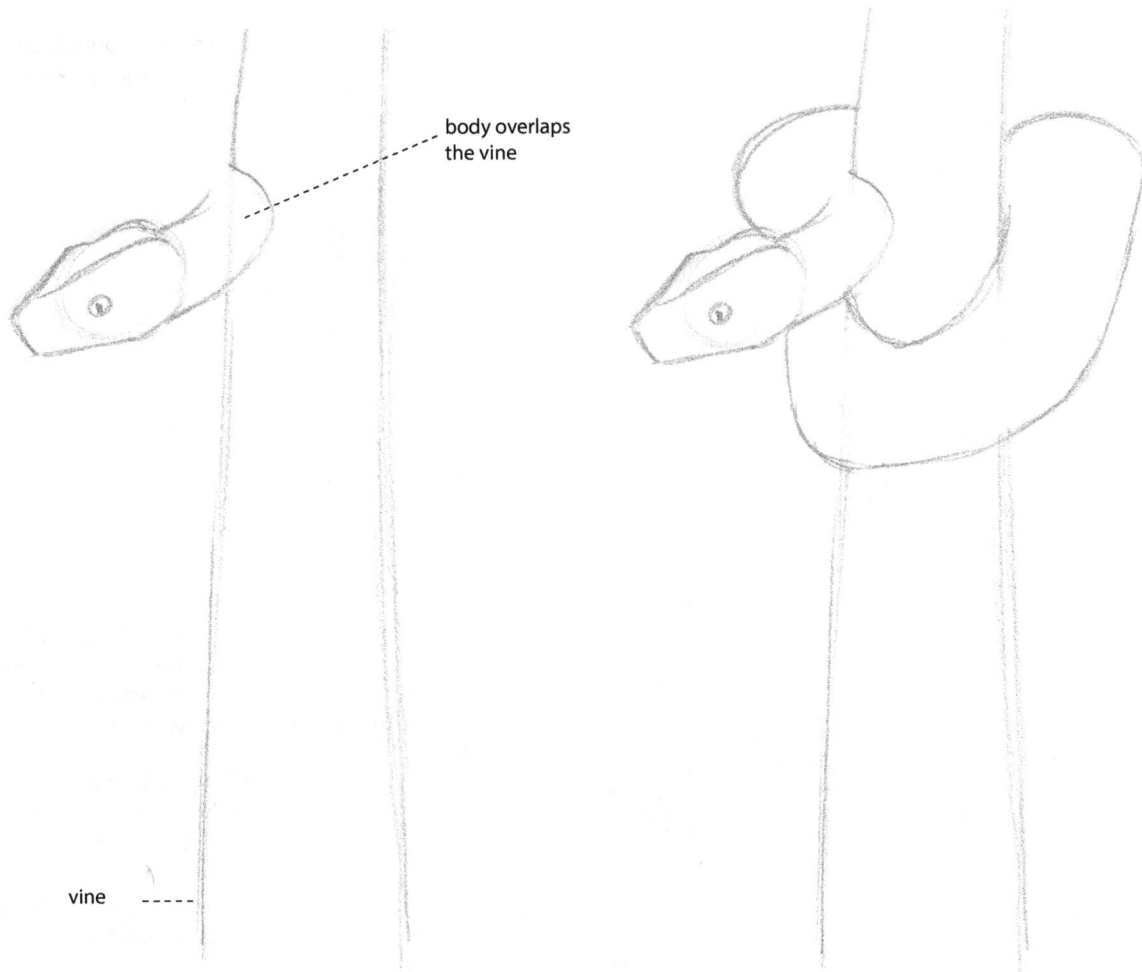

body overlaps the vine

vine

1. Start with two light *vertical* lines for the vine. Draw the head with eye, and the first section of the body, *overlapping* part of the vine.

   Make the front of the head blunt. Notice how the eyebrow bulges slightly.

2. Add the next section of the body, forming a rough U shape. Be creative! Draw this snake in different positions. You don't have to follow my drawing exactly!

> **!** Turn your paper as you draw to avoid smudging it with your hand.

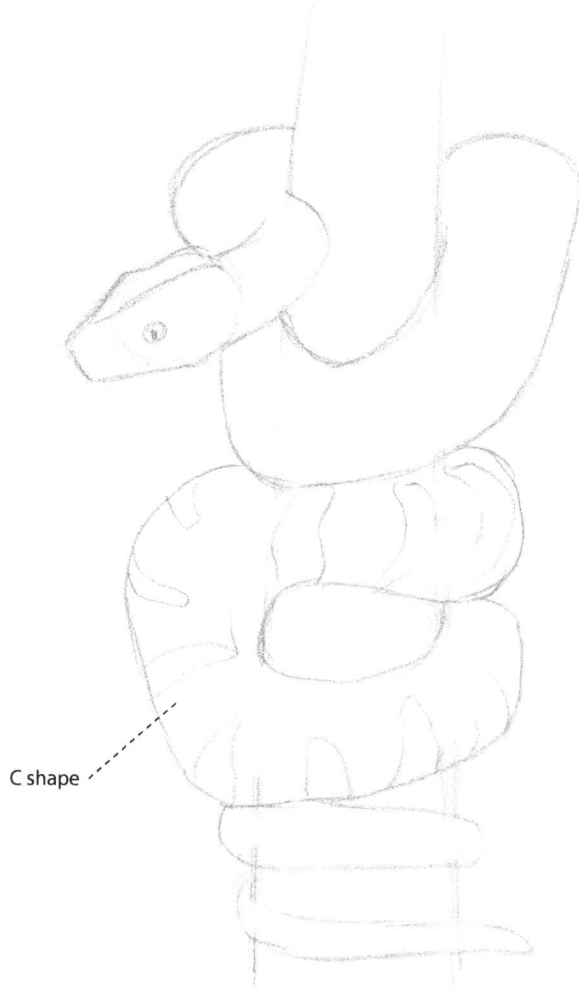

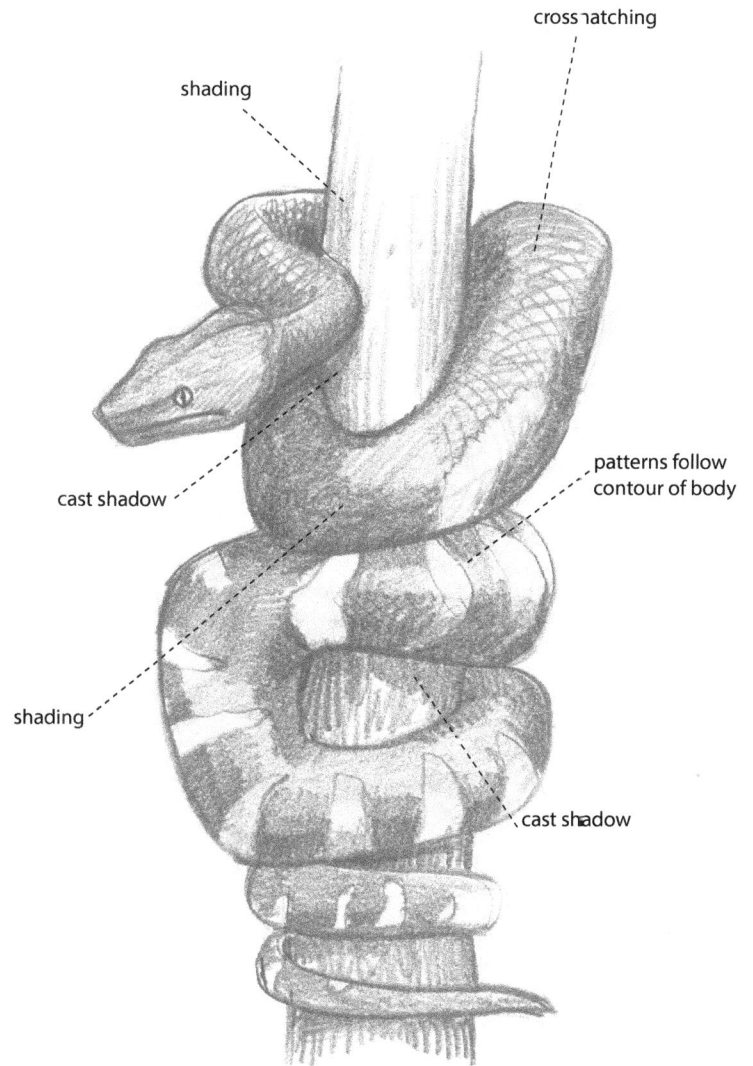

cross hatching

shading

cast shadow

patterns follow contour of body

shading

cast shadow

C shape

3. Below the U shape, make another section of the body, this time a fat C shape. Add a couple more sections, getting smaller and smaller.

   Notice that the snake doesn't wrap around the vine in one continuous spiral. The tail wraps all the way around, but the larger parts of the body reverse direction to form 'clamps' to hold to the vine.

4. Now try to make the snake and vine look round.

   Look carefully for:

   • the pattern of curving white spots,
   • crosshatching to suggest scales,
   • shading on the snake and the vine, and
   • cast shadows on the vine and snake.

   You're on your own! Keep shading until it looks like it's ready to jump off the page!

   Good looking boa!

Flying Squirrel

Anomalurus beecrofti (Beecroft's flying squirrel): West and central Africa.

Size: 53-84 cm (20-33 inches) overall length. Lives in trees. Feeds mostly on berries, seeds and fruit. Glides up to 90 m (300 ft) from tree to tree.

Use the clock face to compare angles of lines and ovals.

1. Draw a tilted oval, with two extended front legs. Make them bend slightly.

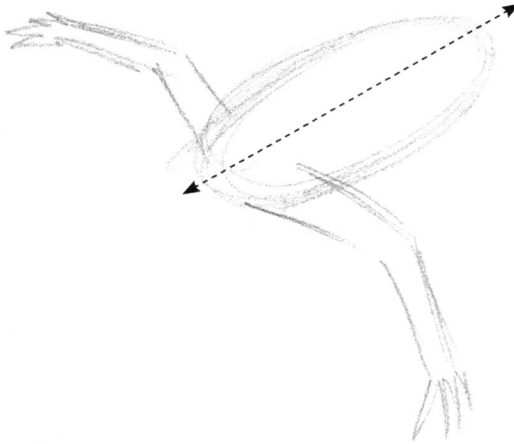

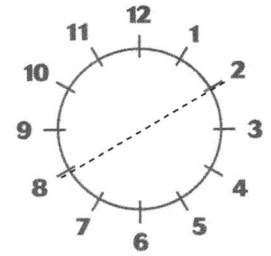

2. Add the rear legs, with two bends (knee and ankle).

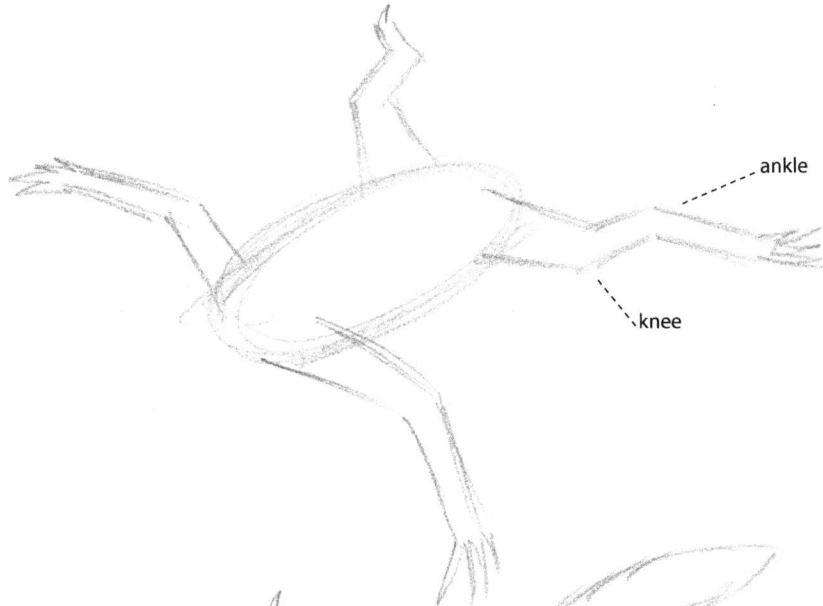

ankle

knee

3. Draw slightly curved lines to connect front and rear feet. Use short pencil strokes for th bushy tail.

4. Draw an oval for the head, slightly pointed at the nose. Add the eye and ears.

5. Draw the fur, using short pencil strokes. Leave some areas white. Add detail to the eye. Draw whiskers. Sharpen details. Clean up any smudges with your eraser.

Idea: add some leaves behind the squirrel. Draw the branch the squirrel just launched from.

Frog 1 (Arrow Poison)

Dendrobates auratus: Central and South America.

Size: 4 cm (1.5 inches). Bright red coloring warns predators that this frog is poisonous! Local tribesman know how to extract the poison, which they use on the tips of hunting arrows.

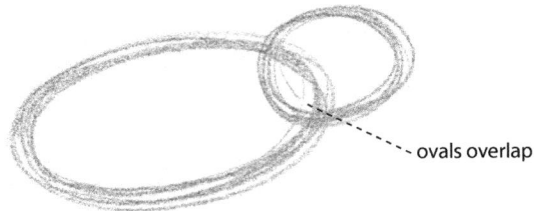

1. Draw two overlapping ovals. Draw them very lightly! You'll see why in a moment.

ovals overlap

hip

throat

2. Add a bump for the hip, a bump at the top of the head, a bump for the nose, and one more for the throat. Erase the ovals where they overlap. Draw a circle for the eye, leaving a small white spot when you darken it. Add the curving lines for the top and bottom of the eye.

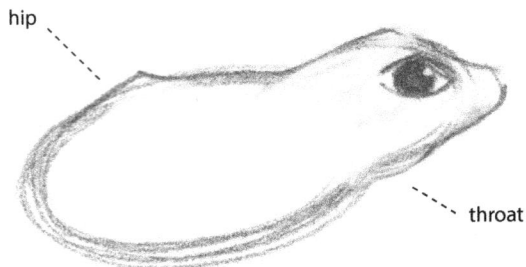

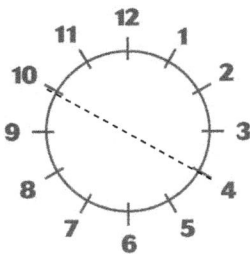

Use the clock face to compare angles of lines and ovals.

3. Add the legs. Look where and how each leg attaches to the body, and the angles of each segment of the legs. Erase the oval where the leg overlaps it.

4. As your pencil gets dull, add shading. Leave part of the back very light to help make it look shiny. When you sharpen your pencil, go over details and outlines to make them sharper.

   Add the cast shadow under the frog. Clean up any smudges with your eraser.

If you use color, make the frog bright orange and the spots black.

cast shadow

Frog 2 (Flying)

Rhacophorus nigropalmatus (Wallace's flying frog): Southeast Asia. This 10-cm (4-inch) long frog glides from tree to tree. The webs and skin flaps act like a parachute.

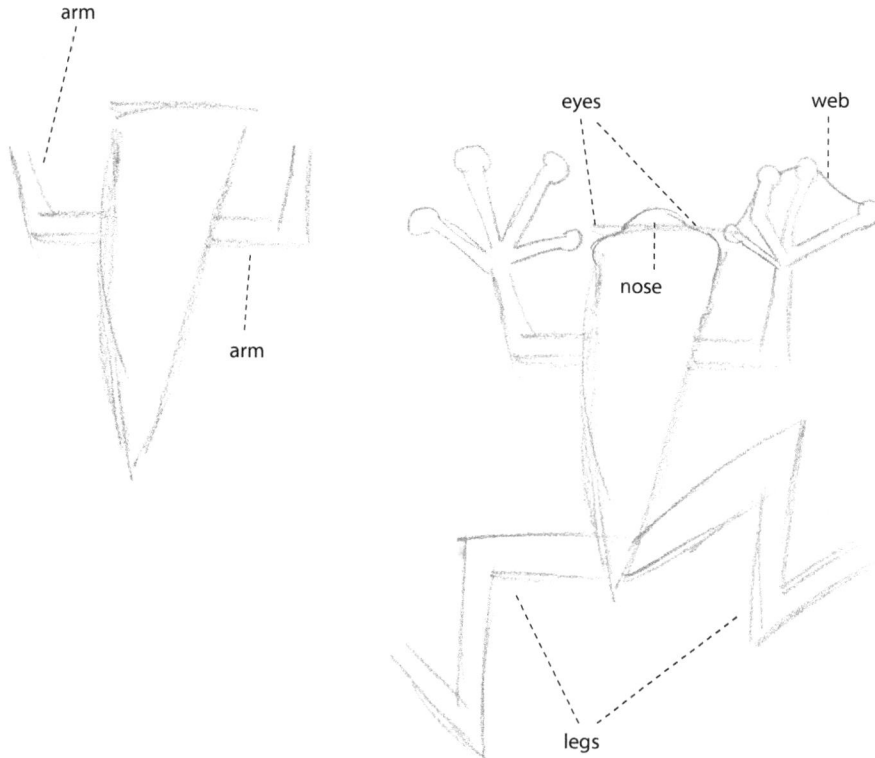

arm

arm

eyes

nose

web

1. Draw a tall, narrow triangle for the body. Add two L-shaped arms to it.

2. Add bumps on the triangle for the nose and eyes. Draw four fingers to each arm. Connect the ends of the fingers to make the webs. Draw Z-shaped legs.

3. Add toes and webbing to the legs. Draw curves in the arms and legs.

4. Shade the dark, webbed parts of the feet. Add shading to the rest of the frog.

   Clean up any smudges with your eraser.

legs

Idea: you're looking down on a frog gliding high above the ground. What would you see below it? Can you draw that?

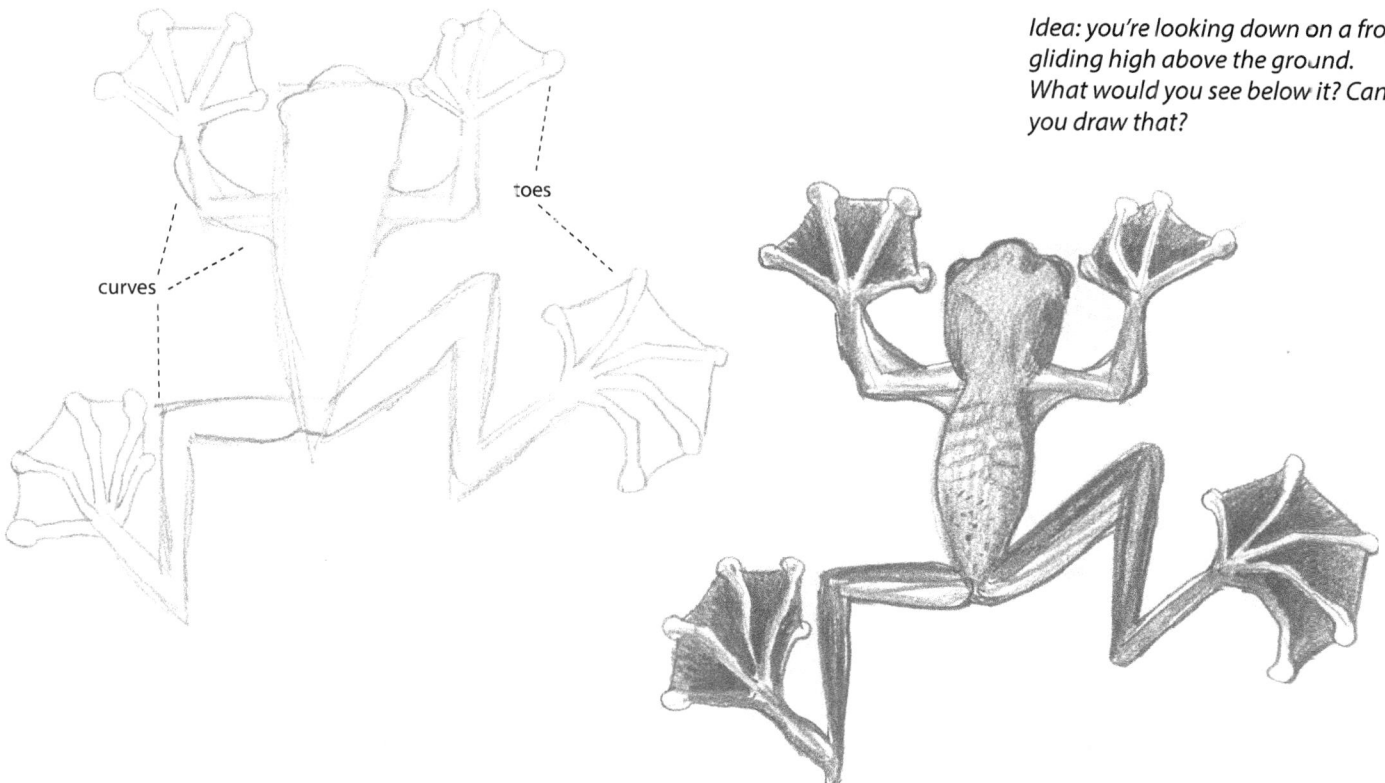

curves

toes

Frog 3 (Tree)

Phyllomedusa appendiculata (Lutz's Phyllomedusa): Southeast Brazil.

Size: 4 cm (1.5 inches). Lives in trees, feeds on insects. Lays eggs in a protective leaf over water. When the tadpoles hatch, they fall into the water.

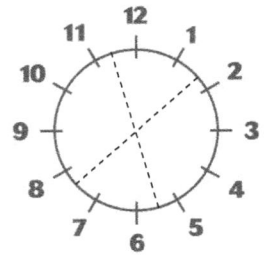

Use the clock face to compare angles of lines and ovals.

In this view, you don't see the whole frog. Look at the final drawing. See how many parts of the body *overlap*.

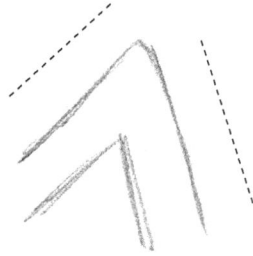

1. Start with 2 upside-down V shapes for the front leg.

mouth

bottom of body

2. Add three fingers. Draw a curving line for the bottom part of the body, then a straight line for the mouth.

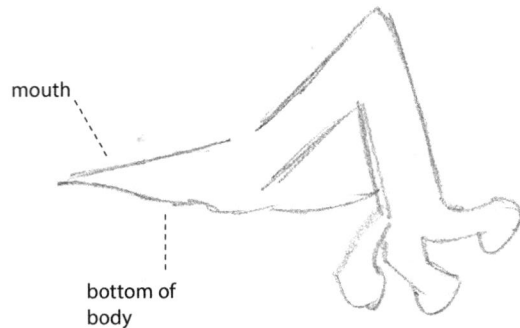

rear toes

3. Add two sideways V shapes for the other front leg. Draw the rear toes.

other front leg

4. Draw toes for the other front leg, then carefully draw curving lines for the branch.

With so many toes overlapping the branch, it's easier to draw them first, then add the branch behind them.

bump for eye

rear leg

rear leg

rear toes

vertical oval for
pupil of eye

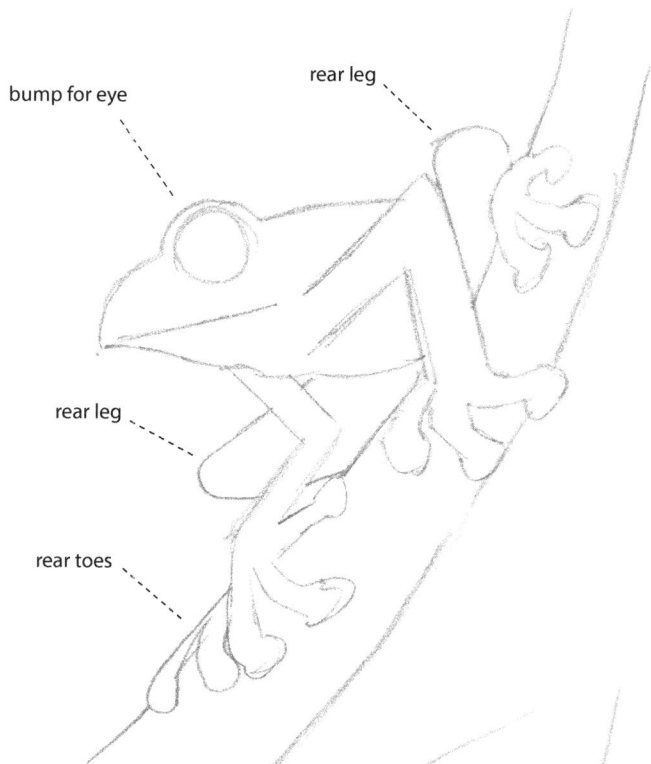

5. From the end of the mouth, draw the outline of the head and back, making a bump for the eye. Draw a circle for the eye inside that bump.

   Draw the two rear legs. Add the other rear toes.

6. Draw the pupil inside the eye. Draw the bump of the other eye. Outline the leaf behind the frog. Lightly draw spots on the frog's back to leave white when you shade the back. Begin shading the darkest area of the drawing, which is the bottom part of the frog.

7. Continue to add shading and details. Clean up any smudges with your eraser.

   Add color if you wish. An online image search will give you ideas for colors.

Cute froggie.

Kribittt…

Gorilla

Gorilla gorilla: Africa, in rain forests to fairly high elevations.

Size: male height 1.7-1.8 m (5.5-6 ft); female height 1.4-1.5 m (4.5-5 ft). Largest of the primat es, gorillas are gentle animals unless threatened. They eat mainly plants. They live in small groups. This has an easy scientific name to remember!

1. Draw two small circles on top of a larger oval. Make a line across them to help emphasize the strong brow of the gorilla.

2. Draw a line for the mouth. Add eyes, with lines under them. Draw slanting nostrils.

3. From the edge of the eyebrow, draw a line up to a point and back down. This part of the head is almost as high as the face! Add the ear, and short pencil lines on the chin, face, and forehead.

4. From the back of the head, make a long swooping line for the back, joined by another swooping line for the back of the leg.

5. Lightly draw the leg and arm, with toes and fingers. Notice the shape of the arm. Look how close the shoulder comes to the face. Add the belly.

another curve

another leg

guide lines

another arm

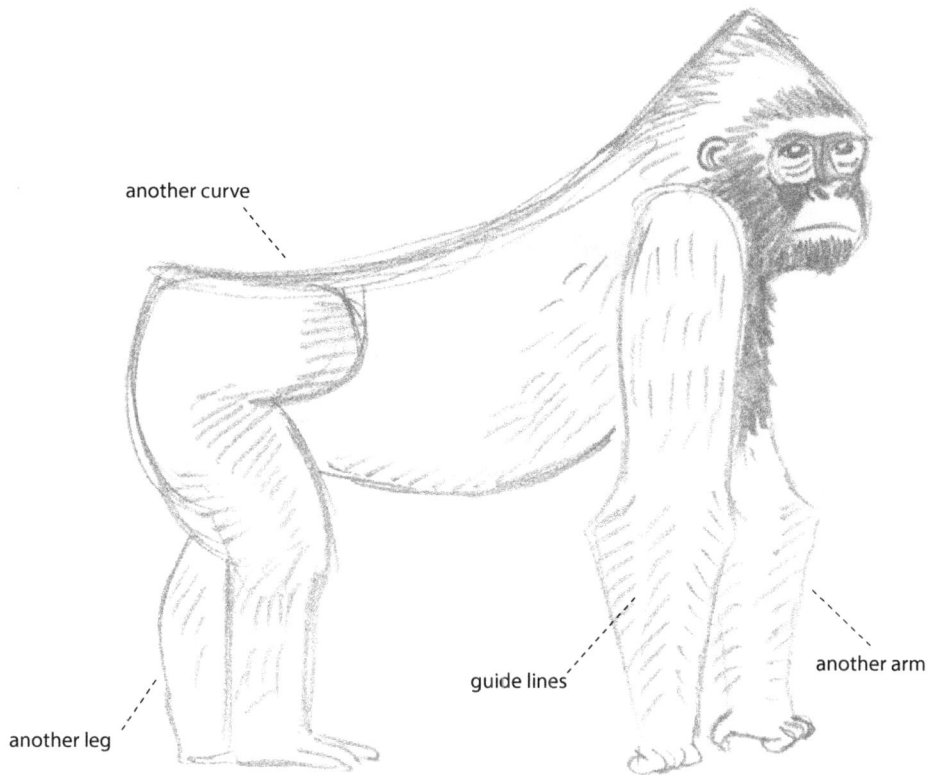

6. Add the other leg and arm. Before you add fur, make light *guide lines* to remind you which direction the shading needs to go.

Which areas are lightest? Which areas are darkest?

cast shadow

7. Cover the whole body with short pencil strokes. Be sure to follow the direction of your *guide lines*.

Pay attention to areas that are lighter and darker. Go over lines that need to be darker or sharper, and refine details of the face if you need to.

Add a cast shadow underneath.

Bright idea: if a gorilla charges you in the wild, stand your ground. If you run, you'll be in big trouble.

Hoatzin

Opisthocomus hoazin: South America.

Size: 61 cm (24 inches). Bizarre bird lives in trees, and doesn't fly well. Eats fruit and leaves. Young can swim, and have claws on the hook of each wing to help them climb trees. Nests are built over water so they can drop to safety if a snake approaches!

1. Draw a tilted oval. At the top, add a curve like an upside-down smile. This will become the top of the head.

2. From the top of the head, draw the neck and breast. Add the mouth, and the eye.

    Lightly draw curved lines to show where the first three layers of wing feathers end. The longest feathers extend beyond the oval. Draw the outline of the wing, then add light lines for the feathers.

    breast

    wing

3. Draw the wild feathers sticking out the top of the head. Outline the eye and beak and light feathers running down the neck. Darken the top of the head. 'Ruffle' the breast feathers with short pencil strokes.

    Add feathers on the back. Outline a small space at the end of each layer of feathers on the wing, which you will leave white. Add points on the end of the longest feathers.

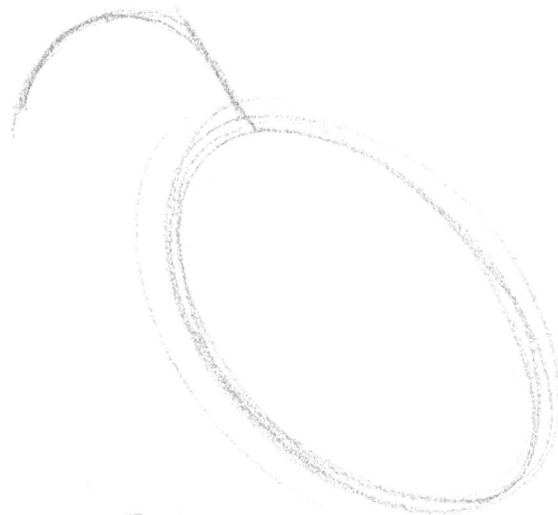

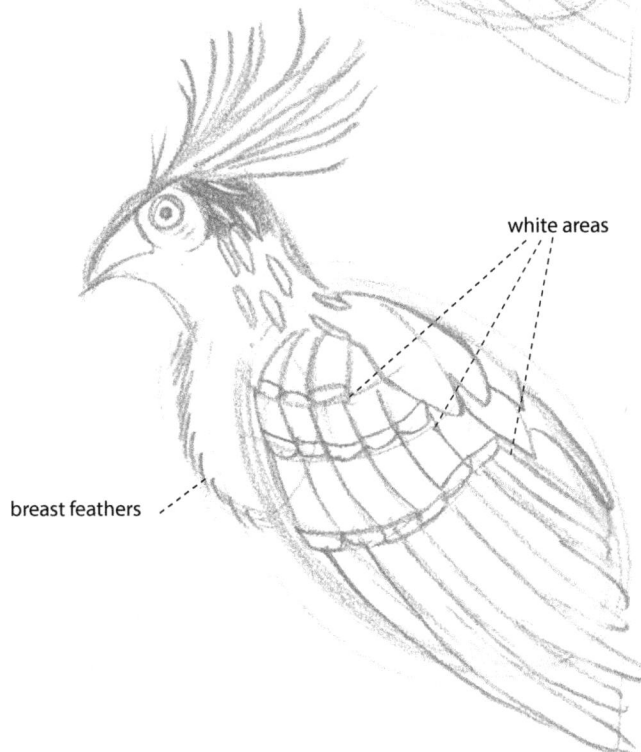

    white areas

    breast feathers

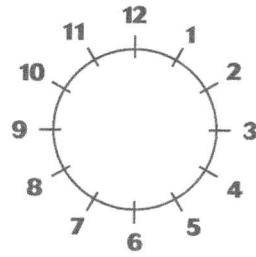

12
11 1
10 2
9 3
8 4
7 5
6

! Turn your paper as you draw to avoid smudging it with your hand.

tail feathers - - - - - - -

4. Add a tree branch, with the bird's claws. Lightly craw the tail feathers.

5. Take a moment to look at the final drawing, noticing white and dark areas. Add shading. Finish the tail feathers, leaving the ends white.

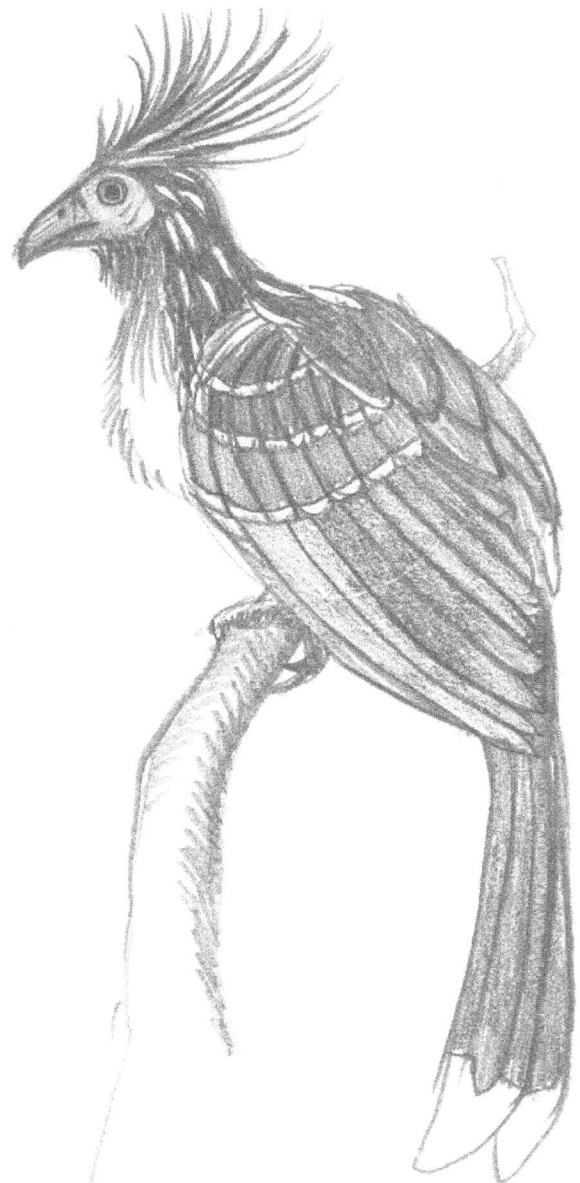

Handsome hoatzin!

Howler Monkey

Alouatta seniculus (red howler monkey): northern South America, mainly Colombia.

Size: 160-180 cm (63-71 inches). Lives in trees, eats leaves and some fruit. Sturdily built, with prehensile tail. They're loud! Male howler monkeys shout to let other monkeys know their territory.

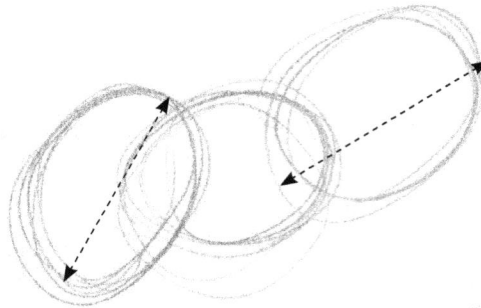

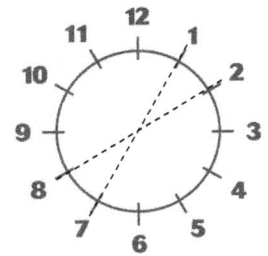

Use the clock face to compare angles of lines and ovals.

1. Start by drawing three overlapping ovals. Notice how each tilts at a different angle.

2. Draw the face, one feature at a time, starting with the mouth.

3. Add the outline of the head, and join the ovals to make the curved back. Draw the arm and leg on the side closest to you; pay attention to the way they bend. Add fur to the chin.

4. Draw the remaining arm and leg, and the tail. As you draw them, add branches. Can you see how the tail curls around one branch?

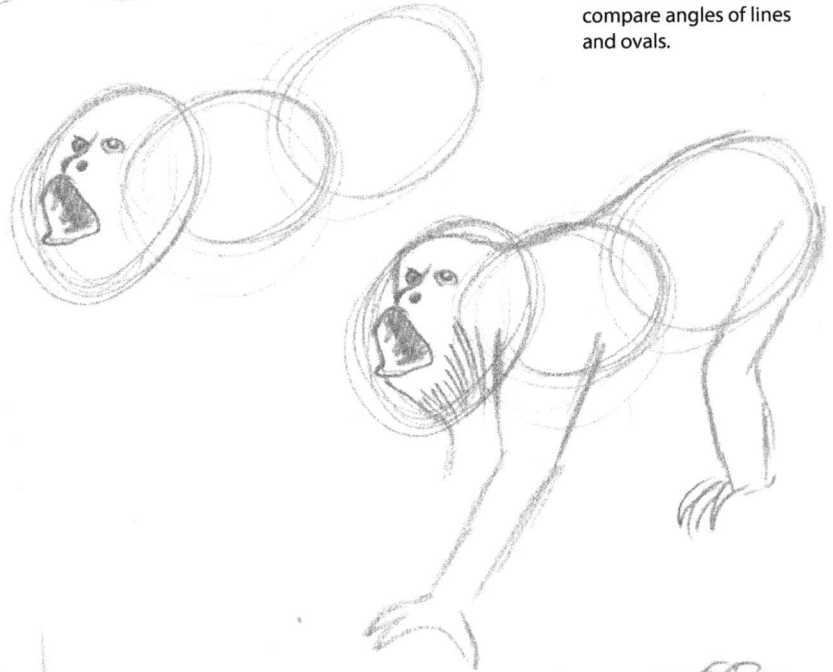

5. Use your eraser to clean up lines you won't need in the finished drawing. Starting with the darkest areas, make short pencil lines for fur.

! Turn your paper as you draw to avoid smudging it with your hand.

6. Look carefully at which parts of the monkey are darkest, and which are lightest. Continue adding fur. Draw shading on the branches.

While your pencil is sharp, go over fine details. As it gets duller, add shading.

Clean up smudges with your eraser. Add color if you wish.

Iguana

Iguana iguana (common iguana): Central and South America.

Size: 1-2 m (3.5-6.5 ft). Iguanas live in trees, but lay eggs in holes they dig in the ground. They feed on plants, but can defend themselves from other animals with sharp teeth and claws. They drop from trees into water to escape—they're great swimmers! Easy scientific name!

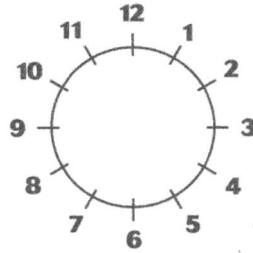

Use the clock face to compare angles of lines and ovals.

1. Begin with the swooping shape for the body. Notice how the bottom line becomes almost vertical at the head. Don't join the lines at the tail yet—it gets a lot longer!

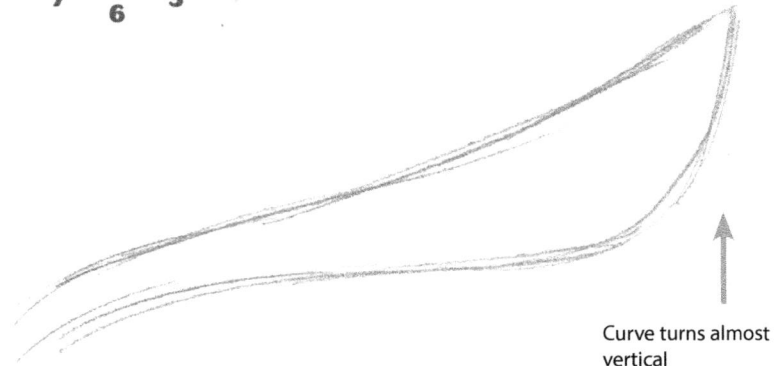

Curve turns almost vertical

2. Look at the legs. The front leg starts at the shoulder, goes down, back, then down again. The back leg is foreshortened. This means that part of it (the part connecting to the body) comes straight towards you. Now draw the legs, and add toes and claws.

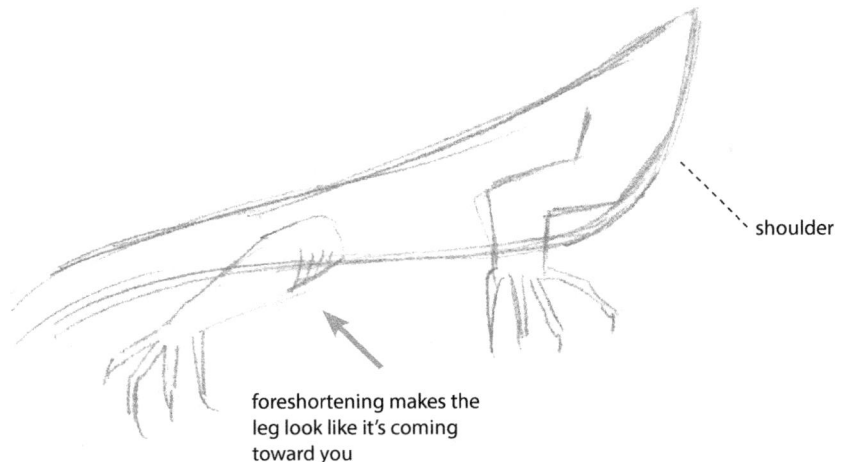

shoulder

foreshortening makes the leg look like it's coming toward you

3. Add the top of the head, and eye. Draw a line for the mouth, then add the flaps of skin beneath the mouth. Add the distinct, jagged row of spikes along the iguana's back. They don't need to be even.

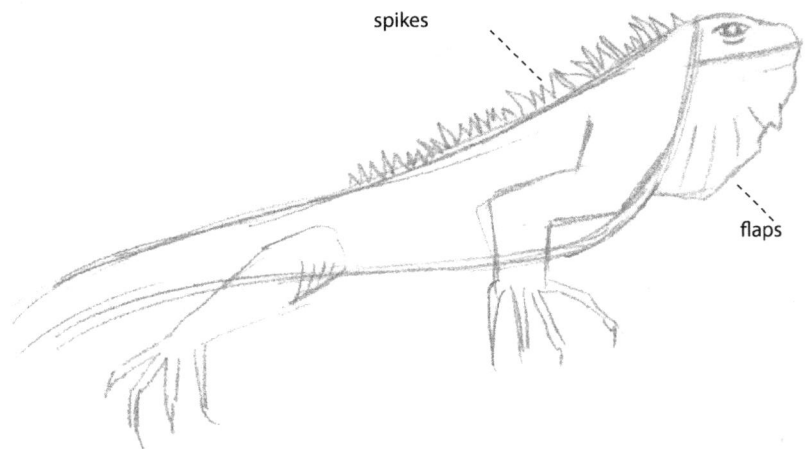

spikes

flaps

crosshatching

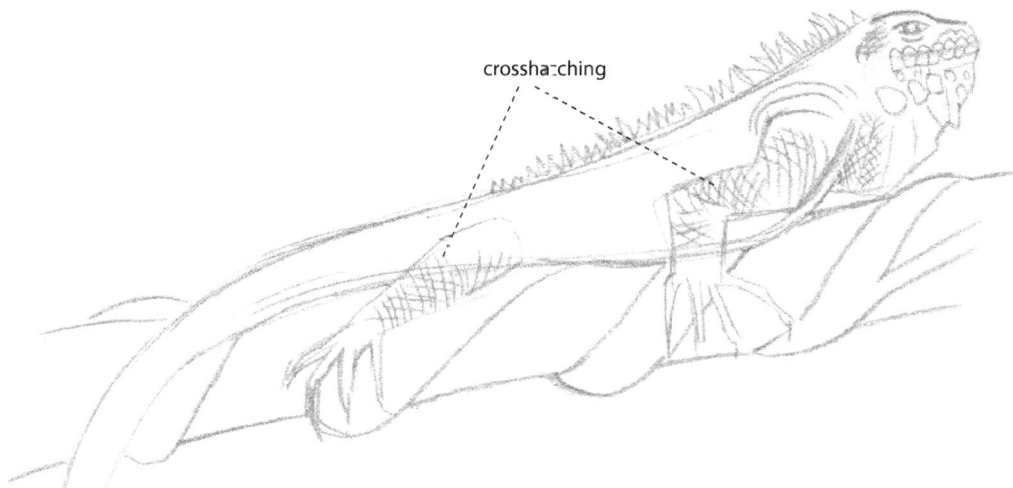

4. Looking closely at my example (or at a photo, or better yet, a real iguana if you have one handy!), add the tail and details. Crosshatching suggests scales on the legs and head. Around the mouth add shapes you see in the example.

    Add a branch under the iguana. To make it more interesting, add a vine or two spiraling around it.

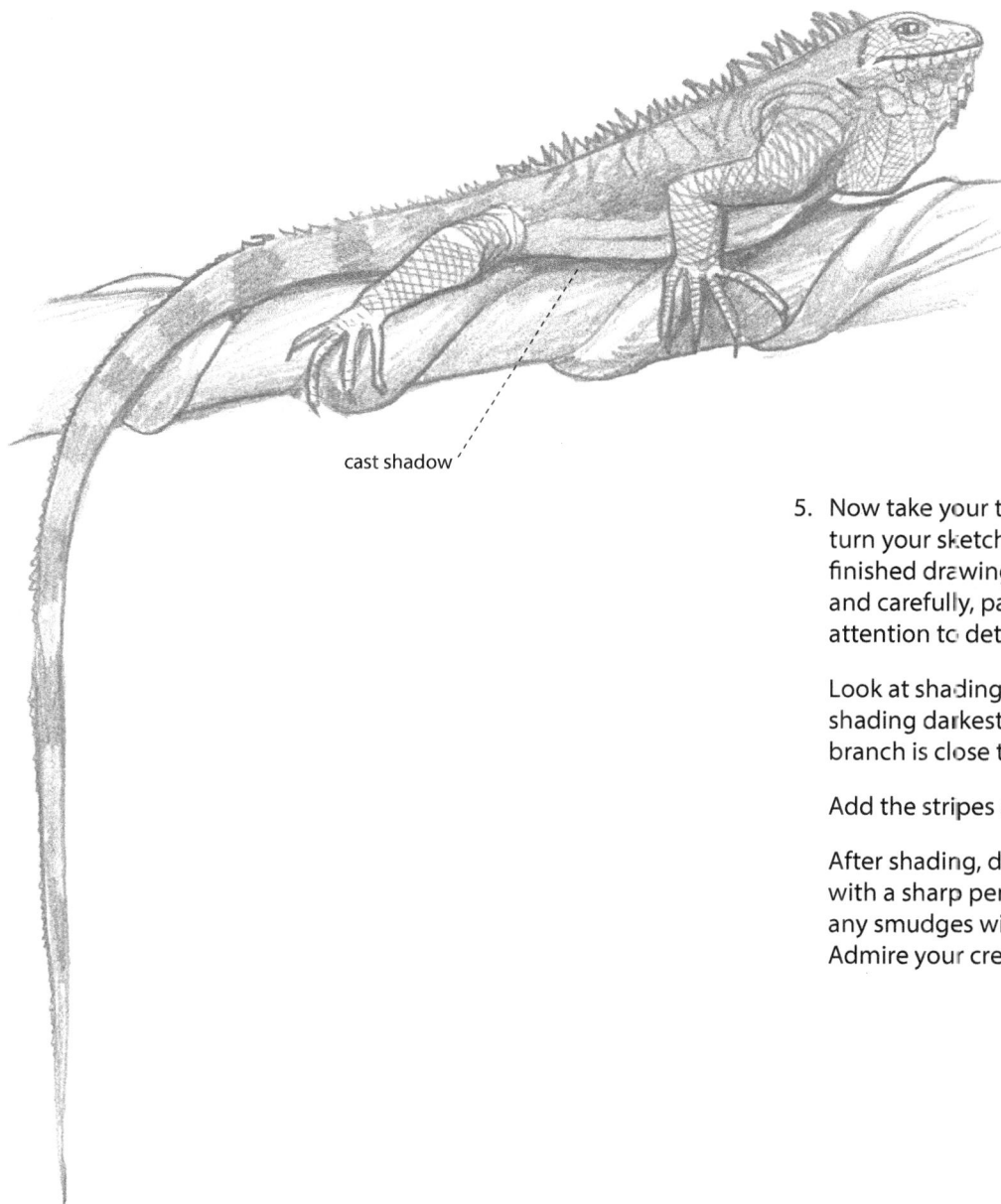

cast shadow

5. Now take your time as you turn your sketch into a finished drawing. Work slowly and carefully, paying close attention to details.

    Look at shading. Make the shading darkest where the branch is close to the body.

    Add the stripes on the tail!

    After shading, darken lines with a sharp pencil. Clean up any smudges with your eraser. Admire your creation!

Jaguar

Panthera onca: Central and South America.

Size: 1.5-1.8 m ((5-6 ft). Climbs trees to lie in wait for prey. Feeds on a variety of animals, even fish. Powerful animal with deep chest and strong limbs.

1. Start by drawing two light, *overlapping* circles.

2. Add the two sides of the mouth slanting downward, with the small vertical line in the center.

3. Add a triangle for the nose.

4. Directly above the outside of the nose, draw two upside-down L shapes.

5. Make eyes by drawing curves down from the outside of the L shapes. Add the ears.

6. Make a circle for the center of the eye. Leave a small highlight in it.

7. Darken the rest of each eye. Add rows of dots on the muzzle and whiskers.

    When you have the face mastered, look ahead to steps 8-10. Remember to leave enough room on your paper for the body!

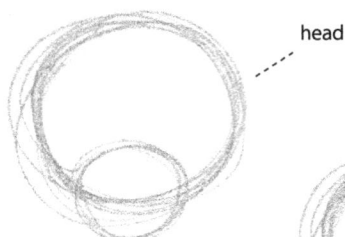

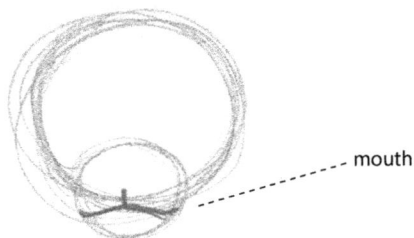

head

mouth

The secret to drawing the jaguar, and other cats, is getting the face right. Rather than trying to draw this perfectly the first time, try it several times on scratch paper. Draw a little larger than you normally do. Pay attention to proportions.

(1)　　　　(2)　　　　(3)

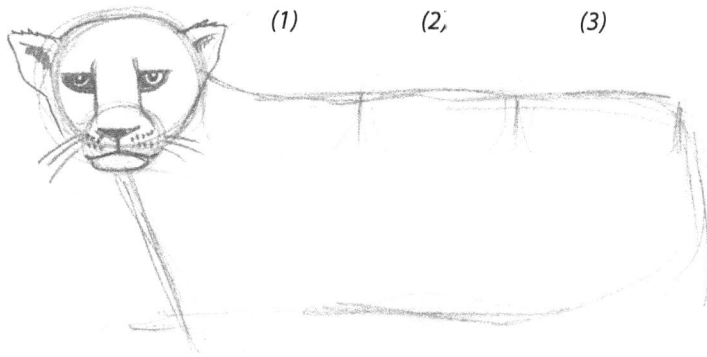

8. Measure three heads back for the length of the body. Make the back level with the bottom of the eyes, with a little curve at the neck. Make the front of the body slant slightly.

9. Add the legs and paws. Draw lightly at first. Look at your jaguar. Is everything the way you want it?

   If something looks wrong, try looking at your picture in a mirror, or hold it up to a light and look through the back.

10. Next add spots to the jaguar: dark patches with one or more darker spots inside. These large spots become smaller spots and stripes on the legs and tail.

   Lightly lay out the pattern, then carefully add shading. It takes a while, but it's worth it!

   While your pencil is sharp, go over fine details. As it gets duller, add shading. Add color if you wish.

   Clean up any smudges with your eraser.

Here, kitty…nice kitty…

Kinkajou

Potos flavus: Central and South America.

Size: 81-113 cm (32-45 inches). Kinkajous live in trees, feeding at night on fruit and insects. Agile climbers, they use their prehensile tail to hold onto branches, leaving their hands free for gathering food.

1. Start by drawing downward-curving lines for the branch, and a titled oval. The angle of the branch emphasizes the kinkajou's prehensile tail in this drawing.

head

2. Lightly draw an oval for the upper body and a small circle for the head.

overlapping

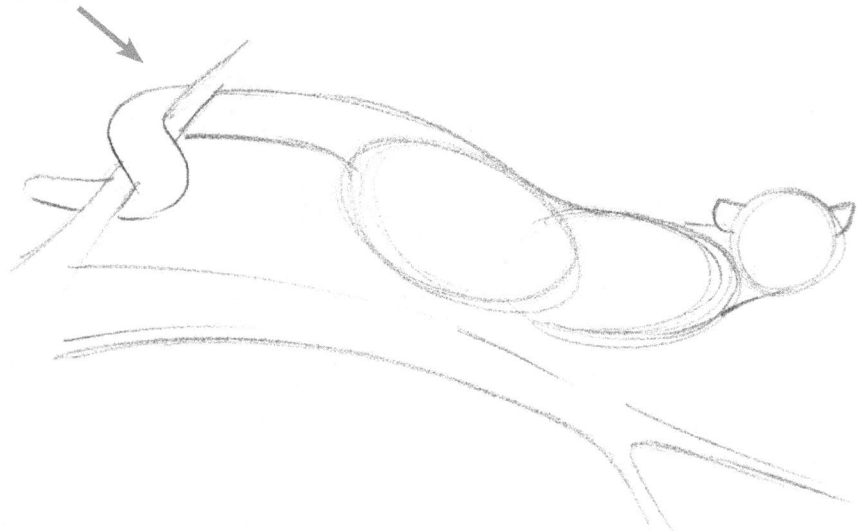

3. Add another small branch behind the animal, and draw the tail curling around it (look closely at my example to see how to do this!). Add ears and the outline of the back and neck.

4. Sketch in the legs, one at a time. You can't see all of each leg, so this takes careful observation. Draw very lightly at first!

5. When you get the legs just right, draw the face. Place the eyes halfway between the top and bottom of the circle, then add nose, mouth, and whiskers below them.

    Carefully erase lines you no longer need. Begin drawing the fur on what will be the darkest parts of the body. Use loose, short pencil marks to capture the texture and direction of the fur.

eyes halfway between top and bottom of circle

6. Keep drawing fur until the whole body is covered. Add leaves to the branches. Look at your drawing in a mirror (or through the back of the paper) to spot any areas you can make better. Go over parts that you didn't get dark enough the first time.

    Finally, clean up any smudges with your eraser.

Ruffed Lemur

Varecia variegata: Madagascar.

Size: 120 cm (47 inches) including tail. This agile climber rarely comes to the ground. It eats fruit, leaves and bark, and is most active at dusk and early part of the night.

1. Start with the eyes. Make small circles with a spot inside them. Around them draw wider, darker circles.

2. Draw the outline of the head, rectangular above the eyes, and a rounded triangle below the eyes.

3. Add the nose and mouth.

4. From the top sides of the head, lightly draw lines going out and up. Then draw the outline of the curving ruff, or collar, or beard, or whatever you want to call it.

   Draw lightly at first!

   Once you have the light outline in place, add radiating lines for the fur.

5. Draw a light curving line for the back. Continue adding lines for fur around the face.

6. Draw the curve of the leg. What number does this look like? Add five radiating curved lines for the toes.

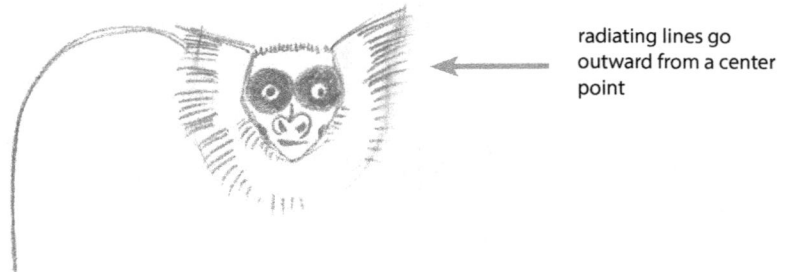

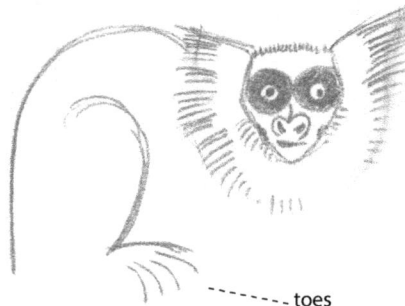

ruff

radiating lines go outward from a center point

toes

7. Complete the rear foot. Draw the front arm and hand, with all five fingers. Draw the lines of the branch, adding a tiny bit of the thumb of the other hand.

8. Add a small upward curve for the lemur's belly, and the dark fur of the other arm. With short pencil strokes radiating from the shoulder, draw more fur. Add jagged lines along the back for texture, and a few fur lines on the face and body.

   What's missing?

belly curves upward

9. A fat, long tail! Try drawing it using only short lines, to show texture of the fur.

   While your pencil is sharp, go over fine details. As it gets duller, add shading.

   Clean up any smudges with your eraser.

! Turn your paper as you draw to avoid smudging it with your hand.

Idea: add leaves and other branches in the background. Draw a dark background to make a night setting for this nocturnal animal.

Macaw

Ara macao (Scarlet macaw): Mexico to northern South America.

Size: 85 cm (33.5 inches). Most familiar of South American parrots. Threatened by destruction of rain forest and people stealing baby birds to sell as pets. Don't buy them!

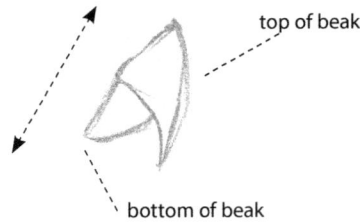

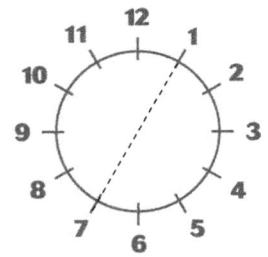

top of beak

bottom of beak

Use the clock face to compare angles of lines and ovals.

1. Lightly draw the top part of the beak, then the bottom.

2. Add a roughly triangular shape for the macaw's face. At the top, draw the eye. Add the pattern of spots on the cheek, and curved lines to suggest the texture of the beak.

head

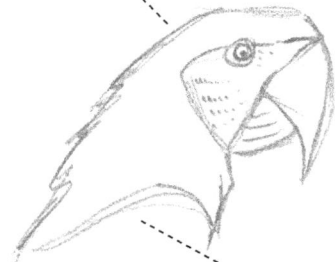

shoulder line

3. From the top of the beak, draw the outline of the macaw's head. From the bottom of the beak, draw the throat. Add a shoulder line.

4. LIghtly draw an oval for the bird's body. Draw two claws grasping a branch.

claws

5. Sketch in the tail feathers. Notice that they stick out a bit, rather than pointing straight down.

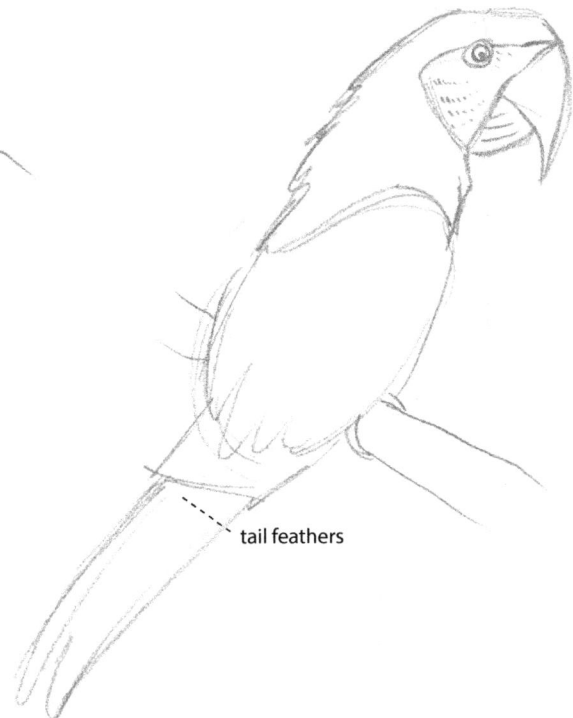

tail feathers

layers

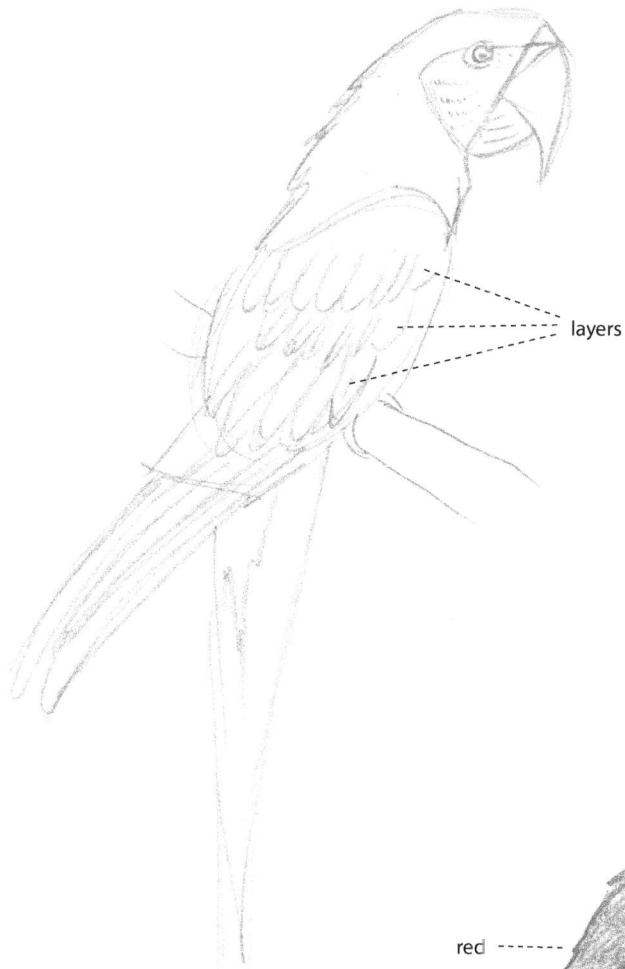

6. Add lines to these wing feathers, then draw the tail feathers, pointing downward underneath the wing feathers. Add three layers of feathers on the wing.

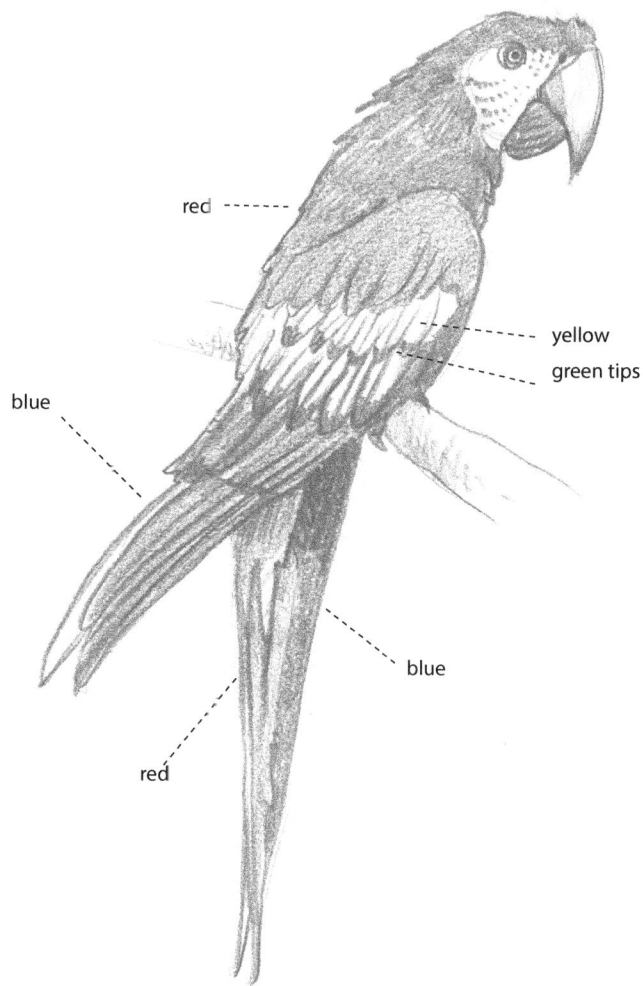

7. Carefully shade the feathers. While your pencil is sharp, go over fine details. As it gets duller, add shading.

Look at your drawing in a mirror (or through the back of the paper) to spot any areas you can make better.

Clean up any smudges with your eraser.

red

yellow

green tips

blue

blue

red

Idea: draw it in color!

Margay

Felis Wiedii: Central and South America.

Size: 1.1-1.7 m (43-67 inches), including tail. Margays usually hunt at night for small mammals, birds, and snakes. They're good at not being seen, either by their prey or by people. During the day, they sleep on a branch or in vegetation.

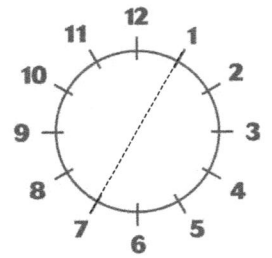

Use the clock face to compare angles of lines and ovals.

1. Begin by lightly drawing a titled oval. Add a triangle for one eye, and an oval shape with a circle inside for the other eye.

2. Draw a triangle for the nose. Add the mouth, and facial markings. Spend some time with the face to get it right.

3. Add ears and more facial markings. Lightly draw the front leg, and a horizontal line for the chest.

4. Lightly sketch the other front leg and paw. Look carefully at the angles!

paws

5. From the ear, draw the curving back, and the line on the bottom, curving into what will become the closer rear leg.

   Now add the rear leg. Pay close attention to where the lines connect to the body.

back

6. Look how far back the other rear leg goes! Draw it. Add the tail; notice where it intersects the edge of the leg. Draw whiskers, and a branch for the margay to stand on.

   Last chance to fix the basic shapes of your cat! Look at it carefully—is everything OK?

   Look at your drawing in a mirror (or through the back of the paper) to spot any areas you can make better.

7. Before drawing spots, look closely at this drawing. Notice how some spots curve to show the contour of the body. Which parts of the drawing are dark, and which are light? Is the tail as dark as the ears? What's the darkest part of the drawing?

   Be patient as you finish the drawing. Work slowly and carefully as you add the spots.

   Clean up any smudges with your eraser.

Magnificent Margay!

Okapi

Okapia johnstoni: Zaire.

Size: 1.5-2.3 m (5-7.5 ft). Lives alone except in breeding season. Has a long tongue. In fact, an okapi can clean its own eyes and eyelids with its tongue! Feeds on leaves, shoots, grass and fruit.

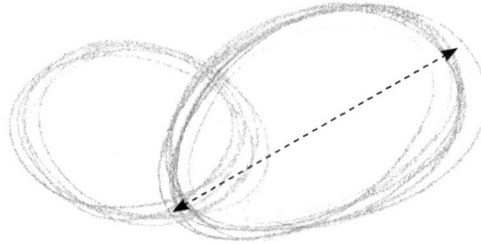

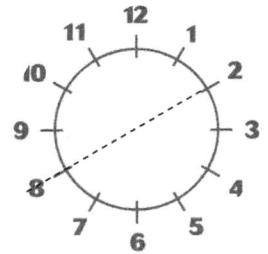

Use the clock face to compare angles of lines and ovals.

1. Start by drawing two light ovals for the body.

   Notice that :

   • they overlap,
   • they're tilted, and
   • they're different sizes.

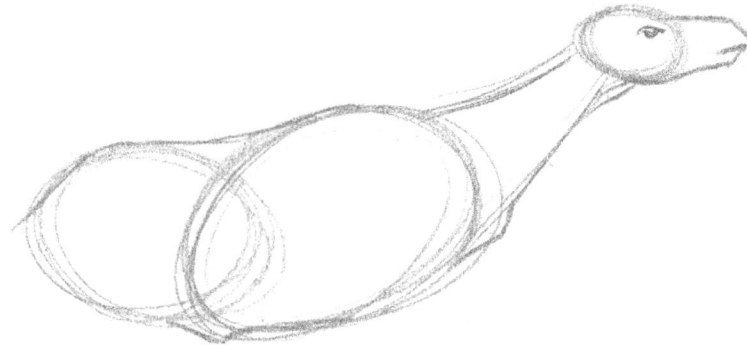

2. Add the lines to join the two ovals, on top and bottom. Draw the neck, then very lightly add an oval for the main part of the head. Add the front of the head, with the mouth and eye.

3. Add the ear and small horns at the top of the head. Draw the rear leg and the front leg, looking closely at the angles in the drawing. Add the tail.

! Turn your paper as you draw to avoid smudging it with your hand.

4. Carefully erase the body ovals where they *overlap*. (You did draw them *lightly*, didn't you?) Draw the other two legs. Lightly outline the distinctive stripes on the upper legs. Add the dark part on the lower legs. Draw some jagged lines for grass.

5. To complete your drawing, shade the body with pencil strokes showing the direction of the fur. Carefully erase the head oval, then add details and shade the head.

Take a good look at your drawing. Are there areas that need to be darker? Darken them. Are details getting fuzzy?

While your pencil is sharp, go over fine details. As it gets duller, add shading.

Clean up any smudges with your eraser.

Idea: the okapi looks like it's stretching to reach food. Add a branch with leaves on it. Draw the okapi's long tongue grabbing a leaf.

Orangutan

Pongo pygmaeus: Sumatra, Borneo.

Size: 1.2-1.5 m (4-5 ft). The orangutan's arms are larger and stronger than its legs, and it is an agile climber. All adults have fatty throat pouches; only mature males have the distinctive cheek flaps surrounding the face. The shaggy fur is reddish-brown.

1. Draw the outline of the face, a tilted rectangle with a rounded bottom. Draw two lines near the middle of the rectangle for the mouth.

2. At the top of the rectangle, draw a series of curved lines to make the eyes. Draw two nostrils, and two lines to define the outside of the nose. Add radiating pencil strokes to make the 'beard.'

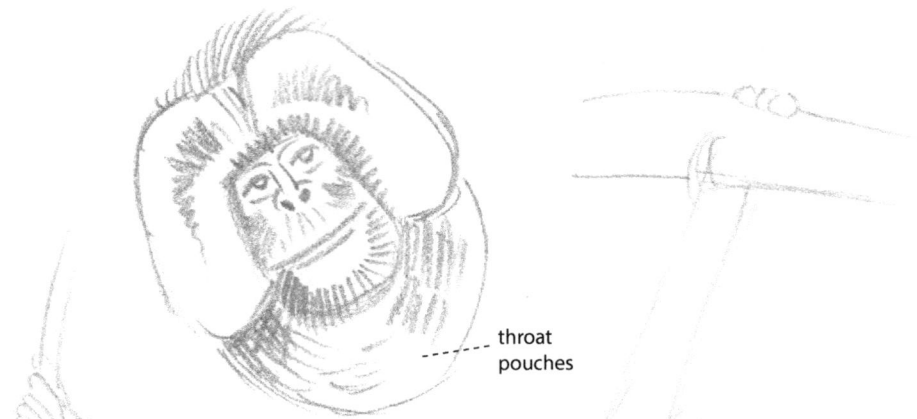

    Add hair at the top of the head. Lightly sketch the cheek flaps that surround the face. It may take you a try or two to get them just right.

3. Add the throat pouches, which look like a collar. Add shading to the face, cheek flaps, and throat pouches.

4. Here's a big jump! *Draw lightly at first*, and redraw any parts that don't look right the first time. Draw an oval for the body. Add the legs, looking carefully at the position and the way the lines run. Add the outstretched arms, then draw the branch and vine for the orangutan to swing on.

beard

throat pouches

5. Add another branch or two. Using short pencil strokes, draw the hair on the body. Pay close attention to the direction of the hair. Draw hair on arms and legs, pointing outward from the body. Add shading and texture to the branch and vine.

Notice areas that are darker and areas that are lighter. Go over any lines that need darkening.

While your pencil is sharp, go over fine details. As it gets duller, add shading.

Clean up any smudges with your eraser.

Idea: turn to pages 114-115. and fill the space around the orangutan with leaves, trees, and vines.

! Turn your paper as you draw to avoid smudging it with your hand.

Ouakari

Cacajao calvus (bald ouakari): West Brazil.

Size: 66-73 cm (26-29 inches) including tail. Lives in treetops. Bald head, red face and a beard! Walks on all fours; has a short tail and doesn't leap much. Eats mainly fruit. Active in the daytime.

1. Look carefully at the shapes in this drawing before you draw. Start with the branch, then add the banana-like oval of the body.

2. Add (lightly!) a second *overlapping* oval for the top of the leg. Draw the bottom part of the leg, with toes curling around the branch.

other leg

tail connects here

3. Erase the first oval where the leg *overlaps* it. Draw the arm, with fingers.

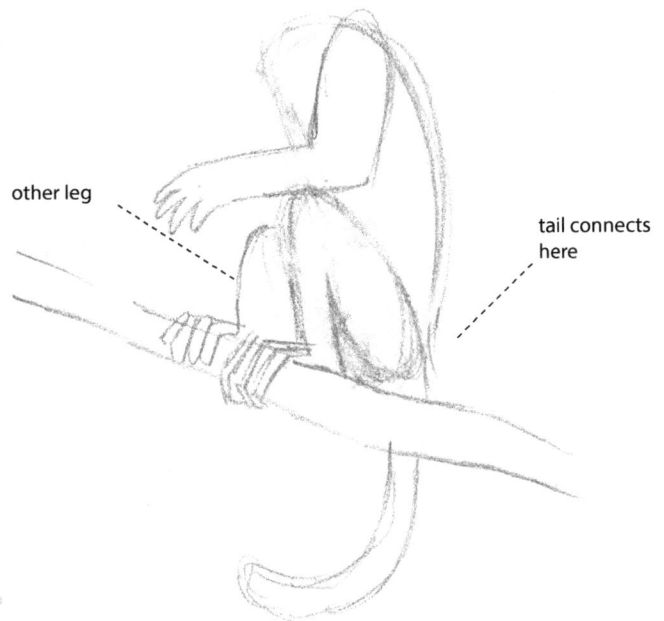

4. Draw a small curved line for the other leg. Add toes. Draw the tail, starting from the base of the back.

eyes in middle of head

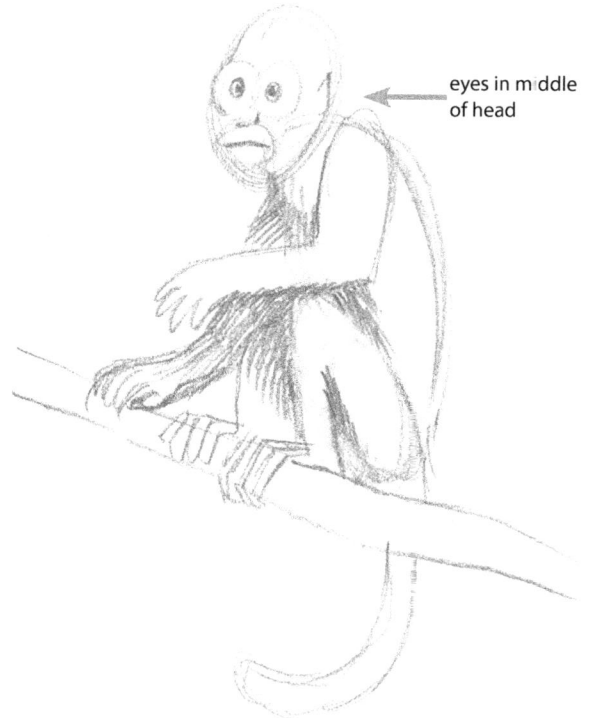

5. Add the second arm. Darken it with short pencil strokes for hair. Notice the direction of the hair.

6. Draw an oval for the head. In the middle, add two circles for the eyes, and an oval beneath them, with a line through the middle, for the mouth.

7. Carefully shade the face and add long hair. Shade lightly at first! You can always make it darker.

8. Add lots and lots of hair! Make some areas darker. Use short pencil lines to make the back and tail look shaggy.

Pangolin

Manis tricuspis (tree pangolin): Central Africa.

Size: 84-105 cm (33-41 inches, including tail). Good climber w ith distinctive pointed scales. Feeds at night on ant and termite nests in trees, which it tears open with its sharp claws. Sleeps during the day in a tree, or in a hole it digs in the ground.

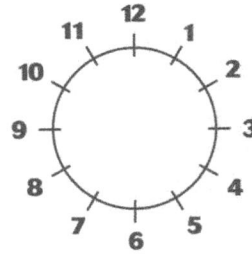

Use the clock face to compare angles of lines and ovals.

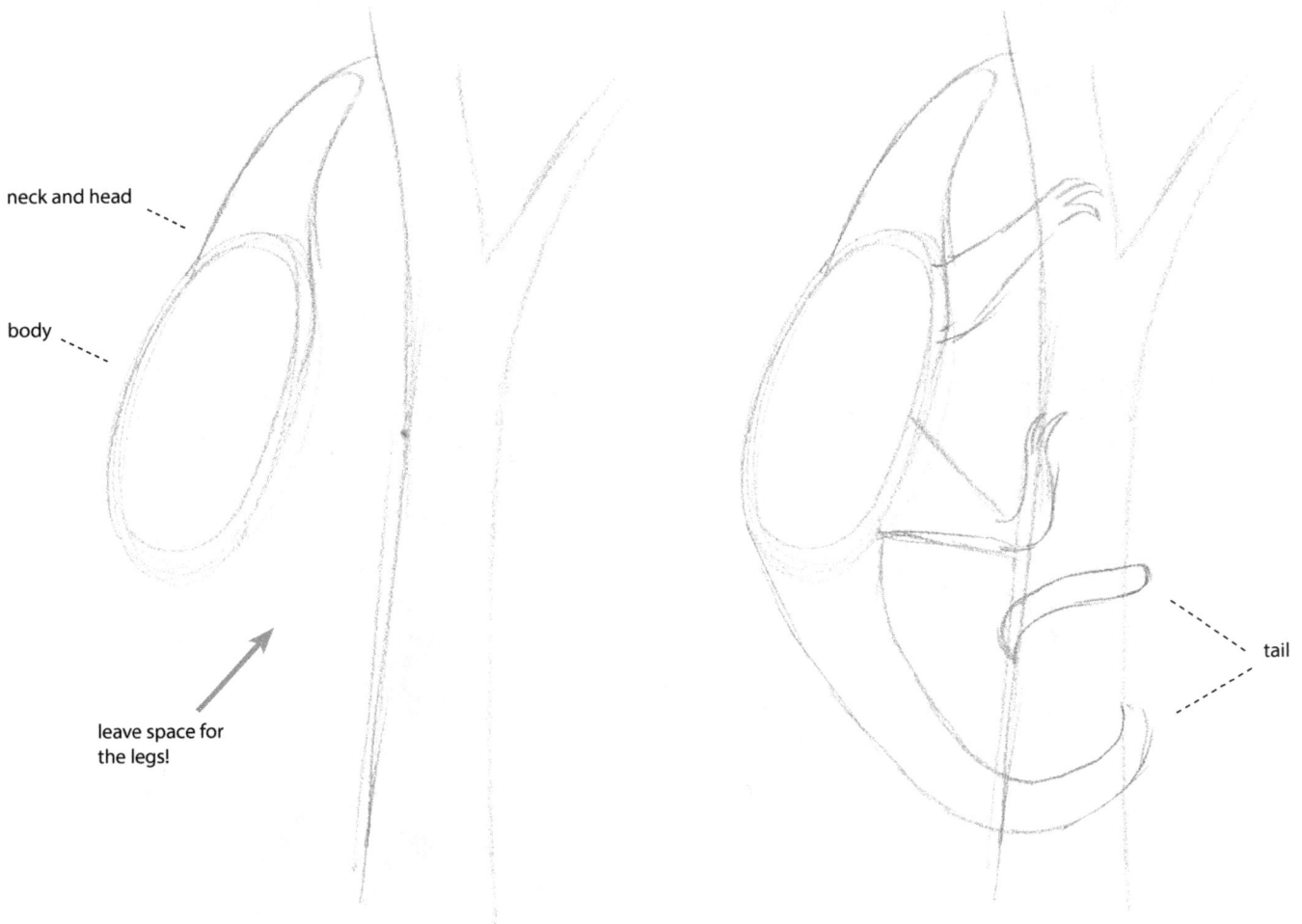

neck and head

body

leave space for the legs!

tail

1. Lightly sketch the tree. Leaving room for the legs, draw a vertical, slightly tilted oval for the body.

   Draw a long curving shape for the neck and head.

2. Add the front leg, with its sharp claws. Draw the L-shaped rear leg. Extend the lower end of the oval to make the tail, curling around the tree.

Turn your paper as you draw to avoid smudging it with your hand.

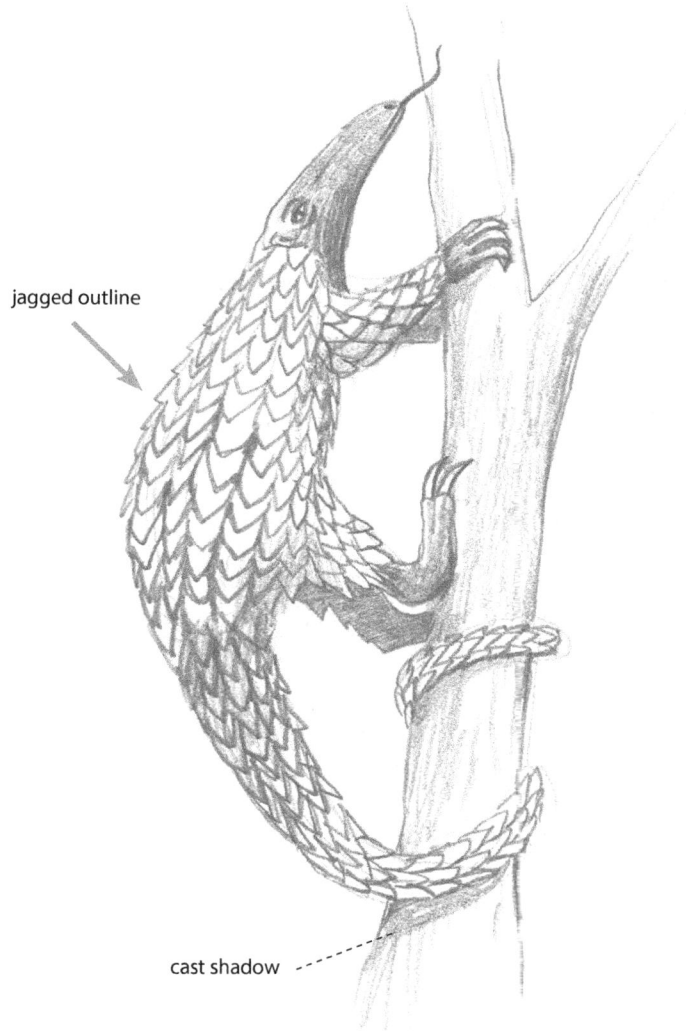

tongue

eye

jagged outline

cast shadow

3. Add the little bit you can see of the other two legs. Draw the long tongue *(termites—yum!)*. Add the eye. Now you have the basic body parts in place. Next draw the scales. Start with light guide lines, like stripes, and draw little V shapes inside them. Notice how they make the back jagged.

4. Cover all but the face and feet with scales. Shade the head and feet, making the legs farthest away darker. Add some texture to the tree with light pencil strokes. Draw a little bit of *cast shadow* on the tree from the tail and legs.

Idea: add some termites on the tree for the pangolin to eat!

Quetzal

Pharomachrus mocinno: Mexico, Central America.

Size: 30 cm (12 inches); tail feathers 61 cm (24 inches). Lives in lower layers of rainforest trees. Feeds on fruit and small animals like lizards and frogs. Long tail feathers, shed every year, were prized by the Maya, to whom the bird was sacred.

1. Start by drawing a light circle for the head. Add the eye and beak.

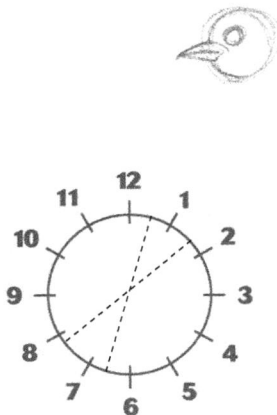

Use the clock face to compare angles of lines and ovals.

2. Make two short lines for the neck and back of the head, then draw a line for the front edge of each wing. Notice the direction each line points; think of a clock face.

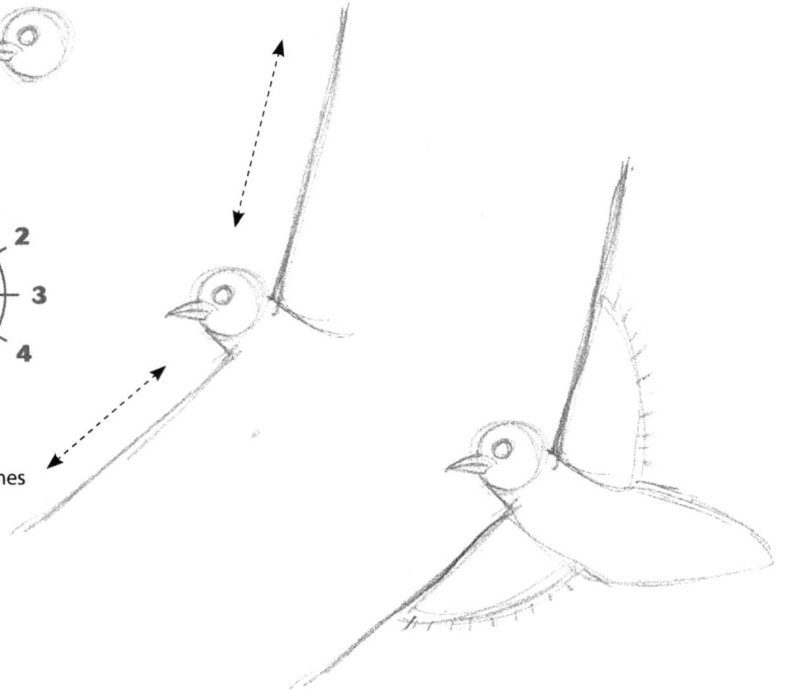

3. Continue the lines of the head to form the body. Add curved lines for the inside part of each wing. Make light marks to plan the spacing of the feathers.

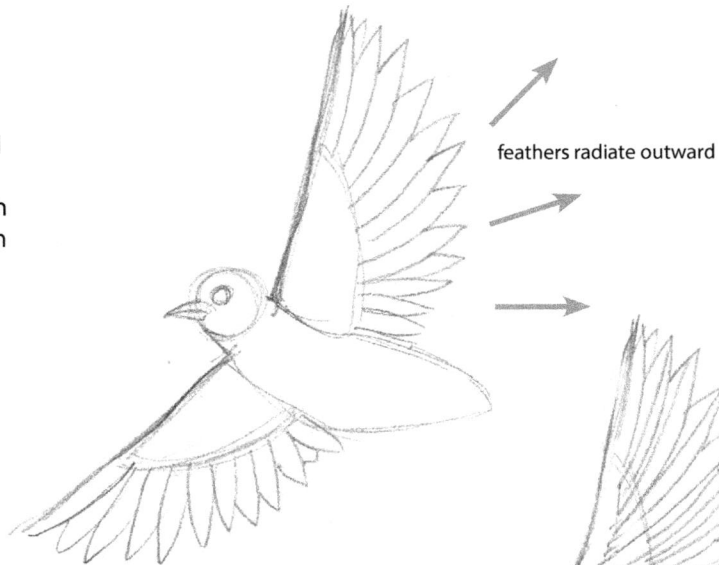

feathers radiate outward

4. Draw the feathers.

5. Add feet and the main tail feathers. Draw short, radiating lines for feathers on the head. Darken the eye, leaving a white spot in it. Add more lines, in the center of each feather. Use short dark pencil strokes for feathers on the head, neck, and breast.

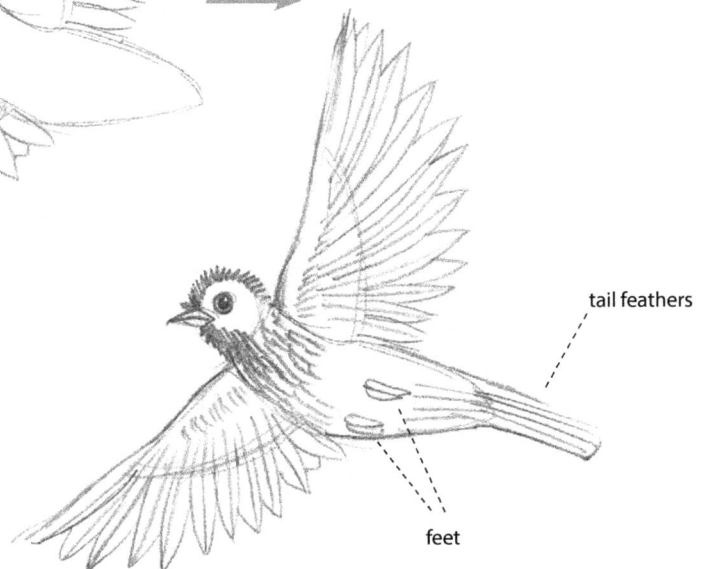

tail feathers

feet

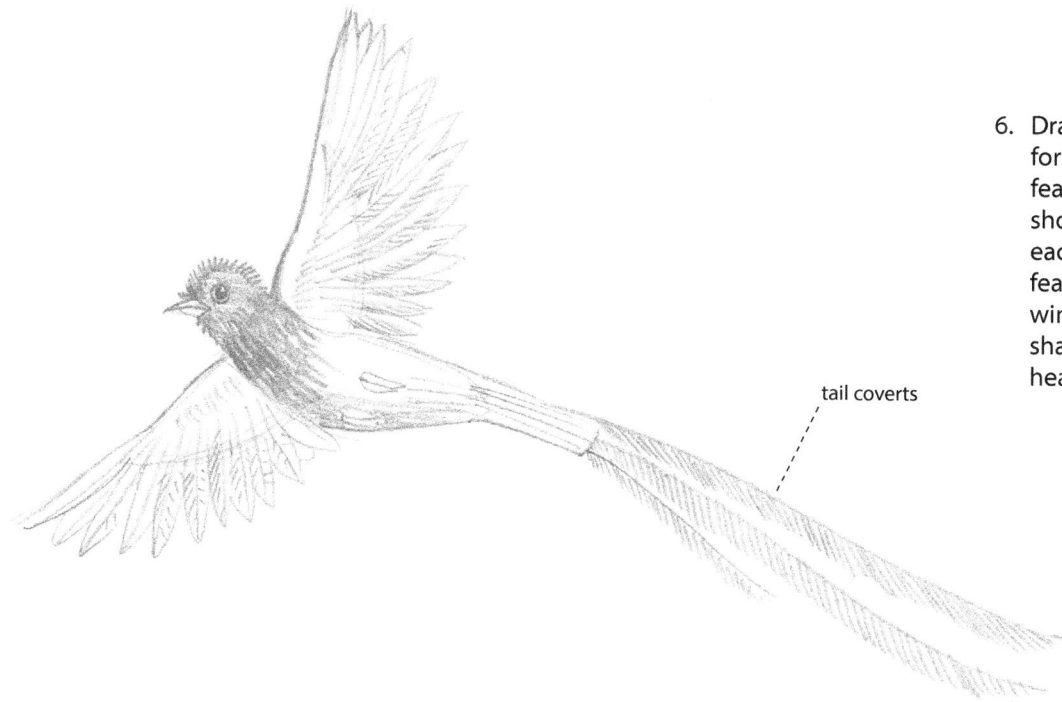

6. Draw long swooping lines for the tail coverts, the long feathers. Make a series of short diagonal lines on each to create the look of a feather. Do the same on the wing feathers. Add more shading and feathers to the head and body.

tail coverts

7. Continue shading the body with short pencil strokes. Go over details and outlines, making them darker and sharper. Quetzals are strikingly colored birds. Add color to your drawing if you wish.

Otherwise, continue to darken shading and feathers.

While your pencil is sharp, go over fine details. As it gets duller, add shading.

When you're satisfied with your drawing, clean up any smudges with your eraser.

! Turn your paper as you draw to avoid smudging it with your hand.

Quite the quetzal!

Slender Loris

Loris tardigradus: Sri Lanka, southern India.

Size: 18-25 cm (7-10 inches). Lives in trees, grasping carefully with its hands. Feeds at night; sleeps during the day in a tree, rolled up in a ball. To eat, it grabs insects (grasshoppers are a favorite), lizards, and small birds with its hands.

leave space for legs!

1. Draw two lines for a branch. Make it interesting by adding a curve or two. Above the branch, lightly draw a rectangle.

Use the clock face to compare angles of lines and ovals.

2. Draw the front legs. The one closest to you has two parts. Notice how you can only see part of the other leg.

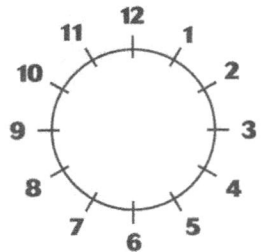

3. Add the rear legs. Notice that they bend opposite to the front legs. Draw the foot.

one leg overlaps the other

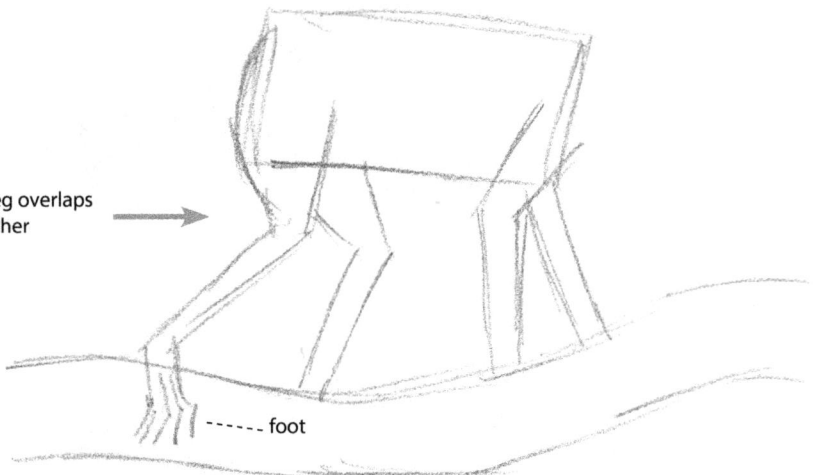

------ foot

space
between eyes

erase

nose

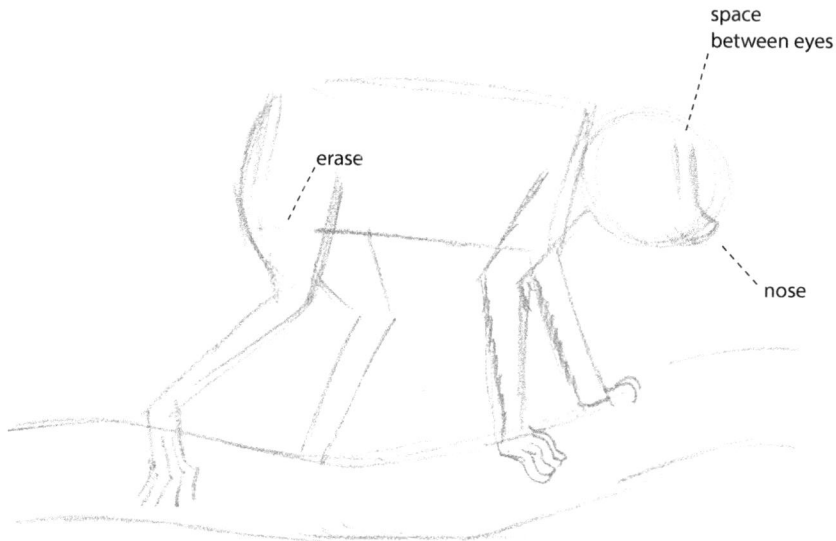

4. Erase the rectangle where the
   rear leg *overlaps* it. Add the
   front feet. Lightly draw an oval
   for the head. Draw two lines to
   leave a white space between
   the eyes. Add a bump for the
   nose.

ears

5. Darken the tip of the nose.
   Add mouth and eyes. Add dark
   areas around each eye. Draw
   the ears. Because you're seeing
   the ears from different angles,
   one looks like a triangle while
   the other appears rounded.
   Add short pencil strokes for fur.
   Start with the darkest areas.

! Turn your paper as you
  draw to avoid smudging
  it with your hand.

6. Add fur to cover the whole
   body. Add texture and shading
   to the branch. Sharper details
   such as the feet.

   Clean up your drawing by
   erasing any smudges.

   *Idea: add epiphytes (see page 115)
   and other vegetation.*

Sloth

Bradypus tridactylus: Central and South America.

Size: 56-67 cm (20-26 in). Ve-ee-ee-ry slo-o-ow mo-oo-ving animal. Spends most of its life hanging upside down in trees. Eats leaves and tender buds.

leave space for the legs!

1. Draw two lines for the tree branch. Make it interesting by adding curves. Below the branch, draw an oval for the sloth's body

2. Draw straight lines upward for the legs, at angles. Notice how one leg *overlaps* part of the one behind it. Draw just part of one front leg, to save space for the head.

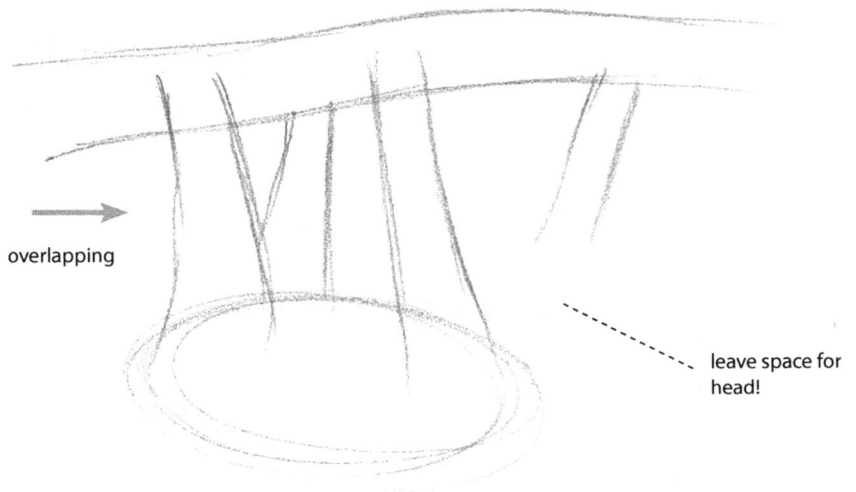

overlapping

leave space for head!

3. Lightly draw a circle for the head. Where is it in relation to the body?

4. Add claws curving around the branch. Begin to add fur with short, downward strokes. The fur on a sloth grows this way because the sloth spends most of its life upside down!

5. Draw the face by starting with a small line for the mouth, at an angle, in the *center* of the circle. Add the nose, and the eyes just to the side of the nose. Draw dark fur areas extending from the eyes.

   Add short pencil strokes for the fur on the arms and legs, and on the back and neck.

6. Keep drawing short pencil lines to add fur to the rest of the body. Notice the areas that are darker, and the direction of the lines. Shade the tree branch. Fix any details you might have missed. Finally, clean up any smudges with your eraser.

Idea: add epiphytes (see p. 115) and other vegetation for this slo-o-ow sloth to hang out with.

Spider Monkey

Ateles paniscus (black spider monkey): Northern South America.

Size: 1-1.4 m (39-55 inches). Tree dweller. Very agile, with a long reach and strong prehensile tail. Spider monkeys eat mostly fruit and nuts, and live in groups of 15-30.

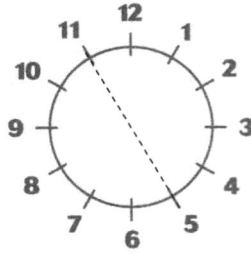

Use the clock face to compare angles of lines and ovals.

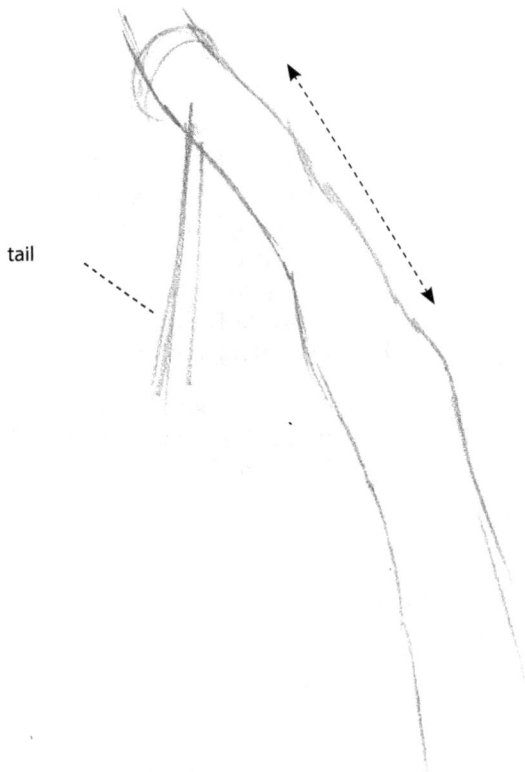

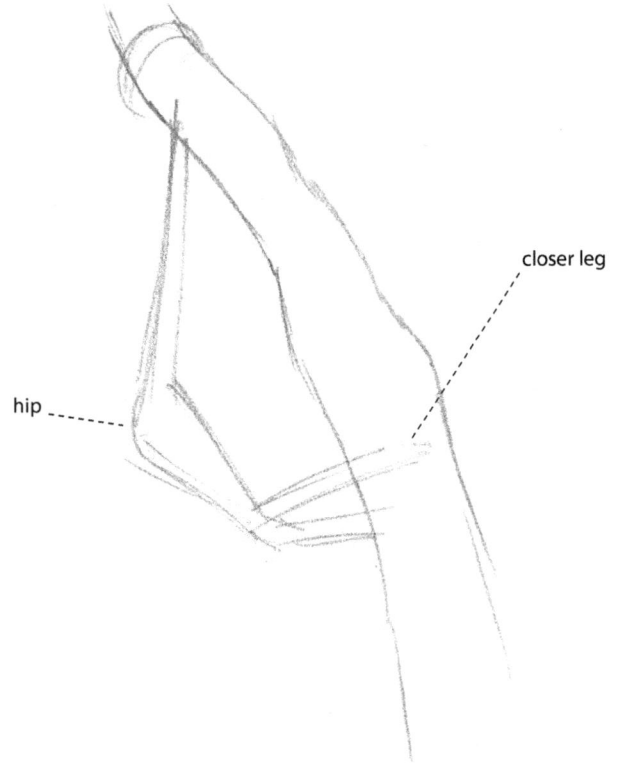

tail

closer leg

hip

1. Draw the tree trunk, lightly. Make the lines interesting, not just straight! Draw two lines straight up for the tail. Then make the tail curling around the tree.

2. Add the hip and rear legs. The leg closer to you *overlaps* part of the one behind.

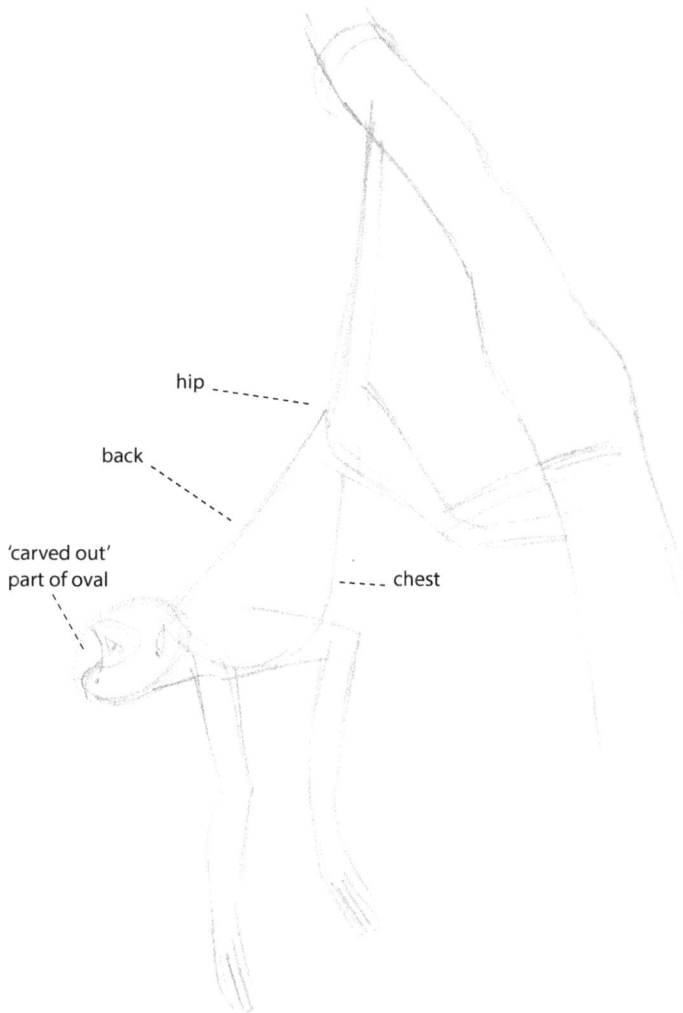

hip

back

'carved out' part of oval

chest

3. From the hip, draw a straight line for the back, and a swooping curve for the chest.

Next, add long, spindly arms.

Lightly draw an oval for the head, then 'carve out' part of it to make the space above the nose. Draw the ear, eye, and nose. Draw a line to connect the head with the body.

4. With many short pencil strokes, add the fur. Notice the direction of the fur on different parts of the body. Also, notice that it's darker in some places.

Look for any lines that might need to be darkened. Add some shadows to the tree trunk. Clean up any smudges with your eraser.

Idea: this monkey looks like it's ready to reach for something, perhaps a vine or a branch. Add vegetation to your drawing, including whatever the spider monkey is about to reach for.

Tamandua

Tamandua mexicana: Southern Mexico to South America.

Size: 1.1 m (43 in) including tail. Tree-dwelling anteater with prehensile tail. Tears open nests with its strong claws, grabs ants and termites with its long, sticky tongue.

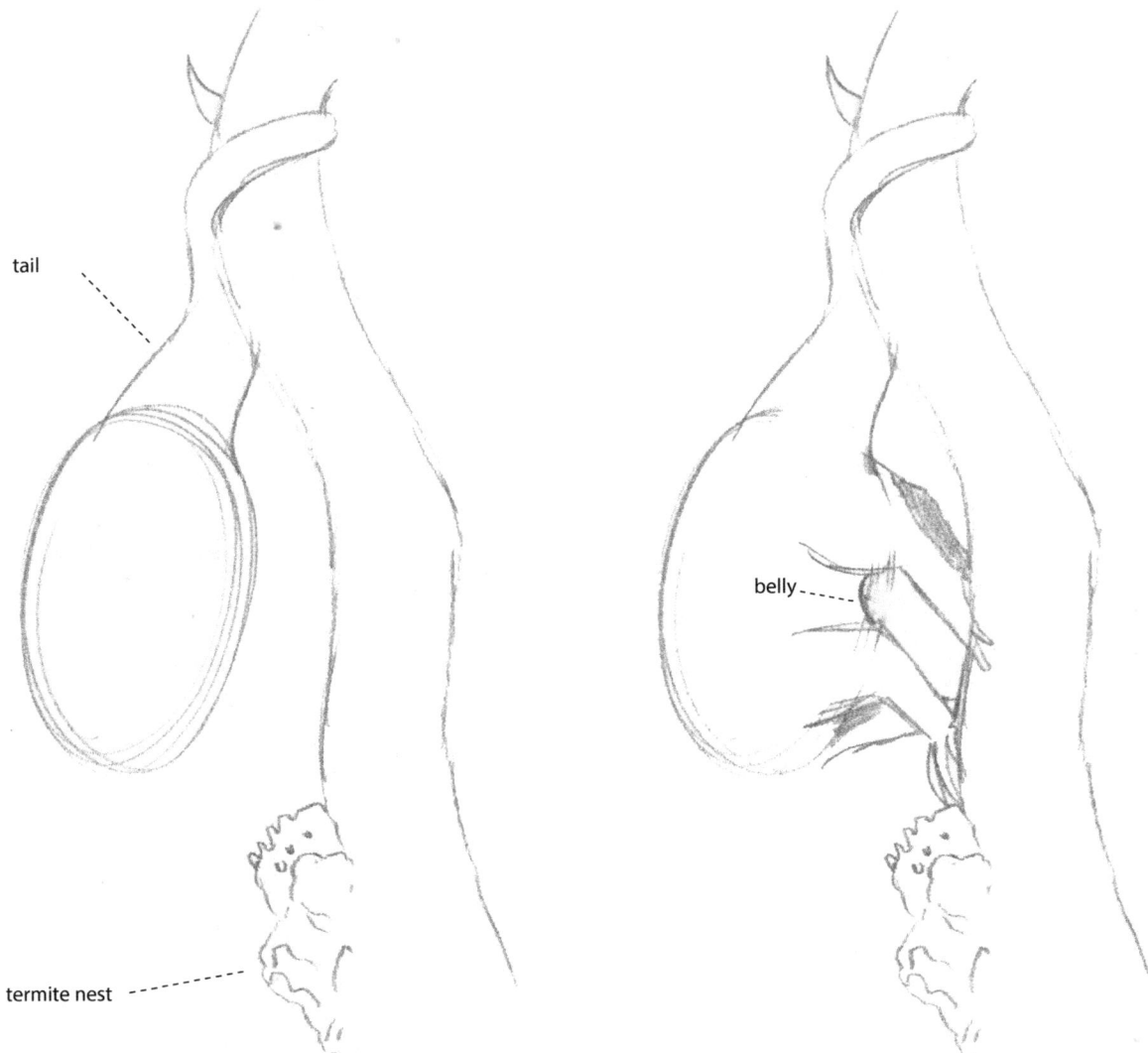

tail

termite nest

belly

1. Start by drawing an interesting tree trunk, which curves back and forth a little. At the bottom, draw a termite nest—it doesn't have to be fancy.

    Drawing lightly, make an oval for the tamandua's body. Then add the tail, curling up and around the tree.

2. Add the legs. Watch where they *overlap* each other. Draw lightly: remember, you can always make lines darker. Draw the sharp claws that the tamandua uses to tear open termite nests.

    Lightly erase parts of the oval where it *overlaps* the legs and tail. Make the belly curve inward between the front and rear legs.

! Turn your paper as you draw to avoid smudging it with your hand.

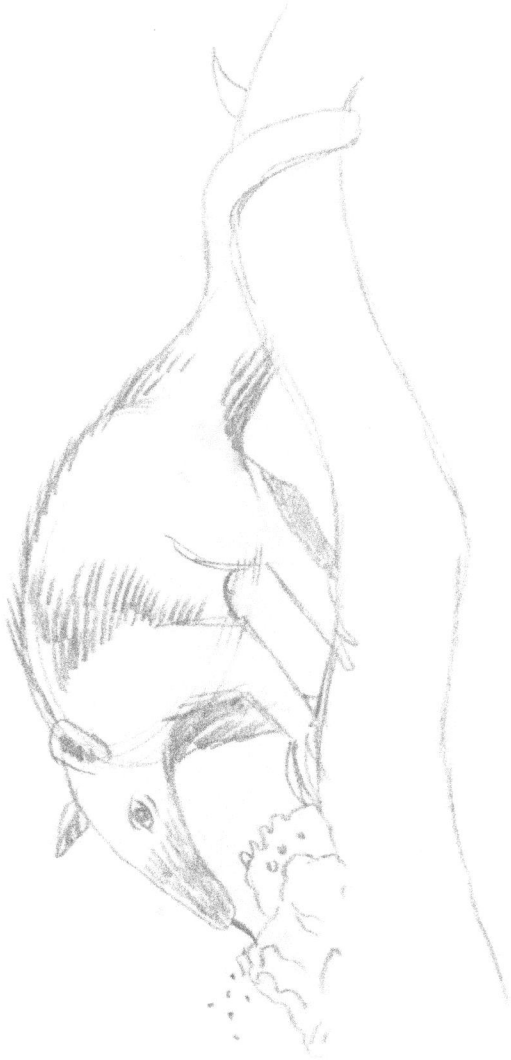

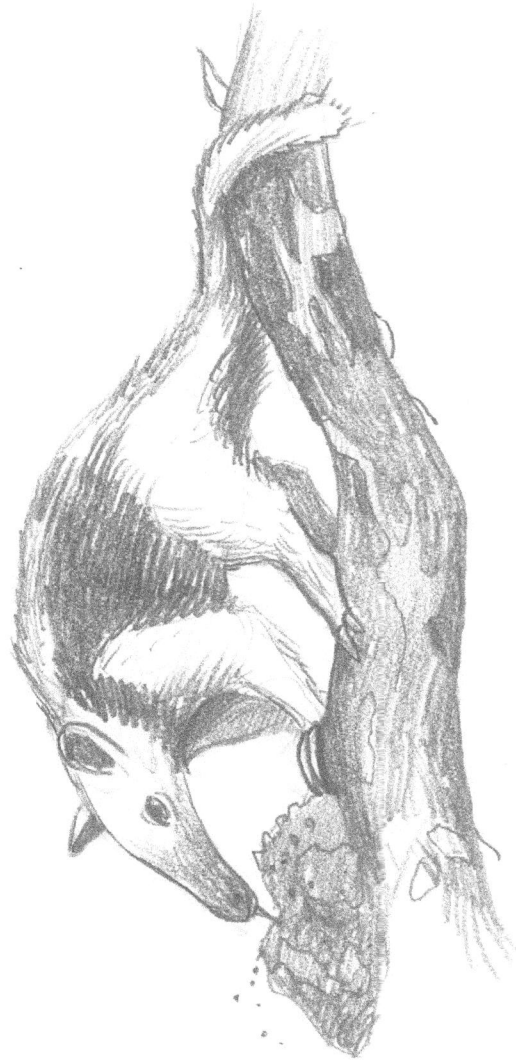

3. Draw the head, two curved lines with a rounded end where the tongue sticks out, scooping up delicious termites (yum!).

    Add the almond-shaped eye and the ears.

    Look at the final drawing, noticing light and dark areas. Draw the dark fur with short pencil strokes.

4. Add more dark fur on the body. Leave the legs light. Draw shapes on the tree trunk to suggest peeling bark. Shade the tree trunk.

    With a sharp pencil, sharpen important details such as the face and claws.

    Use your eraser to clean up any smudges.

    Extra bright idea: when you're finished, put your drawing on the wall where you can admire it the next time you and your friends are snacking on termites.

Tapir

Tapirus terrestris (Brazilian tapir): South America.

Size: 2m (6.5 ft). Covered with short, bristly hair. Found near water (good swimmer). Feeds at night on leaves, buds, shoots, and small branches.

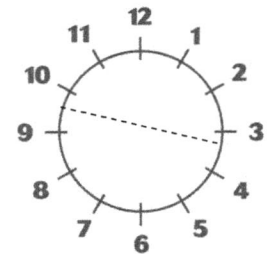

Use the clock face to compare angles of lines and ovals.

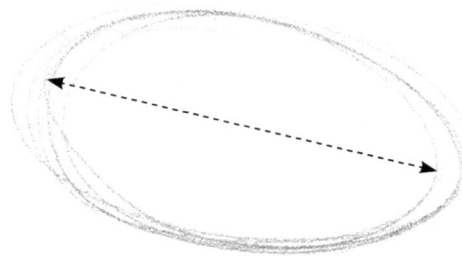

1. Drawing a tapir is quite easy. Start with a line for the ground, and above it, draw a slightly tilted oval.

2. From the right side of the oval, draw the front leg with a bend in the middle, where it crosses the bottom of the oval. Erase the oval where the leg *overlaps* it. Draw the other front leg.

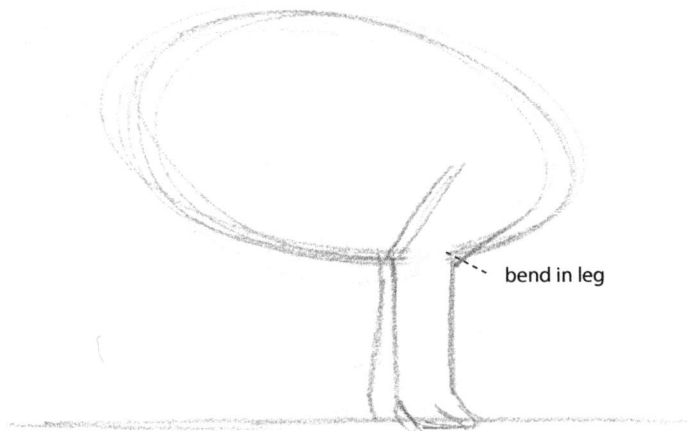

bend in leg

3. Draw the short tail, and the rear legs. Notice that the bend in the rear legs occurs well below the oval of the body, unlike the front legs.

4. Lightly draw another oval for the head. Connect it to the body with two lines for the neck.

5. In the middle of the oval, draw an almond shape for the eye. Extend the top of the head to make the nose. From the nose, draw the mouth and the neck. Carefully erase what's left of the head oval.

   Draw some leaves in the tapir's mouth. Add the short fur strokes above the eye. Draw the ears.

   What a pretty face!

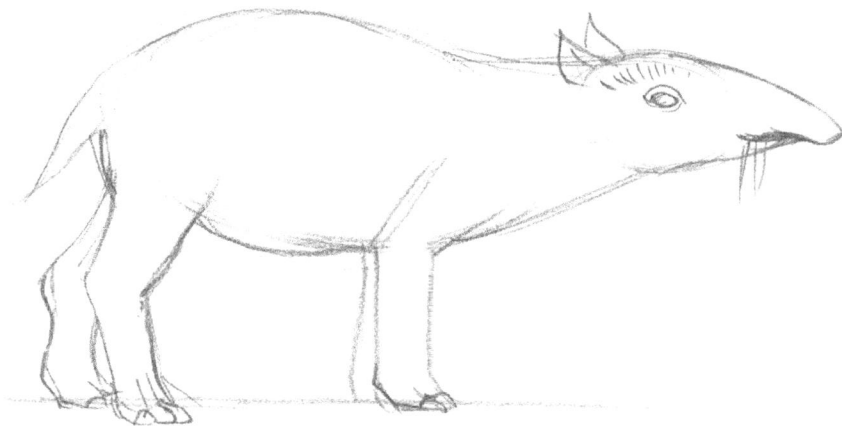

6. To finish your drawing, make many short pencil lines for the fur. Notice which places are dark, and which are light. Darken outlines in shadow areas, such as underneath the body. Add bristly marks on the outline of the back.

   Add grass on the ground, and a bit of *cast shadow*, then clean up any smudges with your eraser and you're done!

! Turn your paper as you draw to avoid smudging it with your hand.

Idea: add bushes and trees in the background.

Toucan

Ramphastos toco (Toco toucan): South America, mainly Amazon basin.

Size: 61 cm (24 inches). Toucans eat a variety of fruits and large insects. Strong claws help them hang onto tree branches. Toucans grab food with their beak, then toss their head backwards to get it into their mouth.

Use the clock face to compare angles of lines and ovals.

1. Draw the horizontal branch.

   Above it, at an angle, draw a titled oval, not quite touching the branch.

   Add vertical lines for the legs, with claws wrapping around the branch.

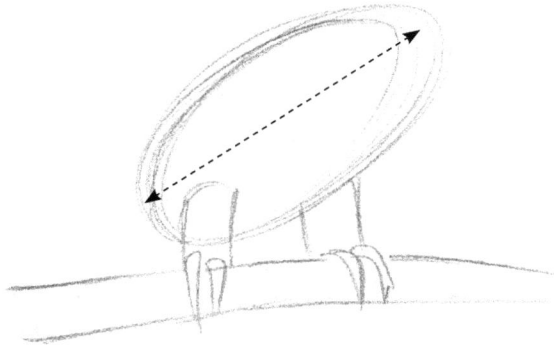

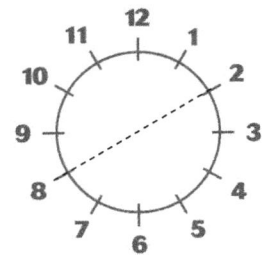

shoulder

2. Add the wing, with a slight bulge at the shoulder.

   Draw lines on the wing to suggest feathers.

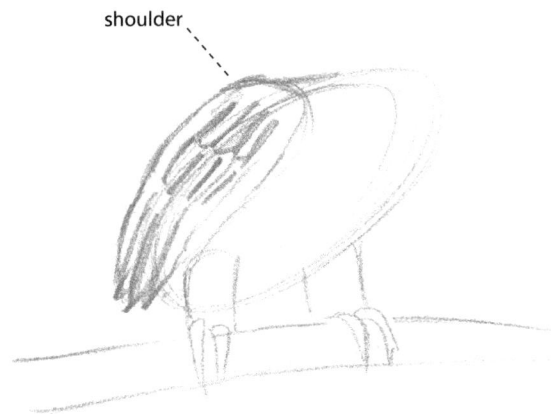

3. Extend the bottom of the oval for the tail. Draw the end of the tail behind and below the branch, with lines for feathers. Add small curved lines on the claws. Shade the leg.

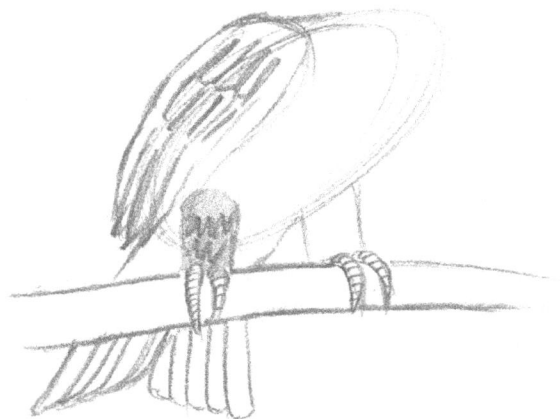

> **!** Turn your paper as you draw to avoid smudging it with your hand.

vertical!

throat

white area

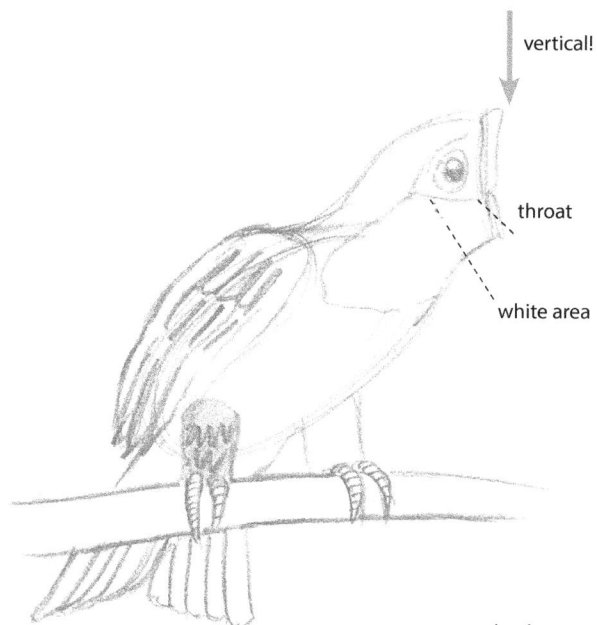

4. Draw a line from the shoulder for the top of the head. Make the front of the head vertical where the beak attaches. Draw the throat. Add the eye, and the triangle around it. Outline the white area on the front of the body.

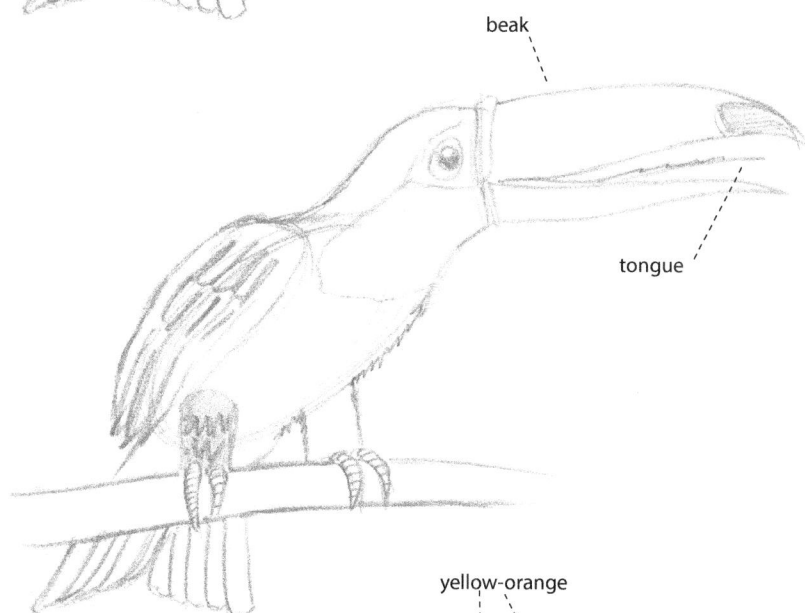

beak

tongue

5. Now draw the beak, looking carefully at how it curves. Make the top part of the beak wider than the bottom. Add the dark spot at the tip. Draw the tongue.

yellow-orange

red

6. Look at the final drawing. Shade or color the dark areas of the bird. Add the pattern to the beak. Darken lines that seem important. Add shading to the branch.

While your pencil is sharp, go over fine details. As it gets duller, add shading.

Look at your drawing in a mirror (or through the back of the paper) to spot any areas you can make better.

Clean up any smudges with your eraser.

Idea: draw a berry in the toucan's beak. Add color to your drawing…

Vine Snake

Oxybelis fulgidus: Central America and part of South America.

Size: 1.5-2 m (5-6.5 feet). Slow-moving predator barely a half inch (1.25 cm) wide. Hard to see because it looks like a vine. Eats lizards and steals young birds from nests.

1. Start by drawing a thin branch with a few leaves. Your drawing doesn't have to look exactly like mine!

   Draw lightly at first!

2. Lightly sketch the outline of the snake. Make it curve this way and that. Position the snake's body so that it *overlaps* branches and leaves in several places. This drawing works best when the snake looks like it's slithering behind and in front of the branches.

> ❗ Turn your paper as you draw to avoid smudging it with your hand.

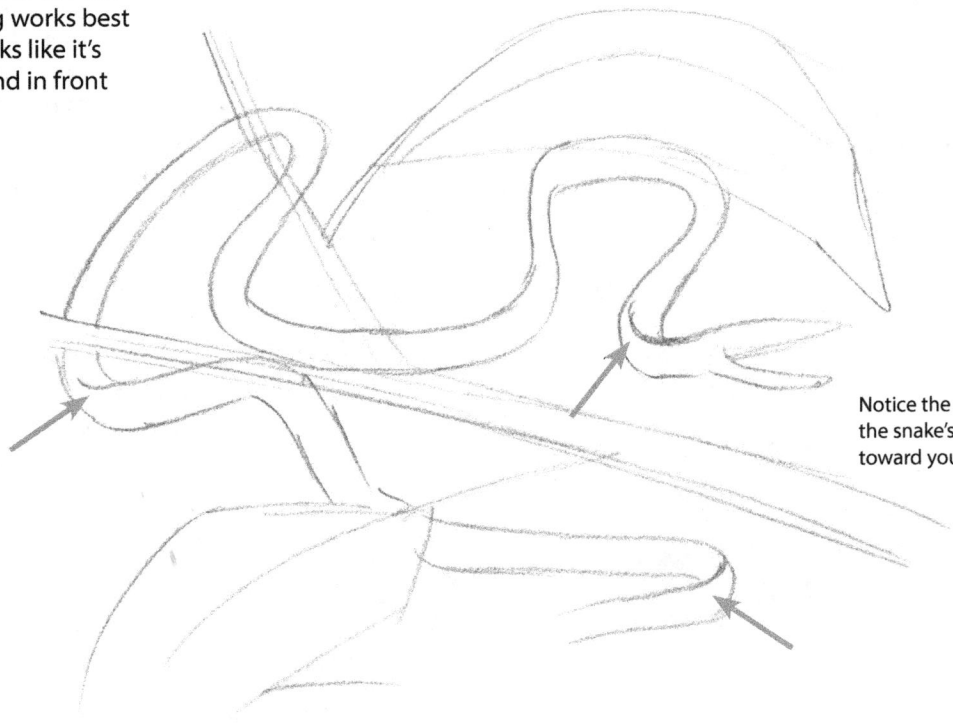

Notice the extra lines where the snake's body comes toward you (arrows).

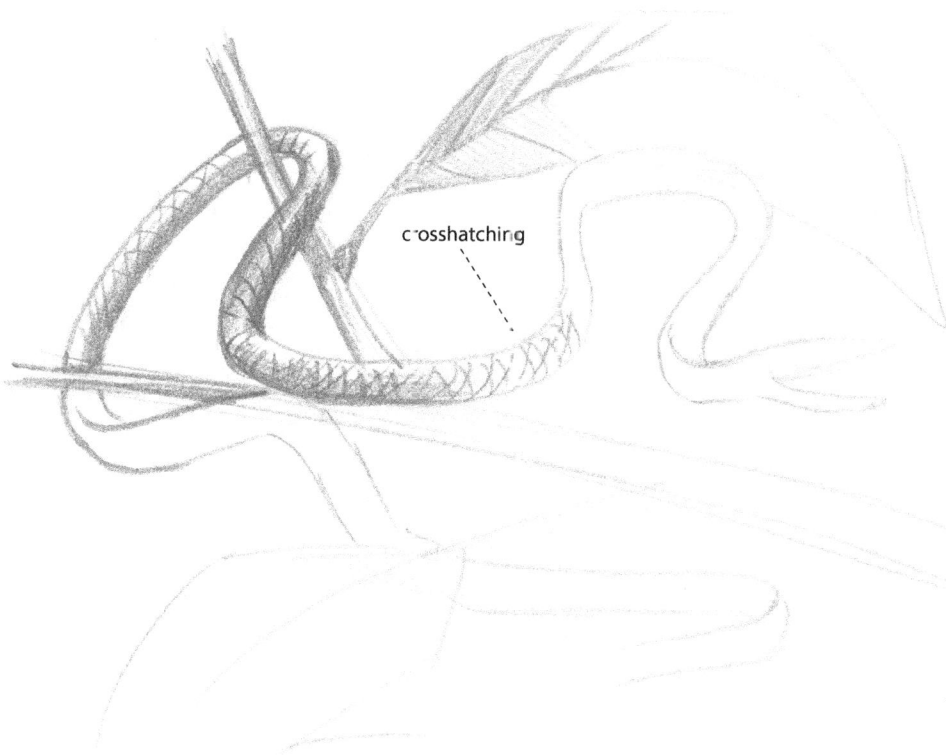

3. Once you have the shape of the snake sketched lightly, the next step is to go over it, bit by bit:

- Darken outlines

- Add curved crosshatching to suggest scales

- Shade the bottom parts darker than the top parts.

- Add extra shading for cast shadows

  While your pencil is sharp, go over fine details. As it gets duller, add shading.

crosshatching

4. Work slowly. Take your time to get details right! Every few minutes, take a look at your whole drawing—are parts too dark? Too light?

   Clean up any smudges with your eraser.

Idea: draw a lizard or young bird in the snake's mouth!

Other ideas

When animals appear in the rainforest, chances are you won't see the whole animal because of the huge amount of vegetation all around them. To make your drawing more interesting, add foliage.

You'll find that it helps to draw the whole animal lightly, then draw the foreground elements, whether trees or leaves. Try not to cover up the most important parts of the drawing—for example, in the picture of the jaguar (right), I wouldn't want a leaf covering its face!

These two drawings are quick sketches—just a way of playing with ideas, to see what looks good and what doesn't. If I wanted to do a finished drawing of the howler monkey (below, right), I might do another sketch first, moving the leaves around to find a better arrangement.

The straight lines on the outside "crop" the drawing, to give a better idea how the finished drawing might appear.

1

2

Try including some of these in your drawings:

1) Two of many leaf forms you can find in the rainforest.
2) Epiphytes: plants that live in the branches of trees high above the forest floor.
3. Buttressed roots that help tall trees stand securely in shallow soil.
4. Vines grow in abundance, and grow into one another over time. This could become a great design for a border for your drawing!

4

3

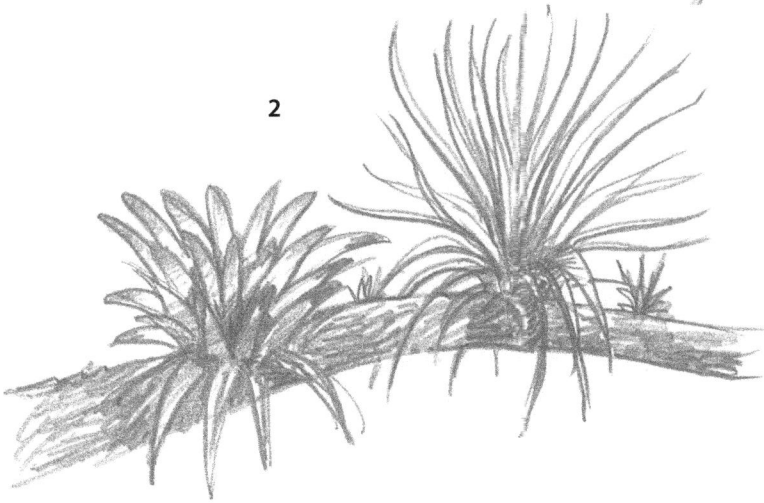

DRAW
DESERT ANIMALS

What you will need

- Draw with a pencil that's longer than your finger. 2B or 3B pencils work well.

- Use colored pencils if you have them.

- Sharpen your pencil when it gets dull!

- Find an eraser – the one on your pencil will disappear quickly. A knead-able one works best.

- For practice drawings, use recycled paper – for example, draw on the back of old photocopies or computer printouts.

- Plan to keep your drawings – put the date on each.

- Positive attitude. Forget "I can't." Say, "I'm learning. I'm figuring this out. I did this part well; now I'm going to work on the harder part. I'm not stopping until I get it RIGHT!"

Three steps to a great drawing

1) Look carefully at your *reference material*. This could be an actual animal, or an image from a book or the internet. See the shapes and pieces and how they fit together. Next, lightly sketch the shapes in the right place.

   When you sketch lightly, you can easily correct any mistakes before they ruin your drawing.

2) Make sure you have all the shapes and pieces in the right place. Adjust lines, redraw pieces that don't look right, and erase sketch lines you no longer need.

3) Finally, spend as much time as you need to make your drawing jump off the page. Darken lines at emphasis points: joints, feet, points of claws, horns, spikes, and eyes, for example. Add fur, feathers, or scales, and shading. Clean up any smudges with your eraser, then date and save your drawing in a portfolio (see below).

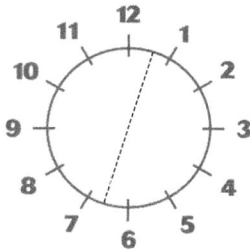

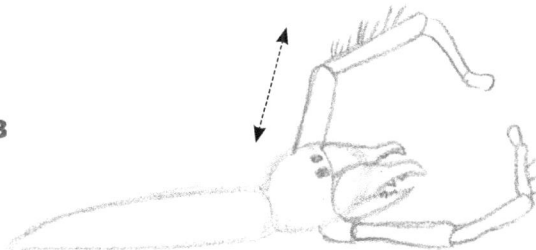

Clock faces appear from time to time. Use them as a reference to see the tilt of ovals, legs, and other angles in the drawing.

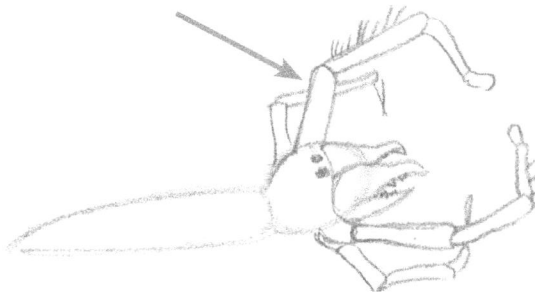

Light arrows point out visual elements of the drawing that may not be obvious to you—in this example, where one leg overlaps another.

pedipalps

Labels will help you identify the parts of the animal mentioned in the text.

For colorful inspiration and ideas, follow our Desert Animals Pinterest feed:

drawbooks.com/desert

Addax antelope

Addax nasomaculatus, Africa.
Height: .9 –1.2 m (3–4')

An addax never drinks, getting all the moisture it needs from its food. Its large, wide-spreading hooves are adapted to walking on soft sand. Addax are nomads, traveling in herds of 20 to 200. They seem to have a special ability to locate the patches of desert vegetation that suddenly sprout after a downpour. Color varies from animal to animal, but they all have a patch of dark brown hair on the forehead.

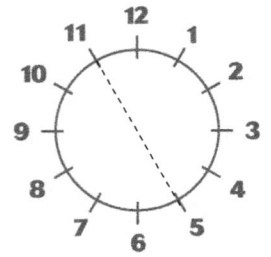

1. Begin with two ovals. Note the tilt of the rear leg oval. Draw lines to connect the ovals, top and bottom.

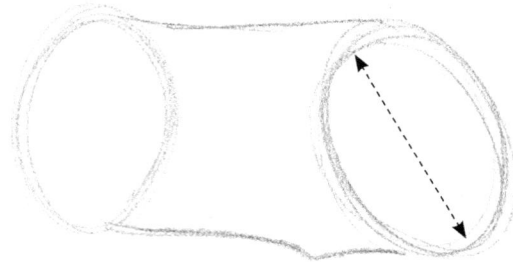

2. Sketch a circle for the head, centered on the top of the shoulder. Sketch a smaller circle for the nose. Draw lines to connect the head and nose. Add ears. Draw jagged lines to connect the head to the body.

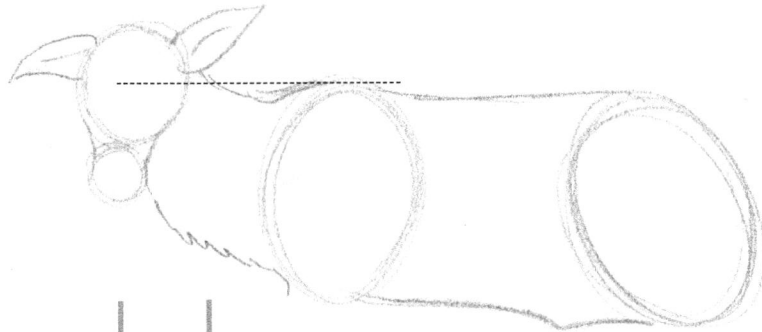

3. Draw the eyes. Notice how one sits on the edge of the circle. Add curved guide lines for the facial pattern.

   Sketch small, light circles for the leg joints. Draw the front and rear legs. Notice how the rear leg follows the tilt of the oval above it. Add the tail.

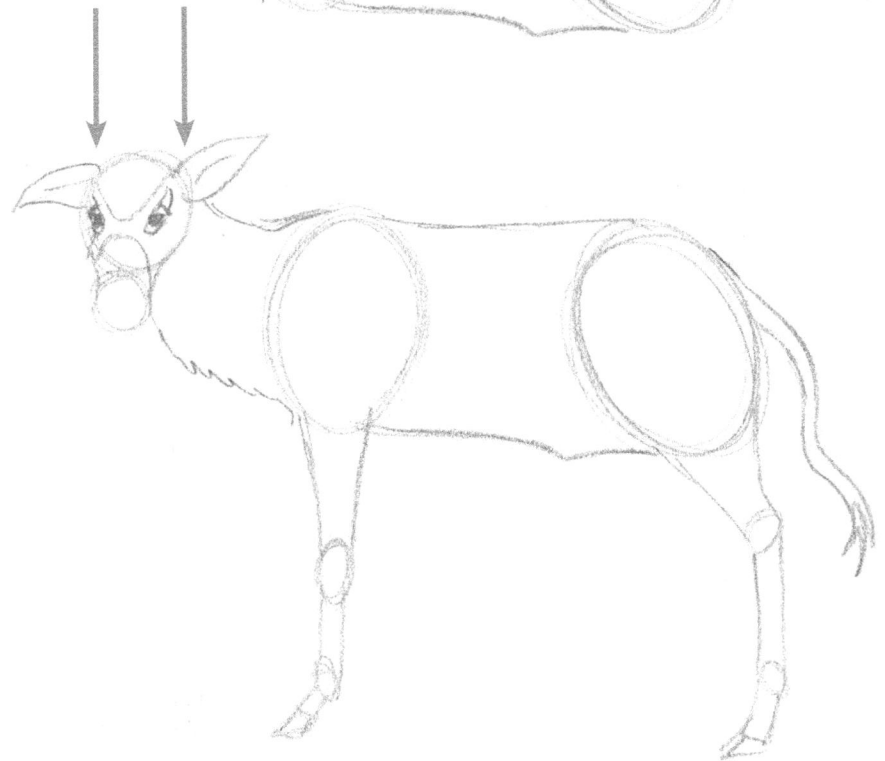

4. Lightly draw the graceful, spiralling horns, then begin to add small curved lines for the ridges on them. Add nostrils and the mouth. Shade the darker area of the face and ear.

Lightly sketch the joints and limbs of the other two legs. Note where each line intersects the overlapping lines of the body or leg.

5. Carefully erase "leftover" ovals before moving to the final step. Starting with the darkest areas of the body, add light, short pencil strokes for fur.

Because the addax is light colored, you don't need to shade the whole body. Make your pencil strokes lighter and lighter into the white highlight area.

Clean up any smudges with your eraser. Put today's date on your drawing and save it in your portfolio!

Arabian Oryx

Oryx leucoryx. E Saudi Arabia.
Size: 2 m (6'3") long

The only oryx found outside Africa, this small, rare animal travels widely in extreme desert conditions to find grass and shrub to eat. It shelters from the sun by scraping a hollow under a bush or on the side of a sand dune. This oryx has been over hunted for its hide, meat, and horns. Protected by law, it may be extinct in the wild (the last wild one seen was in 1972). It lives in captivity though, and hopefully can be reintroduced to its native habitat.

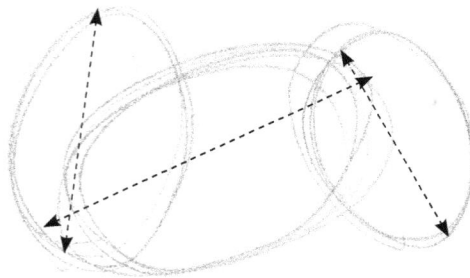

1. Start this drawing by lightly drawing three tilting ovals. Carefully note their angles.

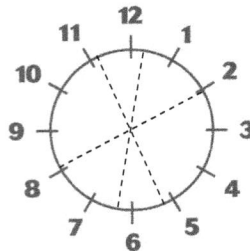

2. Make a light circle for the head, a smaller one for the nose, and curved lines for the neck. Add the eye, halfway up the head circle and to the left. Draw the ears. Add the bottom neck line. Draw a line to connect the head with the top of the body, and continue your line along the top— connecting all body ovals. Add the swishing tail. Draw the bottom of the neck.

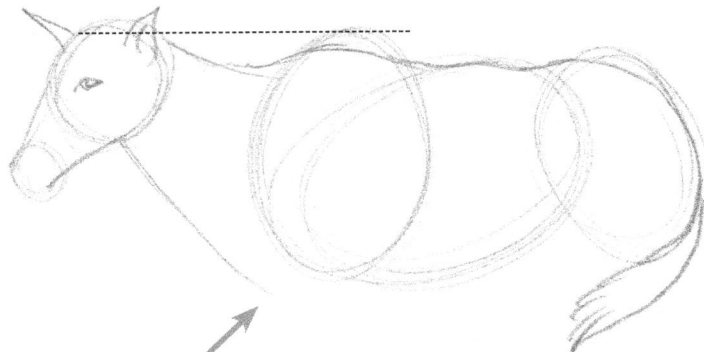

3. Starting with circles for the joints, draw the two closest (left) legs. Note the angles of the rear leg.

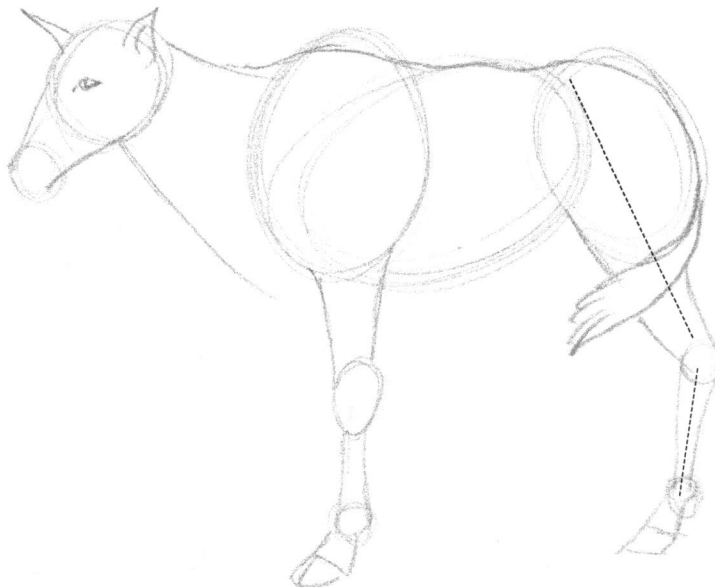

4. In the same way, draw the other two legs. Notice how the bottom of the neck meets the front leg. Connect the belly and the rear leg.

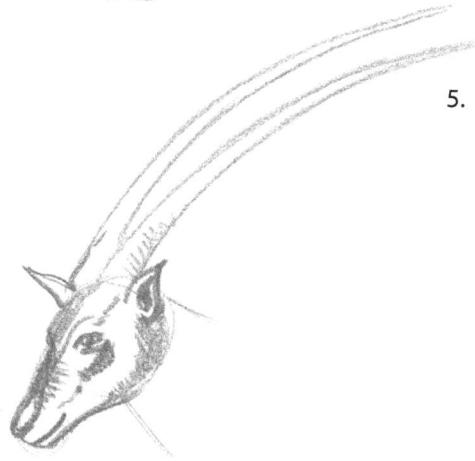

5. Lightly draw the long, curved horns.

   When drawing the horns, turn the paper so that the curve comes naturally.

   To avoid smudging, place a clean paper over the part already drawn. Rest the heel of your hand on this, and keep it still, or it might smudge the drawing underneath.

   Add the mouth and nose. Carefully shade the face to make the facial patterns.

6. Using short pencil strokes, continue shading the body. Pay attention to the direction of the lines and their darkness. Leave the belly light. Darken the hooves and add a little bit of grass. Make a couple of lines for distant sand dunes behind the oryx.

   Add color if you wish.

Orsome Oryx! Clean up any smudges with your eraser, put today's date on your drawing and save it in your portfolio!

Arabian Toad-Headed Agamid

Phrynocephalus nejdensis. SW Asia. Size: up to 12.5 cm (5").

This burrowing lizard digs short tunnels for shelter. It can also bury itself in sand by wriggling from side to side. It eats mainly insects but also some flowers and leaves. If alarmed, it will stand high on its legs, and roll and unroll its tail; this is its defensive posture.

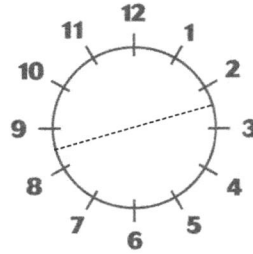

1. Begin by lightly sketching the tilted horizontal oval of the body. Compare the tilt of the oval to the clock face. To the oval, add gently curving lines for the tail. At the other end, draw a rounder oval for the head, and connect it to the body with two short lines for the neck.

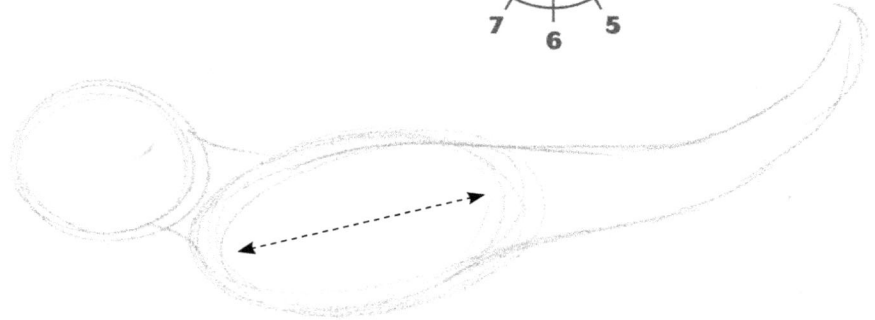

2. Draw one smooth line over the top of the head, neck, and back, connecting the ovals and the tail. Carefully add the spiralling tip of the tail. Draw small curves to locate the attachment points for the legs.

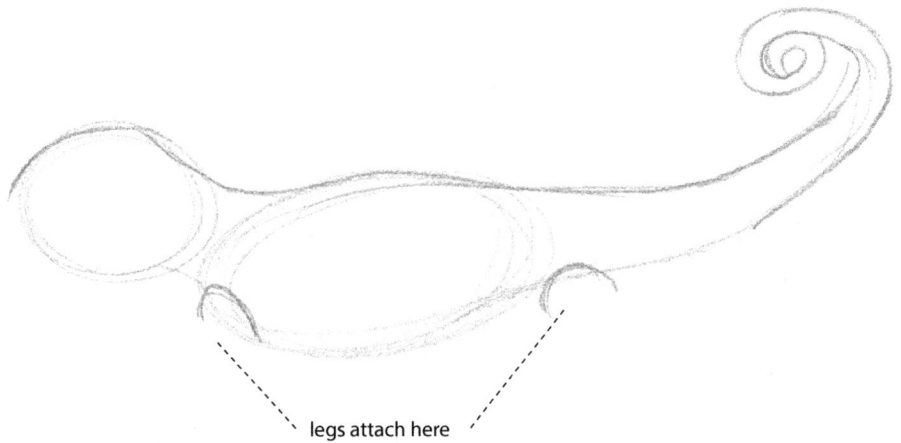

legs attach here

3. As always when drawing limbs, use small, light circles to mark the joints. Add curved lines to finish the legs. Notice the distinct curves in the rear leg. Draw the feet.

right rear leg

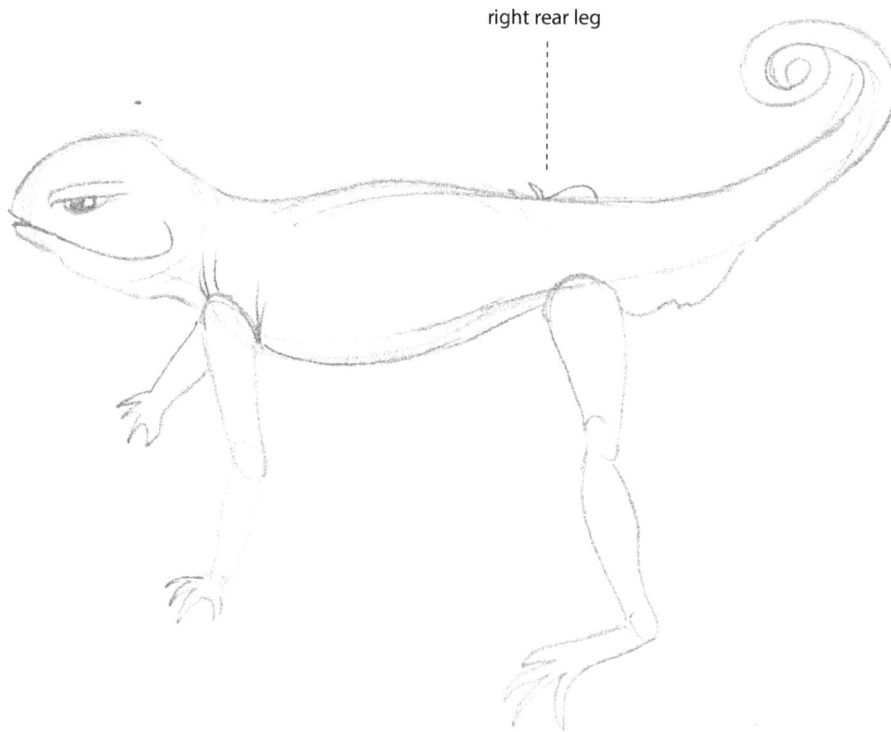

4. Draw the tilted eye with its thick eyebrow above. Add the mouth, swooping down and back into the jaw line. Draw the small visible parts of the two legs on the far side of the lizard. Refine the bottom of the neck, belly, and tail, adding the curved flaps just behind the rear leg.

5. To complete our Toad-Headed friend, lightly outline the stripes on the legs and tail, and the spots on the back. Carefully shade from one end to the other and back again, looking for any details you missed. Add the *cast shadow* beneath.

Go over the outline with a sharpened pencil. Clean up any smudges with your eraser.

Toadally cool, dude! Put today's date on your drawing and save it in your portfolio!

Bactrian camel

Camelus ferus. Central Asia, Northern Africa, Middle East.
Size: 3 m (~10') long, 2 m (6'3") high at shoulder

Bactrian camels have two humps–think of the letter B turned on its side. The humps store fat to help them survive when food is scarce. They eat grass, and foliage of bushes and trees. Their long, shaggy hair keeps them warm in the winter, but they shed it in the summer. They move slowly with a rolling gait, able to lift two legs on the same side at the same time.

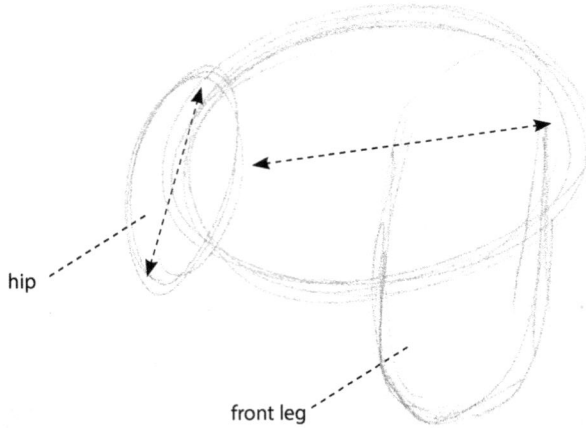

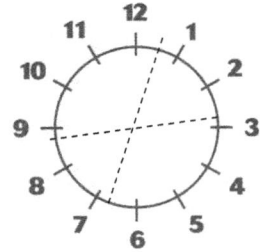

1. Start by lightly sketching the large, slightly tilted oval of the body. *Intersecting* it, draw the small, narrow oval of the hip. Notice how it tilts. Add a U shape for the shaggy front leg, which extends below the body.

2. Add two humps on the back. Sketch a circle for the head. Note how it aligns with the first oval you drew. Add a short line connecting it to the back, and a long, shaggy, U shape for the neck. Draw the tail.

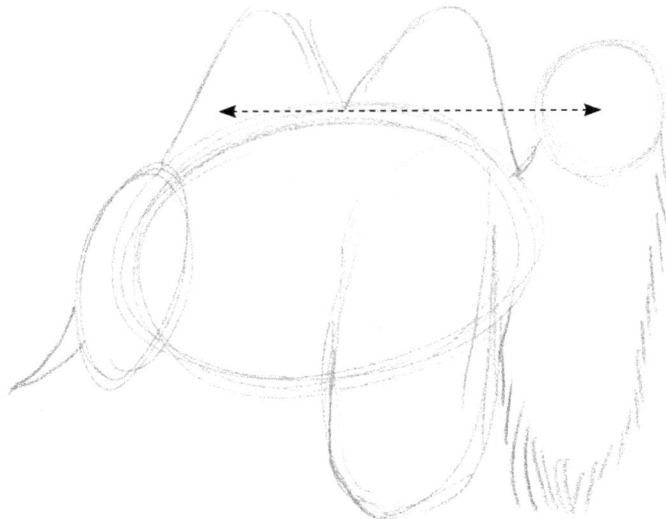

3. Add ears and details to the face. Notice how each detail aligns with the guide.

   Draw the eyes between the nostrils and ears. Use short pencil strokes to make the shaggy hair texture on the face and neck.

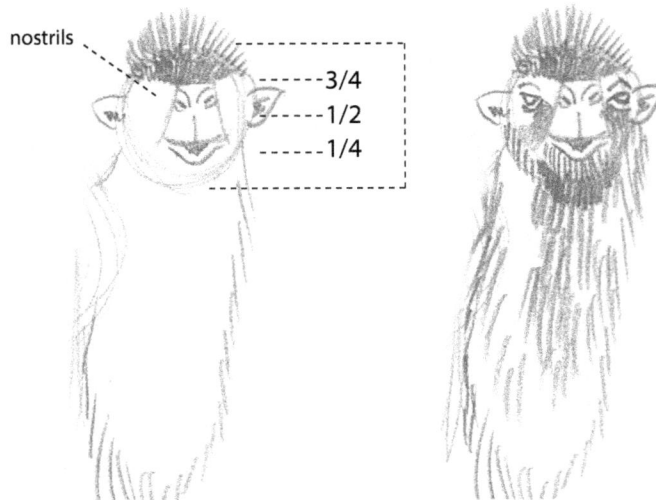

hip

front leg

Where does the head lie in relation to the first oval you drew?

nostrils

3/4
1/2
1/4

4. Continue the front leg with small ovals for the leg joints. Draw wide, low ovals for the hooves, and curving lines connecting them to the top part of the leg. Notice how one leg overlaps part of the other. Add toes.

Using similar ovals and lines, complete the rear legs. Add the tail.

When the camel kneels, thick callus builds up on the legs. On your body, the calluses or the rear leg would be on your knees; the ones in front on the back of your wrists.

toes

5. Finish your drawing by carefully adding short pencil strokes to shade the body and add texture.

Take your time. Which parts are darkest? Which are lightest? What direction do the lines run on each part of the body?

Add a small *cast shadow* under the camel. Clean up any smudges with your eraser.

Oh, by the way, camels spit. Does your camel look like it's about to spit at you?

Camel spider (Wind scorpion)

Solifugida, or Solipugida. Africa, Orient, America, Southern Spain.
Size: up to 15 cm (6") span across outstretched legs

These hairy, fast-moving arachnids (spider relatives) hunt for insects at night, sometimes eating lizards, small mammals and birds. They have strong chelicerae (that's what an arachnid's "jaws" are called), with which they chop, squash, and chew the victim, which ends up a formless lump. They may move as fast as 16 km/h (10 mph). Also known as wind scorpions or sun spiders, they like the drier parts of the desert and stay away from oases.

Yikes! This one looks complicated! Start with the simplest shapes, and add one piece at a time.

1. Sketch the two main body parts: one long and bullet-shaped; the other almost a circle.

2. Add dots for eyes. Draw the huge jaw on the closer side of the head, and the little bit of jaw visible on the other side.

3. Just behind the jaw, add the first segment of the first *pedipalp* (feeler: like legs but without claws), then the next segment.

4. Add remaining segments, and four visible segments of the other pedipalp.

5. Draw the second set of feeler legs. Notice how they go *under* the first set, adding *depth* to your drawing.

6. The third set of legs supports the spider. These walking legs go straight out to the side. Draw them thicker, and stronger.

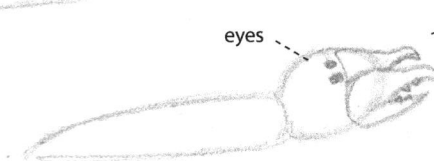

eyes

Jaws (chelicerae)– the biggest in proportion to its body of any living creature!

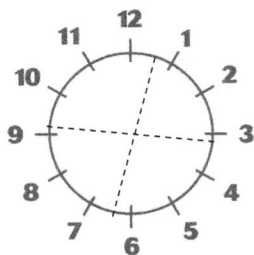

When drawing ovals or angled lines, compare their tilt to the clock face.

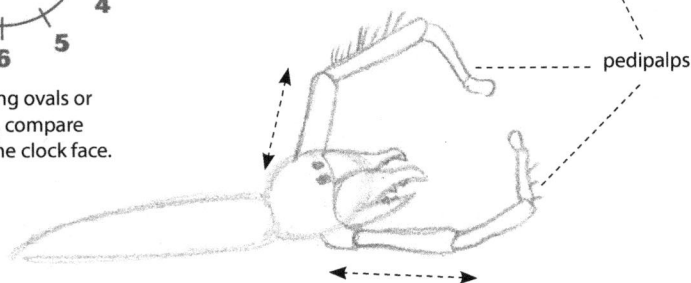

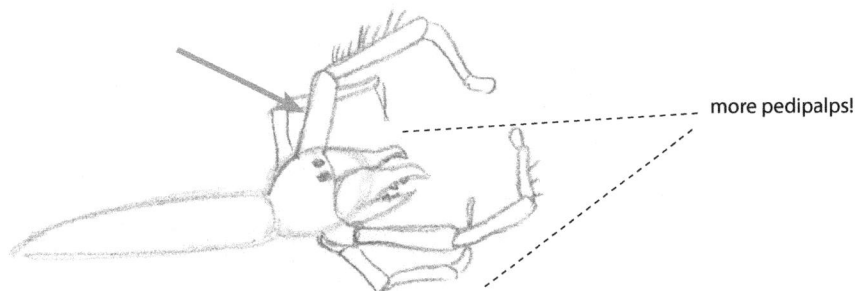

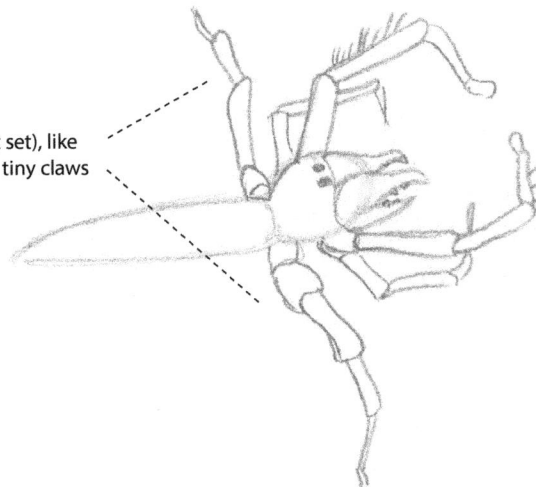

pedipalps

more pedipalps!

walking legs (1st set), like spider legs, with tiny claws

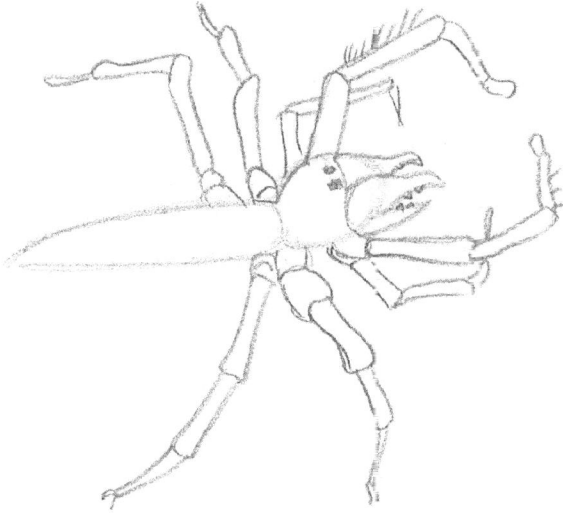

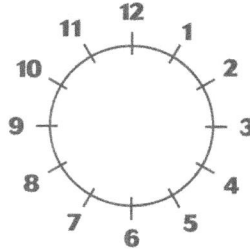

7. Bet you can't guess the next step: another set of legs! Draw them slowly and carefully. Notice the slight curves and angles.

As you draw each segment, check its angle against the clock face.

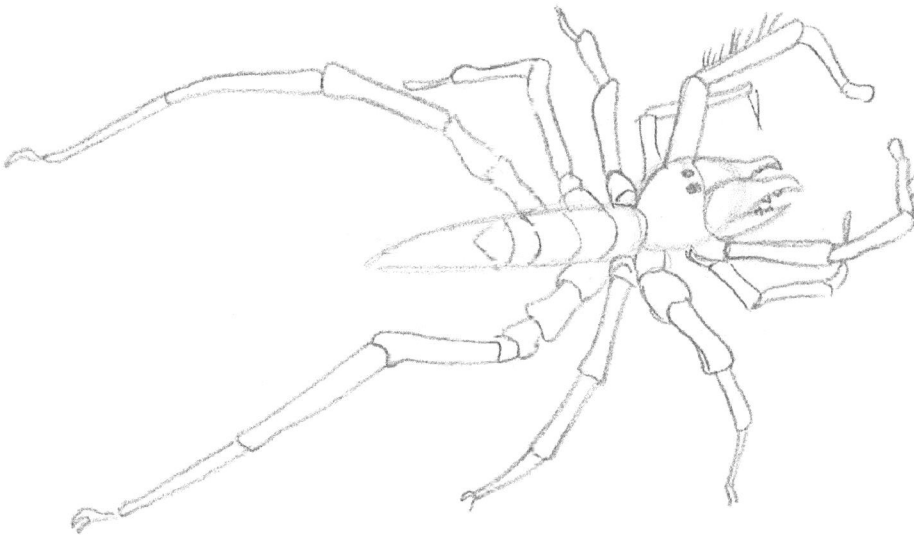

8. Look! What's different about the last set of legs? Draw them!

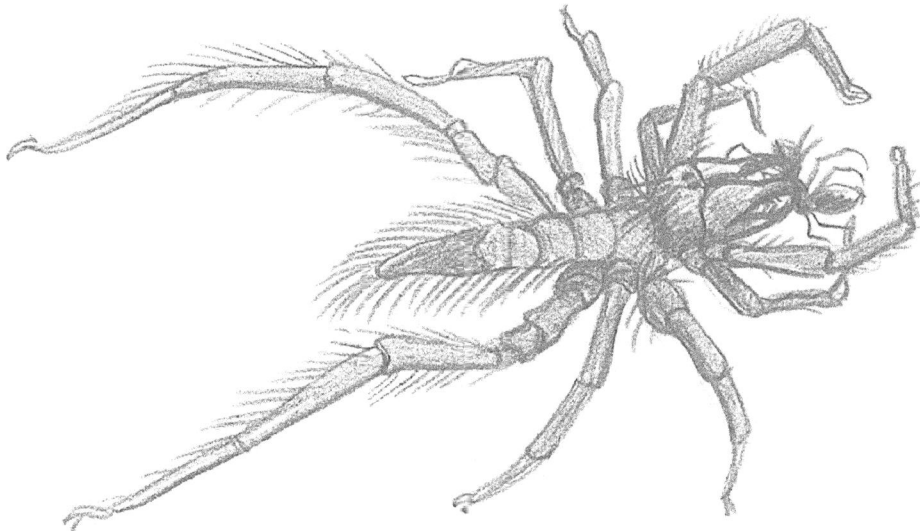

9. To complete this charming character, carefully shade the body and legs. Use short pencil strokes to make the hairs, out from the body.

Perhaps add a hapless ant, being rendered into a formless lump.

Splendiferous arachnid! Clean up any smudges with your eraser, put today's date on your drawing and save it in your portfolio!

Caracal

Felis caracal. Africa, Middle East to India.
Size: .8–1.2 m (33–47") including tail

The solitary caracal patrols a home range, preying on mammals from mice to medium sized antelopes, including birds, reptiles, and smaller domestic animals. Females bear litters of 2-3 young, who don't become independent until they've reached the age of 9-12 months.

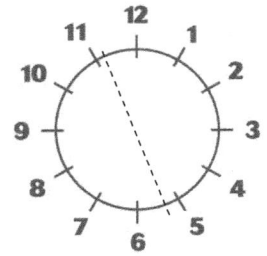

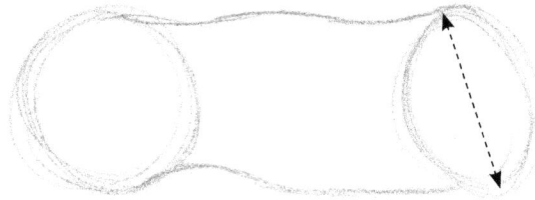

1. Before you draw, look at the distance between the two ovals of the cat's body. Lightly draw the ovals; make one narrower and slightly tilted. Add the curving lines for the top and bottom of the body.

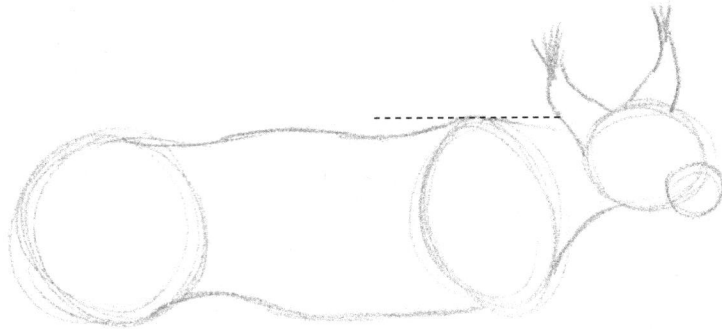

2. Sketch a small circle for the head, just slightly higher than the shoulder. Draw the ears with their tufts of hair at the end. Connect the head to the body with short, curved neck lines. Sketch a smaller circle for the nose.

3. Draw the dark triangle of the nose, with whiskers sticking out either side. Draw the two eyes, each starting with a curved line.

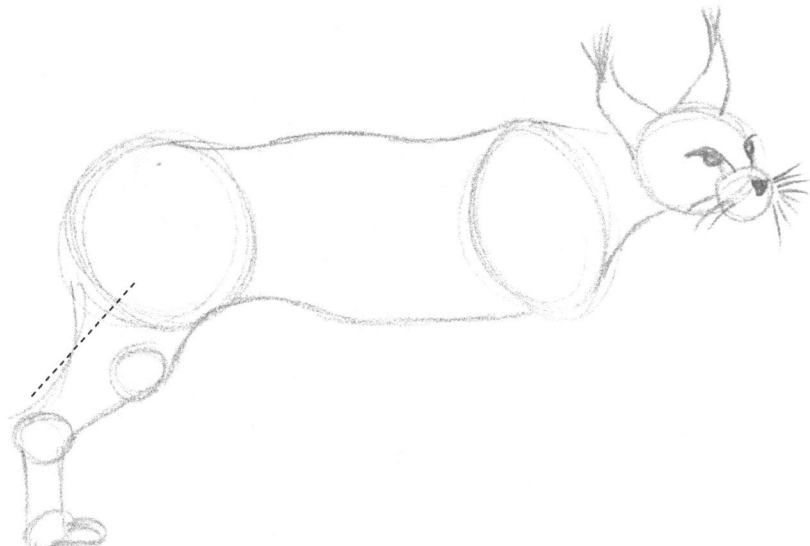

4. Sketch small circles for the joints on the back leg. Draw the leg, paying careful attention to the angle of each section.

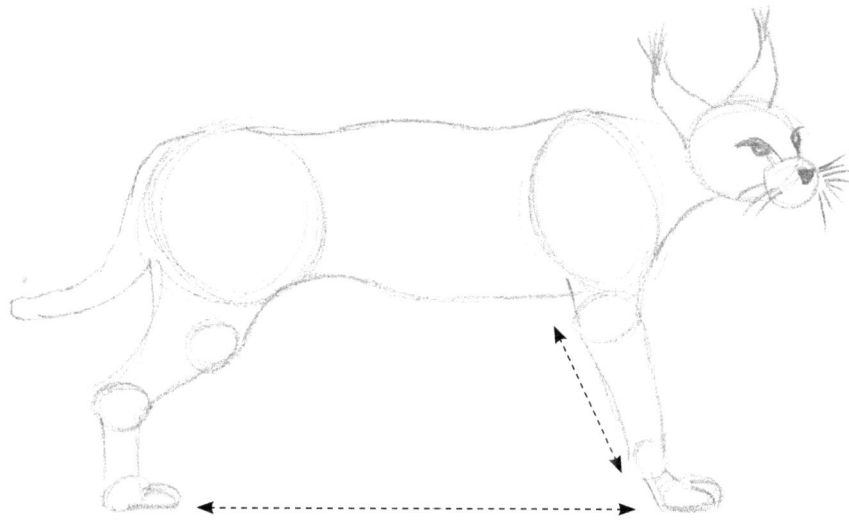

5. Sketch the front leg ovals, then draw the front leg.

Lightly sketching those little circles for the joints forces you to figure out where the limb bends, and also helps you draw the limbs in different positions if needed.

6. Now, in a similar manner, add the other legs.

7. To complete the caracal, make short pencil strokes—in the direction of the fur—over the entire body. Note lighter and darker areas. Take your time.

   Add color if you want.

Desert Cottontail

Sylvilagus auduboni. North America.
Size: 35–45 cm (9-11") incl. tail

Desert cottontails make their shelter in a burrow or shallow depression in the ground. Most active in the late afternoon and evening, they stay close to cover, When alarmed, they dart away quickly, flicking up their tails as they run, showing the white underside. The young are born blind and helpless after a gestation period of 26-30 days.

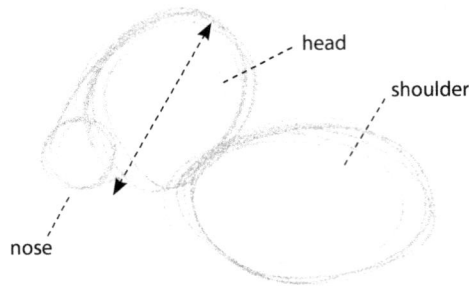

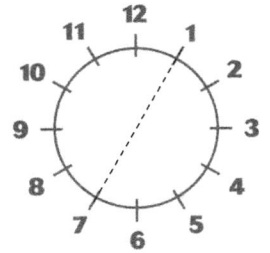

1. Lightly sketch ovals for the rabbit's shoulder and head, and a small circle for the nose. Make lines connecting the nose and the head.

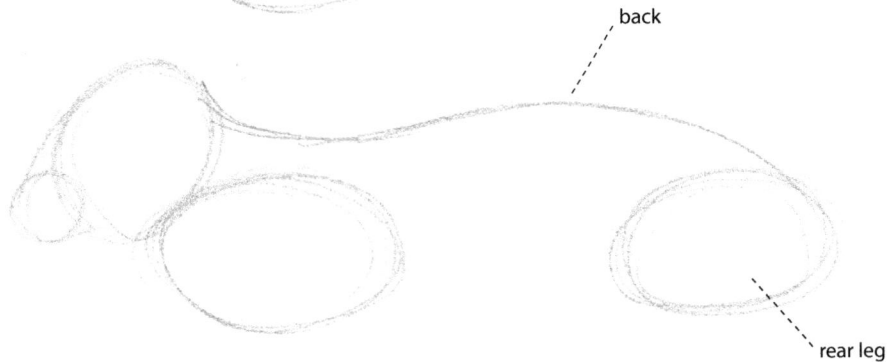

2. Sketch another horizontal oval to begin the rear leg. Connect it to the head with the long, swooping line of the back.

3. Notice where the eye appears in the head. Draw the eye with a circle for the highlight. Add the ear. Notice that the ear is about as long as the rest of the head.

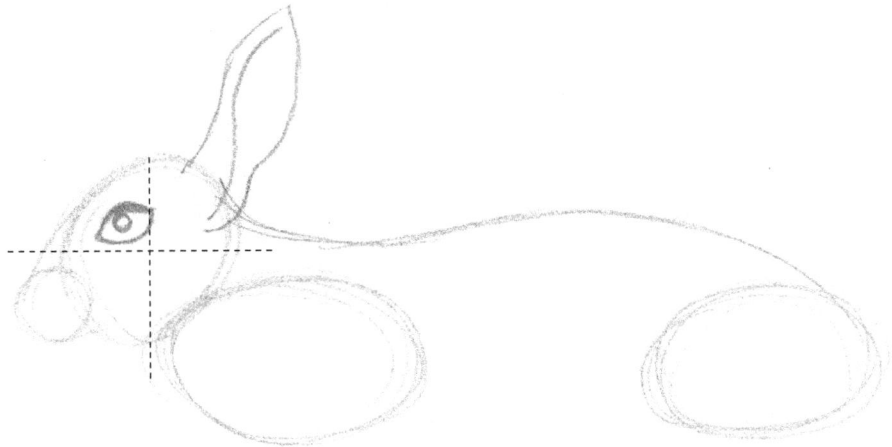

4. Draw the second ear. Darken the eye (except for the small circle). Add lines for the nostril and mouth, and lines for the chin and throat.

5. Draw the closer front leg and paw, then the small visible bit of the other leg.

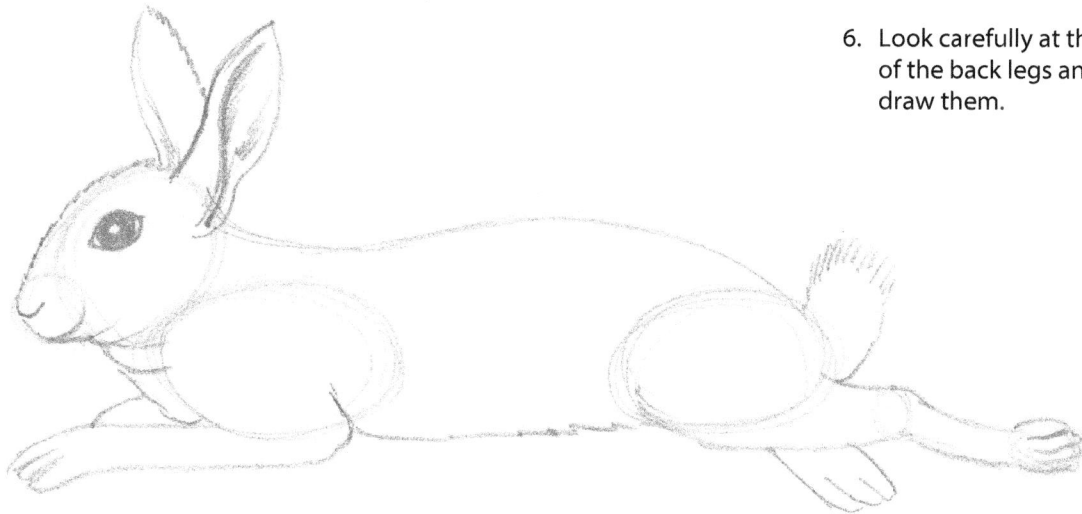

6. Look carefully at the angles of the back legs and tail, then draw them.

7. Complete your drawing, with short pencil strokes over the rabbit's entire body, always in the direction of the fur. Sharpen your pencil as often as you need to in order to make clean, crisp lines.

   Add whiskers, and a shadow underneath.

Wonderful wabbit! Add today's date and save your drawing!

Desert Tortoise

Gopherus agassizi. SW United States.
Size: up to 51 cm (20") long

During the heat of the day, the desert tortoise stays in an underground burrow, which may be up to 9 M (30 ft) long. It gets all its water from plants it eats, such as cactus and succulents. A desert tortoise can exist an entire dry season without water!

1. Sketch an upward arc and a downward arc for the top and bottom of the shell. Connect them with a straight line at the neck.

2. Lightly sketch the front and rear legs, and the lower part of the shell, including the point behind the rear leg.

3. Sketch an oval for the head. Add the neck, eye, and the part of the shell underneath the tortoise's neck, and the visible portion of the other front leg. Add feet and claws.

4. Carefully lay out the row of hexagons (six-sided shapes) on the top of the shell.

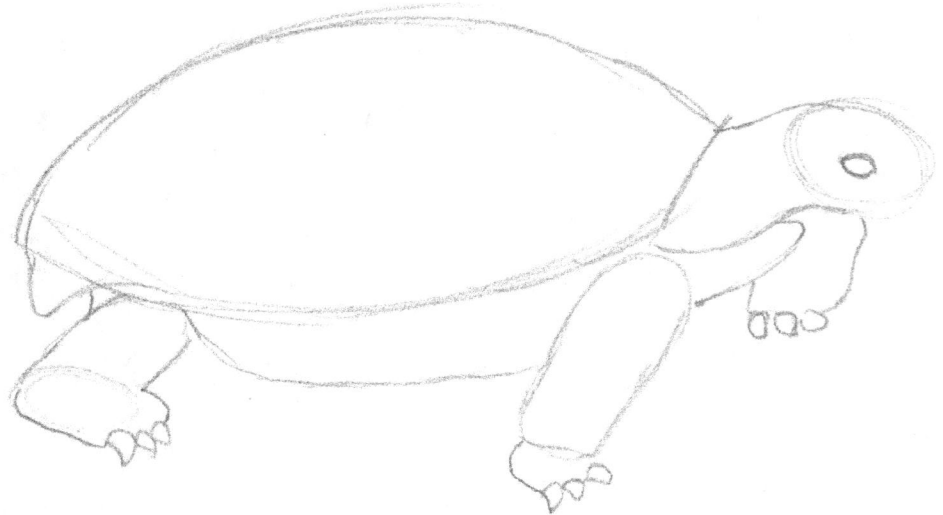

5. Continue the pattern

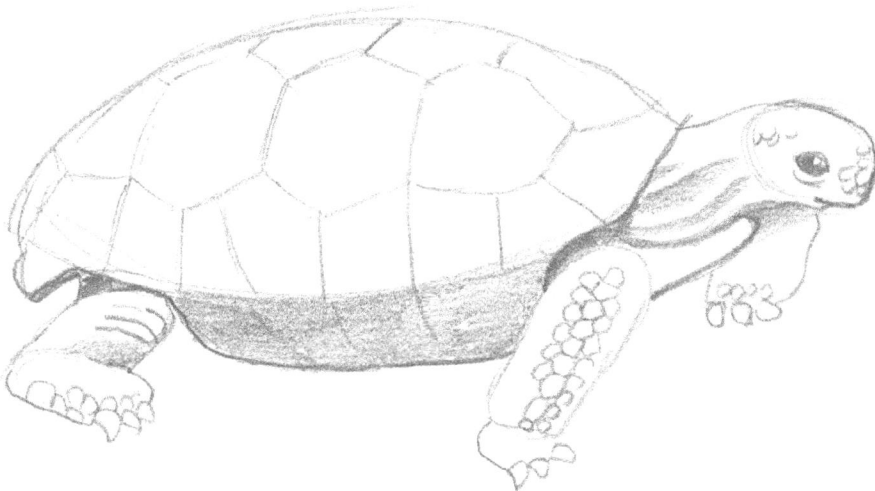

6. Shade the bottom part of the shell. Add shadows to create the folds on the neck. Darken the eye, leaving a small white area. Draw small scaly patterns on the head, front leg, and feet.

7. Add many, many small lines in the patterns of the shell—some lighter, some darker. Add more small scaly patterns on the head, neck, legs, and feet.

Draw a shadow on the ground, and a few small marks for pebbles.

Torrific tortoise.

Diamondback Rattlesnake

Crotalus atrox. Southwest US & northern Mexico.
Size: .76–2.25 m (2'5"–7'4")

The markings on the western diamondback aren't as distinct as you'd think from the name: on the back you'll see diamond-shaped or hexagonal markings, but you may have to look carefully (and by the time you get that close, the snake is probably rattling its tail at you in warning!). Overall, the snake has a speckled or dusty appearance. The tail is set off by broad black and white rings. When rattlesnakes strike, their fangs pierce the victim just for a split second, enough time to inject poison. Then they retreat to their hiding place. Later they look for their kill.

Have fun with this drawing. Enjoy practicing the swooping curves!

1. Sketch gentle, curving lines for the top and bottom of the snake's body. Join them in an upward curve for the fang, and add the lower jaw.

2. Look at the rear portion— then carefully draw it. Add the other fang, and mouth details.

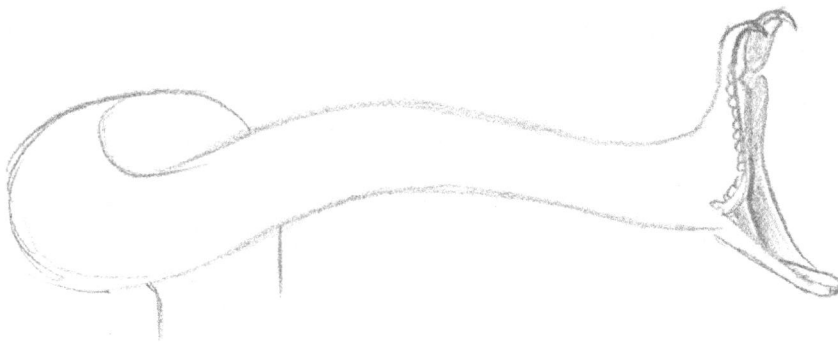

3. Extend the body downward. Study how each line curves. Two of them even run into each other (look).

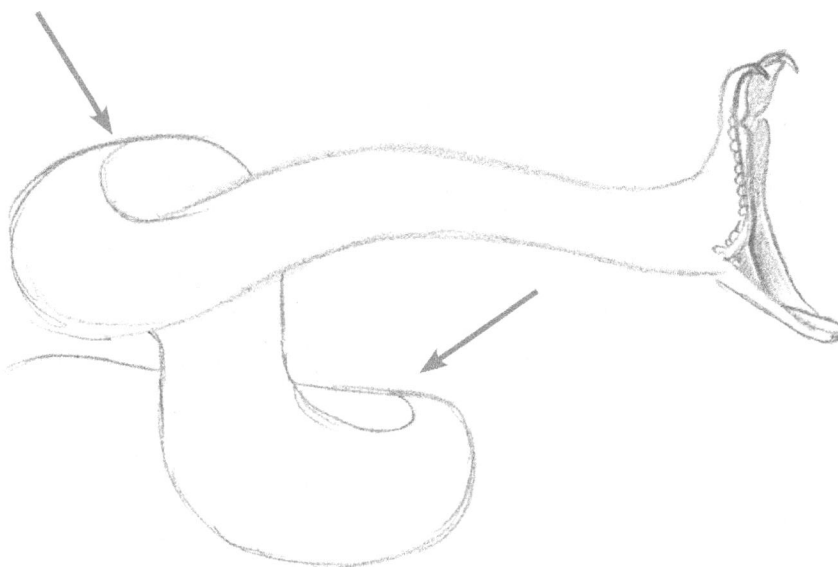

4. Draw curving lines to finish the body and the tail. Draw small ovals for the rattles.

5. Add *crosshatching* (crisscrossing lines), curving around the *contour* to create guide lines for scales. Use short pencil strokes to darken the shadows.

6. Shade the whole body, except for highlights and the faint pattern on the back. Continue shading and adding scales. Go over the outline with a sharpened pencil. Add the distinct light and dark bands on the tail.

Add color if you wish.

Draw a *cast shadow* on the ground. Soften it by rubbing it with your finger or a piece of paper.

Dromedary

Camelus dromedarius. North Africa, Middle East.
Size: body 2.2–3.4 m (7'2"); tail 50 cm (19.5")

Not a wild animal! It's believed that the one-humped camel has been domesticated since 4,000 BC. Today, you'll find two types: heavy, slow-moving beasts of burden, and graceful, fast racers used for riding. They feed on grass and other available plants, and can withstand long periods in areas of tough, sparse vegetation without drinking, thanks to adaptations in their stomach linings and kidneys. In one experiment, a thirsty camel drank 104 liters (27 US gallons) of water in ten minutes! The hump stores fat, not water. Females breed every other year. The long gestation period (365-440 days) results in a single young that can walk after a day.

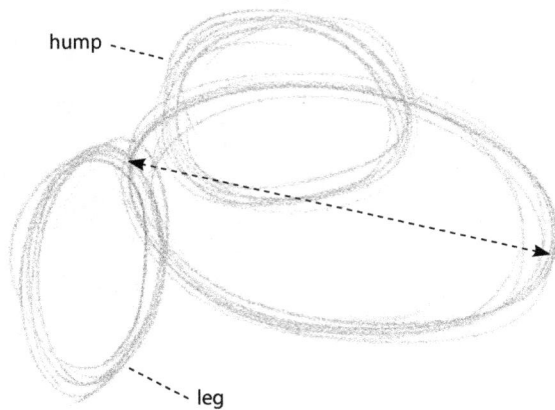

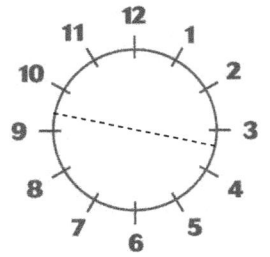

1. Sketch a large, slightly tilted, oval. Sketch a smaller oval, off-center, for the hump. Add a vertical oval for the rear leg.

2. Make a small circle for the head, level with the top of the hump. Add lines to form the front of the head. Draw the mouth, nostril, eye, and ear. Draw the gently curving (and slightly shaggy) lines for the neck.

3. Add the callused knee at the bottom front of the leg oval. Sketch circles for the leg joints. Add curving lines to complete the rear legs. Draw wide, almost triangular shapes for the camel's spreading hoofs.

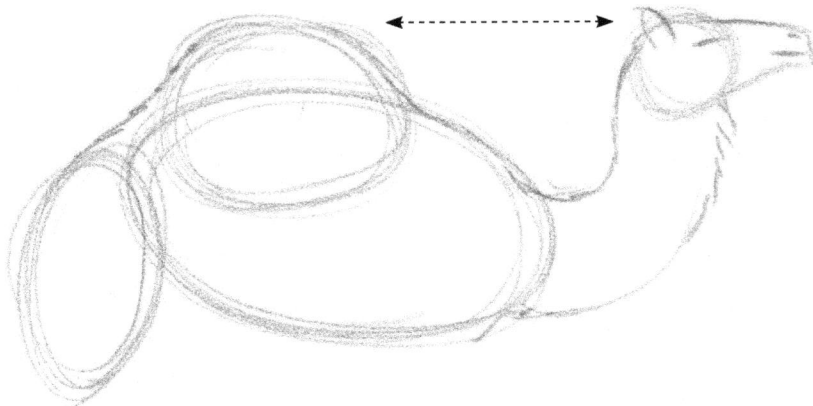

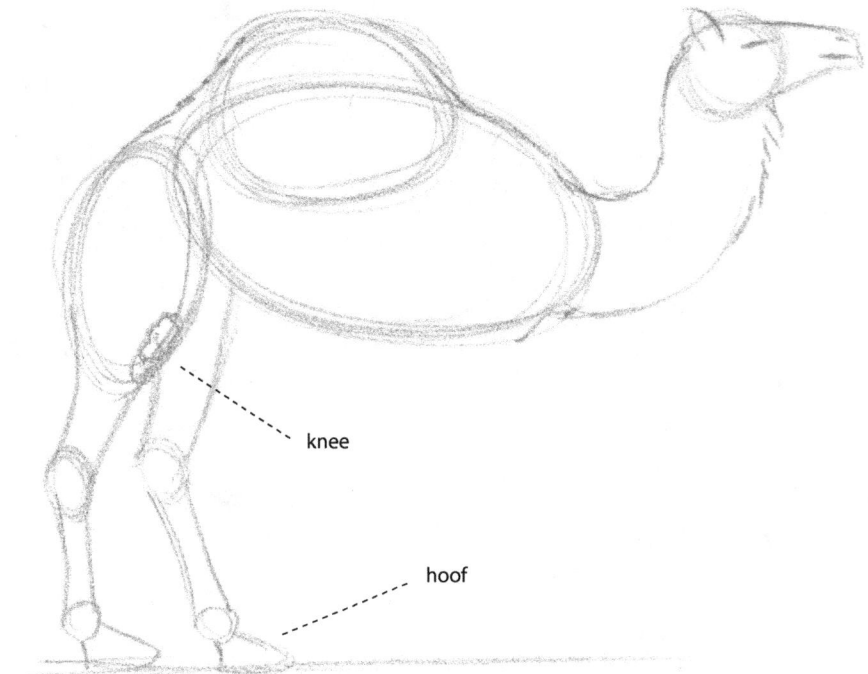

callus

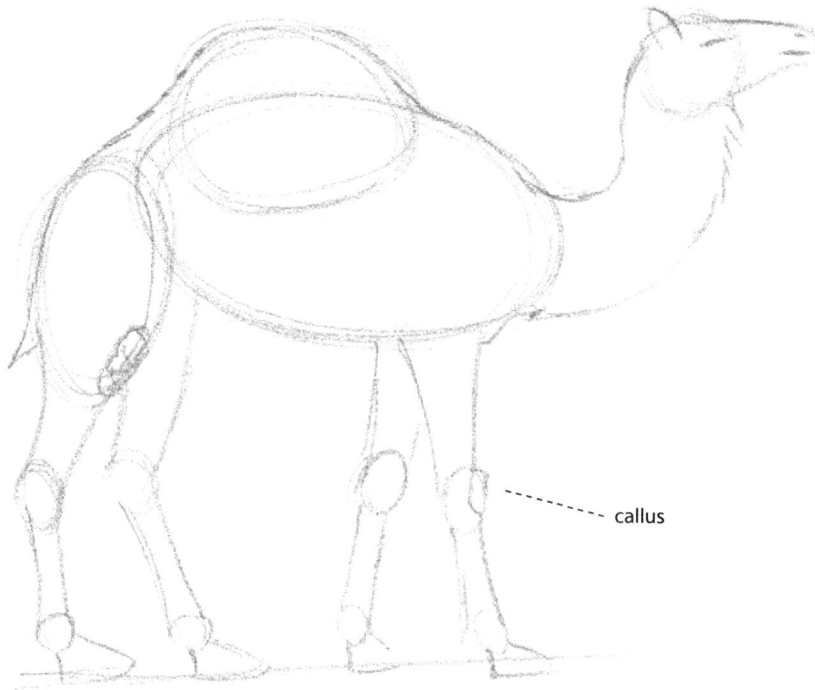

4. Next, add the front legs. Notice the callus on the front of the front leg. The callused areas on the front and rear legs are from kneeling, to lie down and get up again.

Erase sketch lines you no longer need.

At rest, a camel folds its legs underneath to reduce exposure to the hot desert sun. The fat-filled hump on its back helps insulate the body from the sun's heat.

5. Add pencil strokes—always in the direction of the hair and contours of the body—to shade *just* the shadow areas.

Go over the outline with a sharpened pencil. Add a *cast shadow* beneath, and *(why not?)* a couple of pyramids in the distance.

Dazzling dromedary! Clean up any smudges with your eraser, put today's date on your drawing and save it in your portfolio!

Egyptian Slit-Faced Bat

Nycteris thebaica. Middle East, Africa south of Sahara.
Size: body 4.5–7.5 cm (1.8–3"); wingspan 16–28 cm (6.3–11")

Hang around ancient Egyptian temples, and you just may run into a few of these! Slit-faced bats like to catch a variety of invertebrates for supper. Scorpions seem to be a favorite! The bats usually give birth to a single young in January or February; they may do the same later in the year.

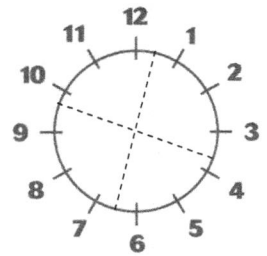

foot

When drawing ovals or angled lines, compare their tilt to the clock face.

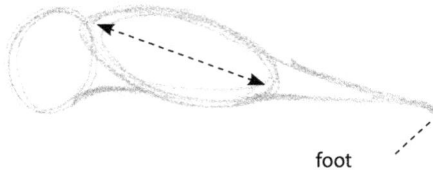

1. Sketch a flat, slightly tilted oval for the bat's body. Sketch a circle at one end for the head. Add a neck line to connect it to the body. Draw two lines tapering to the foot.

2. Draw the front of the wing, up from the top of the body (compare the angle with the clock face). Sketch tiny circles and lines for the bent arm holding it out.

arm

elbow

3. From the point where the arm and wing lines meet, draw the bat's long thin "fingers" spreading out to make triangular shapes. Draw the back edge of the wing, connecting it to the tapered end of the foot.

4. Look closely at the bat's facial features—mouth, nose, the little sensing organ on top of the nose, eyes, and eye slits. Add them. Draw the ears.

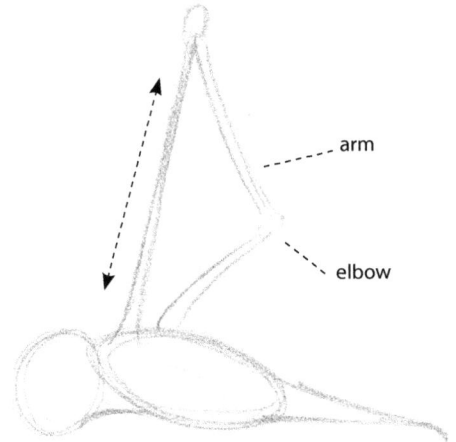

These facial features are part of their "radar," picking up signals, making it possible for them to move and hunt with precision.

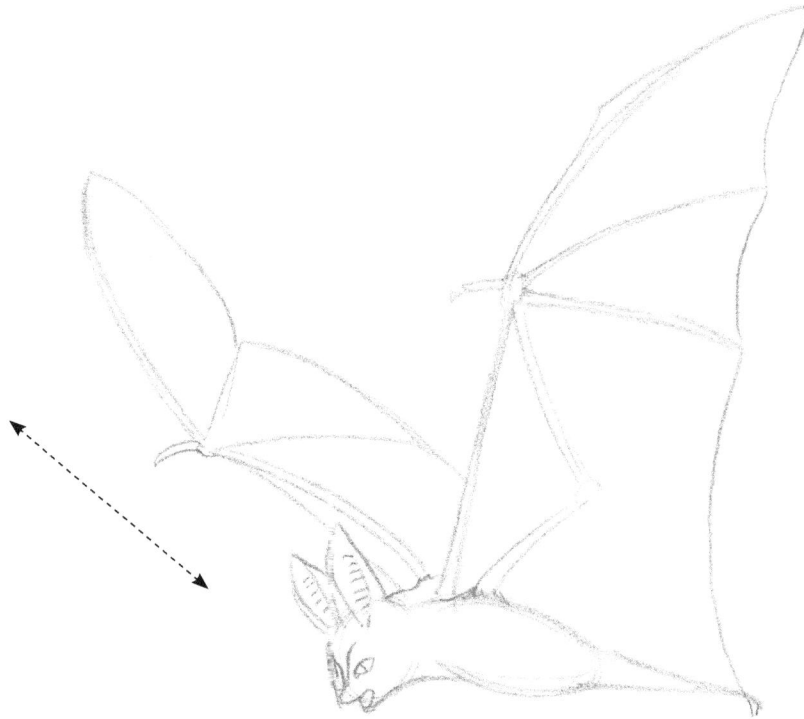

5. Add small lines inside the ears. Behind them, draw a slight hump in the back where the other wing attaches. Look at this drawing carefully (angles!), and draw the second wing.

6. Look at the contrast of light and dark in this final drawing.

    Use *crosshatching* to carefully shade the closer wing. Use short pencil strokes to create the fur on the body. Continue shading, watching for light and dark areas, until you're through. Then take a sharpened pencil and go over lines you want to emphasize.

    Clean up any smudges with your eraser, put today's date on your drawing and save it in your portfolio!

Elf Owl

Micrathene whitneyi. Southwest US & Mexico.
Size: Body 12.5–15 cm (5–6")

Though one of the smallest owls in the world, the elf owl has a loud voice. It lives in wooded canyons and deserts with saguaro cactus, where it roosts in abandoned woodpecker holes. Elf owls use their feet to catch insects in flight; they also catch food on the ground, including grasshoppers and scorpions (they remove or crush the stinger), and sometimes small snakes and lizards.

1. Sketch a horizontal oval for the owl's head. Beneath it, add the slightly tilted vertical oval of the owl's body.

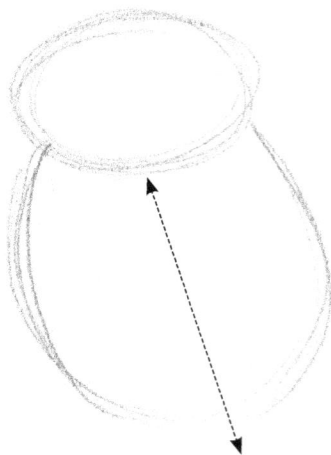

2. Draw the curved beak, slightly off center. Draw two curved lines for each eye.

3. Darken the inside of the eyes, leaving a small white spot. Draw a jagged line to show texture on the side of the head. Add short pencil strokes, up and away from the eye, to shade the head.

4. Add more shading, with short pencil strokes, around the eyes and on the head. Draw the wing, lightly outlining the feathers.

5. Shade the wing, leaving some feather areas white. Draw short, curling strokes to create feathers on the breast and belly.

6. Look closely at the owl's legs, noting where they attach to the body, and their angles. Draw thems. Add two lines for the branch on which the owl perches.

   Draw the tail feathers.

7. Darken the outlines of the feet and branch. Outline the wing and tail feathers. Go over your owl, top to bottom and side to side, adding feathers and shading, and making areas lighter or darker as needed.

8. If owls perch in trees and bushes when they're looking for food or resting. When it's time to nest, they find an old woodpecker hole in a cactus. Try drawing your elf owl nesting in a saguaro cactus!

   Clean up any smudges with your eraser, put today's date on your drawing and save it in your portfolio.

Fat Sand Rat

Psammomys obesus. Algeria, east to Saudi Arabia.
Size: body 14–18.5 cm (5.5–7.3"); tail 12–15 cm (4.7–5.9")

What do you do if you can't be sure when you'll find food? If you're a fat sand rat, you lay down a thick layer of fat all over your body while food is abundant, then live off it when food is scarce. (What other desert animals store fat?) This gerbil is active day and night, collecting seeds and other vegetation to carry back to its burrow.

1. Sketch two light overlapping ovals for the head and face of the rat. Behind the head, sketch part of another oval—the front part of the body. Upward from that oval, sketch the rounded back curving down into the rear leg. Draw a curved line for the belly.

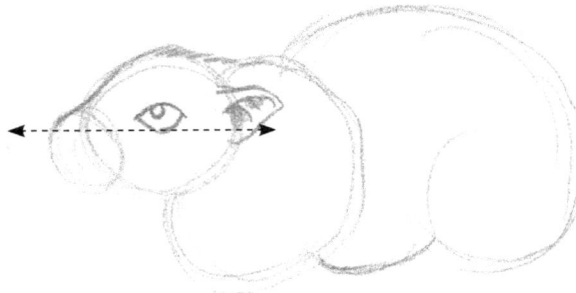

2. Outline the top of the head, making a smooth connection between the ovals. Just above the middle of the head, draw the eye. Add the ear.

3. Darken the eye, leaving a small white spot. Draw the nostrils and mouth. Outline the front of the face.

4. With a sharp pencil, draw lines above and below the eye. Add two short legs, tilting towards the front. Draw feet, then claws.

5. Add the rear legs, making a small circle for the one visible joint. Draw feet and claws.

   Add the tail.

6. Use short pencil strokes and jagged lines to "rough up" the outline.

7. Look at the final drawing, and notice which areas are darkest. Beginning there, start adding short pencil strokes running in the direction of the fur.

   Continue adding fur and shading. Try to match the tones (light and dark) of the final drawing. Add whiskers.

   To make your drawing more realistic, add a cast shadow.

cast shadow

Fennec fox

Vulpes zerda. North Africa, Arabia.
Size: body 36–40 cm (14.2–15.7"); tail
20–30 cm (8–12")

Fennec foxes live in groups of up to
ten, and feed at night on small animals
and insects. Small and agile, they live in
burrows. In soft sand, they dig so quickly
it can look like they're just sinking into the
ground!

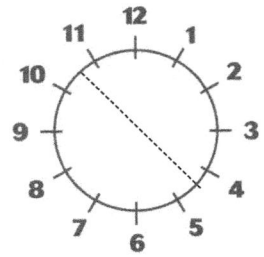

Compare the tilt of ovals
and other angles with the
clock face.

1. Begin by sketching the body
   of the fox—two tall ovals
   connected with curving lines.

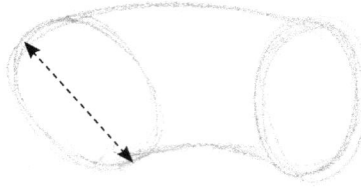

2. Draw a light circle for the
   head, noting where it lies in
   relationship to the shoulder.
   Add the nose and mouth.
   Draw lines for the neck, paying
   attention to how they curve
   outward.

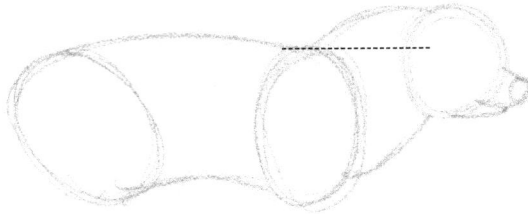

3. Darken the nose and mouth.
   Add the eye, leaving a
   small white circle. Draw the
   distinctive large ears.

4. Draw squiggly lines to form
   the bushy tail.

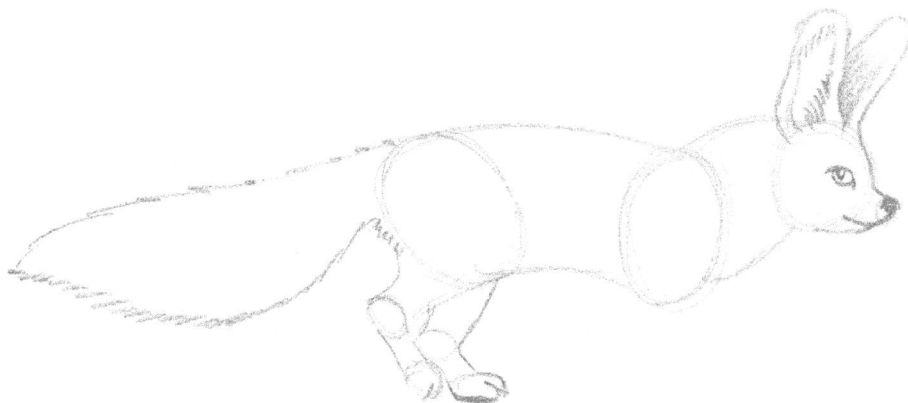

5. Sketch small circles for the leg joints. Draw the rear legs and feet. Add emphasis to the farther one, which is supporting the fox's entire weight.

6. Likewise, draw the front legs and feet. Notice that neither is completely on the ground.

7. Look at the variations in the tones (light and dark). Use short pencil strokes to create the fur of the fennec fox. Leave some areas light. Go over the outline. Note that some parts of the outline are darker for emphasis.

Draw whiskers. Add a slight cast shadow underneath the fox. Clean up any smudges with your eraser.

Fine fox! Put today's date on your drawing and save it!

Gila Monster

Heloderma suspectum. Southwest United States.

Size: 60 cm (23")

The slow-moving Gila (pronounced "heela") moves about mainly at night, feeding on birds' eggs, small reptiles, and small rodents. The large tail stores fat, since food in the desert is not always abundant (what other desert animals store fat?). Gila monsters and their relatives, Mexican Beaded Lizards, are the only venomous lizards. They shelter under rocks or in burrows. The females lay eggs once a year, in a hole, in autumn or winter. The eggs hatch about 30 days later.

other front leg

1. Sketch three flat ovals to begin your Gila drawing.

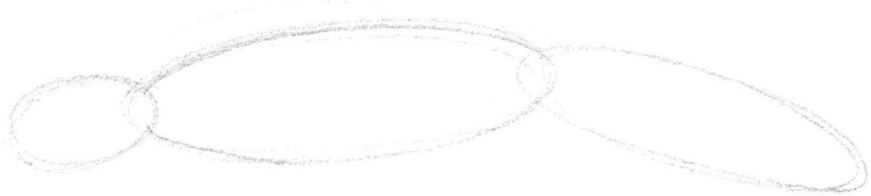

2. Add two legs with claws. Draw the small visible section of the other front leg (behind the head).

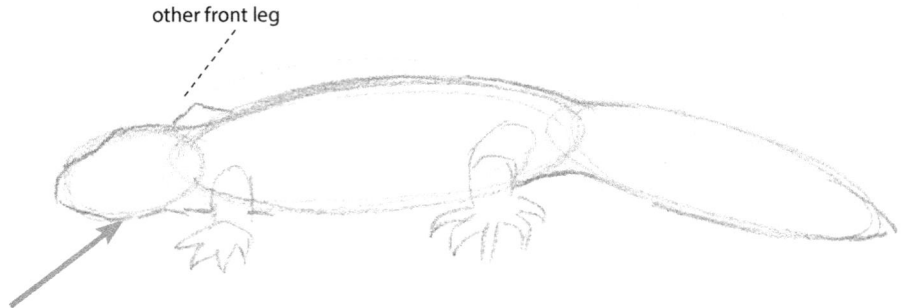

3. Refine the shape of the head, and join the ovals together with smooth curved lines. Draw the forked tongue, eye, and mouth. Add lines to the legs and feet.

4. Erase unnecessary guide lines. Draw the patterns on the Gila's tail—bands of light and dark, with dark or light squarish spots in them. Add scales in the light areas.

scales

5. The body has a less regular pattern. Have fun drawing it! Add a shadow beneath the Gila, and draw some rocks and twigs near it.

    Add color if you want. The lighter color on the gila mimics the ground: reddish brown.

Put today's date on your drawing and save it!

Horned Toad

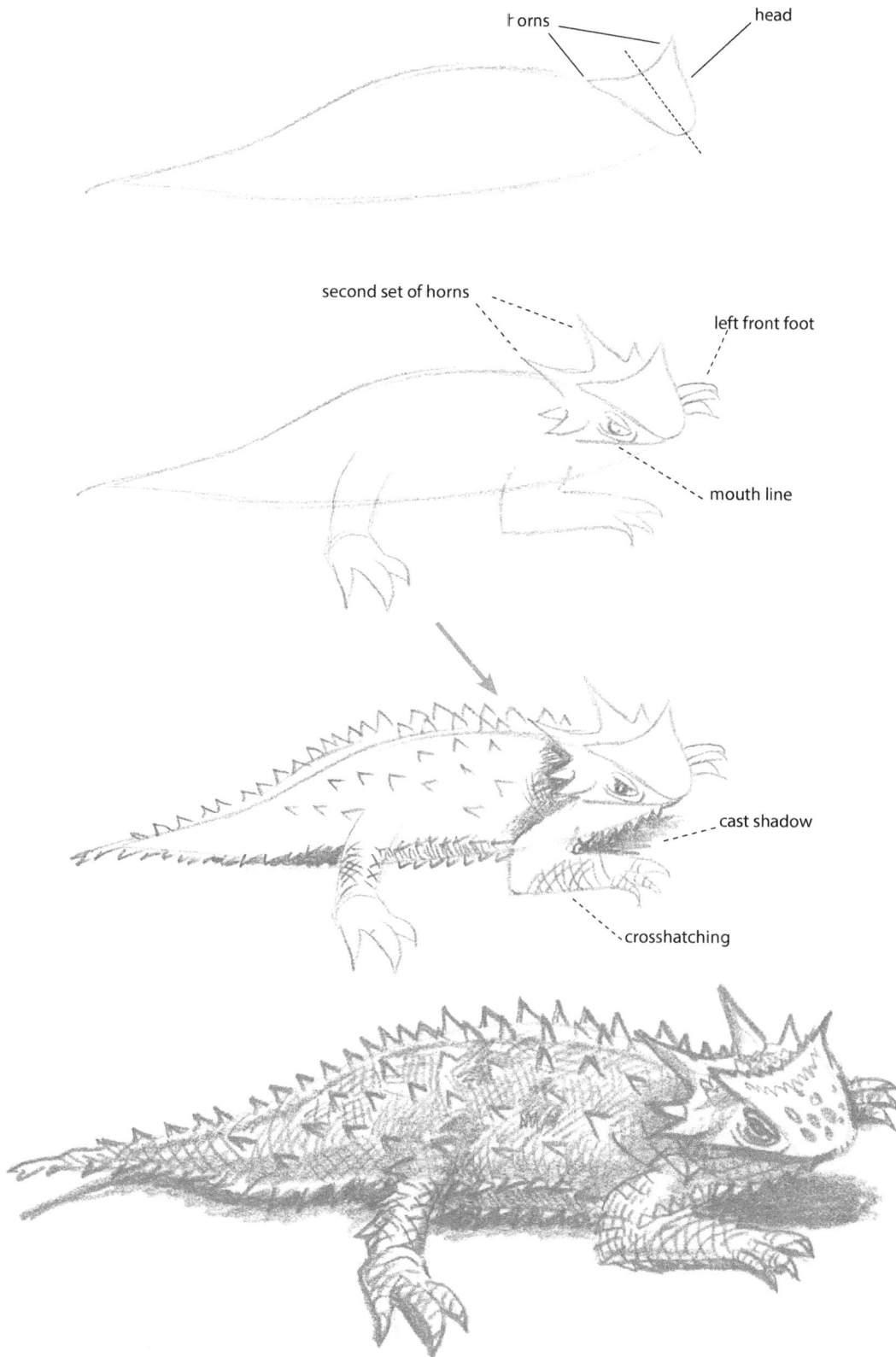

Horns — head

second set of horns

left front foot

mouth line

cast shadow

crosshatching

Phrynosoma douglasii

North America.

Size: 4–13 cm (1.6–5.2")

"That's not a toad!" you say. You're right. The name horned toad is given to a lizard, with horns or spikes on the back of the head (the only other horned lizard is the Thorny Devil of Australia). At night, it wriggles below the sand, during the day it moves about slowly and feeds on insects and ants. Horned toads (also called Texas horned lizards) lie very flat and motionless when disturbed, but can also inflate themselves, jump forward and hiss. And— who knows how—they can even squirt blood from their eyes!

1. Lightly sketch curved lines for the top and bottom of the body. Add the tilted shape that makes the top of the head, rounded at the front and pointed at the back for the horns.

2. Add the second set of horns. Draw the eye and the mouth line. Lightly sketch the two right legs, with claws. Add claws of the left front foot.

3. Add a row of spikes along the back and scattered on the body. Add a cast shadow for contrast under the chin and behind the horns. Use crosshatching to create scales.

4. Complete your drawing with more shading, shadows, and crosshatching. Leave the head lighter than the body. This makes the head, eye, and spikes, the focal point of the drawing.

   Put today's date on your drawing and save it!

Jerboa

Dipus sagitta (northern three-toed). North Africa, Asia.
Size: body 10-13 cm (4–5.2"); tail 15–19 cm (6–7.5")

Like the kangaroo rat of the United States, jerboas live in a burrow, coming out only at night when the surface temperature has cooled off from the heat of the day. In autumn, they dig a deeper burrow to hibernate. In the spring, they may have two litters, with 2-5 young each. A jerboa gets all the water it needs from its food, which includes seeds, roots, and insect larvae.

1. Lightly sketch a horizontal, slightly tilted oval for the jerboa's body. Lightly draw the oval of the leg overlapping the oval of the body. Add another, smaller, rounder oval for the head.

2. From the leg oval, draw the first section of leg, with a small circle for the ankle joint. From there, draw the next section and the foot. Sketch a small circle for the elbow, and draw the front paw.

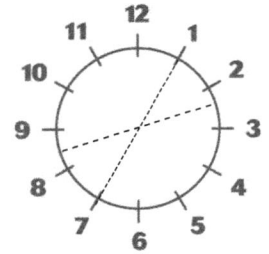

When drawing ovals or angled lines, compare their tilt to the clock face.

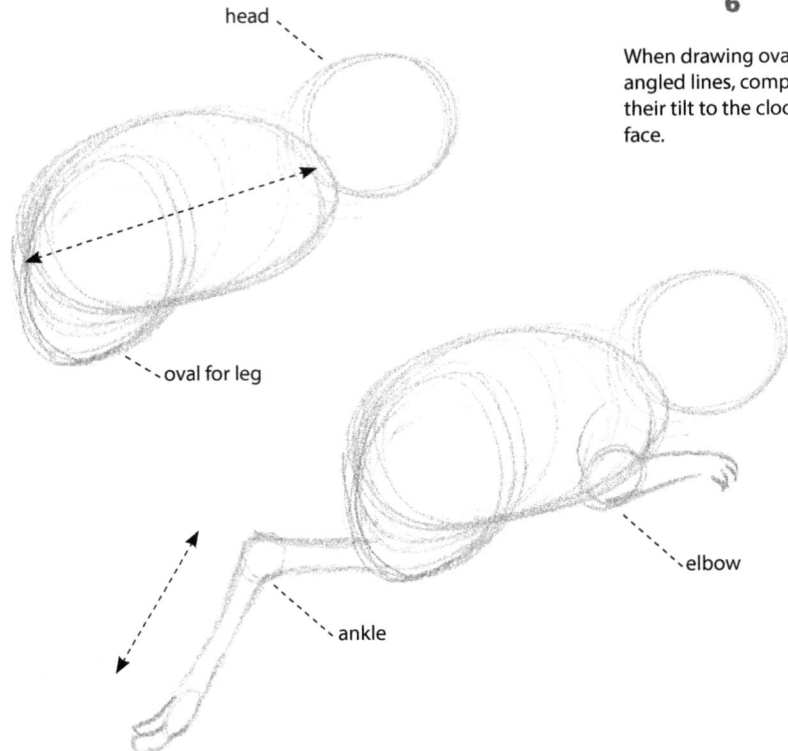

head

oval for leg

ankle

elbow

Climate control: By digging beneath the scorching hot surface of the desert, jerboas and their relatives, kangaroo rats, manage to stay cool during the day. At night, when the surface cools, they emerge to search for food.

3. Draw the other two legs. Note how the closer legs overlap the others. Add fur texture to the outline using short, jagged lines. Draw the eye, ears, and nose. Erase unneeded guide lines.

4. Add a small circle to make the highlight in the eye. Draw whiskers. Add the very long tail. Add more short pencil strokes, in the direction of the fur, on the darkest parts of the body.

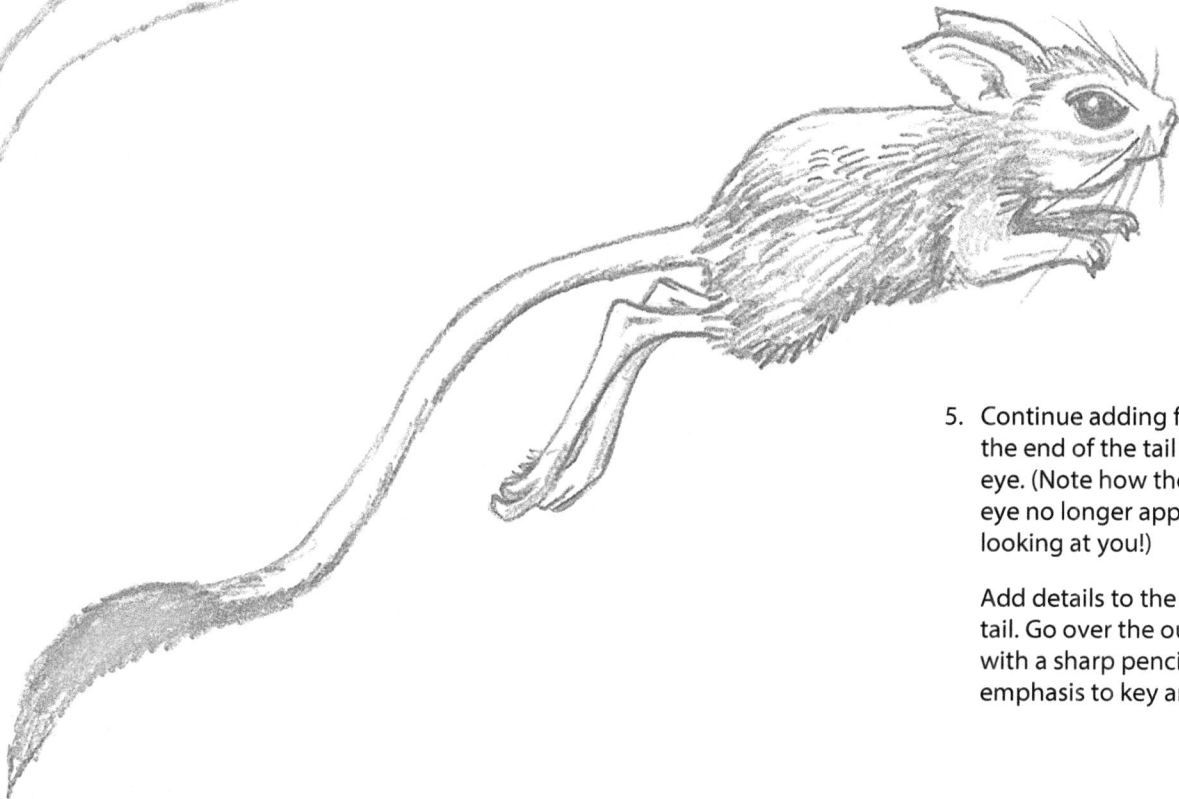

5. Continue adding fur. Darken the end of the tail and the eye. (Note how the darkened eye no longer appears to be looking at you!)

Add details to the legs and tail. Go over the outline, with a sharp pencil, and add emphasis to key areas.

Lanner Falcon

Falco biarmicus. North Africa, Middle East.
Size: Body 40–45 cm (16–18"); wingspan
70–80 cm (25–27")

Falco means sickle, and refers to the curved
claws of falcons. Falcons swoop down
and grab birds out of the air. People have
trained them for thousands of years, to
catch food and also as a sport. Falcons
don't build nests; they either take over an
abandoned nest from another bird, or lay
their eggs on high ledges.

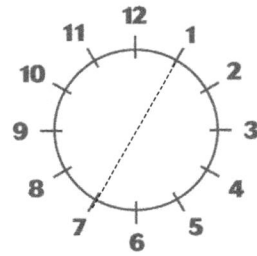

1. Lightly sketch the tall, tilted
   oval of the falcon's body.
   Above it, add a small oval for
   the head. Leaving space for the
   shoulder (arrow), add curving
   lines to connect to the body.

2. Draw the curving beak, with
   the characteristic double notch
   of a falcon. Draw a line back
   for the mouth. In the center of
   the head, draw the curve of the
   eyebrow, and then the round
   eye under it.

3. Sketch the two legs, each with
   a thick feathered portion. Add
   feet, claws, and a jagged line—
   the top of a rock for the falcon
   to perch.

4. Study the falcon's shoulders
   and wings before drawing
   them. Add the shoulder
   beneath the falcon's beak,
   then the outside and inside
   of the wing beneath it. Draw
   the curve of the wing on the
   other side—see how it extends
   behind, to the other side of the
   body (arrows). Draw lines for
   the tail feathers.

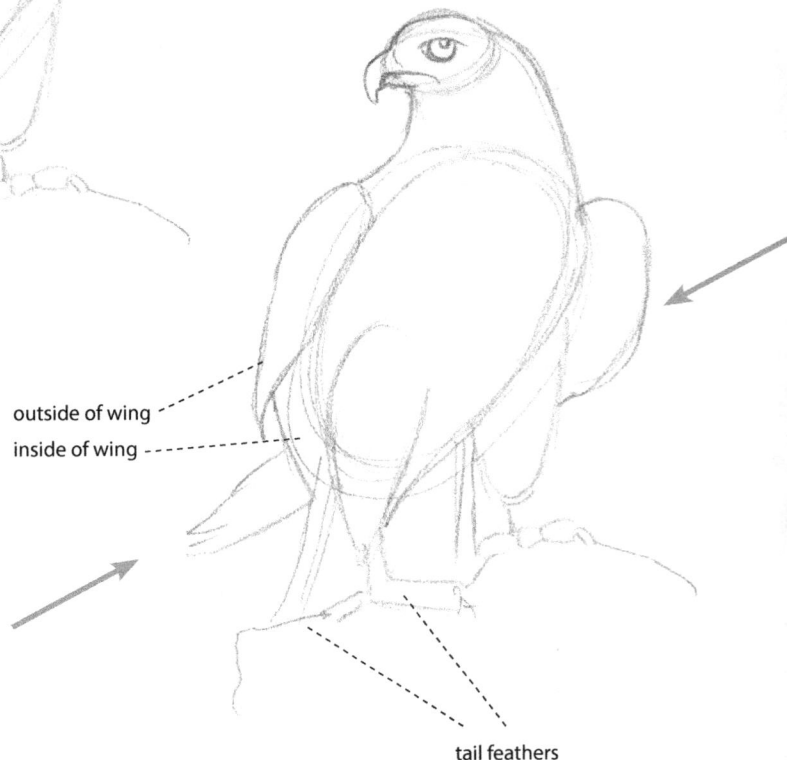

When drawing ovals
or angled lines,
compare their tilt to
the clock face.

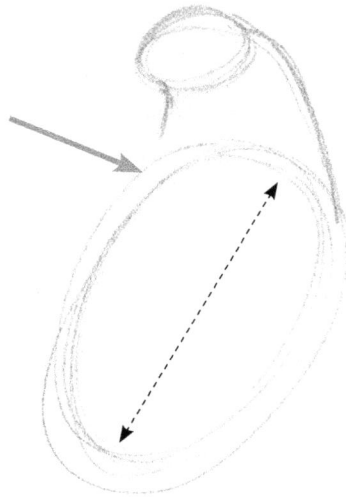

outside of wing

inside of wing

tail feathers

5. Erase guide lines you no longer need.

   Very carefully, with a sharp pencil, shade the head with short strokes radiating from the mouth and beak.

   Shade the tail feathers. Darken parts of the outlines of the wings, legs, and feet with a sharp pencil. Add jagged lines where feathers stick out slightly at the edge of the leg.

6. Notice the details and shading in this drawing. With a sharp pencil, add details: the marks on the breast feathers, claws, or details on the rock. As your pencil becomes duller, add the softer shading.

   Every once in a while, sit back from your drawing and take stock—really look at it and appreciate your progress. Do you see any other details you need to add? Add them, and color if you wish.

Falco fabuloso! Clean up any smudges, date and save your drawing!

Pallas's Cat

Felis manul. Central Asia.
Size: 71–86 cm (28–38")

This elusive cat lives in caves, rock crevices, or burrows taken from other animals such as marmots. It only comes to hunt at night, preying on mice, birds, and small hares. The fur color varies from pale gray to yellowish to reddish-brown. Pallas's cat has the longest, densest fur of any wild cat.

Here's an example of using form to add realism to a drawing. The shape of the cat's body may look like a sack of potatoes, but bones and muscles lie underneath. Understanding them is key.

1. Sketch three light, overlapping circles. You don't need to sketch the hidden part of each circle.

2. The body is fairly easy, but the face may be tricky, so complete it first. Near the center of the head circle, draw a small triangular nose; above it, to either side, draw the expressive eyes.

3. Draw the dark markings on the cheeks. Add the mouth, with a shadow underneath. Draw a line connecting the mouth to the nose.

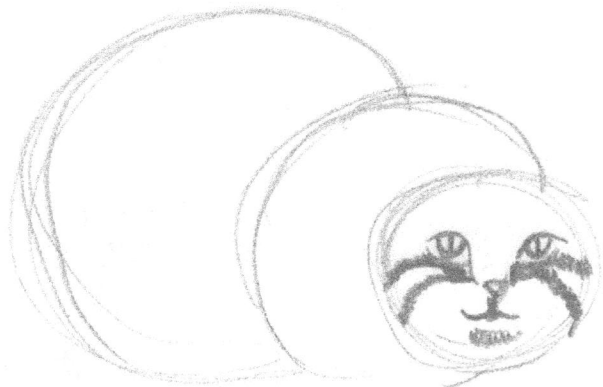

4. From the nose, go up and out, straight past each eye, and draw the short ears. From the nose up, use short upward pencil strokes for fur. Add spots on the forehead. Continue adding fur lines radiating outward around the face.

top of rear leg

ankle

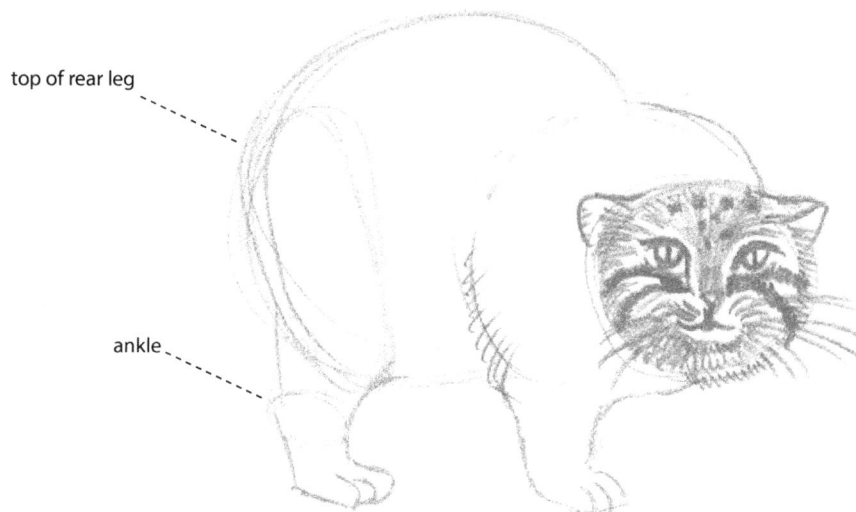

5. Make a tall, tilting oval for the top of the rear leg. Add a small oval for the ankle joint and the rear leg and paw. Draw the front leg and paw. Add a little shading with short pencil strokes to remind you of the form of the leg under the fur, even though you can't really see it.

Finish shading the face, and add whiskers.

6. Sketch the tail, with its dark rings. Carefully add the visible part of the other two legs. Note how the closer legs overlap them.

7. Paying close attention to dark and light areas, go over the entire cat with short pencil strokes in the direction of the fur. Add the stripe marks on the back and side, showing the round *contour*. Draw a *cast shadow* underneath. Notice how the lines in the cast shadow create texture for the ground.

Purrfect! Clean up any smudges with your eraser. Date and save your drawing in your portfolio!

Roadrunner

Geococcyx californianus. North America.
Size: 58 cm (23") including tail

The roadrunner is a species of cuckoo. It makes quick dashes, then stops suddenly and looks around. If it sees food—a lizard, small snake, grasshopper or insect—it dashes after it, making quick turns if necessary. Roadrunners make neat nests in trees or cactus clumps, lining them with leaves, feathers, even snake skins and bones!

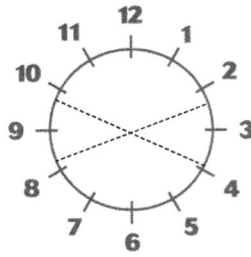

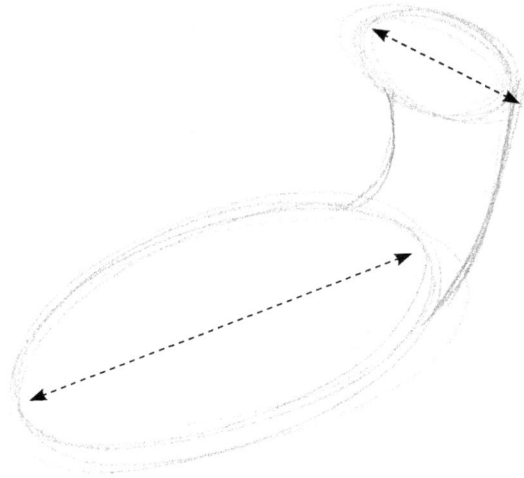

1. Look carefully at the angle of each oval, and compare its tilt to the clock face. Lightly sketch the two ovals. Connect them with curved lines to make the roadrunner's neck.

2. Draw the long and slightly curved beak. Add the eye. Notice the direction the scraggly neck feathers point. Draw them. Add the dark patch behind the eye.

3. See the limp lizard hanging from the roadrunner's beak? Notice how the legs of the lizard hang and point downward. Also notice that part of this lizard's tail is missing!

   Draw the lizard first, *then* the lower part of the beak.

fluffy feathers

edge of wing

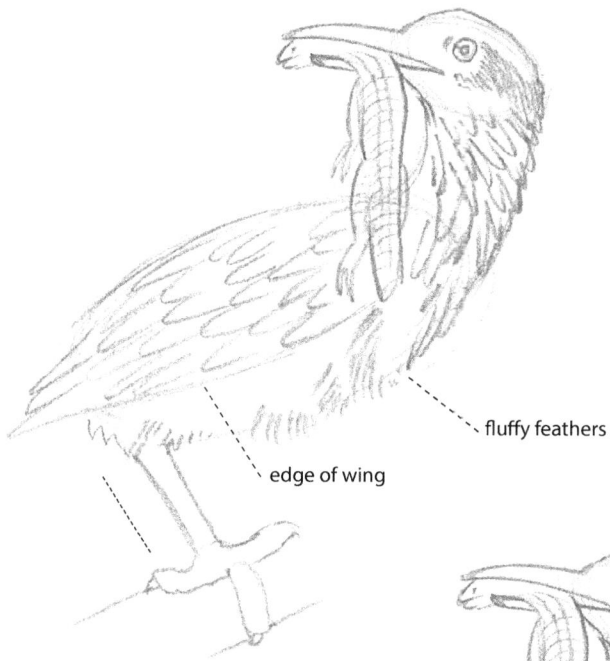

4. Draw a line showing the edge of the wing. Add feathers. On the bird's belly, add short lines to make it look fluffy, in contrast to the neck feathers. Look carefully at the angles of the leg and foot. From the back of the body, draw one leg and foot, with three of its four claws visible.

5. Add the second leg, at a different angle than the first leg. Draw the branch on which the roadrunner sits, and make long pencil strokes to begin the tail.

6. Draw the tail roughly the length of the body. Outline and darken the wing and tail feathers.

Add shading and texture to the branch.

Sandgrouse

Syrrhaptes paradoxus. Central Asia, southern Siberia, southern Mongolia–northern China.
Size: 25–48 cm (10–19")

Sandgrouses are related to doves and pigeons. The desert dwellers eat only very dry seeds, so they need to drink every day. After drinking their fill at a watering spot, they then soak their bellies in water and fly back (as far as 30 km (19 miles)!) to their young, which drink the water from the belly feathers. Pallas's sandgrouse performs "eruptions" every once in a while: suddenly large numbers leave their home and fly tens of thousands of kilometers east or west. No one knows why.

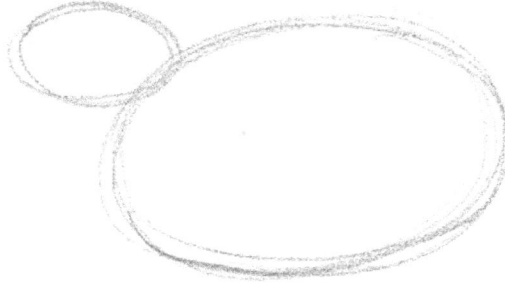

Leave room on your paper for the tail!

1. Look at the finished drawing to see how much room you need to leave on your paper for the tail. Sketch two light ovals, for the body and head.

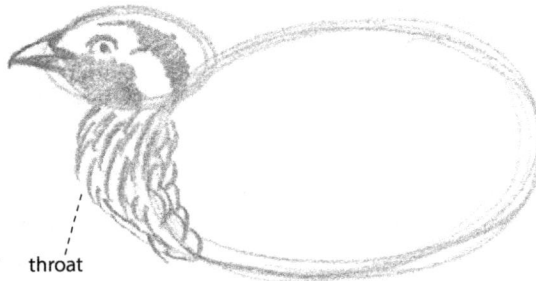

2. Add the beak, eye, and facial markings. Draw short, curving pencil strokes for the feathers of the throat.

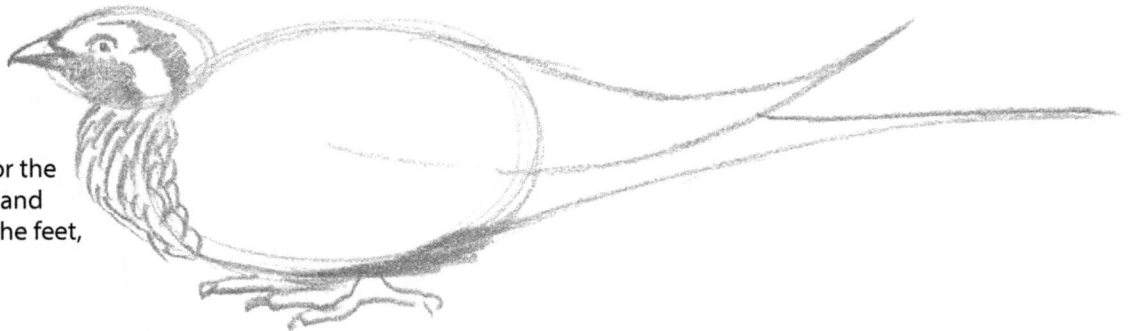

throat

3. Add swooping lines for the upward curving wing and tail. Look carefully at the feet, and draw them.

4. The last step involves observation, patience, and time. Carefully observe the location, direction, and shading of the various wing and tail feathers. Do "soft" shading when your pencil gets dull; use your freshly sharpened point to go over outlines.

Scarab Beetle

Scarabaeus sacer
Mediterranean basin
Size: .2–17 cm (0.08–6.7")

Scarab beetles, also known as dung beetles, roll dung into balls larger than themselves. The female lays eggs in it, and it provides nourishment for the larva after they hatch. The ancient Egyptians considered scarab beetles sacred, since the dung balls reminded them of the sun.

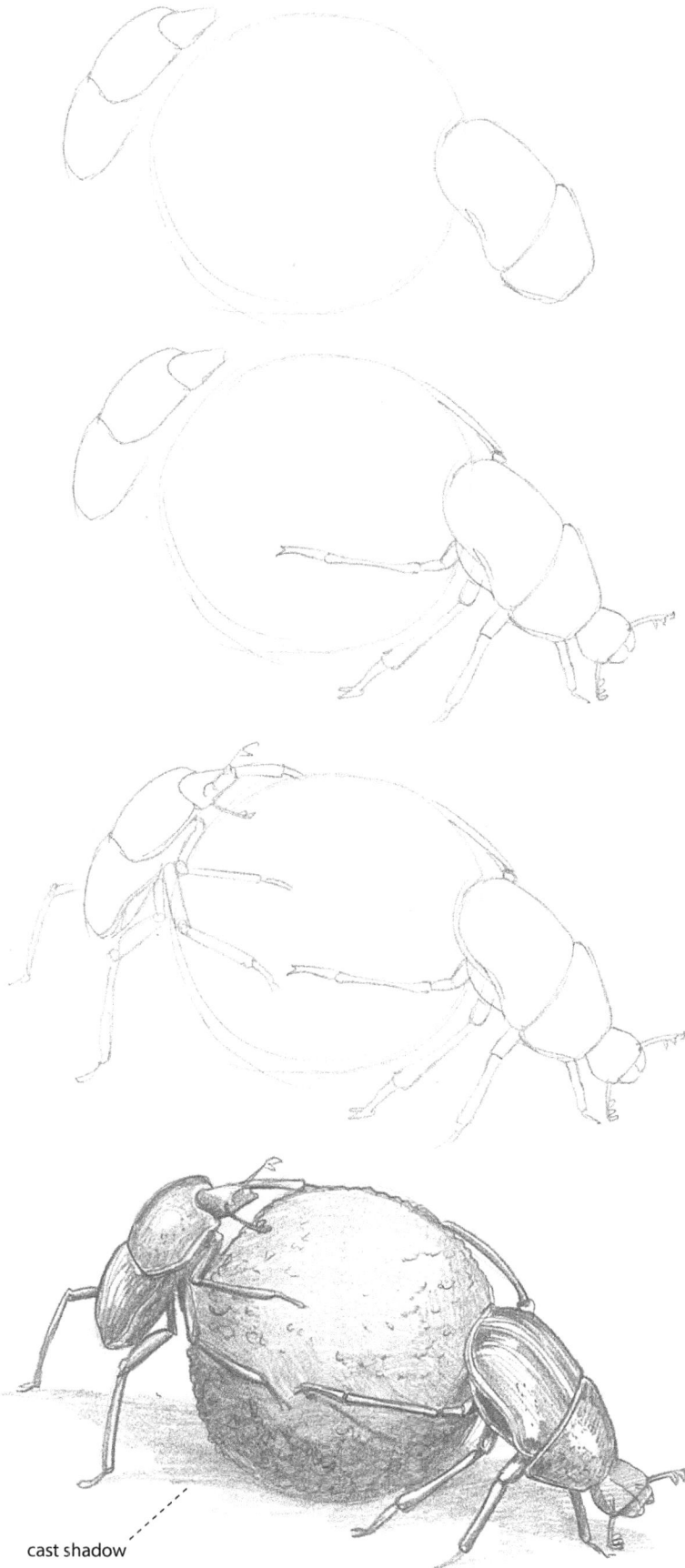

1. Lightly draw the circle for the dung ball. (See if you can get it as round as the beetles do!) Next, add the main body parts of each beetle.

2. Look at the front beetle. Note the angle of each section of each leg. Add the leg segments, a head, and antennae to the beetle.

3. Look at the rear beetle. As with the front beetle, pay close attention to the angle of each section of each leg. Draw the legs, head, and antennae.

4. Notice how the beetles look shiny, while the dung ball looks dull, because the beetles have more contrast between light and dark. Add a *cast shadow* beneath. Look carefully at the example as you finish your drawing, and you'll be able to say ...

... I dung good!

cast shadow

Scorpion

order Scorpiones.
Size: body 3 mm–8 cm (1/8–3")

About 600 different species of scorpion
are known. They have one main part of
their body, then five segments forming the
"tail," at the end of which is a poisonous
stinger. Scorpions live in cracks, but can dig
their own resting places as well. At night,
they eat beetles, cockroaches, and other
arthropods. With their pincers (pedipalps)
they bring prey to their chelicerae (jaws),
which they use to tear it apart. They only
sting when they need to subdue large
or struggling prey. American and North
African desert scorpions have the worst
sting—one Sahara scorpion's sting can kill
a dog in a few seconds.

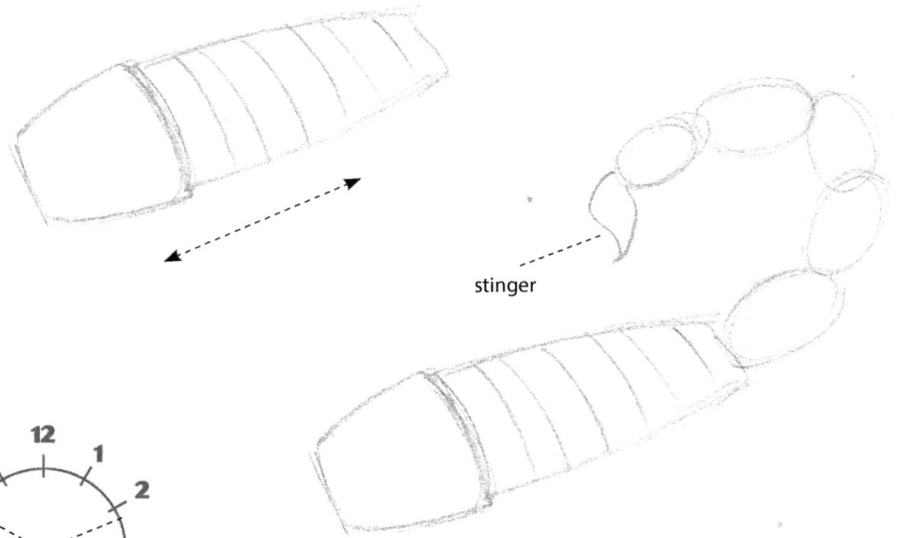

1. Sketch the two main parts
   of the body at an angle
   (compare with clock face).

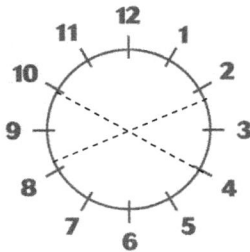

2. Add five connected ovals for
   the tail, the last with a point
   for the stinger.

3. Notice the three main sections
   of the pedipalp, with smaller
   connecting sections. Carefully
   observe the angle of each
   section before drawing.

   Draw the first of the two
   pedipalps, with the large
   pincers at its end.

4. Add the other pedipalp, and
   the first of the walking legs.

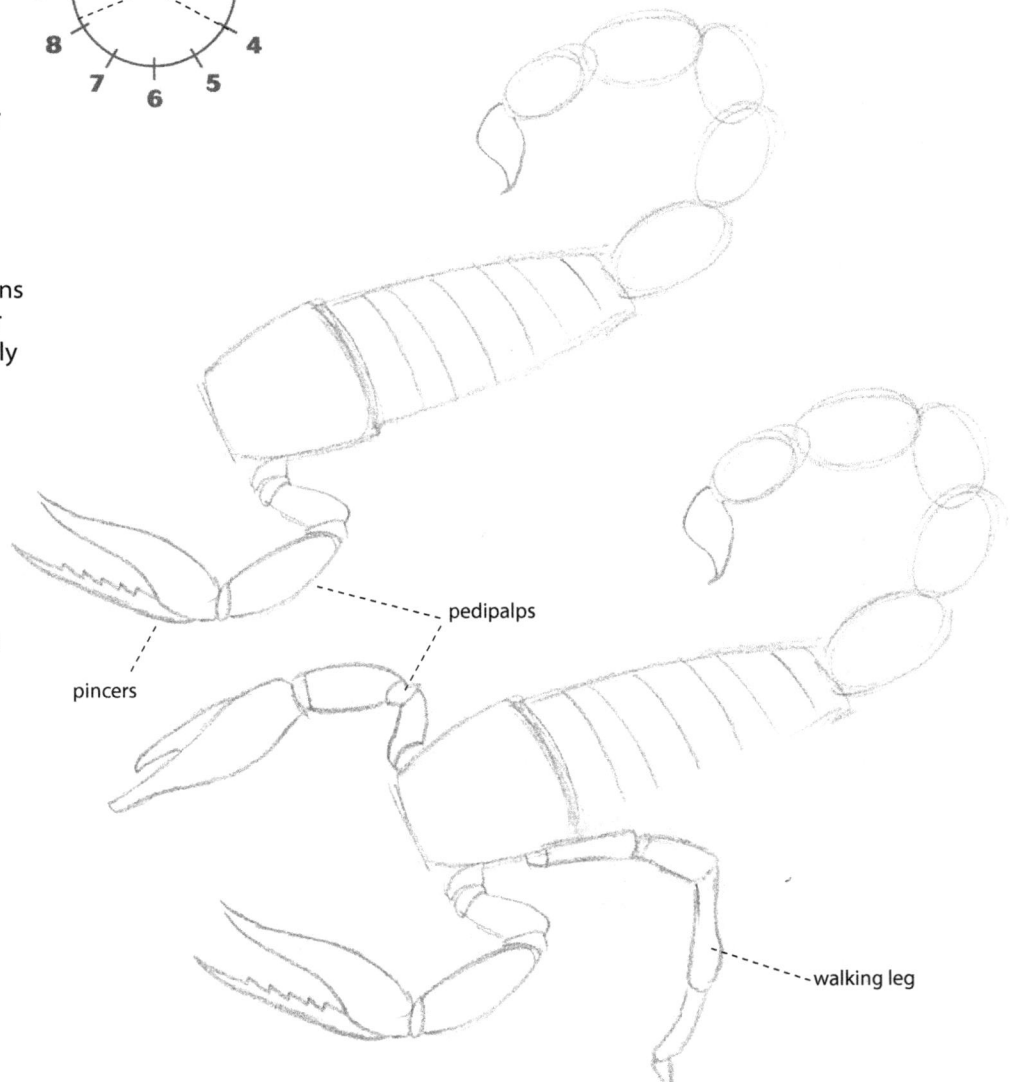

stinger

pedipalps

pincers

walking leg

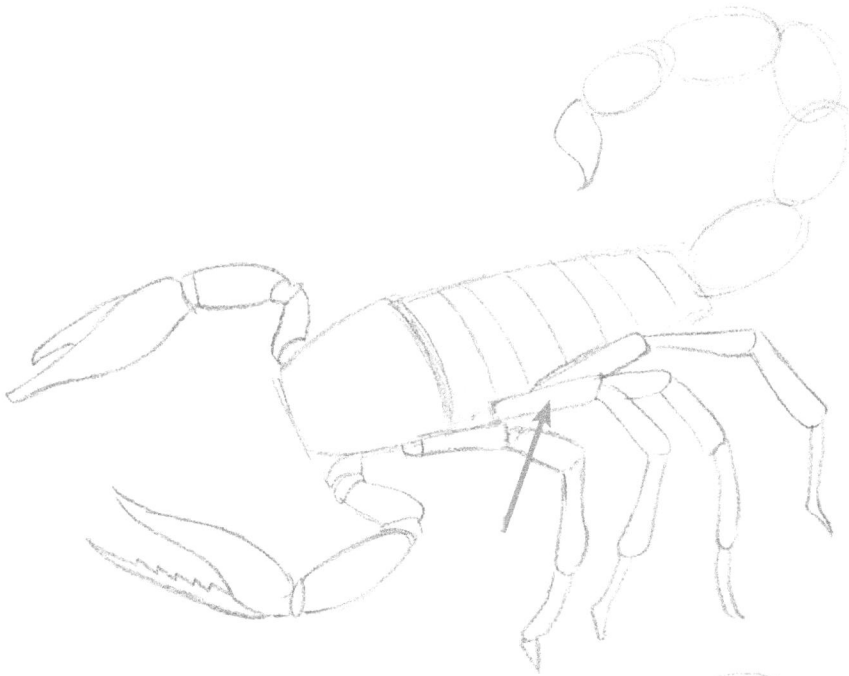

5. Do you see how the remaining three walking legs *overlap* one another? While more difficult to draw, overlapping adds depth and realism to your drawing.

   Draw the remaining three walking legs on the scorpion's left side.

6. On the far side, fewer segments of each leg are visible. Look carefully, and draw them. Compare angles to the clock face to keep your lines running in the right direction.

   Add lines on the tail sections.

7. Add shading, leaving some areas white to make the scorpion look shiny. Draw a cast shadow underneath. Put a few hairs on the tail, and— what has the scorpion caught? Draw part of the pedipalp of another scorpion, which has just lost a fight to yours.

   Put today's date on your drawing and save it!

Sidewinder

Crotalus cerastes. Southwest United States.
Size: 60–70 cm (24–28")

The sidewinder rattlesnake moves uniquely
through the desert sand: only two parts
of its body touch the ground at once!
Sidewinding leaves a series of J-shaped
marks in the sand. Usually sidewinders
hunt at night for small lizards and rodents,
and rest during the day–under a bush or in
another animal's burrow.

1. Start your drawing with two
   curving lines. Make the top line
   connect to the middle of the
   bottom line.

2. Add a second curved line
   below each of the first two.
   Draw the outline of the
   sidewinder's head.

3. Add upward-curving lines to
   connect the ends of the first
   lines you drew. Make sure the
   lower curve aligns with the
   other curving side.

4. Add two more small
   upward-curving lines to
   complete the other side of
   the snake's body. Add the
   end of the tail, with rattles
   on the tip.

5. Look carefully at the curves
   representing the bottom of
   the snake. Add contour lines
   to the snake's underside.

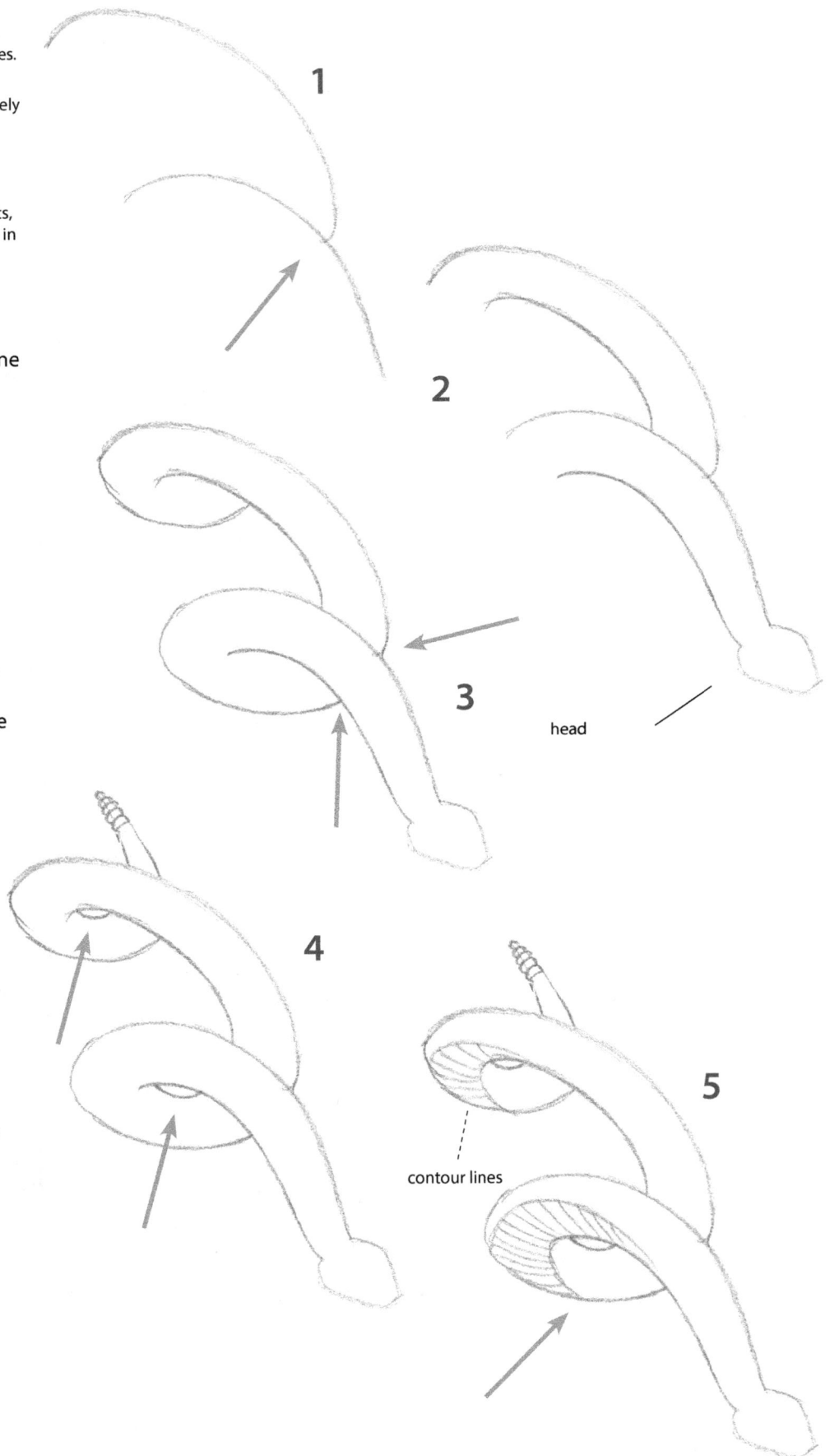

1

2

3

head

4

5

contour lines

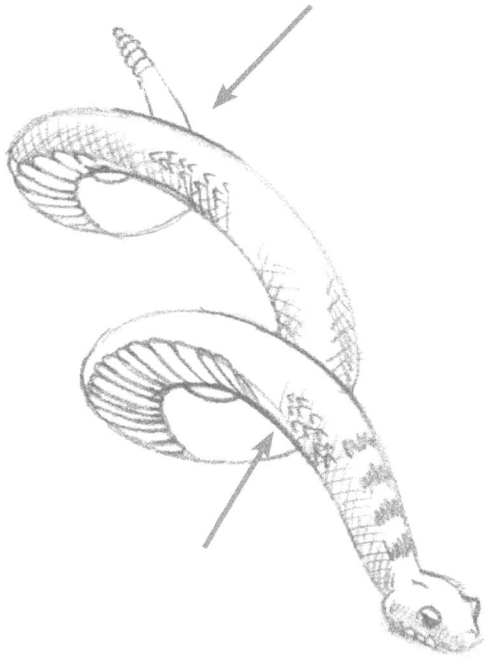

6. Use *crosshatching* to define the *contour* (form) of the snake's body, and to make guide lines for drawing the scales. With a sharp pencil, add emphasis to the outline where parts overlap. Add the eyes, with their pronounced eyebrows.

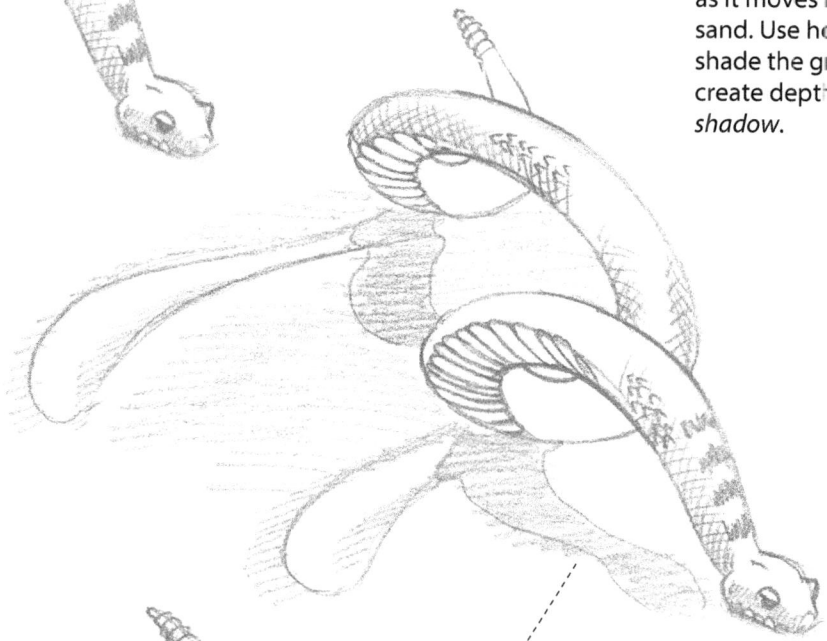

7. Lightly sketch the J-shaped marks the sidewinder leaves as it moves through the desert sand. Use horizontal lines to shade the ground—these help create depth. Draw the *cast shadow*.

cast shadow

8. Darken shadow areas of the snake's track, and add specks for texture as you darken the ground. Carefully go over the snake from end to end, adding scales, the dark band patterns, and shading.

Spectacular sidewinder! Clean up any smudges with your eraser, put today's date on it and save it in your portfolio!

Spotted Skunk

Spilogale gracilis. North America.
Size: 33–56 cm (13–22")

Spotted skunks usually den underground, but also climb trees. No two skunks have exactly the same color pattern. They eat rodents, birds, eggs, insects, and fruit. In the southern part of their range (central Mexico) they give birth any time of the year. Farther north, they give birth in the spring to 4-5 young, after a gestation of 4 months. Before spraying its unpleasant smelly spray, a spotted skunk warns its enemies by doing a handstand.

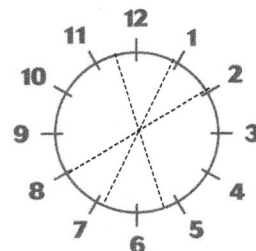

Leave space above!

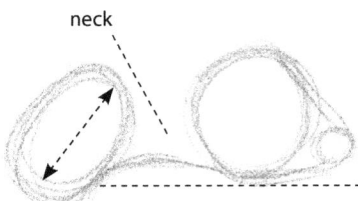

neck

1. Lightly sketch the two small ovals. Leave room above for the rest of the body! Connect the two ovals with a curved line for the neck. Sketch a small circle for the nose, and draw lines to connect it to the head.

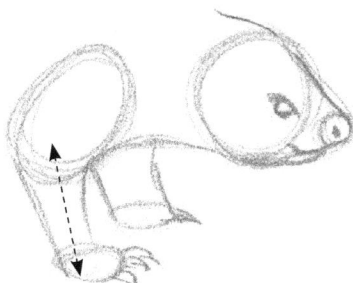

2. From the shoulder oval, draw two lines at a slight angle for the leg. Add an oval for the foot. Draw claws. Add the other leg and foot. Draw the eye, nose, and mouth.

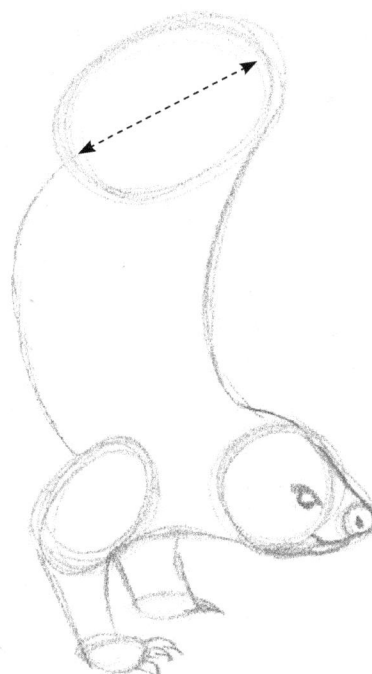

3. Far above the head and leg, sketch a larger, tilted oval. Draw two curved lines to connect the back leg oval with the head and shoulder ovals.

4. Sketch an oval for the rear leg joints. Add the leg and claws. With curving pencil strokes, draw the hairs of the tail, pointing up, then falling back down. Add the ear, whiskers, and short pencil strokes on the front leg for hair.

5. With a sharp pencil, go over the outline, using short back and forth movements—almost like scribbles—to add texture to places where fur sticks out. Lightly "map out" the white spots and stripes for your skunk—remember, each is unique!

To avoid smudging your drawing, put a piece of clean paper under your hand to protect parts you've already drawn.

6. Using short back and forth pencil strokes, always in the direction of the fur, make the whole skunk dark, except for the white spots. Note how the dark areas don't all appear completely black. Leave highlight areas slightly lighter; make shadow areas slightly darker. When the tones are correct, add a few more crisp pencil strokes to emphasize the texture of the fur.

What do you say to a spotted skunk doing a handstand?

"Goodbye."

Yes, but how do you say "goodbye" to a skunk?

As fast as you can!

Tarantula

North America.
Size: body up to 7.5 cm (3") long; leg span to 30 cm (12")

The tarantula is a kind of wolf spider (Lycosa). When threatened, a tarantula might rear up on its hind legs and make a hissing noise. Unlike other spiders, the jaws of the tarantula move up and down instead of sideways. While it is a big, scary looking spider, the tarantula's bite is not as bad as people sometimes think: it's similar to a wasp sting.

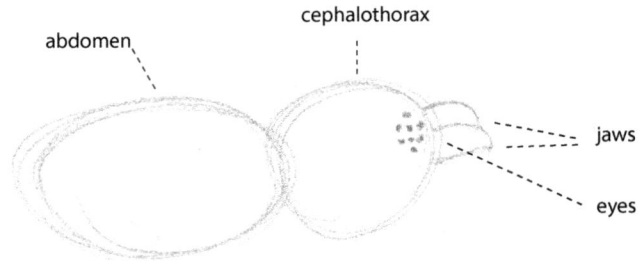

1. Lightly sketch a horizontal oval for the spider's abdomen, and a rounder one for the cephalothorax. Add the eight eyes, and the visible part of the jaws (the fangs point down, so you don't see them from this angle).

2. Draw the two most extended legs first, starting with the coxa and trochanter, then proceeding to depict the femur, patella, tibia, metatarsus, and tarsus.

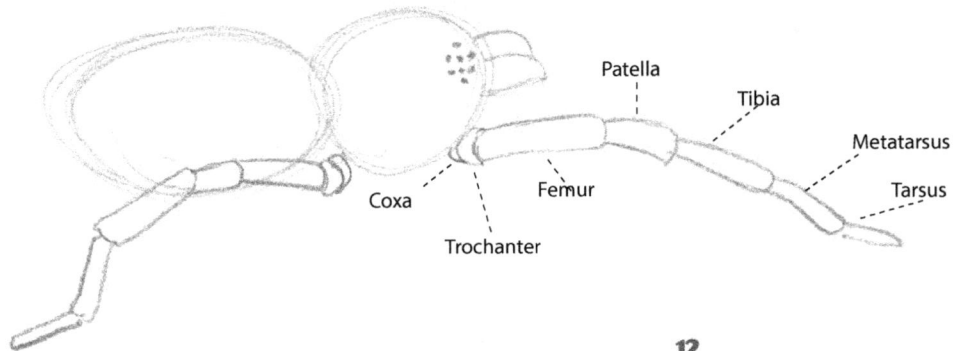

   (You won't be quizzed on them, but pretty cool words to be able to throw around!)

3. The other two legs are *foreshortened* (coming toward you in the picture), so you don't see the full complement of parts. *(I'll bet that's OK with you!)*

   Draw them as you see them, using the clock face as a guide for angles.

   Add a little more definition to the cephalothorax by making slight rounded indents where each leg attaches. Draw the thick pedipalps.

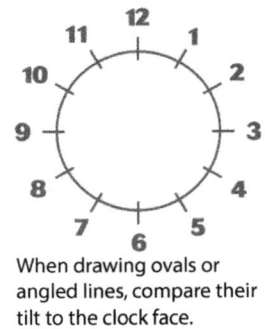

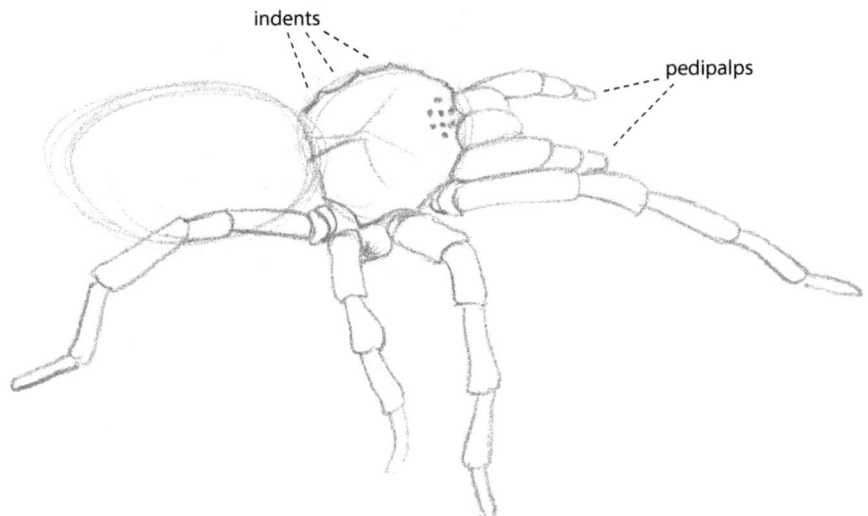

When drawing ovals or angled lines, compare their tilt to the clock face.

4. You'll find the legs on the other side easier to draw, since there is little *foreshortening*. Add them one segment at a time.

As you can see, the last step involves some time. Are you ready to keep going on this drawing, or do you want to keep it as a practice sketch and start another? Your choice. Put the date on this drawing and save it if you want to start over.

5. Finish your tarantula by shading the body parts with a dull pencil, then adding short pencil strokes for hairs when the pencil is sharp.

With a dull pencil (and perhaps smearing it a bit with your finger or a small wad of paper), add the *cast shadow* beneath.

You can have fun adding a hand to your drawing to show scale. Don't know how to draw a hand? Maybe you want to practice on a separate sheet, and draw it before you draw the spider!

Tantalizing tarantula! Clean up any smudges with your eraser, put today's date on it and save it in your portfolio!

Thorny devil

Moloch horridus. Australia.
Size: 15 cm (6")

This small desert lizard (also known as the Australian moloch) looks larger because of the points all over its body. The points keep predators away (would you eat something that thorny?). It moves slowly, and likes to eat ants—one at a time, sitting for hours by an ant nest. At night, dew drops form on the lizard's skin: this is how the Thorny Devil gets water to drink!

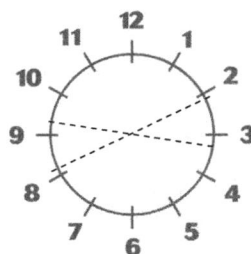

1. Sketch a long, slightly tilted oval for the body. Sketch a smaller oval for the head, tilting the opposite way. Connect them with lines for the neck.

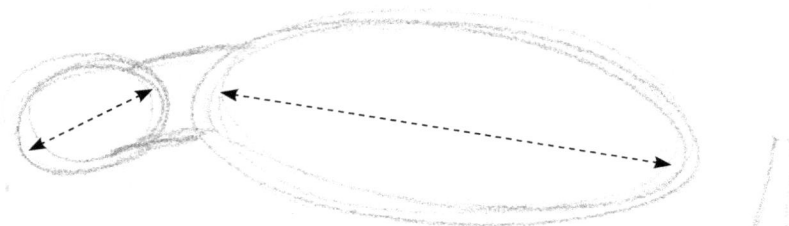

2. Add lines for the legs and claws. Draw the tail. Add a line underneath for the ground.

3. Look at this thorny devil! At the front of the head, draw the eye and mouth. Add spikes on the chin and top of the head.

   Add a jagged edge to the bottom of the tail. Draw spikes on the front and rear leg. Make smaller spikes on each of the claws.

shading

cast shadow

light

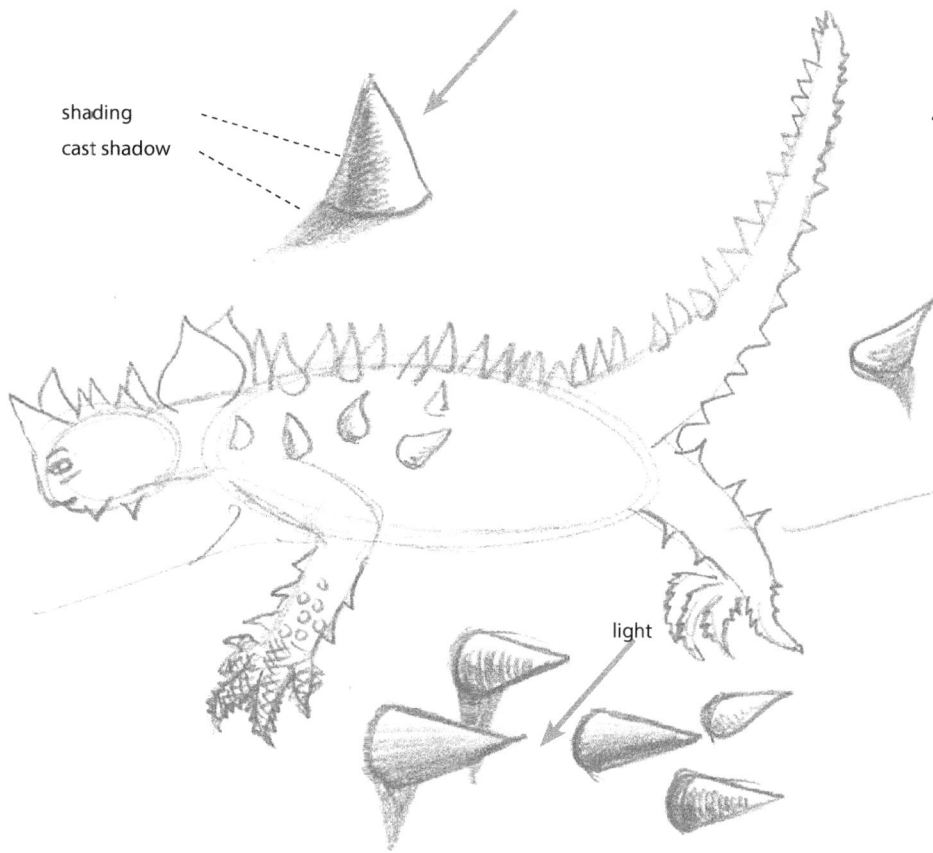

4. Before you start going wild with spikes, take a moment to study the various cones you see here. The rounded spikes on the Moloch's back are really little cones; you don't have to draw them as carefuly as these examples, but you'll find it helpful to see how the shadows of the cones look.

Draw more spikes along the lizard's back, and start adding those little cone-shaped spikes. On the legs, make small circles, tightly packed together, for scales.

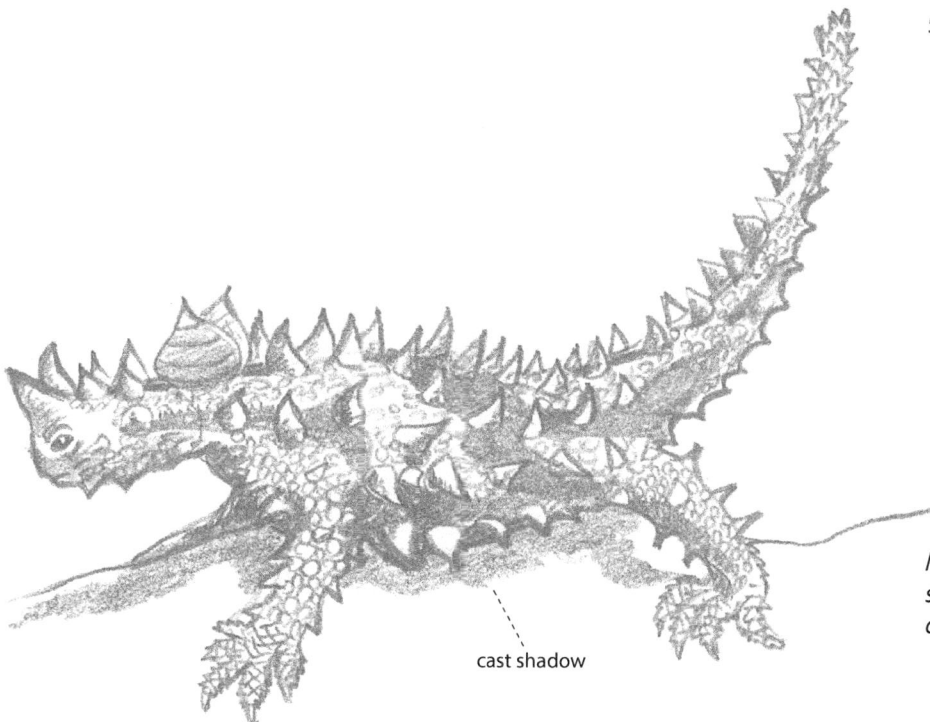

5. Go wild with spikes! Then add shading and the darker areas of the lizard's camouflage pattern. Make a *cast shadow* beneath.

Add color if you want.

Mahvelous Moloch! Clean up any smudges with your eraser. Put the date on your drawing and save it!

cast shadow

Trapdoor Spider

family Ctenizidae. Worldwide, 120 species

Trap-door spiders dig burrows, covering the opening with a hinged flap made from silk and dirt. Then they sit and wait until an unwary insect wanders close to the door, and ZIP!—they push the door open, jump on the insect, and drag it back into the tunnel to kill and eat it.

cephalothorax

abdomen

1. Start your drawing with two upside-down L shapes for the tunnel. Lightly draw the two ovals of the spider's body—the abdomen and cephalothorax.

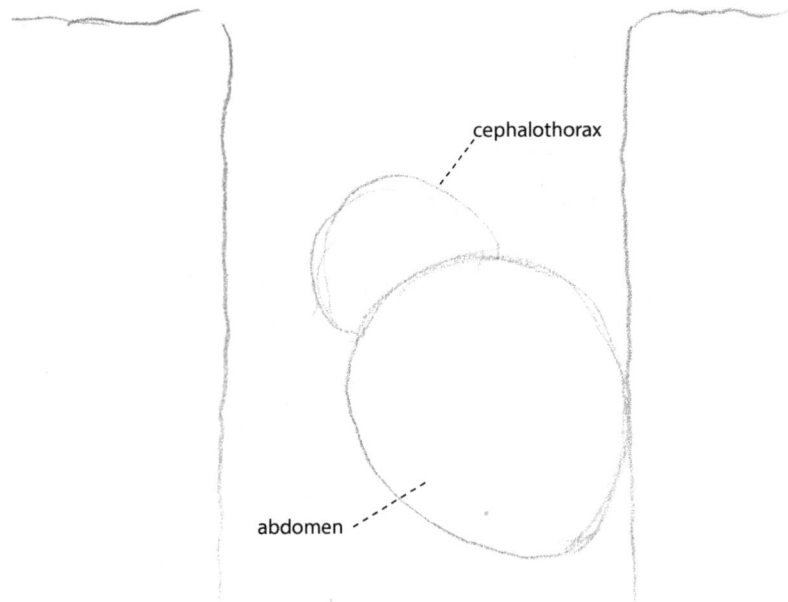

edge of tunnel

pedipalps

jaws

2. From the cephalothorax, draw two segmented legs reaching upward. Add the pedipalps, eight tiny eyes, and jaws (in this top view, you can't see the fangs).

Look at the squiggly shaped trap door. Draw it, and a line for the edge of the tunnel.

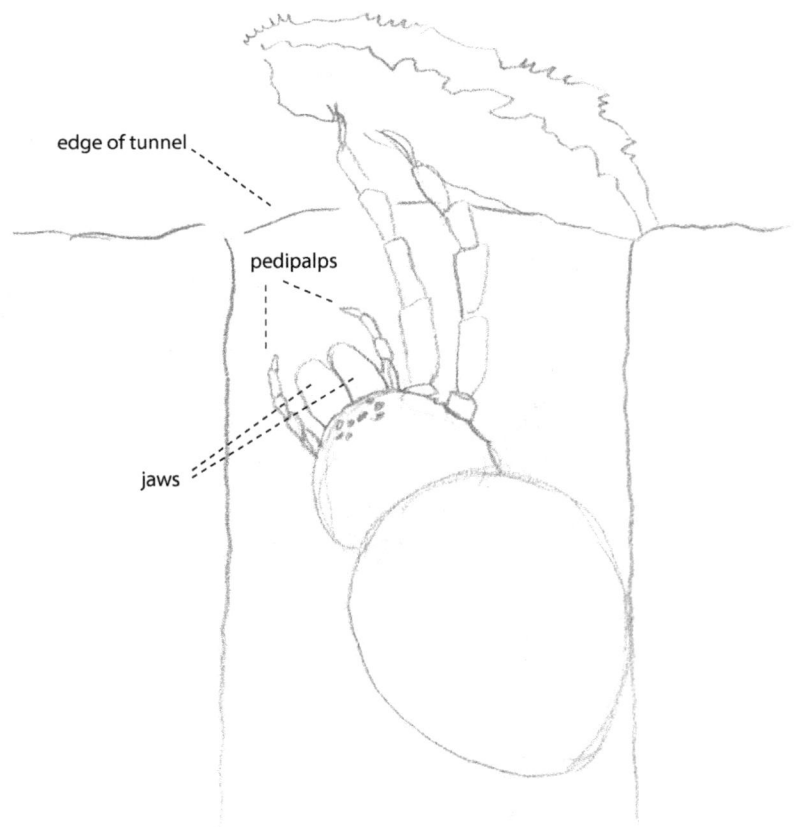

indents

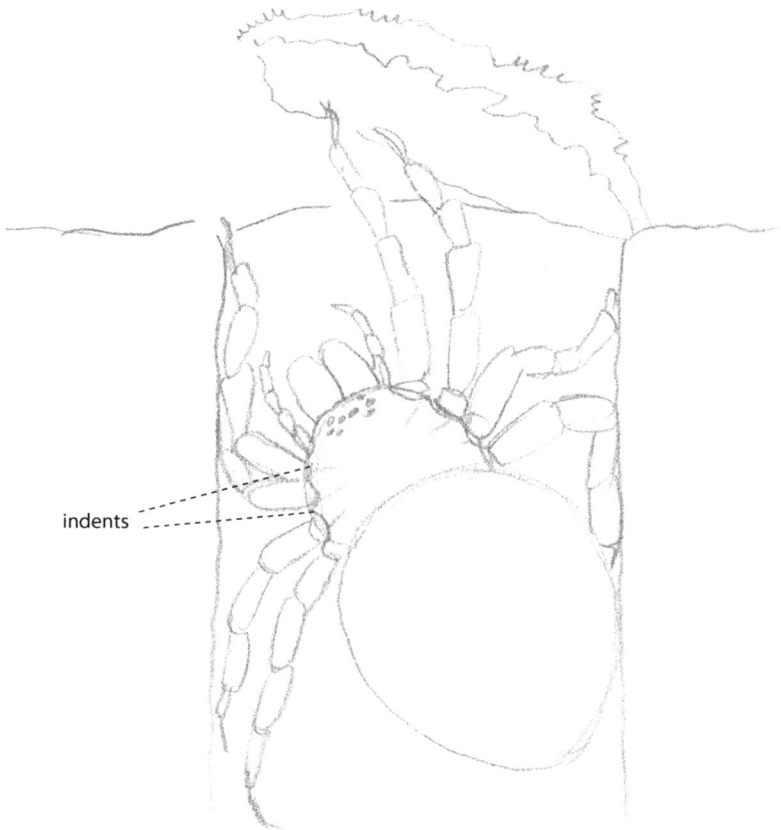

3. Add the remaining legs, one at a time. Draw indents on the cephalothorax at the point where each leg attaches.

4. With a sharp pencil, make short strokes to shade the hairy abdomen and legs. As your pencil gets dull, add to the softer shading of the tunnel and trap door.

Go over outlines, darkening as necessary.

Clean up any smudges with your eraser. Put the date on your drawing and save it in your portfolio!

Knock knock.

Who's there?

Vicuña

Vicugna vicugna. South America: Peru, northern Chile.
Size: 1.4 m long (4.5'), 1m (3' 3") high at shoulder

This smallest member of the camel family lives high in the Andes Mountains, at the edge of the desert near grasslands. Vicuñas are fast, graceful animals who live in groups of up to 15, either one male and females or all male. The females give birth to one young after a gestation period of about ten months. Though long hunted for their wool and meat, it appears that their population is increasing.

1. Sketch two *overlapping* circles for the body. Sketch two smaller circles for the head and nose. Connect head and body with long, curving lines of the neck.

2. Add eyes and nose, paying close attention to where they lie within their circles. Draw a small curved line for the mouth, and add ears.

3. Darken the eye, shade the face, darken the jaw line and make a shadow on the neck. Add jagged lines for the shaggy fur on the chest.

4. Sketch small circles for the leg joints. Draw the front legs and hoofs.

5. Add a rear leg.

6. Draw the other rear leg, noting how the legs overlap. Add the tail. Use short pencil strokes to outline the back. Add hair under the belly.

7. Pay attention to darker and lighter areas as you carefully shade the rest of the body. Add emphasis to outlines. Draw a cast shadow with some rocks and grass on the ground.

Vabulous Vicuña! Clean up any smudges with your eraser, put today's date on it and save it in your portfolio!

Drawing Tips

Start out loose and light

You've seen it enough times in this book: Always sketch lightly at first.

Sketching means trying out ideas, trying out variations, and basically not worrying too much whether the finished product is perfect.

Sketching can vastly improve your drawing skill. Try to do a number of quick sketches to get a feel for the animal: from life, from pictures, or from videos or TV. Then, using your sketch as a guide, carefully put together your final drawing.

You may find—as perhaps all illustrators and artists do—that your lightly drawn sketches have more energy, and capture more of the spirit of the animal, than your final drawing.

So save every drawing, always with the date you drew it!

Timed Drawings

Here's a challenge: pick a subject, and do timed drawings: first, *five seconds* (really, it's possible!). Next, do a 30-second drawing. One more: give yourself two minutes. Now take as long as you need— ten minutes, a half an hour, a day … feel the difference in each? Which is the most fun?

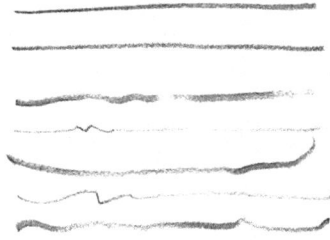

Lines make a difference

Lines are not all created equal. Some lines can make your animal come to life. Try making your lines interesting. Learn to use lines to capture the feel of the animal you're drawing. Here are some suggestions.

Make outlines express

How is the outline of the animal different in each camel? Do you see a technique you can use to make your own drawing more lifelike?

Create texture with lines

What about texture—which drawing gives you an idea what the camel might feel like if you touched it?

Use lines to show form

In addition to showing texture, how do lines help show the form (three-dimensional shape)? Can you see how lines on one of these two Bactrian camels make the drawing look more three-dimensional?

DRAW
GRASSLAND ANIMALS

Giant Anteater

Myrmecophaga tridactyla
South America. Size: 1.5–2 m. (4–6 ft)

Inside that long snout is a long, sticky
tongue which the anteater uses to lick up
termites and ants. With its sharp claws,
it rips open nests, and rapidly flicks its
tongue in and out of its mouth to grab the
insects. The anteater sleeps in the open,
wrapping its hairy tail around its body to
keep warm.

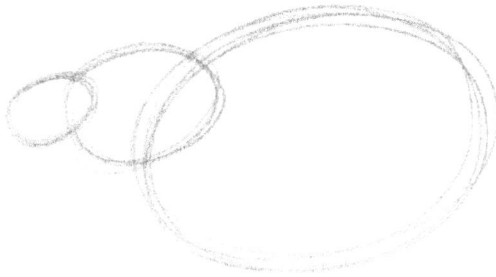

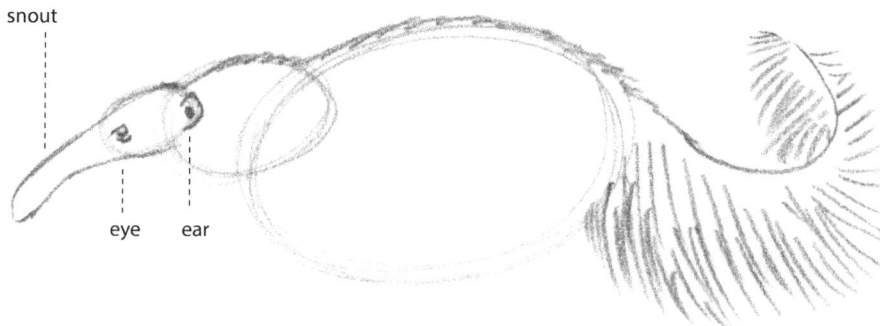

1. Draw three ovals, very lightly.

snout

eye   ear

2. Add the snout to the smallest
   oval. Draw the eye and ear.
   Draw the graceful, curving
   line of the tail from the top of
   the biggest oval. Make pencil
   strokes for the hair on the tail.

3. Draw the curving fronts of the
   two front legs. Create short
   pencil strokes for the hair on
   the back of the front legs. Add
   the claws, curving underneath
   the feet. Draw hair on the
   bottom of the body. Add
   the back legs, and shade the
   distinctive dark area under the
   neck. Add the distinctive band
   of dark fur back from the neck.

4. Finish the drawing by adding
   short pencil strokes and
   shading on the body. Watch
   the direction of the lines!
   Leave the front legs lighter.

*Notice how shading can cover up
the original ovals.*

Nine-banded Armadillo

Dasypus novemcinctus

USA, Central & South America. Size: 70–90 cm (27.5–35.5. inches) including tail. Guess how many bands of plates this armadillo has? Answer: between eight and eleven (good news if you're not a careful drawer!). At night, it digs with its clawed forefeet to find insects, spiders, small reptiles, and amphibians in holes and crevices. During the day, it sleeps in its burrow, often with several other armadillos.

1. Draw a horizontal oval, with two lines at one end to form a thick tail.

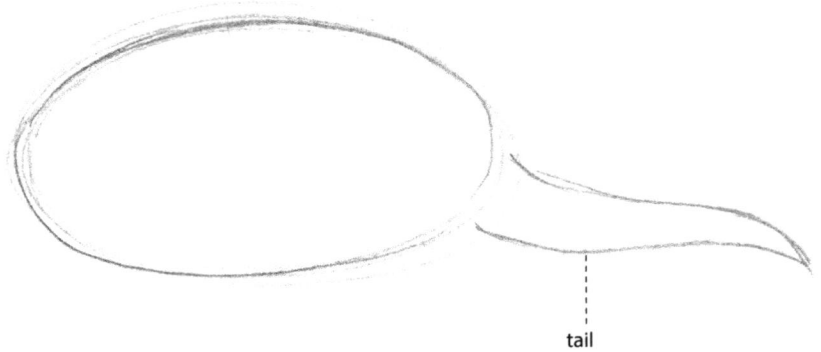

tail

2. Add a rounded, *tapering* (thinner at one end) rectangle for the head. Draw the front and rear leg, with their sharp claws.

head

3. Add ears to the head. Draw a line for the top of the armored part of the head (see final drawing). Add the eye.

   Draw the front and rear legs on the far side of the armadillo.

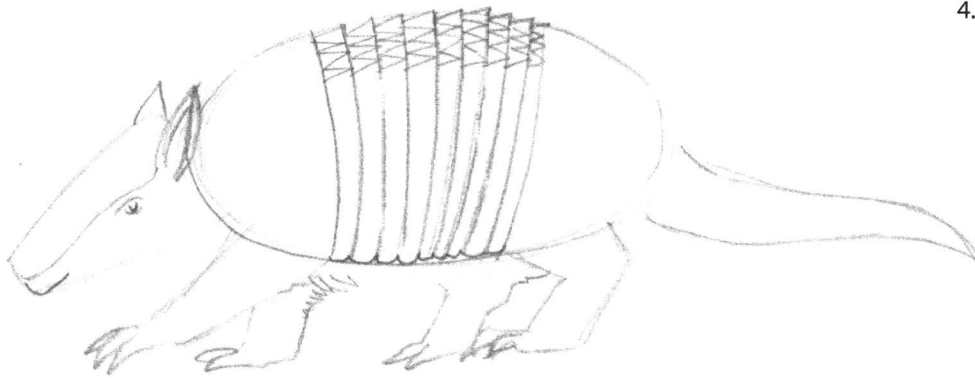

4. From top to bottom of the armadillo's body, draw the nine bands which give it its name. At the top, make them stick out a little from the outline of the body.

Does your drawing have to have exactly nine bands?

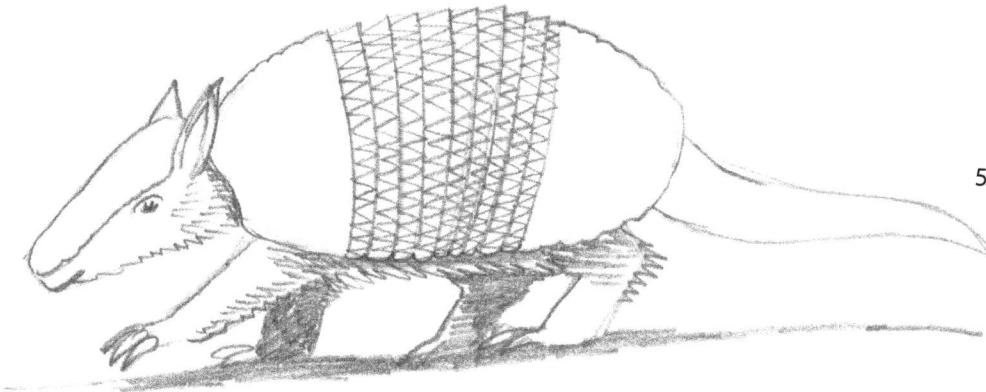

5. Inside each band, carefully add a zigzag line.

Add some short pencil strokes for fur on the face, legs, and body. Shade the legs on the far side of the body. Add a shadow on the ground.

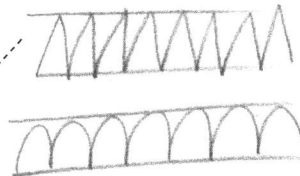

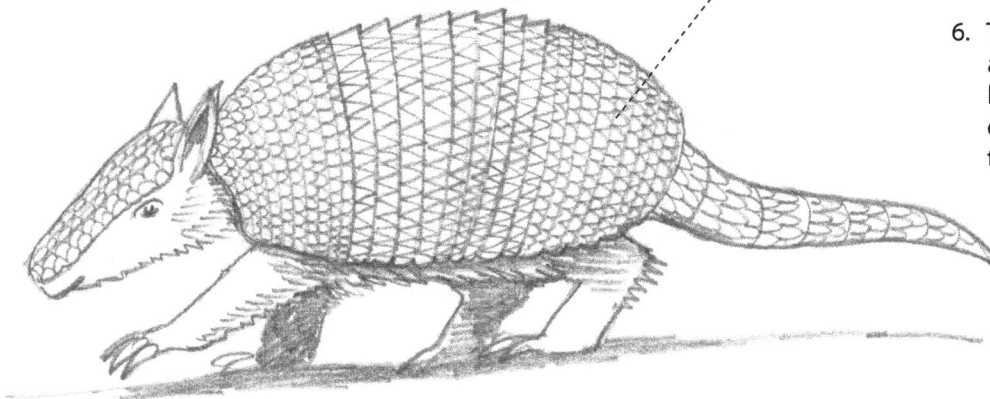

6. To finish your armadillo, simply add more and more narrow bands to the body, and fill each with rounded 'plates.' Do the same on the head and tail.

Awesome armadillo!

Olive Baboon

Papio anubis

Africa. Size, with tail: up to 1.5 m (5 ft).
Baboons live in troops of 20 to 150, finding
safety at night in trees or rocks. They have
strong jaws, and are omnivorous: they eat
grass, seeds, roots, insects, birds' eggs, and
small animals.

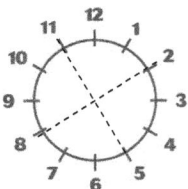

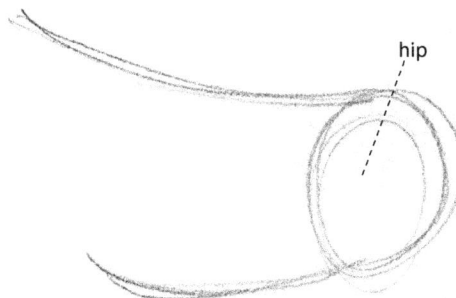

hip

12
11   1
10   2
9   3
8   4
7   5
6

1. Draw a light oval for the hip of
   the baboon. From it, make two
   curving lines, one for the belly
   and one for the back. Look at
   the clock face to make sure
   your lines are running in the
   right direction.

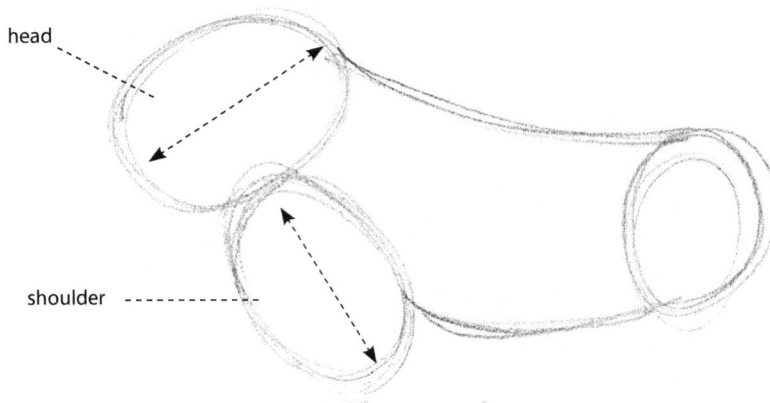

head

shoulder

2. Very lightly, add two more
   ovals—one for the head, and
   one for the shoulder. Again,
   look at the clock face to see
   the direction of the tilt of each
   oval.

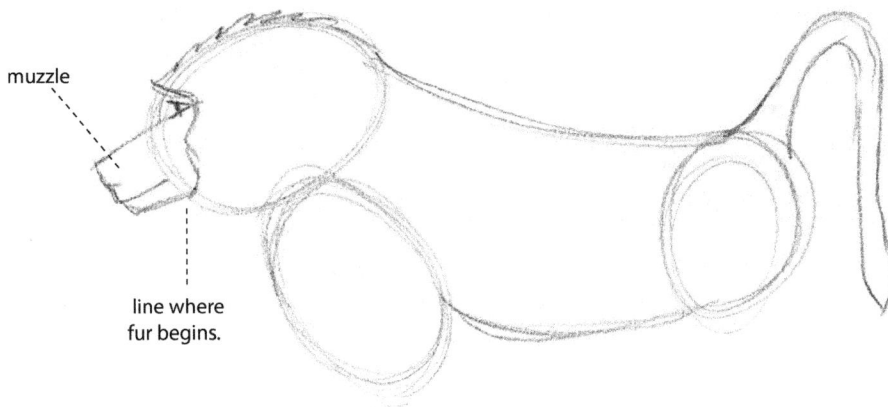

muzzle

line where
fur begins.

3. Add the tail, pointing almost
   straight up and then hanging
   back down. Add the muzzle
   (very much like a dog's
   muzzle), with nostril, mouth,
   eye, and the line where the fur
   begins.

4. Shade the muzzle, and add
   short pencil strokes to create
   the effect of fur, following the
   lines of the body. Shade the
   tail. Add the ear.

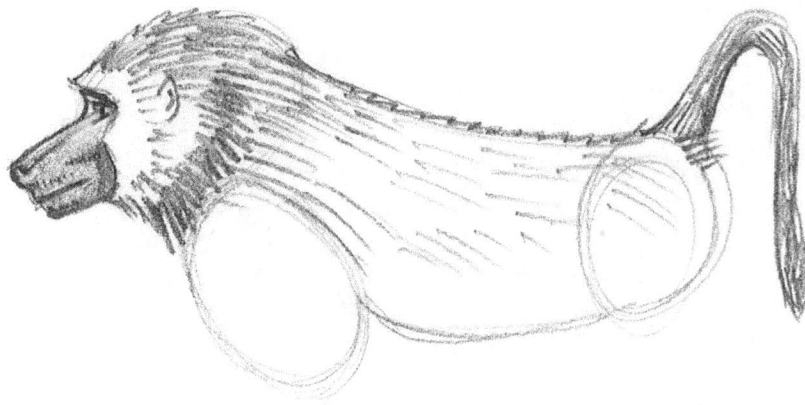

5. From the hip, draw the rear leg and foot closest to you, then add the other. Draw a light line for the ground.

6. From the bottom of the shoulder oval, lightly draw the front legs and feet. Use very light circles to remind you where they bend.

7. Finish your drawing by adding short pencil strokes for fur over the whole body, except for patches on the arms and legs. Look carefully at the directions the fur runs, and pay close attention to lighter and darker areas. Add scribbly lines for grass—grass is great for covering up feet that don't work out well!

Clean up any smudges with your eraser.

Bison

Bison bison

North America. Size: 2.6–4.1 m including
tail; up to 2.9 m (9.5 ft) high at shoulder.
Bison live in herds, which used to number
in the millions. Early European settlers
slaughtered so many that they almost
became extinct by the early 20th century.
Bison are grazers.

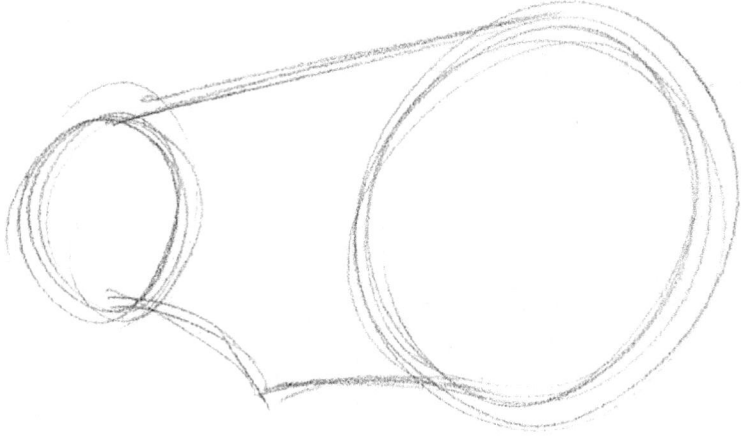

1. Draw two ovals, almost
   circular. Make one much larger
   than the other. Draw a straight
   line for the back of the bison,
   and a curved and straight line
   for its belly.

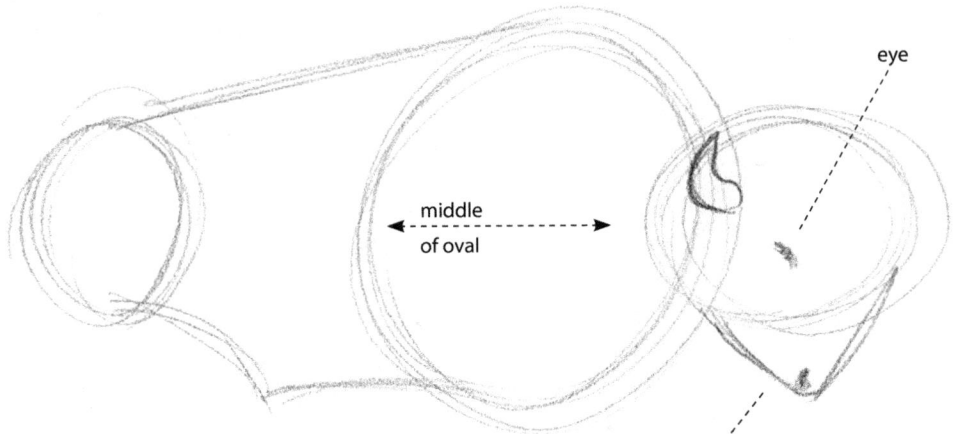

eye

middle
of oval

nostril

2. At the middle of the larger
   oval, draw a smaller oval for
   the head. Add the triangular
   front part of the head,
   pointing downward. Draw the
   horn, eye, and nostril.

3. Using short pencil strokes,
   add fur to the head, neck, and
   back. Add the ear!

4. Before continuing with the fur, add the legs and tail. Draw the legs lightly, using small circles to emphasize the joints. Add a line for the ground.

Notice that the front legs are mostly covered with fur. The rear legs, however, require careful attention to details!

5. Now continue drawing the thick fur on the shoulder, back, and front legs. Lightly shade the rear portion of the bison. Thicken the cast shadow beneath the bison.

Clean up any smudges with your eraser.

Beautiful bison!

African Buffalo

Synceros caffer

Africa. Size: 2.8–4.1 m (9–13.5 ft) including tail. An aggressive animal, and dangerous to hunt–if wounded, it may wait in hiding to attack its hunter! Crocodiles and lions usually are able to kill only young or sick animals. It eats grass, bushes, and leaves.

1. Draw two almost-circular ovals. Make lines connecting the tops and bottoms as you see in the example.

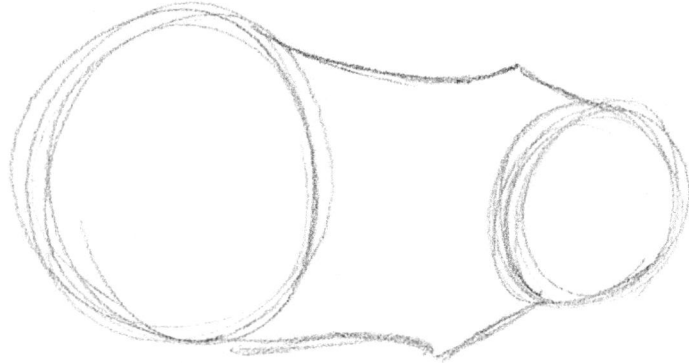

2. Near the top of the larger oval, lightly sketch a circle for the head, then add the flat snout, eye, and horns. Draw the horns very lightly at first—you may need a couple of tries to get them right!

3. When you've got the horns looking right, add ears, nostrils, and mouth. With short pencil strokes, darken parts of the face. Add the curved tail.

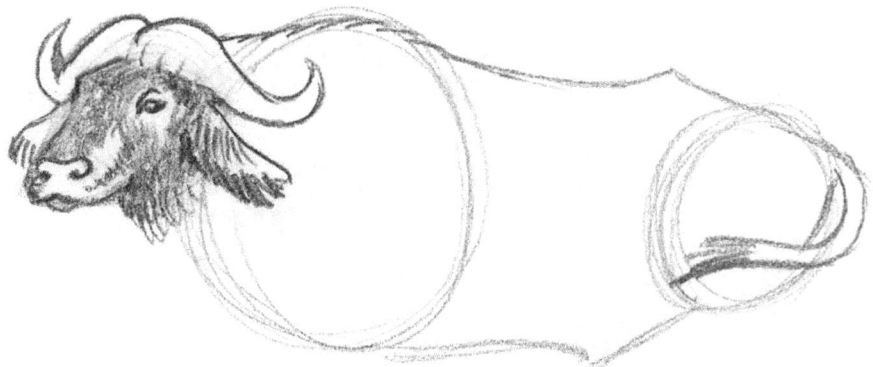

4. Using small circles at the joints, sketch the legs. Pay close attention to the angle of each line. Make a light line for the ground to help you keep the legs the same length.

5. Add the other two legs in the same way.

6. Using short pencil strokes, shade the buffalo. You'll notice you don't have to completely shade the whole body—but also notice how dark the underside is. This *contrast* of light and dark suggests strong light overhead.

Draw some tall grass behind the African buffalo.

Looks kind of friendly, doesn't it? It's not!

Cheetah

Acinonyx jubatus

Africa. Size: 1.7–2.2 m (5.5–7 ft) including tail. The cheetah is the fastest big cat. It can run at 112 km/h (69.5 mph) for short sprints. The cheetah hunts hares, jackals, small antelope, birds, and occasionally larger animals. After a quick chase, it knocks them down and kills them quickly by biting the throat .

1. Draw a small oval, almost straight up and down, for the shoulder. Lightly sketch another, tilted oval for the body, and yet another inside it. Make a small line connecting the tops of the first two ovals.

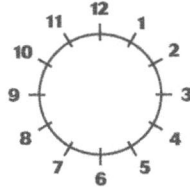

shoulder

Imagine the dotted lines on top of the clock face to see how the ovals tilt.

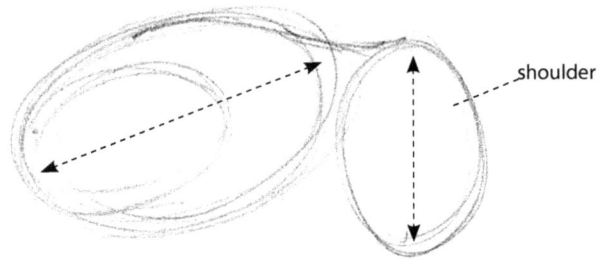

2. Draw a tilted oval for the head. Draw two light lines to connect it to the body. Add the tail. Draw *lightly!*

3. Look carefully at the angles of the rear leg. The leg goes straight down from the front of the 'inside' oval. Where is the bend, compared to the first oval? How far forward does the paw reach?

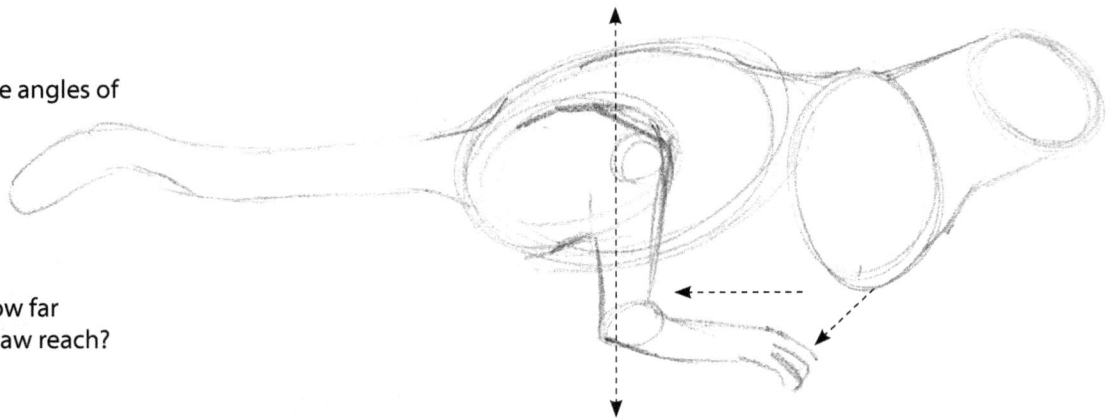

Draw the rear leg.

4. Sketch the front leg, starting from the middle and the bottom of the shoulder oval. Look at the space between the legs as you draw, and notice how the front leg aligns with the rear paw.

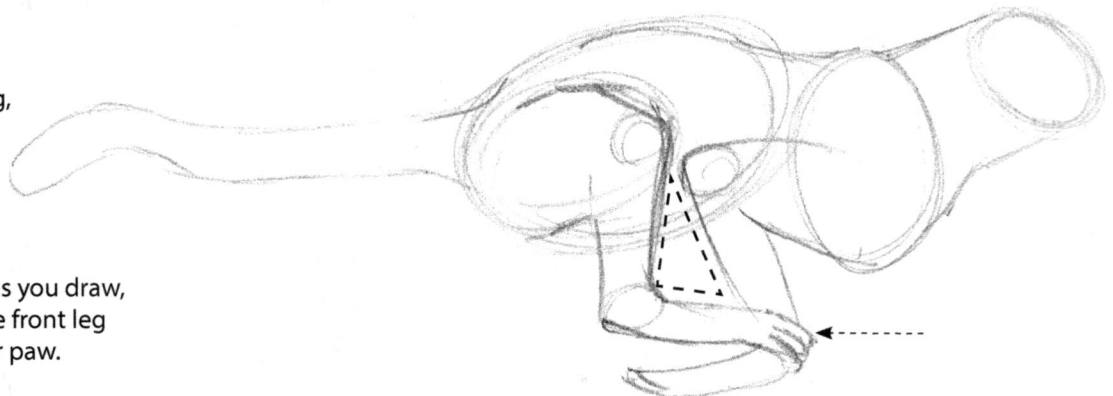

5. On the chest and belly of the cheetah, add short pencil strokes for fur. Draw the other front leg. Draw the head, adding ears, and lines at the mouth and nose.

6. Add the triangular eye, with the cheetah's distinctive tear lines from the eye. Add bumps on the back at the shoulder and hip. Lightly erase oval lines you no longer need. Use the tail as a warmup for drawing spots (there are many more!).

7. Yikes! Lots of spots! Use short pencil strokes in the direction of the fur for shading. Add color if you wish. Take your time with shading and the spots. Sharpen your pencil. Sharpen outlines. Breathe deeply!

Finally, clean up any smudges with your eraser.

Hunting Dog

Lycaon pictus

Africa. Size: 6–9 m (24–30 inches) high at shoulder. These scruffy hunters range widely, ferociously attacking but then letting the youngest pups eat first, and injured dogs as well. They are not closely related to domestic dogs.

1. Start with two tilted ovals. Look at the clock face to make sure you have the right angle for the tilt of the ovals. Connect them at the top with a curving line for the back.

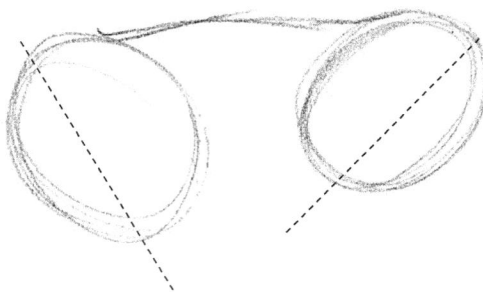

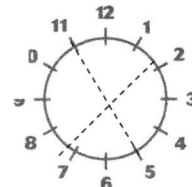

2. Lightly draw an oval for the head. Add ears. Draw lines to form the neck. Sketch the tail.

3. Draw the snout, lower jaw, and eye. With a sharp pencil, make short pencil strokes to 'map out' the direction of the fur on the face, neck, and ears.

4. Look carefully at the legs closest to you. You may find it helpful to make ovals at each joint—just draw them lightly! Draw the top of the front leg, then a longer, narrower section extending downward, ending with a different angle at the paw.

   Now sketch the sections of the back leg, carefully looking at the example. Does the back leg touch the ground?

5. Look carefully at the sections of the legs farther from you. Drawing those little ovals at the joints can really help get the legs right. Notice that you don't see the entire leg.

Add a line for the ground, and spots for dirt kicked up by the running dog.

6. One difference between an OK drawing and a truly awesome drawing is slowing down for details at the end, shading, and cleaning up. Sharpen your pencil, and draw light, short lines to show the direction of the fur. Look closely at my example if you don't have your own hunting dog nearby. Add some low grass.

Since the one front leg is bearing the weight of the dog, give it a little added emphasis.

7. Sharpen your pencil again, and go over the entire drawing, from nose to tail, ear to toe, darkening fur to give the dog its characteristic scruffy look. Don't be scared to get some lead out of that pencil. Just make sure you have a sharp point when you sharpen lines and work on the fur.

African Elephant

Loxodonta africana

Africa. Size: 7–9 m. Elephants can consume up to 200 kg (440 lbs) of plants a day, making them sometimes unwelcome neighbors where people grow food. African elephants have bigger ears and tusks than Indian elephants, and two finger-like extensions at the end of the trunk.

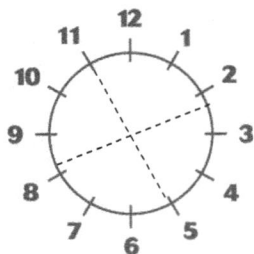

1. *Before you draw, use the clock face to identify the angles of the two ovals you will draw first.*

   Start with a large oval for the body of the elephant. Add a smaller oval for the head.

   Does the head oval touch the oval of the body? How much space is between them?

   Lightly sketch lines to connect the body and head.

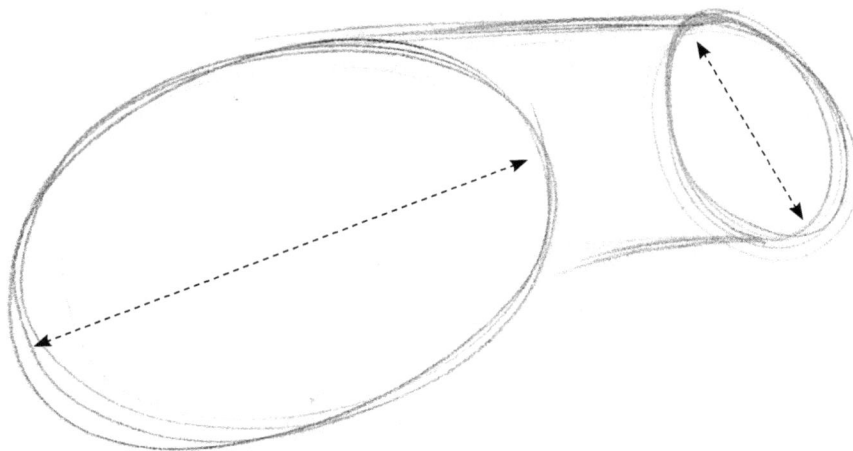

2. Look carefully at the angle of each leg. *Does any leg go straight up and down?*

   Lightly draw a line for the ground. Draw the legs, very lightly at first, using ovals for the knees, as well as the hip and shoulder. From the sides of the head oval, draw gently curving lines for the trunk, reaching almost to the ground.

   Where the trunk joins the head, add a tusk and the mouth (not just a line!). Directly above that, draw the eye. Add a bump on the top of the neck. Draw the ear. Notice how it covers most of the neck.

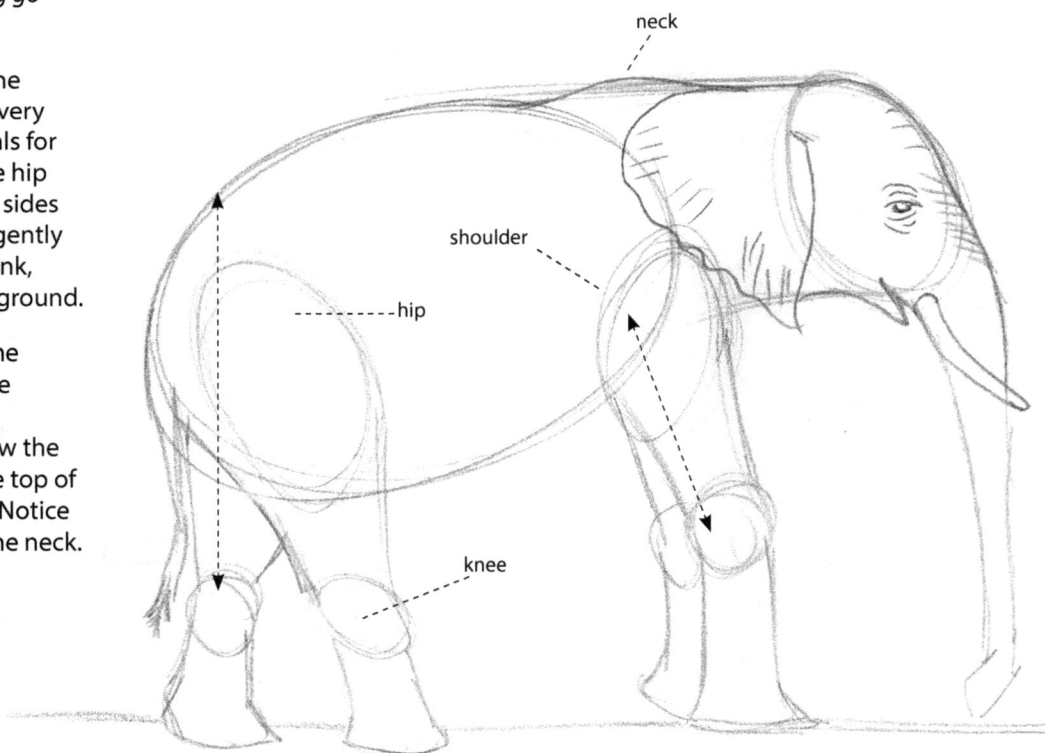

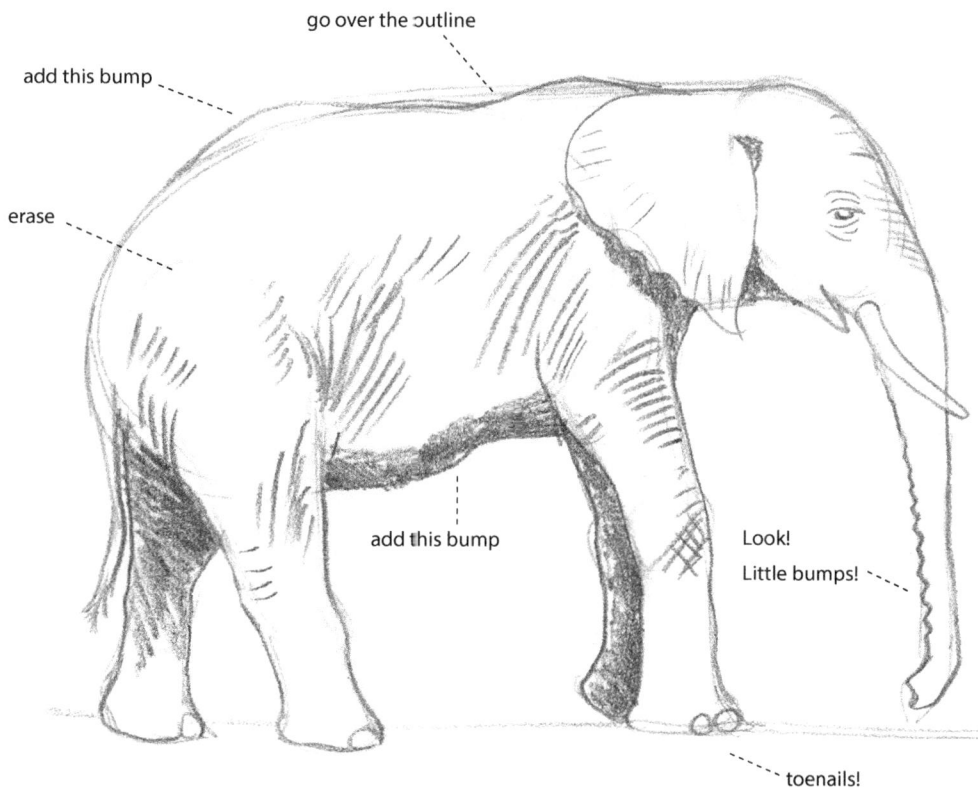

go over the outline

add this bump

erase

add this bump

Look!
Little bumps!

toenails!

When you start to shade, always look for the darkest areas first

3. First, complete the outline of the body: add a bump on the back and a small bump at the stomach. Add toenails! Go over the outline of the elephant, and carefully erase lines you don't need—for example, those ovals you started with.

   Look at the final drawing, or look at a photo of an elephant. Study the wrinkles in the elephant's skin—zillions of them! Can you draw every single wrinkle? Probably not. What you can do is suggest wrinkles, by making plenty of lines running in the direction of the wrinkles.

   Next, add lines showing the direction of the major wrinkles.

   Now begin to shade, starting with the darkest parts of the drawing.

4. *How much white do you see on the final drawing? Not much! Since the elephant is gray, your whole elephant should be gray when you finish.*

   Shade and shade and shade and shade! Use your wrinkle lines to show you which direction to make shading lines.

   When you're satisfied with your drawing, look at it in a mirror—or through the back of the paper—to spot any last minute improvements you can make!

Gerenuk

Litocranius walleri

Africa. Size: (body) 1.4–1.6 m (4.5–5.25
ft). Gerenuks are graceful gazelles
distinguished by a long neck (gerenuk
means 'giraffe-necked' in Somali). They
eat leaves and shoots of thorny bushes
and trees, which they're able to reach
with their long legs and necks. They eat in
the morning and evening, and spend the
hottest part of the day standing still in the
shade.

1. Draw two light ovals, and
   connect them at the top and
   bottom with curving lines.

2. Sketch two circles *(lightly, of
   course!)* for the head and nose.
   Add the eye, near the top of
   the head. Connect the head
   to the body with long, curving
   lines.

   *How long is the neck, compared
   to the length of the body?*

   Add the tail.

3. Draw the nose, mouth, and
   jaw line. Add horns and ears.
   Following the example, add
   shading on the head and ears.

   Using circles at the joints, draw
   the long, slender legs. The
   front leg goes almost straight
   up and down, but not the rear
   leg. Notice how it extends
   beyond the back of the body.

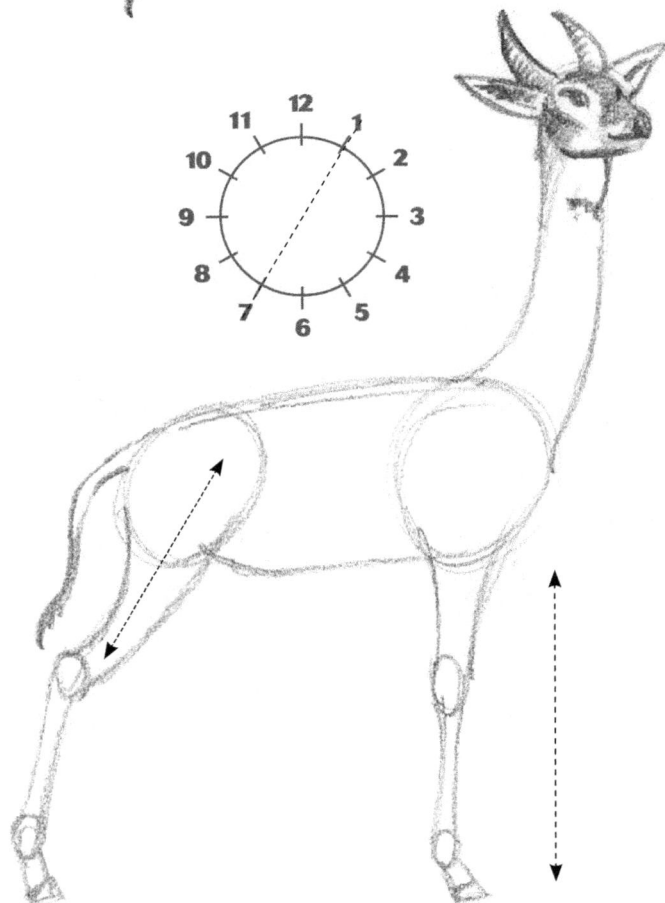

4. Add the other two legs. Go over the outline, using thinner and thicker lines to make it more interesting and emphasize the structure of the body.

5. With short pencil strokes, shade the body. The gerenuk is darkest on top, lighter brown along the side, and white underneath.

Add a background with acacia trees and color if you want to.

Graceful gerenuk!

Where do you suppose the name Gerenuk *comes from?*

Giraffe

Giraffa camelopardalis

Africa. Size: 3.3 m (11 feet) high at shoulder, nearly 6 m (19.5 ft) at crown. Giraffes live in small groups. They eat foliage and fruit from the tops of acacia and thorn trees.

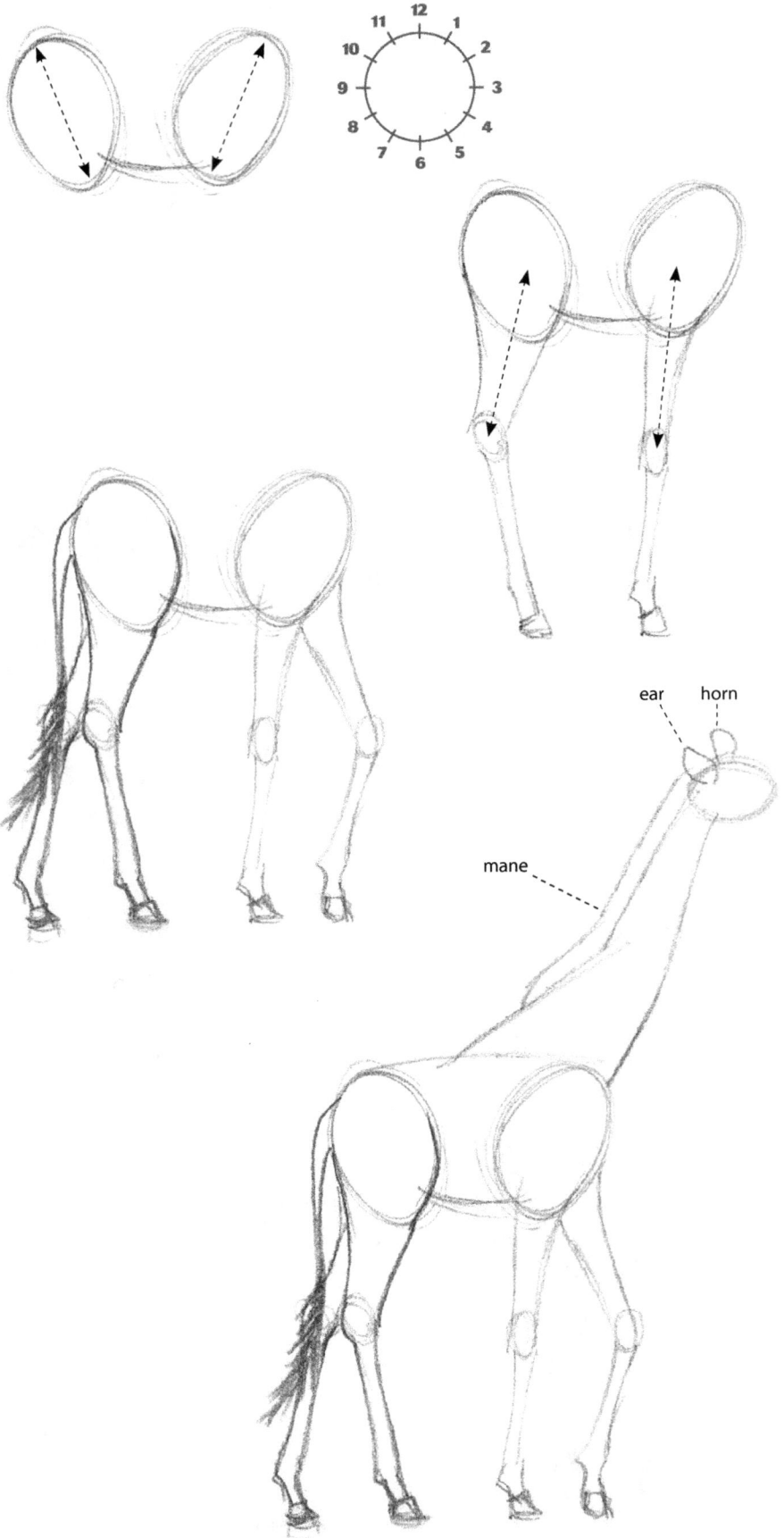

1. Lightly draw two ovals, tilted slightly outward. Use the clock face to help see the correct angles. Connect the ovals with a small curved line on the bottom.

2. Draw the two legs closest to you, using small ovals at the joints. Notice how the rear leg is larger at the top, and how its angles are different than the front leg.

3. Add the two legs further from you. Draw them lightly at first, so that you can change them if you need to—notice I had to adjust the length of the legs at the hooves; fortunately, these get fairly well hidden by grass in the final step!

   Draw the tail.

4. Make a light oval for the head, far above the body. Add the angled lines of the neck. Draw a light line for the back. Sketch the outline of the mane, ear, and horn.

5. Draw the front of the head, with nose and mouth. Make a horizontal line with a curved line below it for the eye, with another curved line above for the eyelid. Use short pencil strokes to create the mane. Go over the whole outline to refine it.

   Lightly erase the ovals and any other lines you no longer need.

6. Study the pattern on the giraffe before drawing it. Note that most of the dark patches are four-sided, but not square. After you draw the patches on the giraffe, add a little shading to help emphasize the form (roundness) of the animal. Make some short pencil strokes for grass. Finish up by cleaning any smudges with your eraser.

In case you were wondering: it takes a little planning to put your head down to a cool stream for a drink when you're a giraffe!

Spotted Hyena

Crocuta crocuta

Africa. Size: 1.5–2.1 m (±5–7 ft) with tail. Hyenas are mostly active at night. Like vultures, they quickly clean up carrion (dead animals) and so help prevent the spread of disease from rotting flesh. The spotted hyena looks like a strong dog, and is found south of the equator in Africa.

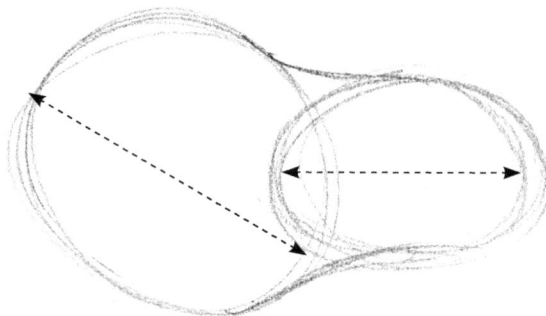

1. Draw two light *overlapping* ovals, and connect them with *concave* curving lines. Notice the different tilt of each oval. (Compare the axis of each oval with the clock face.)

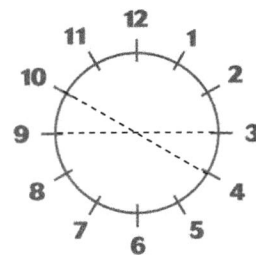

shoulder

2. Draw another *very light* oval for the shoulder. Draw light ovals where the legs bend, then draw the upper legs, lower legs, and paws.

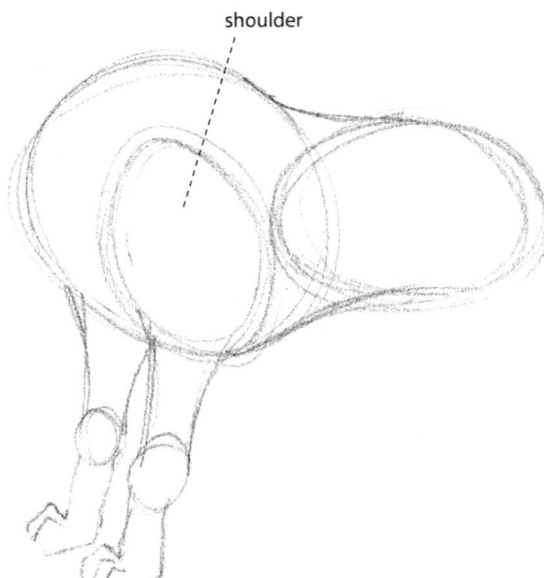

3. Draw small ovals for the *ankles* on the back leg. Add the upper and lower legs, and rear paws. Use short pencil strokes to draw the tail.

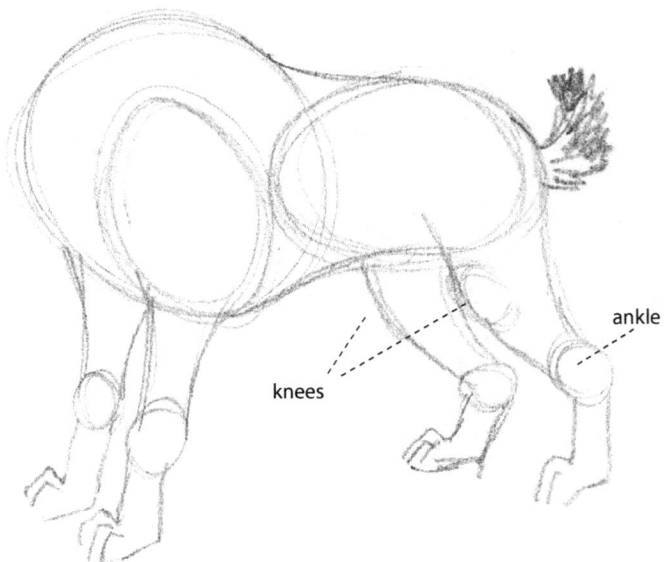

knees

ankle

back of neck

throat

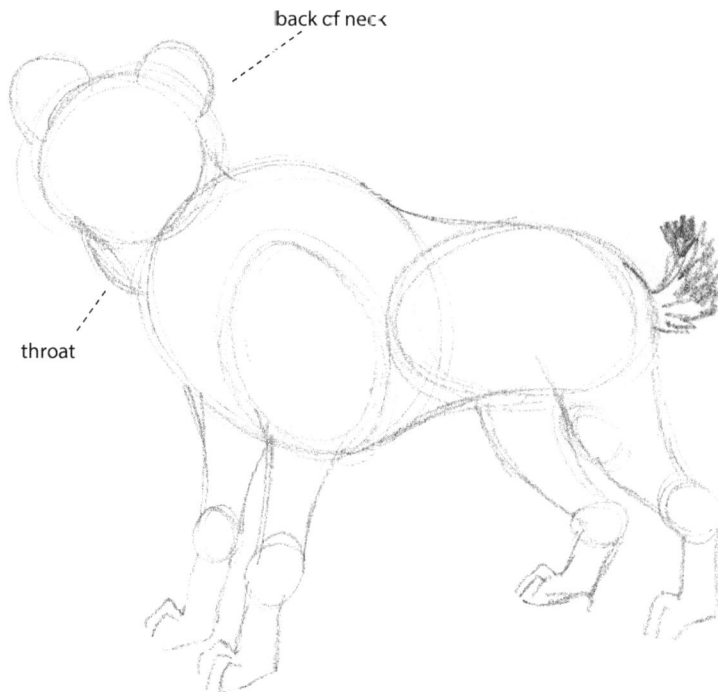

4. Draw a *light* circle, touching the large oval you drew in step one, for the head. Add two partial circles for ears. Lightly sketch lines for the throat and back of neck.

5. At the bottom of the head, draw the nose and mouth. Next, toward the center of the circle, draw the eyes (notice they're at an angle to each other). Add whiskers, and shading around the face and neck.

6. Go over the outline, making it jagged where fur stands out. (Look carefully at the final drawing.) Start at one end and add shading and spots. Draw a *cast shadow* underneath on the ground. Clean up any smudges with your eraser.

Is your drawing perfect? If not, think about trying it again—or hold your drawing up to a mirror, or look at it through the back of the paper to see areas that need improvement.

Red Kangaroo

Macropus rufus

Central Australia. Size: 1.9–2.7 m (6.25–8.75 ft) including tail. Kangaroos stay in shady places during the day, and feed in the evening. Kangaroos are marsupials, meaning the young crawl into a pouch after birth. They stay there about 240 days.

1. Look at the angles of these ovals! Now, draw an oval for the top of the leg, and around it a larger—very light!—oval for the largest part of the body. Draw two vertical lines for the legs, and then add the horizontal part of the leg with foot.

2. From the large oval, draw the tail, angling down toward the ground and then laying flat on it. Add the bit of the other leg that's visible, and begin the pouch where the head of joey (baby kangaroo) will appear.

   Draw another very light oval for the shoulder, with lines connecting it to the rear part of the body.

3. Draw a light oval for the head. Add two lines for the neck. Draw the snout, with nose, mouth, and chin. Lightly draw the two ears, and the eye.

4. Starting at the shoulder, lightly draw the 'mechanics' of the arm, using light straight lines and ovals at the joints (of course you see more of the closer arm than the farther arm). Notice that you can see the claws on the farther arm, but on the closer arm you can't, because they're pointing away from you.

Make a light triangle for the joey's head, with two little triangular shapes for eyes, two ears, and a dark nose. Add lines to complete the pouch.

emphasize important parts of the outline

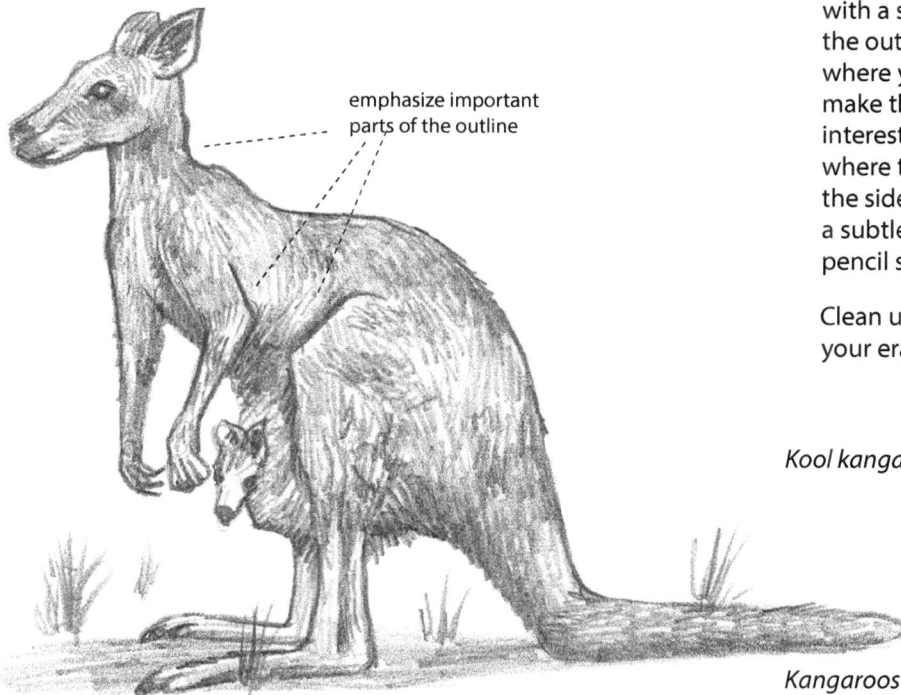

5. To finish your drawing, lightly erase unnecessary lines and fill in the body with short pencil strokes for fur. Refine details (particularly faces) with a sharp pencil. Go over the outline, adding emphasis where you think it will help make the drawing more interesting (for example, where the arm and leg overlap the side of the kangaroo). Add a subtle shadow and some pencil strokes for grass.

Clean up any smudges with your eraser

Kool kangaroo!

Kangaroos travel in herds called mobs, with about a dozen members. Draw a mob of kangaroos—try drawing them in different positions!

Kudu

Tragelaphus strepsiceros

Africa, introduced in N. Mexico. Size: 2.1.–3 m including tail. This attractive antelope feeds on leaves, shoots and seeds. The male has the long, spiraling horns, which lay flat along the back when he's running. Females sometimes have short horns.

shoulder

hip

1. Start with two lightly drawn ovals. Make one (the shoulder) large and almost round. Make the other (the hip) smaller, skinnier, and slightly tilted. Connect the ovals with a *concave* line on the top, and a *convex* line on the bottom.

   Where do these lines connect to the ovals?

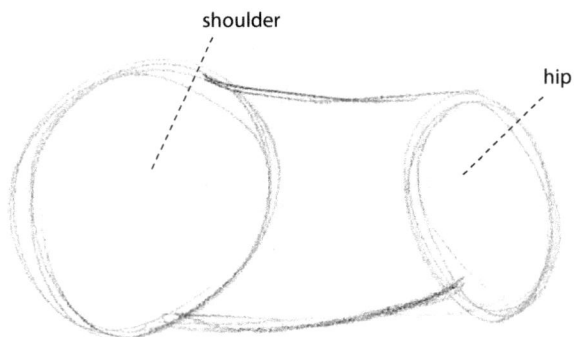

neck

mane

2. First, look: *how much space is there on the neck, between the shoulder and the head?* Draw a very light circle for the head. Add the bulge of the nose. Carefully draw the eye and the ears. Add curving lines for the neck, with short vertical pencil strokes for the mane and the bottom of the neck.

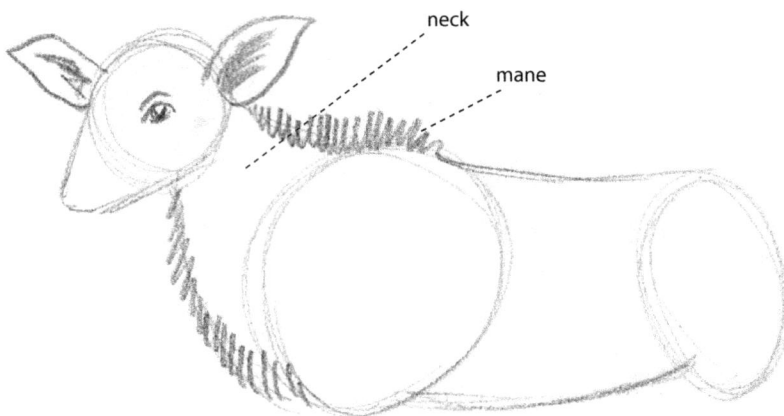

3. Draw curved lines for the horns, joining to make points at the end. Carefully apply shading to create the spiralling effect.

   Add the nose, mouth, and shading on the head.

4. Next, add the legs. Draw a line for the ground, then light circles for knees and ankles. Join them with lines, and add hooves.

   Add the tai .

5. Starting with the darkest areas, carefully shade the entire body. Watch for shadows on the neck and shoulder, representing muscles. Try to leave the white stripes on the back as you shade; you may be able to create them after with your eraser.

   Go over the outline, adding emphasis. Clean up any smudges.

   This final shading may take some time, but will certainly earn you kudos for your kudu!

Lion (female)

Panthera Leo

Africa (south of Sahara), Northwest India. Size: 2–3 m (6.5–10 ft) including tale. The male is larger, with a heavy mane. Lions spend 20 hours or more resting each day. The females hunt gazelles, antelope, and zebras, and sometimes cooperate to kill larger prey like buffaloes and giraffes. Like other cats, they stalk their prey and capture it with a short, quick chase. The males rarely hunt.

1. Draw a vertical oval for the hip. Now, look: *how much space is there between this oval and the shoulder?* Draw the tilted shoulder oval (refer to the clock face for the angle). Add gracefully curving lines to connect them. Draw the tail.

2. Draw a light circle for the head, overlapping the shoulder oval. Add ears.

   Below the shoulder, draw a light circle for the front knee. Add lines upward for the top of the leg, and down for the bottom of the leg, ending with the foot and paws. Now draw the other front leg.

   Draw the rear legs, starting with circles for the ankles (the knee is not as important in this pose—look at the male lion drawing, page 31, to see the rear knee).

3. Study the features of the face, and draw eyes, nose, mouth, and whiskers.

4. Carefully add shading over the entire body, watching for light and dark areas. Add the ground with a few tufts of grass.

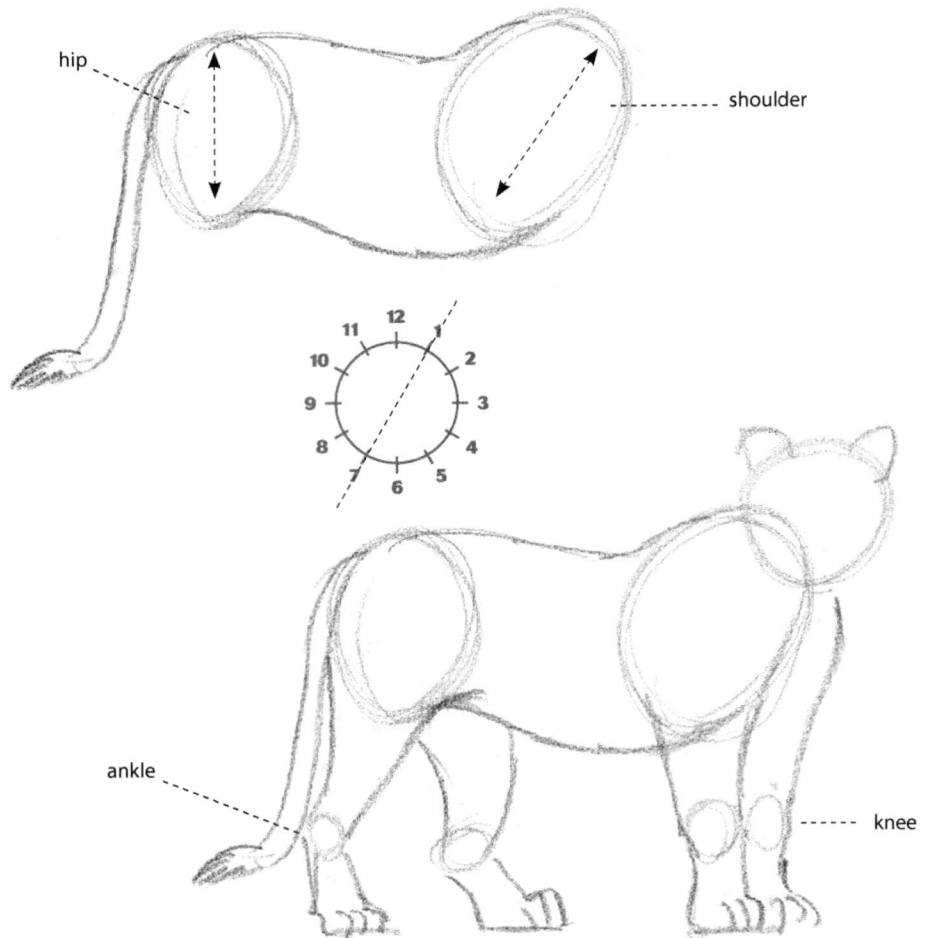

Lion (Male)

shoulder

hip

12 11 1 10 2 9 3 8 4 7 6 5

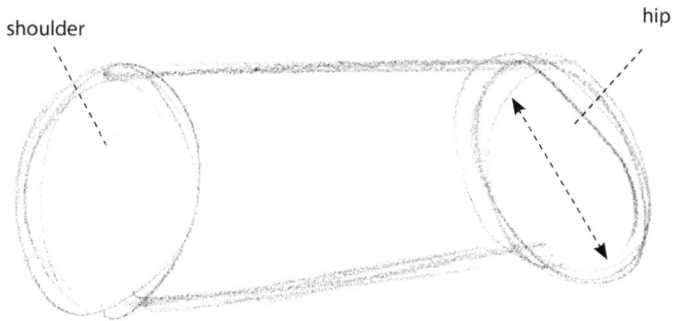

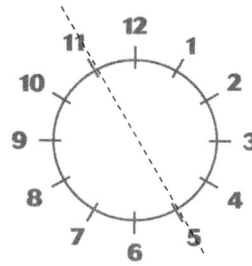

1. Draw a titled oval for the lion's hip. Being careful to leave enough space for the body, draw the shoulder oval, and lines to connect the two ovals. *Where do they connect to each oval?*

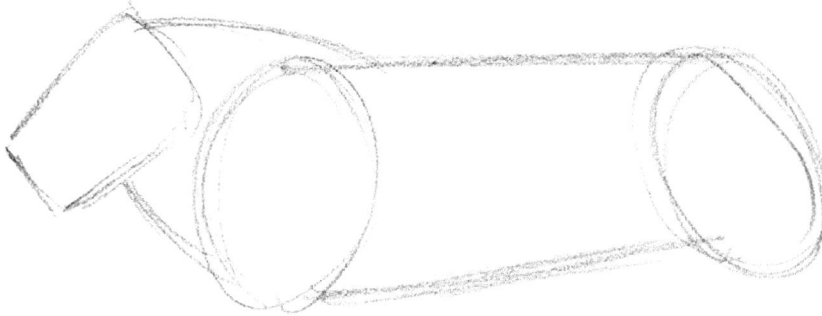

2. Draw the boxy shape of the lion's head, slightly smaller at the mouth end. Notice the angles of the box. Add curving lines for the top and bottom of the neck. *Where do they connect to the body?*

3. Draw a line for the ground, and use light circles and lines to 'map out' the legs. Pay close attention to the angles, and look at the shapes between the legs *(negative space)* as well as the shapes of the legs themselves.

   Add nose, mouth, eye, and ear. Use short pencil strokes for whiskers, mane, bottom of neck and at places on the body where muscles show.

4. Emphasize muscles with shading (and color, if you wish). Leave contrast between light and dark to suggest strong light. Go over the outline, especially on the legs.

Locust

Locusts thrive on every continent. They are the most destructive member of the grasshopper family—a large swarm can eat 3,000 tons of crops each day. No wonder they've been considered a plague since early times! Though locusts can be controlled with pesticides, that raises another problem: locusts provide food for other animals, including storks and rodents.

wing

abdomen

1. Start your locust drawing with the hind leg. It looks somewhat like the leg of a mammal, such as a gazelle, but it bends the opposite way.

thorax

2. Add the wing and abdomen, as well as the next leg.

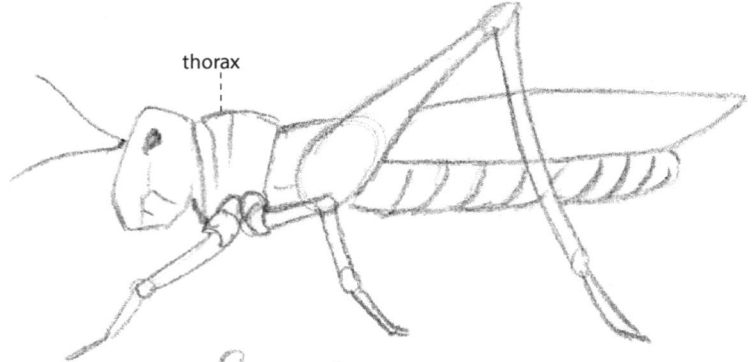

3. Draw the thorax and head (notice where the eye is), antennae and front leg.

4. Add the three legs on the far side of the insect, plus lines on the largest leg and the wing.

5. Shade the locust, paying attention to which areas are darkest and which are lighter.

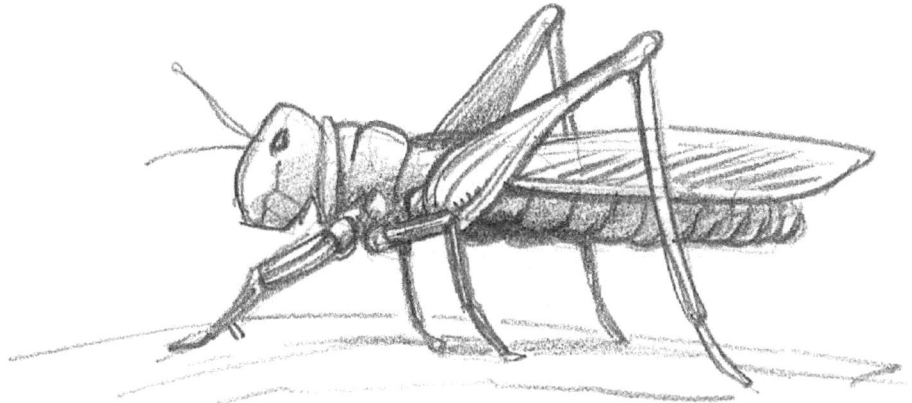

Have you ever eaten an insect? Well, me neither, but they're a great source of protein. Lightly sauté with a little olive oil until slightly crunchy and salt to taste. Nummy!

Locusts in action: imagine each of those dots is a hungry locusts. Very little vegetation remains after they've passed through an area.

Burrowing Owl

Speotyto cunicularia

North, Central and South America. Size: 23–28 cm (9–11 inches). The burrowing owl lives in abandoned burrows of prairie dogs and other mammals, digging out a nesting area with its feet. Its short tail and long legs are well-suited for ground dwelling. They like to follow moving dogs or horses, to catch insects and other small prey disturbed by the larger animal.

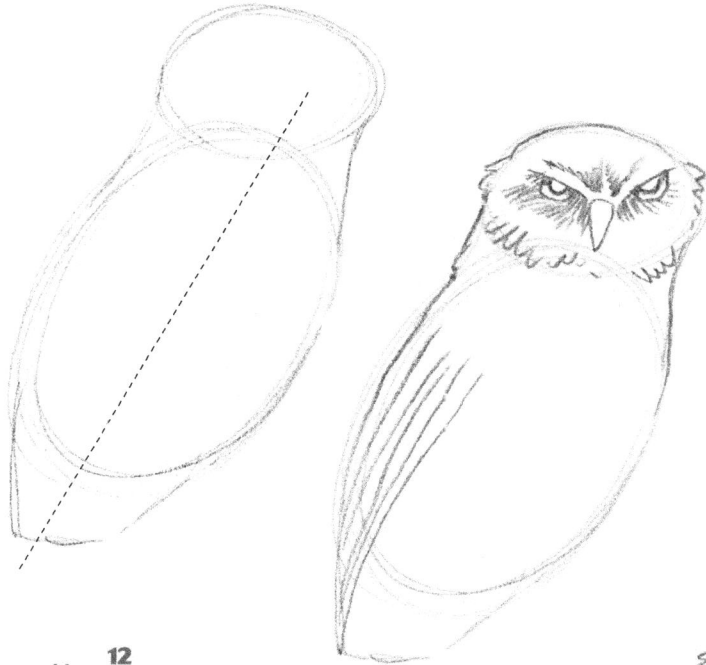

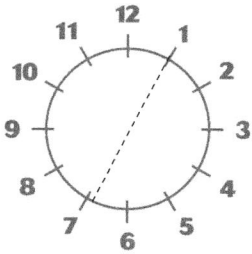

1. Draw a long, tilted oval for the owl's body. Compare the angle of the tilt with the clock face. Above the body, draw a horizontal oval, and connect it to the body with curving lines. Add the squared off section of tail feathers at the bottom.

2. Next draw the face, starting with the beak. Add two lines slanting upward for the eyebrows, with partial circles underneath for the eyes. Draw other details, noticing how they *radiate* from the eyes, adding emphasis to them.

   Add long lines for the wing feathers.

3. Using light circles for the joints, draw the legs, and toes with sharp claws.

4. Darken the eyes, leaving a small bright spot in one (this helps make the owl look alive!). Carefully add shading over the body. Toward the head, white spots appear on a darker background. Toward the tail, darker patterns appear on a light background.

   Add a burrow in the background. You can smear the pencil a bit to contrast with the sharp detail of the owl's face.

Draw Animals **203**

Meerkat

Suricata suricatta

Southern Africa. Size: 45-55 cm (1.5–1.8 ft) including tail. The meerkat, also known as the suricate, has thin fur on its belly. When it wants to get warmer, it sits up so the sun warms its belly. When it wants to cool off, it lies belly-down in a cool, dark burrow. Meerkats eat all kinds of food, mostly animal. Cute as they appear, you wouldn't want one for a pet: they're messy and they don't smell very nice!

1. Draw two tilted ovals, for the hip and shoulder. Use the clock face to check the tilt of each oval. Connect the two ovals with slightly *concave* curving lines.

2. Touching the lower left edge of the hip oval, draw a small circle for the meerkat's knee. Below the hip oval, draw another small circle at the ankle. Connect these circles and the body with curving lines. From the ankle, draw the lower part of the leg, and the foot.

3. Using similar circles, draw the arm (front leg). Add the small bit that shows of the other leg and arm.

4. Draw a light circle for the head, and extend it to make the nose. Add curving lines for the neck. Draw ears, eye, and mouth.

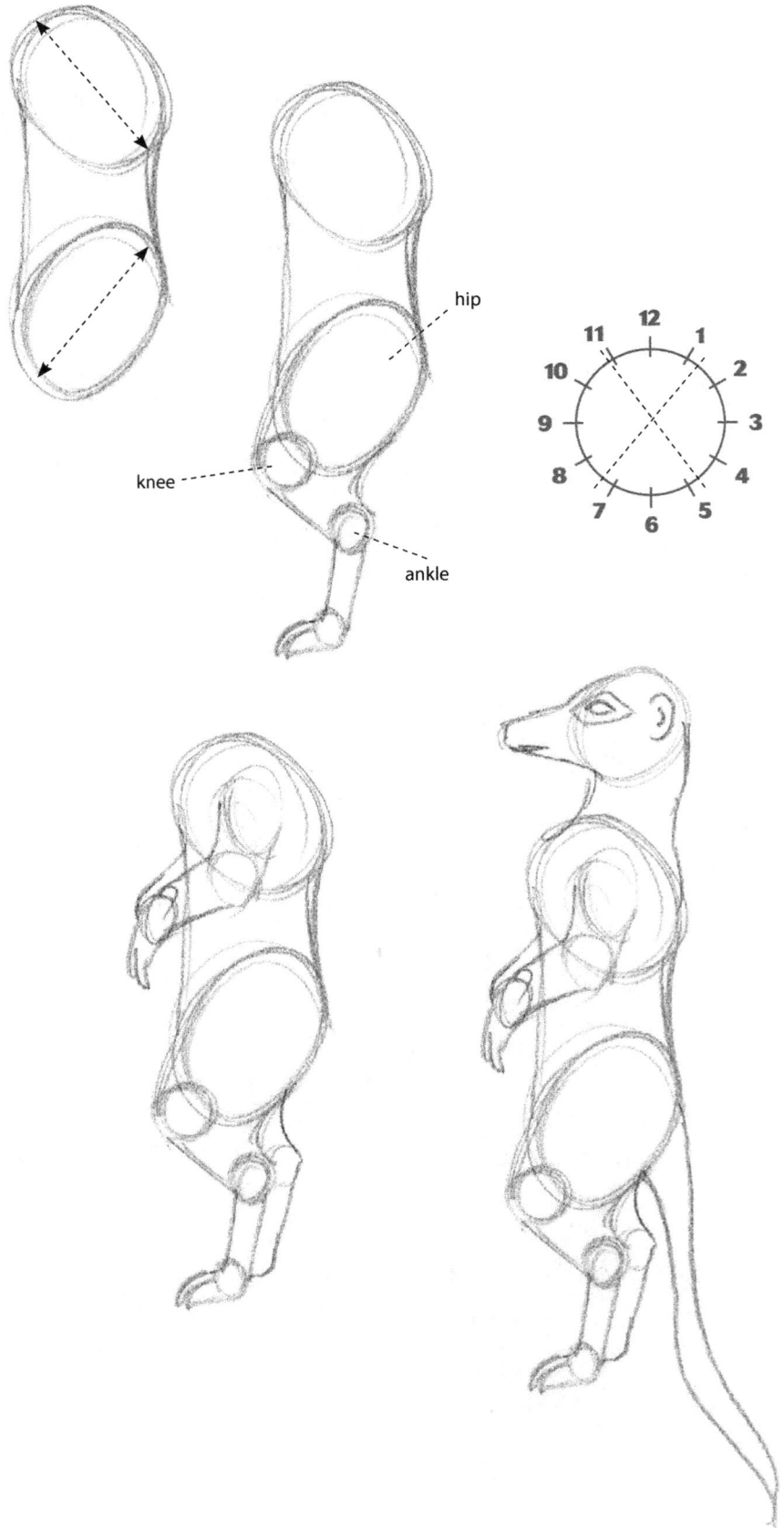

5. Add the nose and whiskers. Sharpen your pencil and go over the outline, adding jagged lines where fur sticks out. Lightly sketch the second meerkat, and lines for the ground.

(Why might one be standing when the other is lying down?)

6. Add short pencil strokes in the direction of the fur, except in parts of the body which remain light. Add the distinctive bands, or stripes, on the back.

Clean up any smudges with your eraser.

Magnificent meerkats!

If at first you don't succeed ....

Black-tailed prairie dog

Cynomys ludovicianus

(Black tailed prairie dog)

Central USA. Size: 36.5–41.5 cm (14.2–16 inches) including tail. Surprise! Prairie dogs aren't dogs. They're sociable rodents who live in burrows. They get their name from their appearance and barking sound. They eat grass and other plants. They form part of the diet of hawks, foxes, ferrets, and coyotes.

1. *Draw very lightly!* Draw two ovals, one for the body and one for the head. Add a short curving line for the top of the neck.

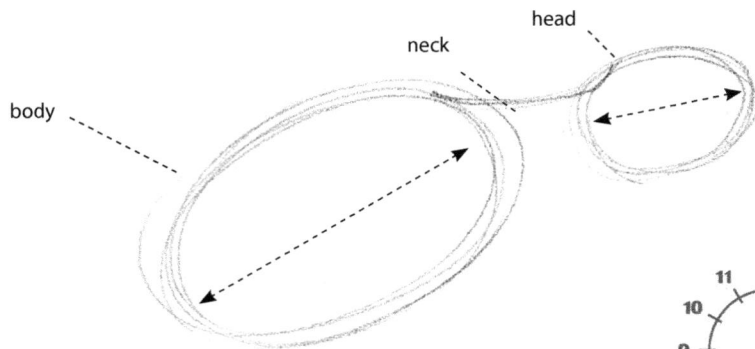

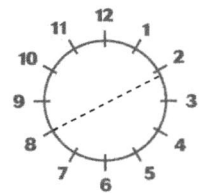

body

neck

head

Compare the main axis (dotted line) of each tilted oval with the clock face.

12 1 2 3 4 5 6 7 8 9 10 11

2. Add the bottom of the neck and the front leg, with claws. Use light, wispy lines to draw the tail.

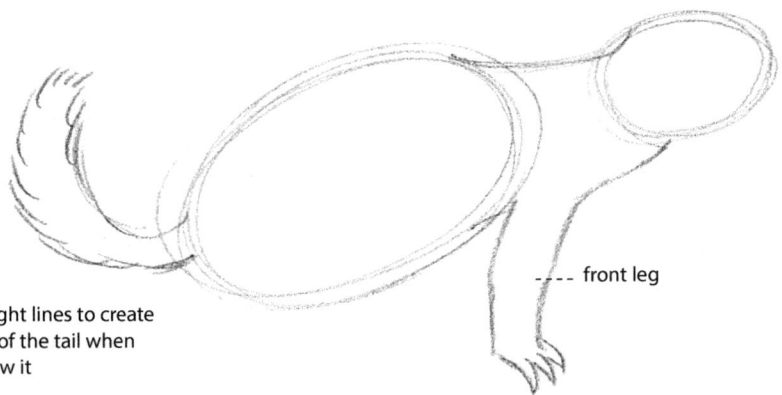

Use many light lines to create the texture of the tail when you first draw it

front leg

3. Draw a jagged line for the edge of the burrow. Make it bumpy, like dirt thrown up by the prairie dog's digging.

4. Lightly add the front of the prairie dog's face. *Do any of the lines go straight up and down (vertical) or straight side to side (horizontal)?*

When you have the shape of the face the way you want it, carefully erase the front part of the oval. Then mark where you want the ear and eye.

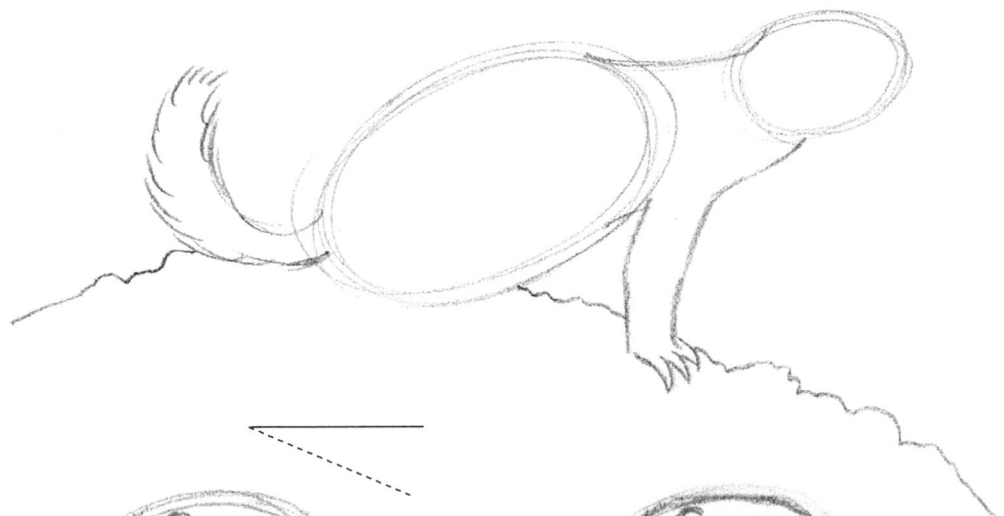

5. Using curving lines, draw the ear and eye. Add whiskers and short pencil strokes for fur.

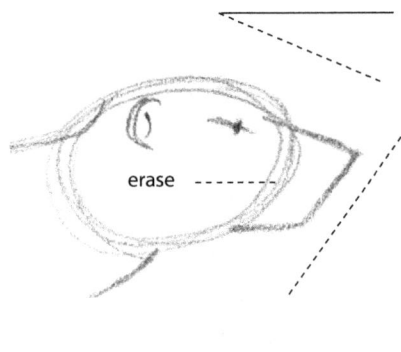

erase

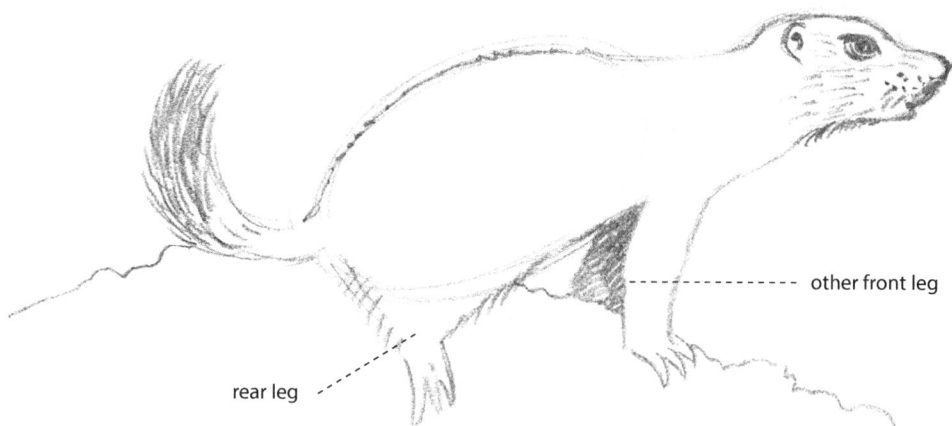

6. Add the other front leg, and shade it. Draw the rear leg. Go over the outline. Notice how you can make it look more like fur by making the line a bit jagged. Add more short, curving pencil strokes to make the tail look furry. Carefully erase parts of the oval that you don't want in the finished drawing.

other front leg

rear leg

7. Look at the final drawing—where are the dark areas? These will be the areas we shade first. Use short pencil strokes going in one direction for the fur in the darkest parts of the body.

Add a bumpy line for the dirt at the edge of the burrow closest to you. Use short pencil strokes going in different directions to shade the entrance to the burrow.

edge of burrow

8. Continue adding short pencil strokes for fur. Watch how they change direction on different parts of the body. Add more shading, rocks, and grass. Clean up any smudges or "leftover" lines with your eraser.

Now, what's that pretty prairie dog looking at?

Pronghorn

Antilocapra americana

North America. Size: 1–1.7 m (3.5–5.5 ft).
Pronghorn antelopes are fast runners and
good swimmers. They eat grasses, weeds,
and shrubs such as sagebrush.

1. Draw two light ovals, one
   vertical and one tilted. Use
   the clock face to see how they
   tilt. Connect the tops and
   bottom with slightly curving
   lines. Note the bit of a hump
   at the hip, and bit of an indent
   underneath.

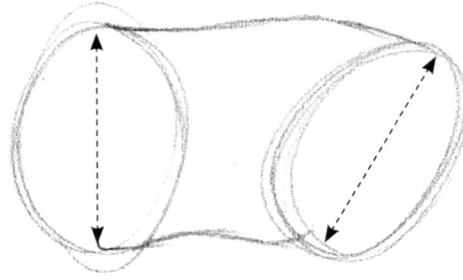

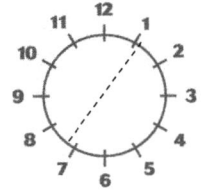

2. Sketch light lines and ovals to
   plot out how the legs bend.
   Pay special attention to the
   angles.

   *Using the ovals at joints will
   help you see how the legs
   bend. Later, you may want to
   try putting the legs in different
   positions, perhaps using a
   photograph as a guide.*

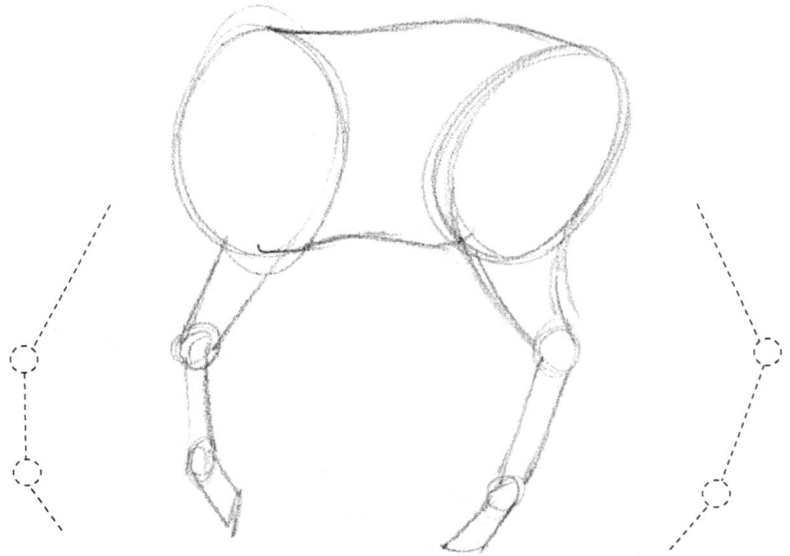

3. Add the other two legs. Draw
   a small oval for the head.
   Connect the head to the top
   of the body with a straight line
   *(look where it connects to the
   body!)*. Draw the bottom of the
   neck, with its two curves.

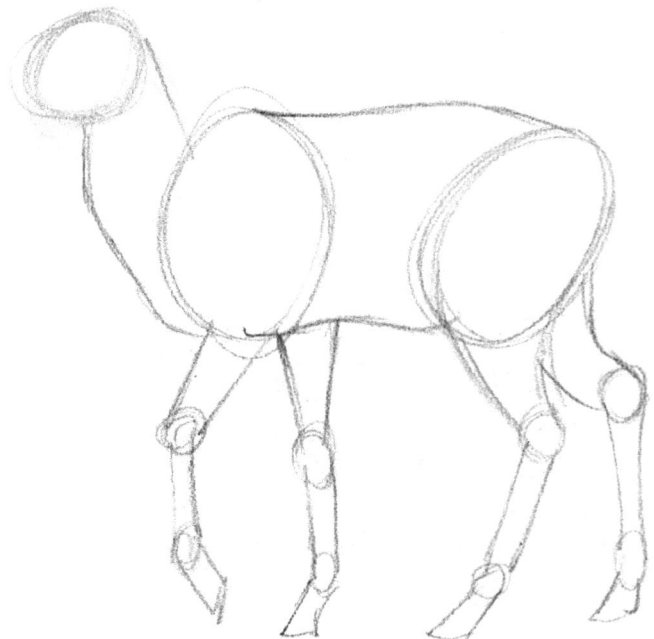

4. Add the snout, with nose and mouth. Draw the eye, high in the head. Add horns and ears.

Lightly erase lines you no longer need. Sharpen your pencil and go over the outline of the animal, making your line thinner in some places and thicker in others. As you draw, you'll develop a feel for where to make lines thin and thick. Pay special attention to where lines meet or curve.

5. Being careful not to smudge your paper, add short pencil strokes for fur over the entire antelope. Leave the rump lighter. Also notice that part of the face and throat are lighter.

This last step may take longer than all the ones leading up to it. Take your time!

Clean up any smudges with your eraser.

Common Rabbit

Oryctolagus cuniculus

Europe, northwest Africa; introduced into other countries. Size: 39–52 cm (15–19.5 inches). This is the ancestor of the domestic rabbit. They live in underground colonies called warrens, and feed on grass and leaves, as well as bark and roots in winter. To warn other rabbits of danger, a rabbit may thump its foot.

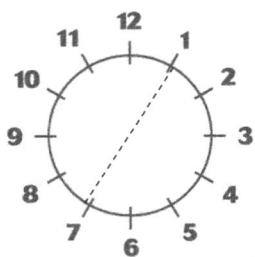

1. Start by lightly drawing three ovals. The top two touch. The bottom two don't touch— connect them with lines for the back and stomach of the rabbit.

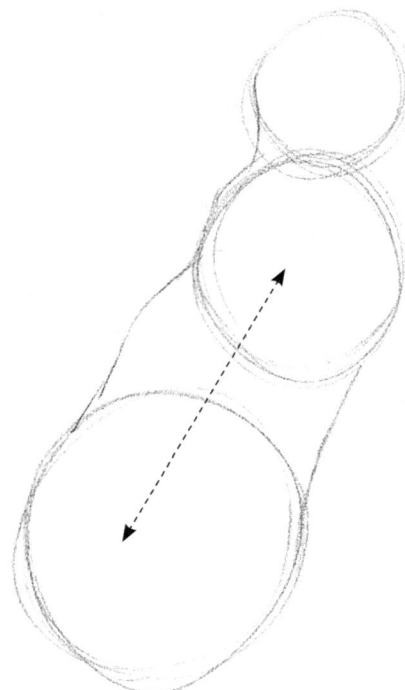

2. Carefully—and *lightly!*— draw the ears. Add the rounded nose and the line for the throat.

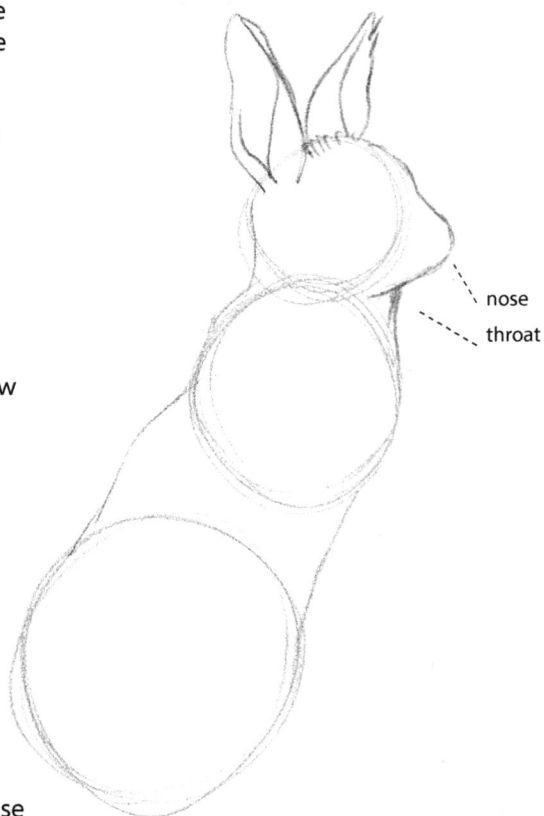

nose

throat

3. Draw the eye, mouth and nose details, and whiskers. Add the feet.

4. Draw the tail and front legs. Notice which are the carkest parts of the final drawing, and start to add shading there.

5. Complete your rabbit by filing the body with short pencil strokes for fur. Add grass. Add color if you wish. Go over any parts of the outline that might need additional emphasis or texture. Clean up any smudges with your eraser.

White Rhinoceros

Ceratotherium simum

Africa. Size: 3.6–5 m (12–16 ft). The only bigger land animal is an elephant! White rhinos are placid, and rarely attack, preferring to flee from trouble. They eat only grass. They're gray, not white—the name comes from their WIDE mouths, which are unlike pointy mouths of other rhinos.

1. Lightly draw a tall, tilted oval for the rhino's hip. Look at the clock face to see the angle of the tilt. Add two bent lines showing the leg nearest you, and another straight line for the leg on the other side. Draw a line for the ground.

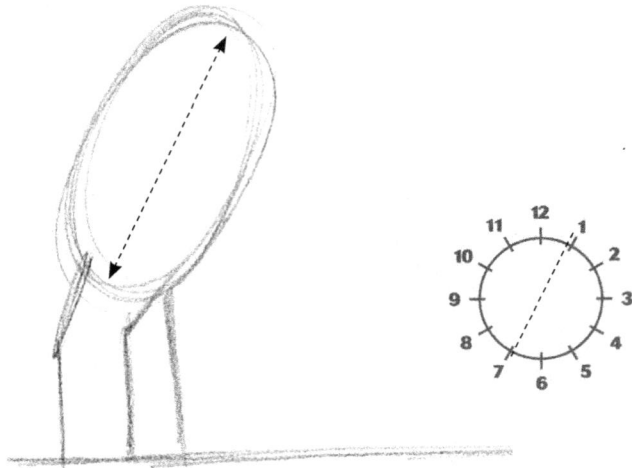

2. From the top of the oval, draw a horizontal line for the back, and a swooping, sagging line underneath for the belly. Extend the line for the ground.

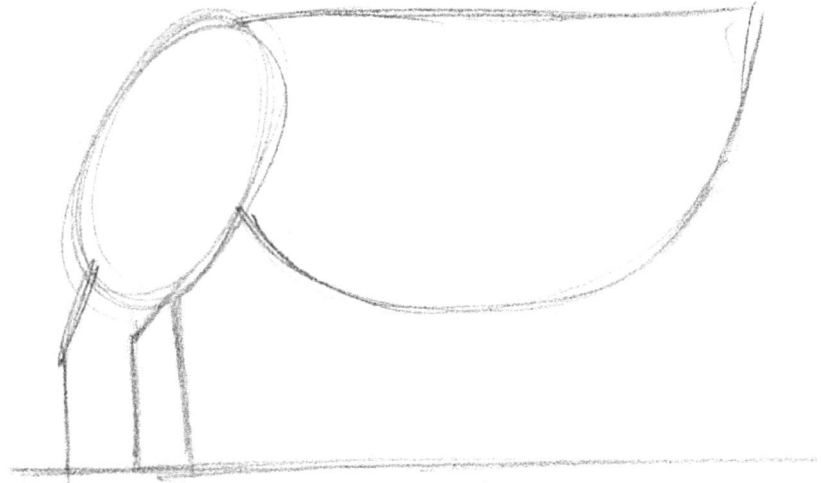

3. From the front of the body, draw a line straight down and back. Under it, add the front leg closest to you, then the one behind it. Sketch the shape for the neck.

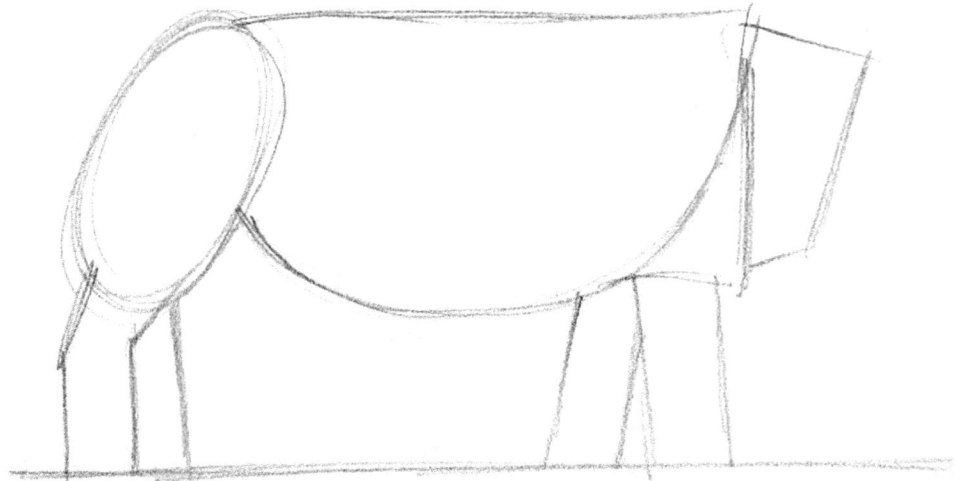

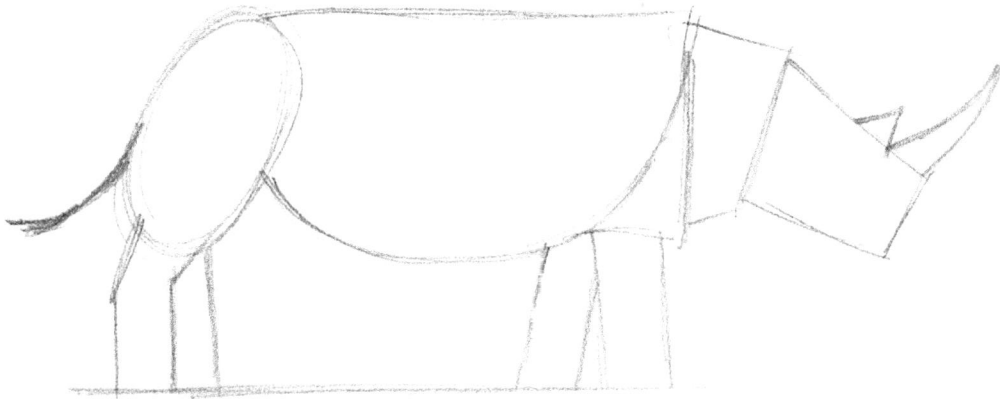

4. Draw a rectangle for the head, getting smaller towards the front. Add the two horns, and the tail.

5. Now you'll find many details to add as you refine the head: draw lightly at first, and observe carefully. Add the eye and arcs around it, below and behind the smaller horn. Make the front of the head bulge out slightly and add a nostril and wrinkles. Add curves to the bottom of the head and neck, and wrinkles. Draw the ears, and bulges at the top of the neck.

6. Look at this finished drawing. Add curves to the legs, widening them to make feet; draw toenails. Draw lines for the ribs, then shade with short pencil strokes. Make the bottom of the body and the inside of the far legs darker. Follow the direction of the wrinkles as you shade the face. Add grass, and an egret to keep the rhino company!

Clean up any smudges with your eraser.

A note about shading: if it doesn't look good, add more!

Saiga

Saiga tatarica

Central Asia. Size: body 1.2–1.7m (4–5.5 ft). Saigas migrate through cold, treeless, windswept plains. Their large noses are thought to help them survive by warming and adding moisture to the air they breathe.

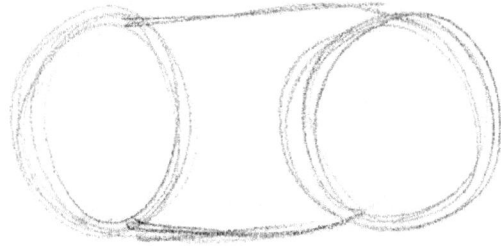

1. Draw two ovals, connected by rounded lines.

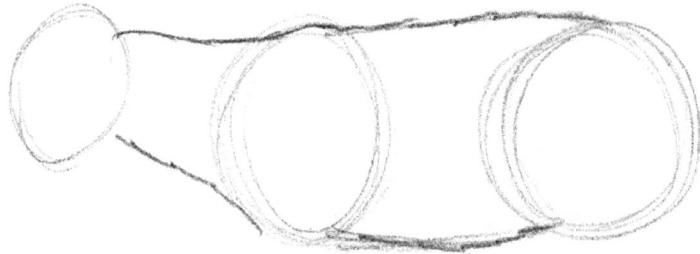

2. Add a third oval for the head, and draw lines for the neck. Notice where they connect to the oval for the head!

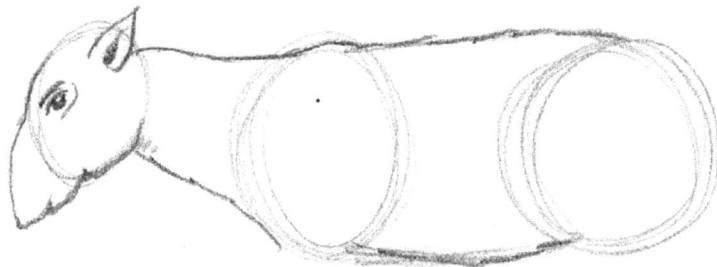

3. Draw the Saiga's large nose, eye, and ear.

4. Using small circles at the joints, outline the front and rear leg.

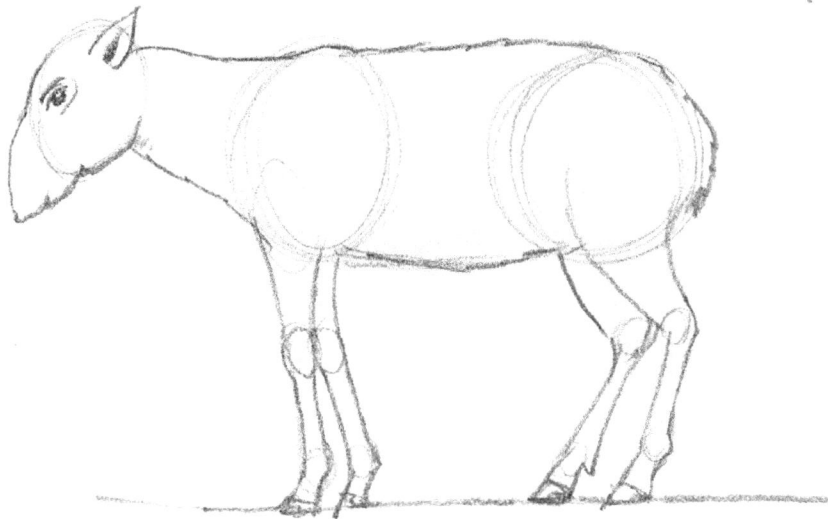

5. Draw the remaining two legs.

6. Add the horns. Lightly erase the parts of the ovals you no longer need. Look carefully at the final drawing. Start shading with the face.

7. Continue shading with short pencil strokes to complete the Saiga. You can create a softer look by gently smudging part of the pencil drawing with your finger, a small rolled up piece of paper, or an artist's stump, which is made for that purpose.

    Just be sure to wash your hands if you get graphite on them; they can make a mess of your picture fast!

    Clean up any smudges with your eraser.

Secretary Bird

Sagittarius serpentarius

Africa. Size: 150 cm (59 inches). The secretary bird mostly walks, covering 30 km (20 miles) a day. It eats just about anything crawling on the ground. It either runs to catch it in its mouth, or stamps it with its foot. The odd name probably comes from the feathers on the head, which look like quill pens stuck behind the ear of a secretary in the old days.

1. Draw a horizontal oval, with the two straight sections of leg extending downward from the middle of it.

    Notice the angle of each leg section—neither is perfectly vertical.

2. Add the second leg.

    Notice how you can't see the entire second leg.

second leg

front of wing

draw these feathers first…

3. Draw the front of the wing. Add the feet, each with four toes and sharp claws.

4. From the front of the wing, draw the triangular back part of the wing, with lines for feathers. Then add the feathers sticking out from underneath. Add shading.

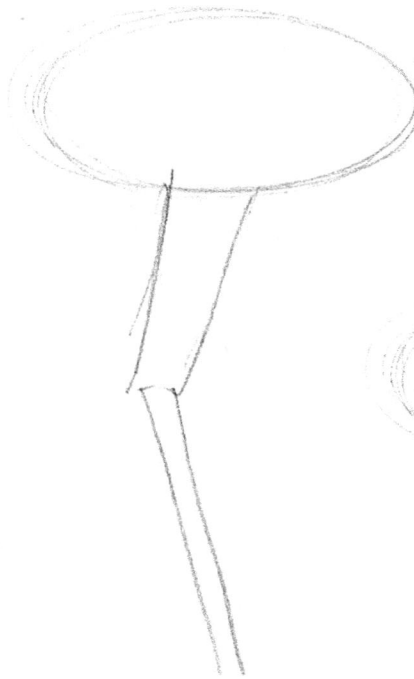

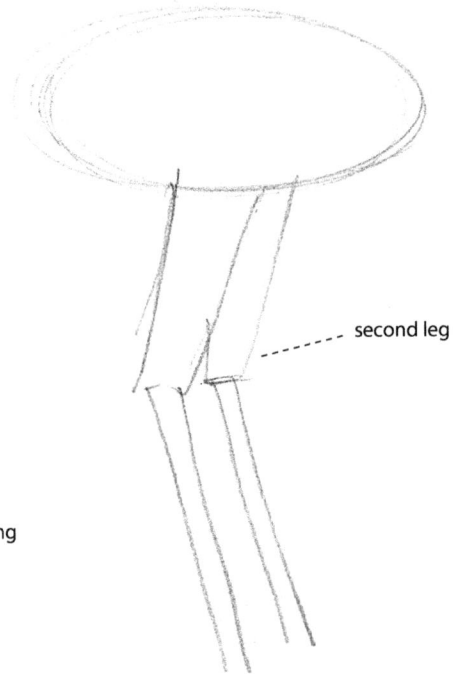

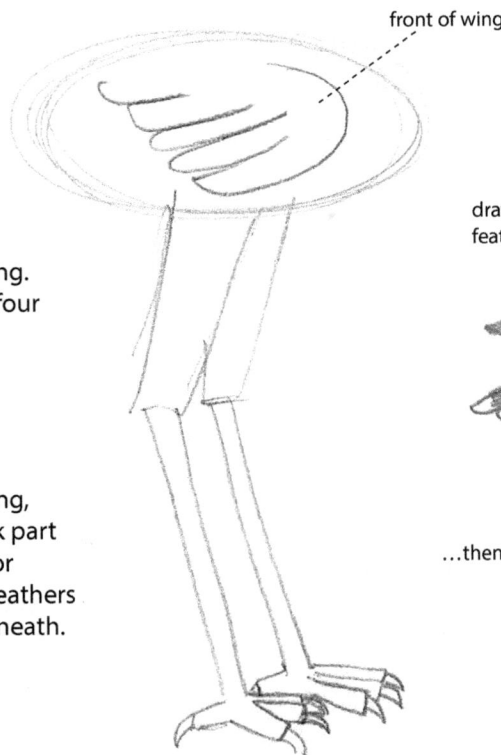

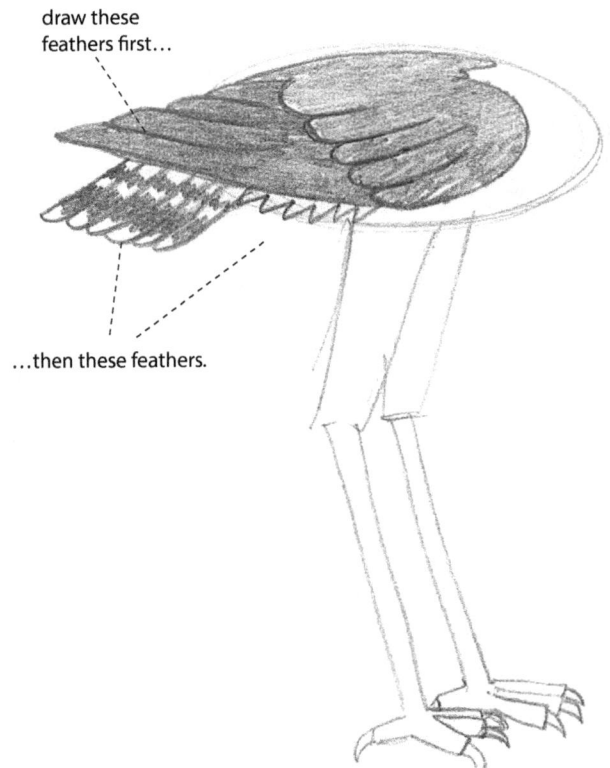

…then these feathers.

5. Add the two long tail feathers. Add shading and jagged lines to fill out the bottom of the body. Shade the top part of the legs with short, dense, vertical pencil strokes. Go over the outline of the lower legs, and make evenly spaced horizontal marks on them.

   Shade the feet. Draw a captured snake. Add the ground and grass.

6. Draw a small, horizontal oval for the head, and connect it to the front of the body with smoothly curved lines. Add the turned-down beak, eye and nose details, and distinctive 'quill' feathers.

7. Add short pencil strokes for neck feathers, shade the beak, head, and feathers. Clean up any smudges with your eraser.

Super Secretary bird!

Thomson's gazelle

Gazella thomsoni

Africa. Size: 1–2.3 m (3.25–7.5 ft) including tail. Gazelles live in groups and eat short grass. They need water only when grazing is dry. They are prey of lions, cheetahs, hunting dogs, and hyenas.

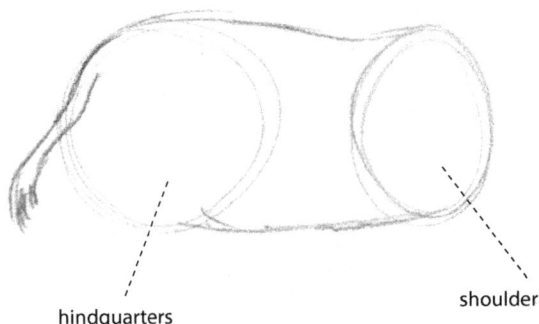

hindquarters

shoulder

1. Draw a light circle for the hindquarters, and a smaller, vertical oval for the shoulder. Connect the two with slightly curved lines, and add the tail.

2. *Look: how much space do you need between the body and the circle for the head? Where is the head in relation to the body (see clock face)?*

   Lightly draw a circle for the head, and connect it to the body with curving lines. Add the eye and ears.

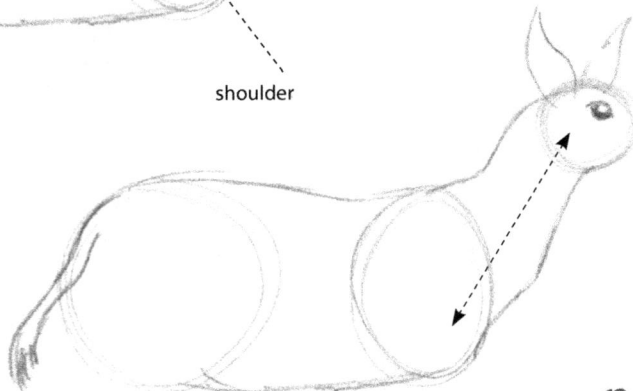

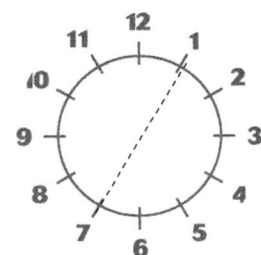

3. Extend the front of the circle for the gazelle's muzzle, and draw the nose and mouth. Sketching very lightly at first— and rotating your paper if it helps—draw the horns, one partly covered by the other. Add the pattern of dark fur inside the ear, and the dark patch extending toward the nose.

4. Using small ovals for the joints, draw the legs and hooves. Look carefully at the angles of each leg section.

5. Draw a line for the ground, and add the other two legs. Notice the shading of the final drawing, and lightly sketch the curve on the rump that separates the lightest fur from the darker fur. Add the distinctive dark patch on the side.

Draw the wrinkles of the neck.

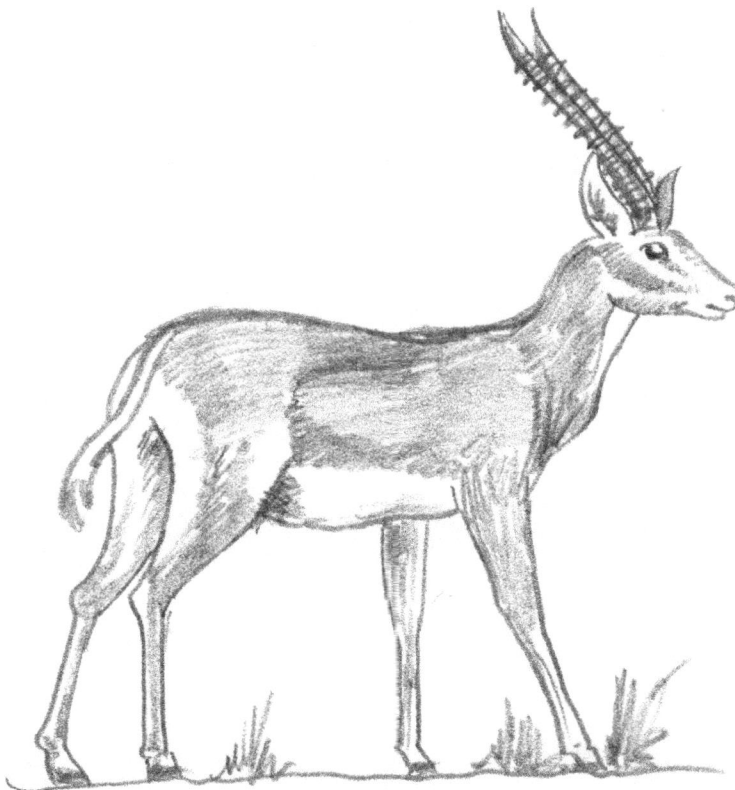

6. Using short pencil strokes in the direction of the fur, shade the entire body, except for the lightest parts. Go over the outline with a sharpened pencil, adding emphasis. Add ridges on the horns.

Clean up any smudges with your eraser.

Try holding your drawing up to the light and looking at it through the back of the picture (or use a mirror). Do you notice any possible improvements you can make?

Vicuña

Vicugna vicugna

South America. Size: 1.4–1.6 m (4.5–5.25 ft). Vicuñas live near the snow line in the Andes (above 4200 m; 14,000 ft). They avoid rocky places, because their hooves are soft and sensitive. The 'flag' of wool on the front is commercially valuable—in Inca times, only royalty were allowed to wear vicuña wool. Though gentle creatures, males defend their territory by biting and spitting regurgitated food.

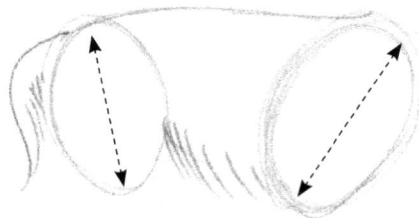

1. Draw two tilted ovals, referring to the clock face for the angle of the tilt. Add a curving line for the back, a curving tail, and long wispy pencil strokes for the fur on the belly.

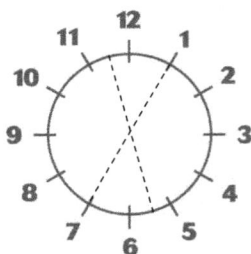

2. Add a small, light circle for the head, and connect it with slightly curved lines for the neck. Extend the front of the head and add the nose and mouth. Draw the eye and ears. Add more long, wispy pencil strokes for the 'flag' of fur on the vicuña's breast.

3. Using small ovals at the joints, draw the legs. Notice the angles of different lines. Also notice that you don't have to draw much of the second rear leg!

4. Shade the vicuña with short pencil strokes. Concentrate first on getting the *values* (light and dark) right, then sharpen your pencil and add small lines to suggest texture. Go over the outline with a sharpened pencil, and add the shadow on the ground.

   Clean up any smudges with your eraser.

Plains viscacha

Lagostomus maximus

Argentina. Size: 62–86 cm (2–3 ft). These large rodents live in complex, underground burrows. They dig with their forefeet and push soil out of the way with their noses. How do they keep dirt out of their noses? They close their nostrils.

shoulder

1. Draw a tilted oval for the shoulder. Add a light, rounder, larger oval near it, and draw curving lines at the top and the bottom of the body.

2. Draw a vertical oval, overlapping the shoulder slightly, for the head. Add the two ears. Below the shoulder, draw the front leg. Under the larger oval, draw the horizontal rear foot. Sketch the tail with short, outward pencil strokes.

foot

eyebrow

3. Draw the eye, then a bump for the eyebrow. Extend the front of the head, and add the nose and mouth. Draw the inside of the ear, and wrinkles on the chin. Add the little visible bit of the other two legs. Now go over the outline with a sharpened pencil.

4. Using short pencil strokes, shade the body of the viscacha, leaving a light patch on the bottom and the tail. Pay close attention to the markings on the face. Add whiskers, and a shadow underneath.

Voila! Viscacha!

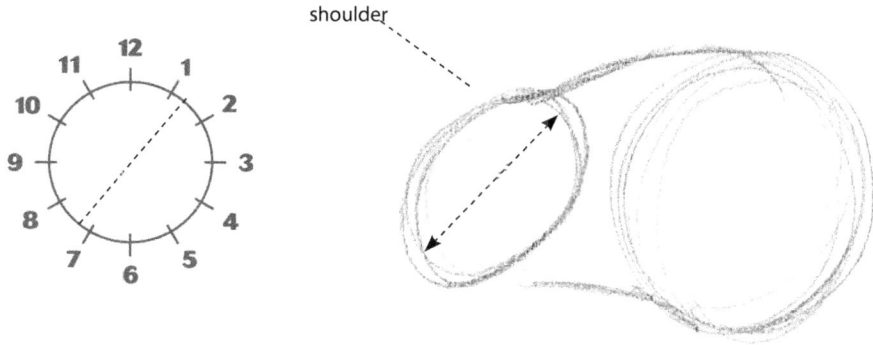

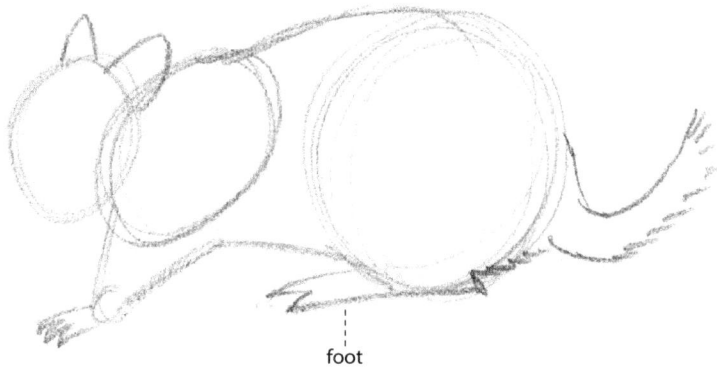

White-backed vulture

Gyps bengalensis

Africa. Size: 81 cm (32 inches); wingspan 2.2 m (7 ft 3 in). Vultures are scavengers. They clean up leftovers from other animal's meals. With keen eyesight, they soar high in the air looking for their next meal. Vultures poke their heads inside dead animals to eat, and so have no feathers on their head or neck—feathers there would become a mess quickly!

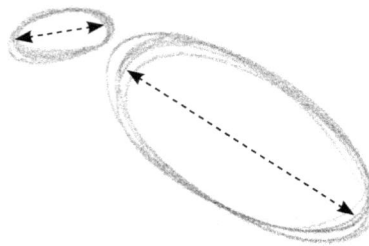

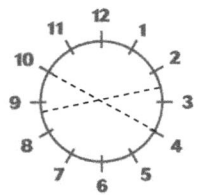

1. Lightly draw two ovals, for the body and the head of the vulture.

   Which is bigger? How much bigger? How is each oval tilted?

Compare the main axis (dotted line) of each tilted oval with the clock face.

2. With a sharp pencil, lightly outline the details of the head, and add the eye—a short straight line with a curved line underneath it. Add curved lines for the top and bottom of the neck.

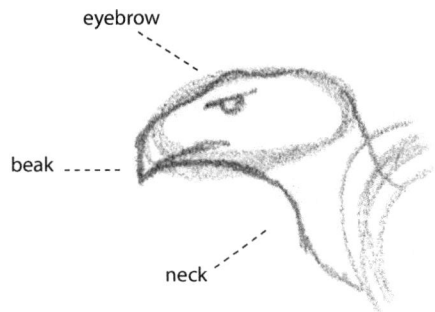

eyebrow

beak

neck

3. At the other end of the large body oval, sketch the tail feathers fanning outward. Add the legs.

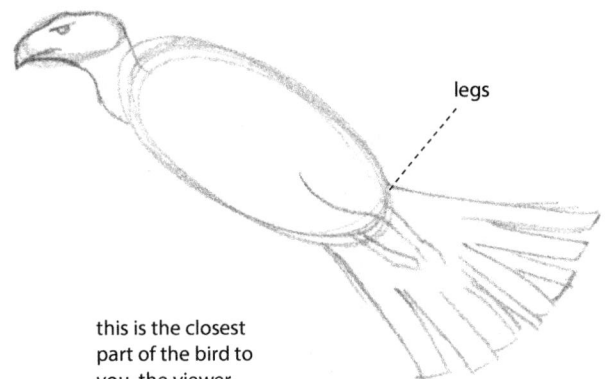

legs

this is the closest part of the bird to you, the viewer

4. Above the body, lightly sketch the part of the wing that is coming toward you. This is a complicated shape, so draw very lightly at first, and do it again if you need to. Connect this shape to the body with a short curved line, running into a bump at the shoulder.

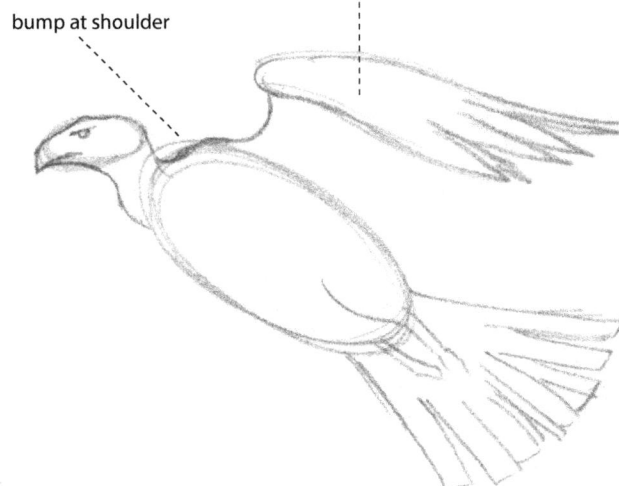

bump at shoulder

5. Look at the dotted line. Compare it to the clock face on the opposite page. Now lightly draw the gently curving line of the top of the wing. Add the curving bottom part on both wings.

6. Sharpen your pencil. Carefully draw the feathers, radiating from the end of the wing, then closer together and parallel as they get closer to the body.

7. Clean up the outline of your vulture, erasing any smudges. Darken the wing and tail feathers, leaving the main part of each wing lighter. Add short pencil strokes to shade the wings, head, and body.

Clean up any smudges with your eraser.

Great venturous vulture!

Warthog

Phacochoerus aethiopicus

Africa. Size: 1.5–2 m (5–7.5 ft). The warthog gets its name from two wart-like bumps on each side of its face. Warthogs like to stay around water. They live in family groups and eat grass, fruit, and sometimes small mammals or dead animals. They can run up to 55 kph (35 mph), and raise their tails when alarmed. They burrow with their teeth, kneel on their calloused knees, and rest in crevices near trees and boulders where they're easy to (almost) step on.

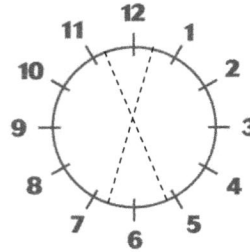

1. Draw two tilted ovals, connected with slightly curved lines.

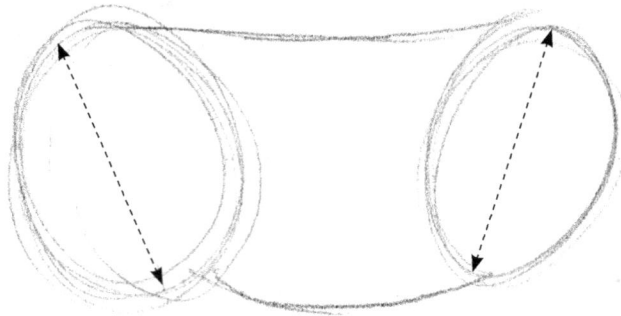

2. Add a light circle, slightly overlapping one of the ovals (not much of a neck on this pup). Extend the face downward, add eye and ears.

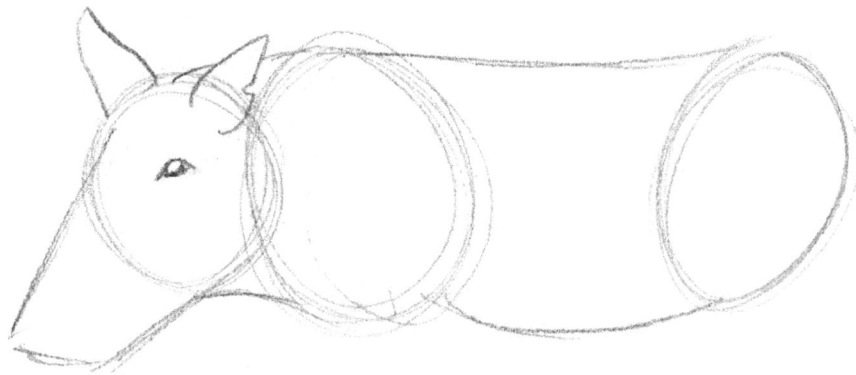

3. At the end of the face, draw two sets of curving tusks. Add two 'warts' and the eyebrows. On the closer side of the face, draw the bump (wart) near the eye, and a crescent shadow for the bump closer to the nose. Add ears, and wrinkles under the chin.

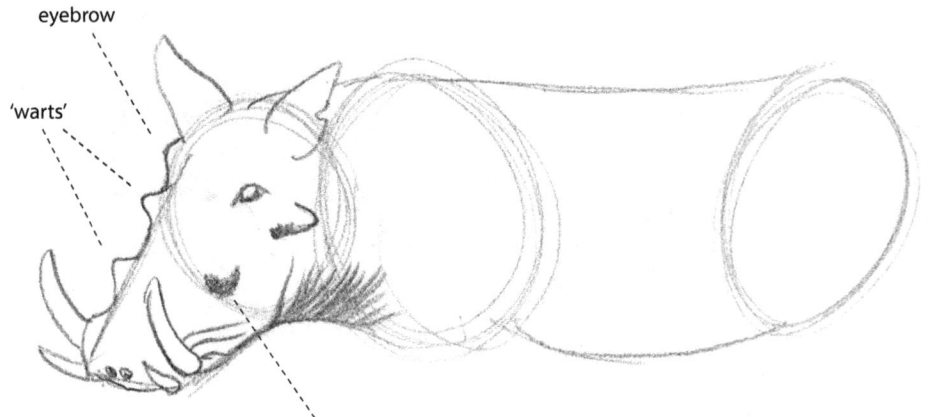

eyebrow

'warts'

Since this 'wart' is pointing at you, you see only its shadow

4. With small ovals at the joints, sketch the legs. Pay attention to the angles, and notice which parts of the legs are hidden by other parts of the body.

5. Go over the outline to clarify lines and add emphasis. With strong, quick strokes, add the wild bristly hair of the mane. Draw the tail.

6. Patiently shade the entire body (notice the very few areas left white in this drawing). As you shade, turn your drawing so the pencil strokes help make the side of the warthog look cylindrical, or rounded. Add more wrinkles around the neck and eyes, and darker shading for the muscles of the rear leg. Draw a cast shadow on the ground.

Keep your hand off the drawing to avoid smudging. If you do make smudges, clean them with your eraser.

Give your warthog a name, preferably starting with a W.

Blue Wildebeest

Connochaetes taurinus

Africa. Size: 2.3–3.4 m (7.5–11 ft)

Wildebeests live in large herds, feeding on grass and often seen among zebras and ostriches. They are prey of lions, cheetahs, hunting dogs, and hyenas. The Blue Wildebeest is also known as the Brindled Gnu. That was gnus to me, but I'll bet you gnu it already.

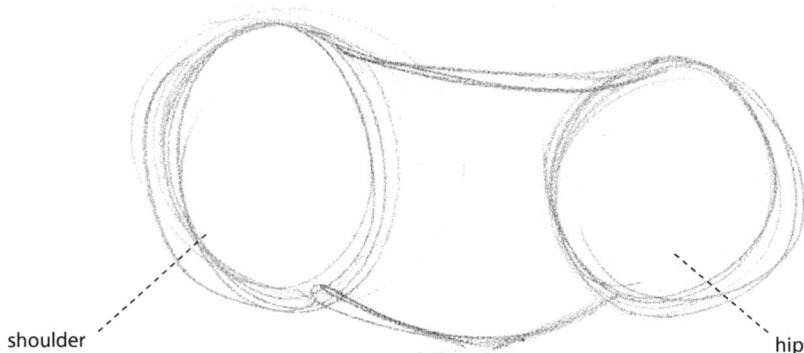

shoulder

hip

1. Draw two light, almost-round ovals, one for the shoulder and the other for the hip. Connect the tops to make the back of the wildebeest, and the bottoms to make the stomach.

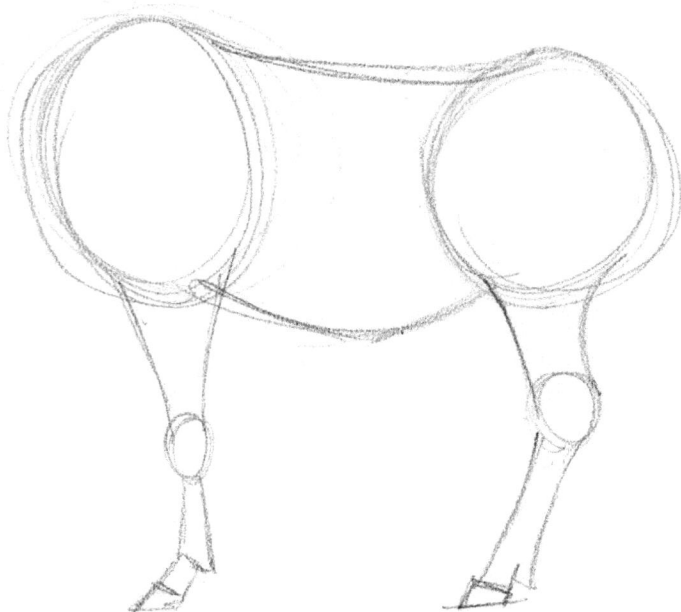

2. Add a front and rear leg, drawing lightly at first. Pay close attention to the angle of each segment of the legs. Add the hooves.

mane

3. Lightly outline the head, roughly a triangle, with the top at the center of the shoulder. Add ears, sticking straight out to the side, the eye and the slit of the nostril. Carefully draw the curving horns on top of the head. Draw the mane, using short, repeated pencil strokes up from the neck. Do the same at the bottom of the neck, making strokes downward.

nostril

4. Lightly draw the other front and rear leg. Add the tail. Looking ahead to the finished drawing, notice which areas are darkest. Begin shading those areas first. Darken the bottom of the neck with more short, vertical pencil strokes.

5. Continue shading, using short pencil strokes. Add shading and grass underneath. Clean up any smudges with your eraser.

Cape Zebra

Equus zebra zebra (go ahead, memorize this one!)

Africa. Size: 1.3 m (4.2 ft) high at shoulder. These endangered zebras came close to extinction in the 1940s. The main threat was habitat loss, when water holes were cut off by fencing for livestock. About 450 now survive.

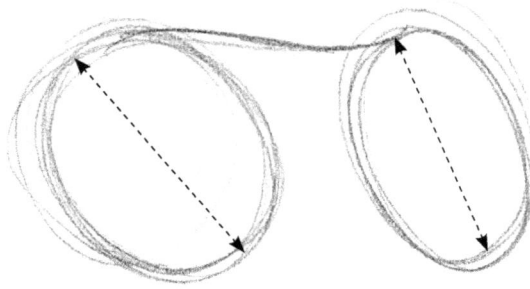

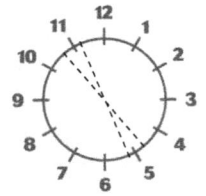

1. Lightly sketch two tilted ovals. Look at the clock face to make sure you have them tilting like the example. Connect them with a curvy line for the back.

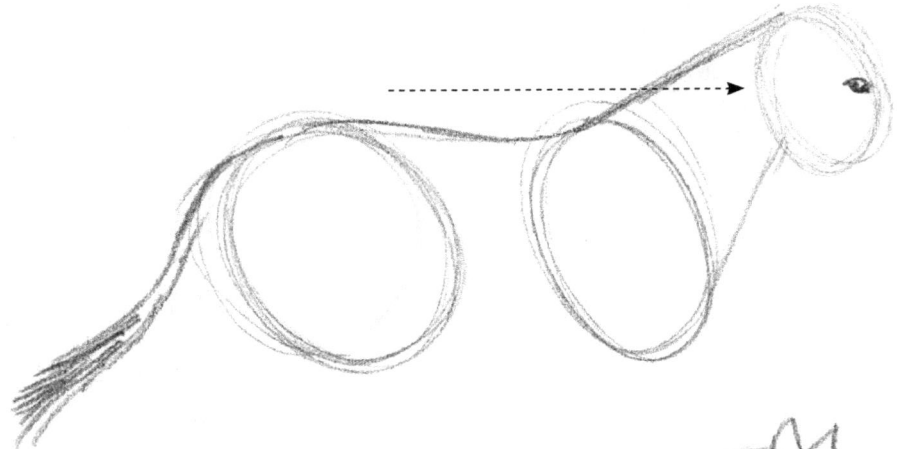

2. Add the tail (easy!). At the opposite end, draw a light oval for the head (again, notice the tilt of the oval). At the very front of the oval, draw the eye. Notice where it lies in relation to the shoulder (above it). Draw the two lines of the neck.

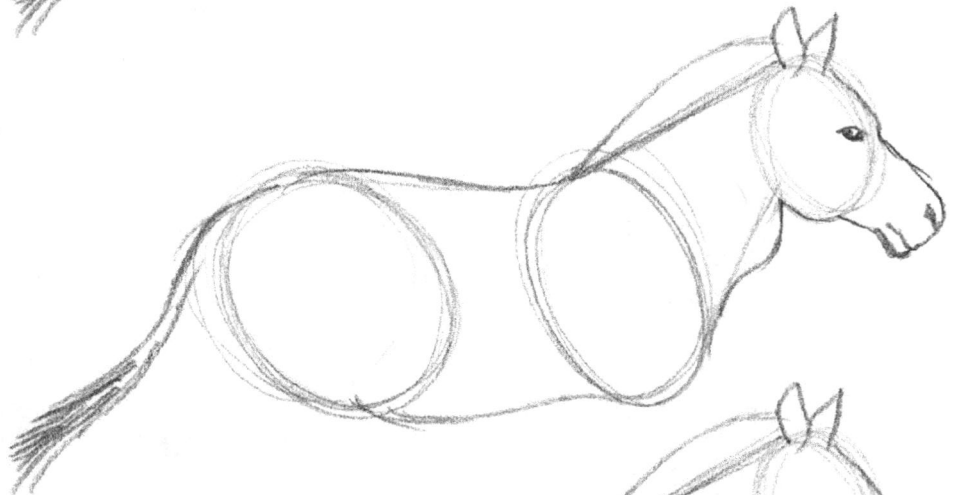

3. Add ears, a light outline of the mane, a bulge at the throat, and a snout, complete with nostril and mouth. Draw lightly until you're sure you have it right!

4. Lightly sketch the legs, using light ovals at each joint to help you understand how the leg bends. The rear leg bends in three places. Look at the clock face and compare angles if you find part of it confusing.

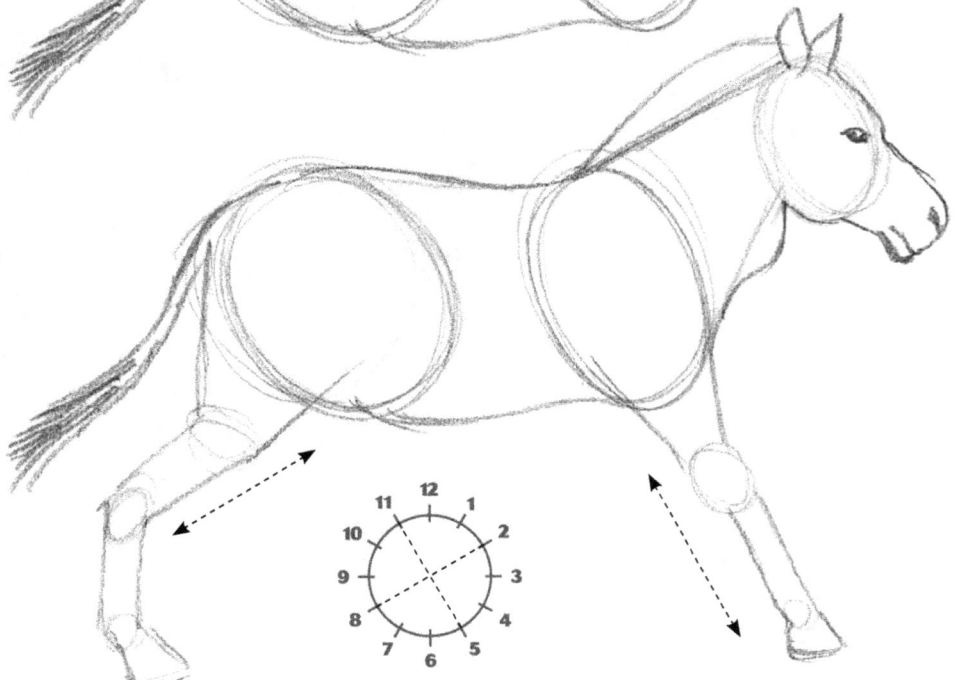

Always draw lightly at first!

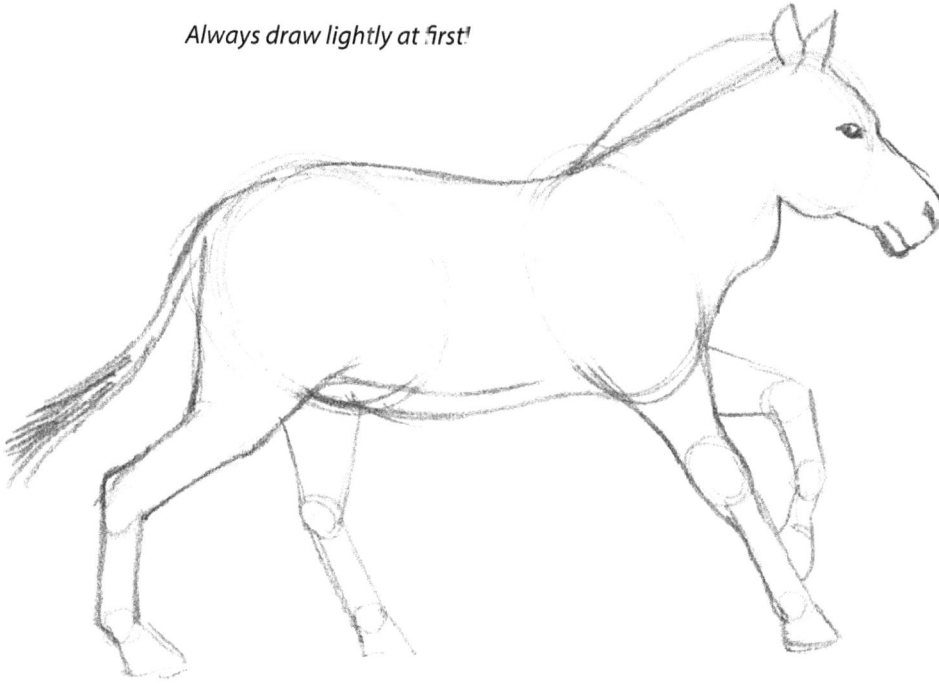

5. Ah, what a difference we see in this drawing! Add the two further legs, lightly at first, observing angles and joints carefully. Lightly erase the ovals—while helpful in getting the drawing started, we don't want them to show through the stripes!

(You did start out lightly, didn't you?)

6. Add stripes and shading, and curving pencil strokes for grass. Be sure to sharpen your pencil when you draw details. Also use a sharp pencil to lightly draw the pattern of the stripes before you darken them. Avoid smudging by keeping your hand off parts you've already drawn. Put a clean piece of paper under your hand to protect drawn areas, or turn the paper around so that your hand is on the white part while you draw.

Another thought: you might want to finish this drawings with a black colored pencil, which will smear less than a normal graphite pencil.

About those stripes: the lone zebra above seems like a pretty obvious target for a hungry lion, but seen in a herd, it's not so easy to see where one zebra starts and another ends!

Drawing tips

Lines make all the difference

Lines are not all created equal. Some lines can make your animal come to life. Try making your lines interesting. Learn to use lines to capture the feel of the animal you're drawing. Here are some suggestions:

The two baboons have the same shape. If both were on display, which would you want to be able to point to and say, "That's mine"?

Make outlines interesting

Specifically, what parts of the outline make one drawing more interesting to look at than the other? Do you see a technique you can use in your drawing?

Create texture with lines

Which drawing seems to have more texture–which drawing gives you an idea what the baboon might feel like if you touched it?

Use lines to show form

In addition to showing texture, how do lines help show the form (form is three-dimensional shape)? Can you see areas on the baboon or hunting dog where lines make the drawing look more three-dimensional?

Drawing tips

Start out loose and light

You've seen it enough times throughout this book: always draw lightly at first. Another way to say this would be always sketch at first.

Sketching means trying out ideas, trying out variations, and basically not worrying too much whether the finished product is perfect.

This very light drawing, or sketching, makes it easier to learn to draw. Ideally, try to do a number of quick sketches to get a feel for the animal: from life, from pictures, or from videos or TV. Learn something from each sketch. Then carefully put together your final drawing, working more methodically and carefully.

You may find–as perhaps all illustrators and artists do–that your lightly drawn sketches have more energy, and capture more of the spirit of the animal, than your final drawing.

Welcome to the club!

Timed Drawings

When drawings are starting to get too tight, or too controlled, try this: pick a subject, and do timed drawings: first, five seconds (really, it's possible!). Next, do a 30-second drawing. One more: give yourself two minutes. Now take as long as you need–ten minutes, a half an hour, a day ... feel the difference in each: which is the most fun?

Learn about other books
in this series online at
drawbooks.com

www.ingramcontent.com/pod-product-compliance
Lightning Source LLC
Chambersburg PA
CBHW062039090426
42740CB00016B/2963